BOLSHEVISM IN TURKESTAN
1917-1927

STUDIES OF THE RUSSIAN INSTITUTE

OF COLUMBIA UNIVERSITY

BOLSHEVISM IN TURKESTAN 1917-1927

ALEXANDER G. PARK

COLUMBIA UNIVERSITY PRESS
NEW YORK, 1957

*The transliteration system used in this series is based on
the Library of Congress system with some modifications*

THE RUSSIAN INSTITUTE
OF COLUMBIA UNIVERSITY

THE RUSSIAN INSTITUTE was established by Columbia University in 1946 to serve two major objectives: the training of a limited number of well-qualified Americans for scholarly and professional careers in the field of Russian studies and the development of research in the social sciences and the humanities as they relate to Russia and the Soviet Union. The research program of the Russian Institute is conducted through the efforts of its faculty members, of scholars invited to participate as Senior Fellows in its program, and of candidates for the Certificate of the Institute and for the degree of Doctor of Philosophy. Some of the results of the research program are presented in the Studies of the Russian Institute of Columbia University. The faculty of the Institute, without necessarily agreeing with the conclusions reached in the Studies, believe that their publication advances the difficult task of promoting systematic research on Russia and the Soviet Union and public understanding of the problems involved.

The faculty of the Russian Institute are grateful to the Rockefeller Foundation for the financial assistance which it has given to the program of research and publication.

STUDIES OF THE RUSSIAN INSTITUTE
OF COLUMBIA UNIVERSITY

SOVIET NATIONAL INCOME AND PRODUCT IN 1937
By Abram Bergson

THROUGH THE GLASS OF SOVIET LITERATURE: VIEWS
OF RUSSIAN SOCIETY
Edited by Ernest J. Simmons

THE PROLETARIAN EPISODE IN RUSSIAN LITERATURE,
1928–1932
By Edward J. Brown

MANAGEMENT OF THE INDUSTRIAL FIRM IN THE USSR:
A STUDY IN SOVIET ECONOMIC PLANNING
By David Granick

SOVIET POLICIES IN CHINA, 1917–1924
By Allen S. Whiting

UKRAINIAN NATIONALISM, 1939–1945
By John A. Armstrong

POLISH POSTWAR ECONOMY
By Thad Paul Alton

LITERARY POLITICS IN THE SOVIET UKRAINE, 1917–1934
By George S. N. Luckyj

THE EMERGENCE OF RUSSIAN PANSLAVISM, 1856–1870
By Michael Boro Petrovich

BOLSHEVISM IN TURKESTAN, 1917–1927
By Alexander G. Park

TO JEANNE

FOREWORD

◆

THE EXTENSION and exercise of Soviet rule over non-Russian peoples have traditionally been described in sweeping terms of unstinting praise or all-out condemnation. For this reason, Dr. Park's detailed and objective study of *Bolshevism in Turkestan, 1917–1927*, is all the more welcome and needed. It cuts through the billowing clouds of variously tinted propagandas to analyze realistically the actual aims, methods, and achievements of Soviet policy in Central Asia during the first decade after the revolution.

By 1917 the ancient Moslem lands of Central Asia, largely conquered by direct force of arms between 1860 and 1890, had been integrated strategically and economically, but not politically or culturally, into the Russian Empire. After 1917 the existence of Russian-populated cities as islands or citadels of Soviet power, and the control by Russian immigrants of major centers of communication, determined the main lines of the struggle of the small educated class of Moslems to enable their countrymen to exercise the Soviet-proclaimed right of national self-determination. These same factors also influenced decisively the course of the struggle by the new regime in Russia to establish its complete control over the people and resources of Central Asia. Dr. Park has given a masterly account of this unequal and intricate struggle.

Once the military supremacy of the new regime had been established, the Bolshevik leaders faced a whole series of new problems in bringing Central Asia within the scope of their

plans for political, economic, and cultural transformation. Dr.
Park has again drawn upon the full range of Soviet sources,
carefully scrutinized, to provide the first detailed picture of the
impact of Bolshevik rule on the lives of the twenty-odd millions
of Moslems situated to the east of the Caspian. To what extent
did the Soviet rulers fulfill the promises of genuine national
equality? To what extent did Soviet Moslems really participate
in the making of decisions which profoundly affected their
future? In this study these and many related questions have
been fully clarified for the first time.

Having been in close touch with Dr. Park's investigations
since he first began them in 1948 in my seminar, I can certify
that he embarked upon his study in a truly scholarly spirit of
open-mindedness. If many of his conclusions now highlight the
seamy side of Moscow's claims to be the sole "liberator" of
weaker peoples, these findings arise solely from Dr. Park's
exhaustive use of all available Soviet sources, especially those
closest to the events which he describes.

PHILIP E. MOSELY

New York, N. Y.
October, 1956

PREFACE

❖

UNTIL RECENT YEARS it has generally been assumed that Soviet nationality policy constitutes one of the great strengths of the regime. This opinion has usually been justified by reference to the achievements of the Soviet government in promoting racial equality, in broadening educational opportunities, and in encouraging technological and industrial advances in the non-Russian republics and regions of the USSR. It has been contended that the general framework of socialist goals within which Soviet society operates had generated or was forging a new unity which superseded and complemented the national and cultural diversity of the Soviet peoples.

The contrary argument that Soviet policy has inspired no greater and in some respects less unity than the policies of the Tsarist government gained ascendancy after the close of World War II. This view emphasizes the repeated Soviet campaigns against "national deviationism," frequent purges of non-Russian political and intellectual leaders, the dissolution of several Soviet autonomous formations on grounds of disloyalty during World War II, the mass deportations of inhabitants from the Western border regions, and the persistent reports of anti-Soviet partisan activities in the western Ukraine.

To some extent this recent shift toward stress upon the coercive aspects of Soviet policy reflects the rise of tensions between the Soviet Union and the Western powers. But the currency of such widely divergent views is also indicative of difficulties which confront research into Soviet nationality policy. One handicap, common to nearly all investigation in the Soviet field, derives from the broad areas of divergence between actual Soviet practices and the doctrinal principles and legal codes which theoretically define and regulate the operations of Soviet society. Soviet efforts to hinder independent observation and investigation have magnified greatly the consequences of this difficulty. Official policy has consistently sought to discourage foreign specialists from visiting and traveling in areas inhabited by Soviet national minorities and it has complicated the problem of research by affixing the stamp of official secrecy upon data relating to large areas of domestic activity. An equally formidable problem arises from the complex structure of national relationships within the USSR. Comprised of nearly 200 separate national strains, the Soviet peoples represented numerous levels of political, economic, and cultural development at the time of the Russian Revolution. In dealing with them, the Soviet government felt compelled not only to establish an elaborate hierarchy of political and administrative divisions but to adopt a bewildering variety of economic and cultural practices.

The present study cannot claim to have overcome the difficulties inherent in attacking so vast a problem as that of Soviet nationality policy. But, by narrowing the field of inquiry in time and space, it seeks to gain insights into the actual operation of that policy. In scope the work is limited to a description and analysis of certain policies and practices which the Soviet government pursued in a specific region—the Tsarist colony of Turkestan—during the first and formative decade of Bolshevik rule. In this respect it is a case study concerned with the working relationship between the living institutions of Soviet rule and the political, economic, and social goals toward which the Bolshevik rulers aspire.

This investigation also bears upon a second problem. The record of Soviet rule has been fashioned largely from interplay between the abstract force of Bolshevik doctrine and the practical demands encountered in operating and controlling a going social system. The initial test of the real meaning of the Soviet nationalities theory resides in the extent to which established Bolshevik doctrinal propositions influenced the conduct of Bolshevik revolutionary activities in the Tsarist colony of Turkestan. To be sure, a reconstruction of events which took place in Central Asia during the Russian Revolution and civil war is but a small part of the problem involved in a quest for insights into the operating relationship of Soviet nationality policy in theory and practice. Nonetheless, it does establish a useful point of departure for an investigation of the form and substance as well as the limitations of the political, economic, and cultural policies which the Soviet government adopted in its effort to foster national equality in the "backward" borderlands.

In searching out the implications and practical consequences of the Soviet concept of national rights and obligations in a socialist state, it is hoped too that this study may provide at least a tentative answer to a larger question. Has the Soviet system been able to create a new and mutually satisfying order of relationships between dominant and minor nationalities in the territories of the former Russian Empire? Or has the Soviet regime, despite its development of novel forms of political and social organization, succeeded only in establishing a colonial system of its own?

Admittedly, no single study limited to the experience of the peoples of a single region during the first decade of Soviet rule can be conclusive. It is nevertheless the contention of this writer that Soviet policy, as revealed in Turkestan, did not vary significantly from the policy pursued in other former colonies of the Russian Empire and that the essential characteristics of that policy had become manifest by the end of 1927. This work is dedicated to the discovery of these characteristics and of their relative importance in policy formation and execution in the Soviet Union.

I wish to express my sincere gratitude to the many persons who, as teachers, colleagues, and friends, stimulated my interest in Russian and Soviet studies and who have unstintingly aided me in my work. A special place in this company belongs to Professor Philip E. Mosely, formerly of the Russian Institute, Columbia University, and now of the Council on Foreign Relations. Professor Mosely's warm and patient encouragement, wise advice, and perceptive criticism not only guided this study to completion but led me surely into the field of public law and government. I am also deeply indebted to the members of the staff of the Russian Institute, Columbia University, Professors Geroid T. Robinson, John N. Hazard, Abram Bergson, and Ernest J. Simmons, whose careful teaching and scholarship provided a firm foundation for my study of matters Russian and Soviet.

Other scholars and teachers, of whom but a few can be mentioned, contributed of their time and support in this project. I wish to name especially Professor Clyde Kluckhohn, former director of the Russian Research Center at Harvard University, Professor Merle Fainsod of Harvard University, and Mrs. Xenia Eudin of the Hoover War Memorial Library at Stanford University. The kind assistance rendered to me by the librarians and personnel of the Columbia University libraries, the Harvard University libraries, the Hoover War Memorial Library at Stanford University, the New York Public Library, and the Library of Congress cannot go without mention.

The task of editing and shepherding the manuscript through printing was in the capable hands of Mr. William F. Bernhardt of Columbia University Press. Not the least, I acknowledge the tireless work of my wife in typing, reading, and criticizing the manuscript.

The funds which made this study possible came from two sources. In the years 1947–48 and 1948–49 the Carnegie Corporation, through the Russian Institute at Columbia University, made available to me grants which enabled me to pursue my studies in the Russian and Soviet field and to embark upon the early stages of this work. The bulk of the research was conducted in 1949 and 1950 under an Area Research Training Fellowship of the Social Science Research Council. Without this aid, the study could not have been completed.

Washington, D. C.   ALEXANDER G. PARK
October, 1956

CONTENTS

◈

MAPS

◆

TABLES

◆

BOLSHEVISM IN TURKESTAN

1917-1927

I

THE BOLSHEVIK
REVOLUTION
IN CENTRAL ASIA

◆

FROM the Baltic Sea to Lake Baikal and southward to the High
Pamir and the Caucasian Alps lies the great Russian plain.
Here nature has raised few obstacles against the sweep of the
restless wind or the movement of more restless man. In times
past, successive waves of migration and conquest have swept
across its broad expanse and have spent themselves in its vast-
ness. Empires, arising along its periphery, dominated it from
time to time, cast out frontiers of settlement, and, receding,
bequeathed to the plain their own legacy of ethnic and cultural
diversity. As the last of these declined, Muscovy debouched into
the plain and spread gradually outward along the river valleys
across low-lying watersheds to the highlands of the south and
east. Only in the west where nature had drawn no strong physical frontier was the struggle over the demarcation of a permanent boundary bitter and continuous. Elsewhere the forces of
distance and wilderness played a larger role in retarding the
outward march of Russian settlement and conquest than did the
resistance of indigenous peoples. But neither man nor nature
could stem the tide of Russian expansion, and, at its height, the
Empire of the tsars embraced some eight and a half million
square miles of contiguous territory—approximately one sixth
of the total land surface of the earth.

The origins of a nationality problem which would one day confront the government of the Union of Soviet Socialist Republics were rooted partially in this historical extension of Great Russian political domination across territories inhabited by a host of culturally and linguistically diverse national and ethnic groups. Tsarist census takers, who canvassed the entire country, except Finland, in 1897, reported 104 nationalities speaking 146 languages and dialects. Soviet demographers, operating within the shortened boundaries of the USSR nearly thirty years later, counted 182 ethnic groups speaking 149 languages.[1] At the earlier census, the politically dominant Great Russians constituted only 43 percent of the total population. But in company with the Ukrainians and White Russians, whose languages, history, and culture were linked closely with their own, they not only dominated the non-Slavic peoples numerically but provided the unifying force which held the far-flung nations of Russia together. Among the other peoples of the Empire, several of whom numbered a million or more, there existed neither a pole of attraction strong enough to threaten the supremacy of the Russian core nor even the bond of a common history or culture.

It is significant too that the spirit of the Russian Empire—although the Empire itself was founded on a national Muscovite state—was dynastic and supranational. Until the last quarter of the nineteenth century, Great Russian nationalism did not express itself in extreme political forms. Government policy had disapproved of non-Orthodox religious sects; it had discouraged the use of local languages in public institutions; and it had denied certain privileges to non-Great Russians. But it had balanced these disabilities within the European parts of the Empire by throwing open the ranks of the ruling military and bureaucratic caste to those of its non-Russian subjects who would adopt the Great Russian language and assimilate themselves to the Russian culture. Consequently, groups which otherwise might have assumed the leadership of incipient na-

---

[1] Avrahm Yarmolinsky, *The Jews and Other Minor Nationalities under the Soviets* (New York, 1928), pp. 141, 183; for a listing of peoples as shown in the 1926 census, see Frank Lorimer, *The Population of the Soviet Union: History and Prospects* (Geneva, 1946), pp. 55–61.

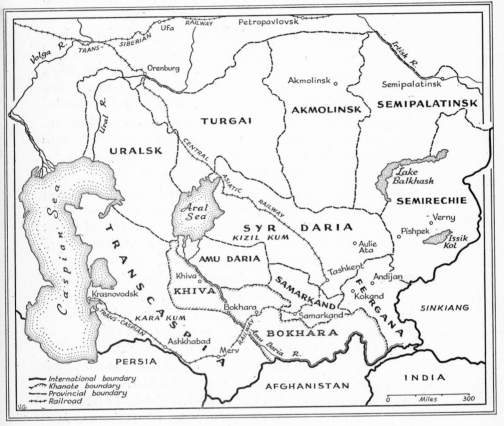

PRE-SOVIET CENTRAL ASIA

tional movements tended to find a place in the bulging apparatus of government and to assume an interest in the preservation
of the regime.

In the Asiatic parts of the Empire, typically colonial methods
of administration prevailed. Guarantees of protection and
privilege were in most cases sufficient to transform native ruling
classes into agents of Tsarist rule. But the government also
planted its military garrisons on the headwaters of the principal
rivers and along the main routes of trade and travel and encouraged the settlement of European immigrant communities in
close proximity to—but nearly always separated physically from
—the chief towns of non-Russian districts.[2]

Administrative procedures and policies in Russian Central
Asia—a region whose fortunes during the first decade of Soviet
rule will form a central part of our story—were typical of the
Tsarist colonial system. The region itself, known before 1917
as Russian Turkestan, consists of a broad strip of territory
stretching eastward from the Caspian Sea along the borders of
Persia and Afghanistan to the mountain frontiers of western
China. Ethnically its peoples were Turkic in origin, with a
strong admixture of Mongolian—except for a small group of
Iranian Tajiks in the southeast. While nomadism still prevailed
among the Turcoman, Kazakh, and Kirghiz tribes as late as the
Soviet period, the fertile valleys and oases had encouraged the
growth of sedentary civilizations in ancient times. There, at the
time of the Russian conquest, the cities of Tashkent, Samarkand, Kokand, Bokhara, and Merv—rich with the traditions
and monuments of past magnificence—still flourished as centers
of Moslem culture and learning.

The Russian advance into Central Asia was carried out
mainly in the nineteenth century and was completed only with
the capture of Merv in 1884. Formal incorporation of parts of
the region into the Tsarist Empire had begun nearly twenty
years earlier and progressed rapidly after the formation of a
government-general of Turkestan in 1867. The sole exceptions

---

[2] For an excellent description and analysis of the policy of the Tsarist regime
and its effects upon the non-Great Russian peoples, see Sir John Maynard, *Russia in Flux* (New York, 1948), pp. 444–56.

were the khanates of Khiva and Bokhara. In these principalities, the Tsarist government maintained the native khans in their rule but exercised the power of life and death over them by direct control over their sources of water supply. Even in areas of direct Russian rule, the Tsarist administrative system interfered little in the accustomed way of life of the native community. The official staffs and language were Russian but the administrators themselves avoided rigid enforcement of the policy of Russification. In large measure the Moslem community continued to govern itself according to the centuries-old theocratic laws of social organization and conduct laid down in the Shariat, or canon law of Islam. The kadi continued to hold court and to dispense Koranic justice. The time-honored system of Moslem education, which consisted largely of memorizing and reciting the Koran and other sacred texts of Islam; the bride price and the seclusion of women; and, in the more remote regions, even the primitive law of vendetta remained in force.

The conciliatory aspects of Tsarist colonial rule were nonetheless considerably outweighed by official efforts to extend the frontier of Russian colonization and to establish quasi-garrisons of permanent European settlement at strategic points. Along the northern borders of Turkestan, where nature favored extensive forms of agriculture, the Russian government transformed the land outright into state property and after 1890 opened it to peasant and Cossack immigrants from European Russia. The colonists, aided by the government, seized the most fertile plowlands in these districts and gradually drove the native tribes and peoples into the surrounding deserts and mountains. Throughout most of Turkestan proper, however, Russian colonization followed a pattern which saw the emergence of urban European settlements side by side with, but isolated physically and culturally from, the principal native communities. In these centers lived not only the soldiers, officials, and merchants usually associated with colonial rule, but the nucleus of a working class which had been imported into Central Asia to operate the Russian-built railways and industries.

One fact stands out clearly at the outset. Turkestan represented precisely the type of environment which Marxists before
1917 had considered most unsuitable for the promotion of a
social revolution. In many districts nomadism still prevailed at
the time of the Russian Revolution and the primitive tribal organization, in which even private property existed only in rudimentary forms, was not extinct. Among the settled peoples,
primitive forms of agriculture and land tenure still retained
their vitality. Russian influence nonetheless had left its own
impression on the economic and social life of the people.

In the four decades between the incorporation of Turkestan
into the Russian Empire and the outbreak of World War I,
Russian enterprise had converted the region into the primary
source of cotton in the Empire (it supplied 80 percent of the
total domestic crop) and Tashkent, its principal city, had developed as the railroad center of Central Asia. Alongside the
local system of economic supply and distribution and undermining its foundation, a modern economic apparatus had come
into being. Even the rudiments of an industrial structure had
grown up around the railway shops and the cotton ginning
plants. The influx of Russian goods and capital, moreover, had
evoked consumer demands that could not be satisfied on the
local market; after the Russian conquest cheap manufactured
goods began to flood the bazaars and slowly drove the products
of the inefficient kustar', or artisan, off the market. The small
agricultural producer suffered even more and in many cases was
driven off the land entirely. In consequence of these conditions,
the old tribal and semifeudal pattern of social relationships was
in the process of dissolution when the Bolsheviks seized power
in Petrograd. But the breakdown was by no means complete.

The independent khanates of Khiva and Bokhara too had
felt the shock of Russian economic expansion in Central Asia,
but, unlike Turkestan, they had not been subjected to complete
domination by St. Petersburg. Administrative functions remained in native hands, existing social institutions were disturbed relatively little, and Russian capital had penetrated
their economies on a much smaller scale than in Turkestan. In
the less fertile regions of these countries, as well as in the drier

regions of Turkestan, nomadism still prevailed among the Kirghiz, Kazakhs, and Turcomans. The more numerous Uzbek population, on the other hand, was largely sedentary and generally more advanced. It provided the greatest proportion of native industrial laborers for the cotton ginning plants and the railroads. Similarly it was from Uzbek stock primarily that the beginnings of a middle class and its concomitant, a middle-class intelligentsia, were emerging. "Capitalism," however, was in a rudimentary stage and was confined basically to usury, retail trade, and private ownership in land.

These trends had not proved to be a divisive factor in the non-Russian community. For the most part, natives of every political and social persuasion were united by a common aspiration to be rid of Russian colonial domination. The Russian settlement in Turkestan, on the other hand, was just as firmly committed to maintaining the region on a colonial footing. The stake of the Russian administrators and officials in the preservation of the *status quo* was obvious; but all other categories of the immigrant population had benefited as well. The Russo-Ukrainian peasantry, whom the Tsarist government had settled on lands seized from the natives, saw in the regime a source of protection and future aggrandizement. The immigrant workingmen had acquired status by the mere fact of membership in the ruling nationality, and they monopolized the skilled and supervisory positions which local industry offered.[3] These interests, moreover, were intensified by the physical and spiritual isolation of the entire Russian community from the native population. And their effect upon the character of the Russian Revolution in Central Asia was decisive.

THE OCTOBER REVOLUTION IN TURKESTAN

The collapse of the Romanov dynasty in February, 1917, was followed in Tashkent, as it had been in Petrograd, by a period of dual power which pitted an official Turkestan Committee, composed of former Tsarist administrators and supporters of the Provisional Government, against a radical Soviet of Work-

[3] Economic data gathered in 1914 showed that the Russians, representing one fifth of the industrial workers in Turkestan, held three fourths of the jobs requiring skilled labor. Lorimer, *Population of the Soviet Union*, p. 23.

ers' and Peasants' Deputies. Both of these bodies were Russian in composition and origin and represented conflicting interests within the immigrant community in Turkestan. In the Moslem community, the general breakdown of authority, which attended the February events, also precipitated a demand for autonomy, but the Moslems of Turkestan, unlike the Russian colonists, found themselves unable during the early months of the revolution to create an effective political instrumentality for registering their claims. It was, in fact, only the rise of the Tashkent Soviet to power which gave a sharp delineation to the native demand for national self-determination and brought it into direct and open conflict with the demand of the Russian railway workers for a socialist regime in Turkestan. Already in September, 1917, the dichotomy in the aims of these rival camps had become evident.

In that month the Tashkent Soviet, under Bolshevik leadership, made its first bid for power. Mass demonstrations of railway workers and soldiers, who demanded worker control of production, nationalization of the banks, and the transfer of the land to the toiling peasantry, took place from September 12–16. While workers marched through the streets demanding "All Power to the Soviets," a temporary revolutionary committee was formed and prepared to seize the government. The revolutionary outburst resulted in a general strike that brought the economic activity of the city to a standstill. But it failed in its purpose. Largely because the Provisional Government in Petrograd was able to rush reinforcements to the scene, but partly because the natives took no part in the uprising, the revolutionary bid was crushed and its leaders were jailed. Native reaction, however, was not confined to nonparticipation. At month's end an extraordinary All-Moslem Conference, guided by Uzbek intellectuals, convened in the city and demanded the establishment of a Moslem government, an end to the interference of foreigners in the internal affairs of Turkestan, and autonomy for Turkestan within a Russian federated republic.[4]

[4] Georgii Safarov, *Kolonial'naia revoliutsiia: opyt Turkestana* (Moscow, 1921), p. 62.

Curiously, the demands set forth at the Moslem Conference fell within the limits prescribed in the Bolshevik Party's own program in the nationality question. Two propositions were central to the Bolshevik position as it affected the colonial regions of the Tsarist Empire. One was a demand for political and civil liberties, the complete equality of the rights of all nations and languages, and a wide measure of regional autonomy and local self-government. The other involved the right of all the oppressed nations of the Tsarist Empire to national self-determination, which the Bolsheviks defined as the right to secede and form an independent state. Support of the latter principle did not also commit the Bolsheviks to support every demand, or any particular demand, for separation, but it did place that decision firmly in the hands of the oppressed nation. The nation might secede if it so desired. If it did not, it possessed no right which did not belong to all other citizens of the state. Since equality of language, education, and culture would naturally accompany the formation of a workers' republic in Russia, the nations had no need for special devices to protect them against national oppression.[5]

The nationality plank in the Bolshevik platform underwent no basic revision in the interim between the February and October Revolutions in Russia. At its Seventh Conference in April, 1917, the Party reaffirmed its support of the right of "all nations forming part of Russia" to "free separation and the right to form their own independent states." [6] Joseph Stalin,

---

[5] From the resolution on the nationality question adopted at the August Conference of the Central Committee of the Bolshevik wing of the Russian Social Democratic Labor Party in 1913. Text in *Vse-Soiuznaia Kommunisticheskaia Partiia v rezoliutsiiakh i resheniiakh s'ezdov, soveshchanii i plenumov Tsentral'nogo Komiteta (1898–1932)* (4th ed., Moscow, 1932), I, 238–40. The resolution of the conference related specifically to "capitalistic conditions," but Lenin in theses propounded in 1916 in his article on "The Socialist Revolution and the Right of Nations to Self-Determination" (Vladimir I. Lenin, *Sochineniia* [2d ed., Moscow, 1930–35], XIX, 37–48), argued that "victorious socialism" must still support the "right of oppressed nations to self-determination." In this same article he specifically assigned the right of exercising self-determination in colonies and dependent countries to the rising middle class which, he wrote, was not only the most progressive class but the only class capable of leading a militant struggle for democracy.

[6] Text of resolution in *Vse-Soiuznaia Kommunisticheskaia Partiia v rezoliutsiiakh* (4th ed.), I, 271–72.

who appeared at the conference as reporter on the nationality question, repeated Lenin's frequent admonition that recognition of the right of separation did not also commit the Bolsheviks to support every demand for separation. But he neither denied the privilege of exercising the right to any nationality in the Empire nor indicated that the Bolsheviks would condone the use of force in opposing national claims. For the Bolshevik Party, doctrine permitted only "freedom of agitation for or against separation, depending upon the interests of the proletariat and the proletarian revolution." [7]

The principles of national equality and self-determination which the Bolshevik program supported had no influence in Turkestan upon the policy of the Tashkent Soviet or upon the Russian Bolsheviks and Left Social Revolutionaries who dominated it. Neither before nor after the miscarriage of the September coup did the leaders of the Soviet solicit or expect Moslem support in overthrowing the Turkestan Committee. Instead they directed their revolutionary appeals to the military forces stationed in the district. At the end of October (a week before the revolution in Petrograd), after the Soviets had won over the Tashkent military garrison, the Soviet seizure of power took place. Thereafter, the new regime took immediate steps to consolidate its authority and to exclude both native and European competitors from power. In mid-November the Third Congress of Soviets, whose task was to lay the foundation of the Soviet power in Turkestan, convened in Tashkent.

One of the strangest peculiarities of this congress [wrote Chokaiev, who later became president of the Kokand Autonomous Govern-

---

[7] Joseph V. Stalin, *Sochineniia* (Moscow, 1946—), III, 52–53. Stalin repeated these strictures in August, 1917, in an article which called the Provisional Government to account for its opposition to the national claims of non-Great Russian peoples. He denounced specifically the government's forcible dissolution of the Finnish Seim. Stalin agreed that duty compelled the Russian Marxists to point out the "mistakes" of those nations which sought independence, but he wrote, "*no one* has the right to interfere *forcibly* in the internal life of nations and to 'correct' their mistakes by force." *Ibid.*, III, 206–9. Lenin also continued to insist upon "the right of free separation" for the peoples of Russia and promised as late as October to recognize this right "immediately and unconditionally with regard to Finland, the Ukraine, Armenia and any other nationality oppressed by Tsarism" if the Bolsheviks won power. V. I. Lenin, *Collected Works* (London, 1927—), XXI, Part II, 93–94.

ment] was the fact that no representative of the native population of Turkestan took part in its deliberations. The soldiers sent thither from the interior provinces of Russia, the peasants settled therein by the old [Tsarist] regime on the lands confiscated from our people, and the workers accustomed to regard us haughtily from above —these were the people who were to decide at this moment the fate of Turkestan.[8]

The character of the representatives determined the attitude of the congress toward native participation in the regime. By an overwhelming vote, ninety-seven to seventeen, the congress adopted a special resolution excluding Moslems from governmental posts.[9]

To the Moslems of Turkestan this was proof enough that the change in the faces of the rulers had not altered Russian policy toward Turkestan. Even earlier their hopes in the February Revolution had been disappointed, for the Provisional Government had continued the repressions against the natives begun by the Tsarist regime in retaliation for the native uprisings of 1916. Throughout 1917 arrests had persisted and punitive expeditions against the rebels still went out regularly from the Russian garrison towns. Even General Kuropatkin's notorious plan for removing the Kirghiz and the Kazakhs into the mountainous regions was put into effect, and unscrupulous peasants, assisted by "revolutionary soldiers" who had returned from the front, took advantage of the turmoil to plunder natives of their possessions.[10] These policies, moreover, received the support of nearly all elements within the immigrant European community

[8] Mustapha Chokaiev, "Turkestan and the Soviet Regime," *Journal of the Royal Central Asian Society*, XVIII (1931), 406. According to a Soviet account, three natives were present at the congress, but the figure was cited in a condemnation, not approbation, of the policy of the early Soviet regime toward the native population. See S. Dimanshtein, "Po povodu uchrezhdeniia narkomnatsa Turkrespubliki," *Zhizn' Natsional'nostei*, No. 28 (126) (December 3, 1921).

[9] Soviet hostility was not addressed exclusively to native groups seeking a voice in government. The Tashkent government opposed every attempt on the part of outsiders to gain admittance to positions of authority. A peasant congress petition to merge with the Congress of Soviets was rejected on the ground that the merger would result in a peasant majority. See Safarov, *Kolonial'naia revoliutsiia: opyt Turkestana*, pp. 76–77.

[10] Chokaiev, "Turkestan and the Soviet Regime," *Journal of the Royal Central Asian Society*, XVIII (1931), 405.

in Turkestan. In early summer the First Congress of Soviets of Turkestan had insisted upon government action to remove the turbulent part of the Kirghiz (Kazakh) population, to prevent the return of fugitives from China, and to maintain military units in the villages to prevent hunger riots.[11] Throughout the entire period, the Social Revolutionary press had opposed distribution of land to landless natives; the solution to the agrarian problem, it had argued, lay in the extension of the irrigation system.

Although European hostility to the Moslem community provoked no outbreaks of native violence in 1917, it had excited a wave of native resentment and appears to have contributed to the demand for Turkestanian autonomy at the Second Pan-Islam Congress in September, 1917. After the Soviet seizure of power in Tashkent, Moslem bitterness, enflamed by fear of the social revolution and indignation at the exclusion of natives from the new government, led to a complete break. In mid-November, while the Third Congress of Soviets was meeting to organize the Tashkent Council of People's Commissars, a Third All-Moslem Congress, which had convened in another part of Tashkent, repeated the previous demand for autonomy and ordered the formation of a Moslem government. Although a small minority (sixteen representatives) spoke for recognition of the all-Russian and local councils of people's commissars and for participation in the soviets, the congress expressed overwhelming hostility to the October Revolution.[12]

To be sure, the Moslem Congress voiced aspirations which

---

[11] This solution to the so-called Kirghiz problem was the one generally accepted by the Russian immigrant population in Central Asia. In April, 1917, a peasant congress, which met at Vernyi (Alma Ata), adopted a similar resolution. "National antagonism," it read, "ought to be overcome through agitation. In those localities where a complete reconciliation cannot be achieved the Kirghiz population must be isolated from the Russian. If necessary, recourse must be had to the removal of the Kirghiz to other localities. In order to prevent a possible collision in the Przheval'sk district the staff of the bodyguards, companies, and Cossack troops must be augmented and outposts established in the passes." Quoted in M. Belotskii, *Kirgizskaia Respublika* (Moscow, 1936), pp. 29–30.

[12] Safarov, *Kolonial'naia revoliutsiia: opyt Turkestana*, p. 64; also "Ocherk po razvitiiu revoliutsii v Turkestane," *Zhizn' Natsional'nostei*, No. 3 (November 24, 1918).

had previously been identified more with a coterie of national-istic Moslem intellectuals than with the native population at large, but its demand for Turkestanian autonomy under a native government soon gained the backing of every important element within the Moslem community. Initially, Moslem re-ligious leaders,[13] who spoke for the conservative element in the native community, had not contested the right of the Soviet regime to exercise temporal power in Turkestan. But when the Tashkent Soviet refused to entertain their petition for a civil administration based on the precepts of Moslem law, they quickly took the side of the nationalists. The native peasants followed suit. To them the revolution appeared to have brought into power nothing more than a new regime of Euro-pean exploiters. Even the native working class refused to sup-port the new government.[14] Except for the immigrant Russian working class, the local military garrison, and certain European petit-bourgeois elements, nearly every group in Turkestan turned against the Soviet regime.

Such was the situation when in early December, 1917, the Fourth Extraordinary Regional Moslem Congress met in Ko-kand to proclaim the autonomy of Turkestan.[15] Present were 150 representatives from Fergana, twenty-two from Syr-Daria, twenty-one from Samarkand, four from Bokhara, and one from Transcaspia.[16] Although one faction insisted upon a unilateral proclamation of autonomy such as the Ukrainian Rada already had made, the majority adopted a more conciliatory attitude. Hopes still ran high that the Soviet government in Petrograd would honor its promises of self-determination by interceding in Turkestan in behalf of the Moslem claimants. If it did not,

[13] Most early Soviet accounts mention an "Ulema party" and define it as a political instrument of the Moslem religious community and the large land-owners. It appears likely that these references erroneously ascribe a political character to the Turkestanian ulema, or body of Islamic scholars who achieved their position in the group on the basis of their knowledge and training in Moslem religion and law.

[14] P. Alekseenkov, "Kokandskaia Avtonomiia," in Istpart Sredazbiuro Ts.K., V.K.P. (b), *Revoliutsiia v Srednei Asii: sbornik* (Tashkent, 1928), I, 31.

[15] For a Soviet account of the deliberations of the congress, see *ibid.,* pp. 28–36.

[16] Joseph Castagné, "Le Turkestan depuis la révolution russe," *Revue du Monde Musulman,* L (June, 1922), 47–48.

all expected the forthcoming All-Russian Constituent Assembly to effect a satisfactory settlement. As yet, hostility to the Bolsheviks had not hardened into implacable opposition, and the nationalist leadership, according to Chokaiev, was concerned less with "the creation of barriers between our own and the Russian peoples" than with "the reconstruction of the life of our people on new lines." [17] These considerations weighed heavily in the decisions of the congress and tempered its declaration of Turkestanian autonomy.

The Fourth Extraordinary Regional Congress [the proclamation read] expresses the will of the peoples of Turkestan to self-determination in accordance with the principle proclaimed by the great Russian revolution, [and] proclaims Turkestan territorially autonomous in union with the federal democratic Republic of Russia. The elaboration of the form of autonomy is entrusted to the Constituent Assembly of Turkestan, which must be convened as soon as possible. The congress solemnly declares herewith that the rights of national minorities [Russians] settled in Turkestan will be fully safeguarded.[18]

To reinforce this decision the congress elected a thirty-two member delegation to the Constituent Assembly and chose a government consisting of a twelve-member "Council of Ministers of Autonomous Turkestan" and a "Council of Toilers." [19] At midnight of December 11, the autonomy of Turkestan was proclaimed, and the new government installed itself in Old Kokand.

Although the Tashkent Soviet was not immediately aware of the significance of the events which had transpired in Kokand, it was soon brought face to face with the reality of united Moslem opposition. On December 13, on the occasion of Mohammed's birthday, the autonomy of Turkestan was declared in Tashkent and eleven days later a Moslem mass demonstration took place. On that day a virtual sea of white-turbaned Moslems bearing green and light-blue standards surged through

[17] Chokaiev, "Turkestan and the Soviet Regime," *Journal of the Royal Central Asian Society*, XVIII (1931), 407.

[18] *Ibid.*

[19] S. B. Ginzberg, "Basmachestvo v Fergane," *Novyi Vostok*, Nos. 10–11 (1925), p. 183.

the streets in the direction of the government palace. There, with the approval of the crowd, a protest was voted against the dissolution of the municipal duma, against searches, violation of households, and requisitions. However, the much feared and expected revolution did not occur. After a few speeches and the protest, the crowd broke up, leaving the Tashkent Soviet still in control.

Up to this point the Kokand government, lacking military power, was little more than an annoyance to the Tashkent Soviet. The situation became serious, however, when a people's militia began to take form at Kokand and the Moslem government began negotiations for the issuance of a three-million-ruble internal loan. Early in January the organized Moslem workers and peasants of Turkestan convened at Kokand to express their support for the autonomy of Turkestan. The Kokand government utilized the occasion to appeal again to Petrograd "to recognize the Provisional Government of autonomous Turkestan as the only government of Turkestan" and to demand the dissolution of the Tashkent Soviet "which relies on foreign elements hostile to the native population of the country, contrary to the principle of the self-determination of peoples proclaimed by the October Revolution." [20]

Petrograd's response to this petition, while not encouraging to the autonomists of Kokand, was no more reassuring to the Tashkent Soviet. In a declaration of its position, which amounted to an invitation to open warfare between the natives of Turkestan and the regional Soviet government—it was written by Stalin—the center replied:

The soviets are autonomous in their internal affairs and discharge their duties by relying on their actual forces. Therefore, it will not behoove the native proletarians of Turkestan to appeal to the central Soviet authority with petitions to dissolve the Turkestan Council of People's Commissars which, in their opinion, is leaning upon the non-Moslem army elements, but they should themselves dissolve it by force, if such force is available to the native proletarians and peasants.[21]

[20] Chokaiev, "Turkestan and the Soviet Regime," *Journal of the Royal Central Asian Society*, XVIII (1931) , 408.
[21] Quoted in Vadim Chaikan, *K istorii Rossiiskoi Revoliutsii:* Vol. I, *Kazn' 26 Bakinskikh Komissarov* (Moscow, 1922) , p. 133.

Released thus from the obligation to defer to the authority of the central Soviet government on the matter of autonomy, Kokand moved one step closer to independent action.

There remained the commitment to accept the decision of the All-Russian Constituent Assembly, but when Bolshevik sailors dispersed that body at the end of its first session, the last objection to unilateral Moslem action disappeared. On January 23, 1918, Kokand telegraphed to the Tashkent Soviet its decision to convoke a "Turkestan Constituent Assembly" composed of the elected representatives of every district in Turkestan and "summoned to resolve all the expectations and desires of the people and to promulgate democratic principles in autonomous Turkestan." Unlike the Soviet regime in Turkestan, which had proclaimed the equality of all peoples but had banned Moslems from government posts, the Kokand autonomists reserved one third of the seats of their Constituent Assembly to the "non-Moslem population" and pledged themselves to enact legislation which would "guarantee the rights of minorities . . . and of the laboring peoples." [22]

After this the Tashkent Soviet could afford no longer to ignore the challenge. For one thing, Tashkent, confronted by almost daily reminders of its own isolation, could not overlook the growing belief among Russians as well as Moslems that Kokand represented the aspirations of the majority of the population better than did the Tashkent Soviet. Even its internationalism met indictment in the columns of the independent socialist press of Turkestan.[23] Moreover, Kokand's effort to convoke a Constituent Assembly which, no one doubted, would give an overwhelming endorsement to the dissolution of the Tashkent Soviet presented a direct challenge to the survival of

[22] *Svobodnyi Turkestan,* January 24, 1918.

[23] *Svobodnyi Turkestan,* a Tashkent newspaper which was devoted to independent socialist thought, was especially critical of the Tashkent government. In its issue of January 24, 1918, it charged that the world of Islam, united under the slogan "Moslems of the World Unite," was "much more 'internationalist' than those Turkestanian 'socialists' who understand one another badly but who are outwardly united by the cry 'Proletarians of the World Unite' and who violate the freedom of the natives in spite of this slogan." The newspaper itself was suppressed shortly thereafter. It reemerged briefly under the name *Novyi Turkestan,* then disappeared completely.

the Soviet regime in Turkestan. In any case, the Soviet government was beginning to find the presence of dual authority in
Turkestan intolerable. Not only had it drawn a sharp line between competing classes—a "bourgeois" government in Kokand
versus a "proletarian" government in Tashkent—but it expressed vividly the dichotomy between the numerically overwhelming native population and the Europeans.

At the Fourth Regional Congress of Soviets which met in
Tashkent at the end of January, 1918, Kolesov, president of the
Turkestan Council of People's Commissars, accepted the challenge. Classing the Kokand government as a threat no less dangerous to Soviet power than anti-Soviet agitators and Ataman
Dutov's counterrevolutionary Cossack army which had severed
communications between Europe and Turkestan, he demanded
immediate Soviet action to crush the "counterfeit autonomy"
of the Moslem nationalists.[24] The congress seconded his demands. In a declaration reminiscent of the resolutions of the
Third All-Russian Congress of Soviets, it ordered subordination of "the principle of self-determination of peoples wholly
to socialism" and defined "the self-determination of peoples
solely as the self-determination of the toiling classes." [25] Demanding a "soviet autonomy" for Turkestan, the resolution
concluded with a declaration of war against Kokand.[26]

Much as Stalin had done at the Third Congress of Soviets,[27]
the Turkestanian Soviet government insisted that the conflict
had arisen on class, not national, grounds. And it could point
to organizational work among lower-class Moslems in substan-

[24] *Svobodnyi Turkestan*, January 25, 1918.
[25] The authors of this resolution, in evident imitation of Stalin's logic at the
Third Congress of Soviets, took pains to deny that the conflict between Tashkent and Kokand had a national implication. "This conflict has no national
basis," the declaration read. "It is a clash between the socialist government of
Russia and this autonomous government, the whole power of which is actually
in the hands of the bourgeoisie." Text of the resolution in "Vopros ob avtonomii
Turkestana na Kraevom Sovetskom S'ezde," *Svobodnyi Turkestan*, January 25,
1918. Compare with the resolution on self-determination of the toilers adopted
by the Third All-Russian Congress of Soviets. Text in *Tretii Vserossiiskii S'ezd
Sovetov Rabochikh, Soldatskikh i Krest'ianskikh Deputatov* (Peterburg, 1918),
p. 94.
[26] P. G. Antropov, *Materialy i dokumenty I S'ezda Kompartii Turkestana*
(Tashkent, 1934), pp. 67–68.
[27] For Stalin's report, see Stalin, *Sochineniia*, IV, 30–37.

tiation of its argument. Even before the Soviet seizure of power, local Bolsheviks, unlike the Social Revolutionaries whose support of the immigrant peasantry had brought them into conflict with the native population, had sent organizers grouped in *piaterki* (groups of five) to gain native support for the social revolution. In Tashkent they had won some influence over native workers in the construction and leather industries and over segments of the kustar' workers. In Fergana a "Union of Toiling Moslems" emerged and a similar organization arose in Samarkand; both were composed of native industrial workers, kustar' workers, and urban poor.[28] After the revolution in Tashkent, moreover, a regional Soviet of Moslem Workers' and Soldiers' Deputies was formed around the sixteen who had voted for recognition of the revolution at the Third All-Moslem Congress.[29] But this was no legislative or administrative agency as the name would seem to imply. Its work consisted merely of educating native workers, offering them some economic protection, and propagating the ideas of social revolution. When the issue of Kokand put the "Union" to the test, it split and one faction went over to the nationalists.[30]

The Tashkent Soviet, in any case, did not count on active native support in its campaign against the Kokand government. The existence of pro-Soviet organizations, composed of Moslem laborers, was useful to the Soviet effort to shift the dispute to class grounds, but the conduct of actual military operations fell to more reliable Russian Red Guard detachments from Tashkent and the Orenburg front.[31] On February 14, these troops,

---

[28] F. Bozhko, *Grazhdanskaia Voina v Srednei Azii* (Tashkent, 1930), p. 15.

[29] "Ocherk po razvitiiu revoliutsii v Turkestane," *Zhizn' Natsional'nostei*, No. 3 (November 24, 1918).

[30] Alekseenkov, "Kokandskaia Avtonomiia," in Istpart Sredazbiuro Ts.K., V.K.P.(b), *Revoliutsiia v Srednei Azii*, I, 32–33.

[31] The detachment from Tashkent contained a large number of Austrian and Rumanian prisoners-of-war whom the Tashkent government had impressed into service. The Soviet practice of using prisoners-of-war to augment its own forces, incidentally, was followed so flagrantly in Central Asia that it aroused a storm of protest from the home governments of the prisoners. The protests of these governments finally compelled the Soviet government to issue an order—it was signed by Lenin, Trotsky, and Chicherin—which forbade the Red Army to recruit prisoners and ordered it to muster out those already in service. But when Captain A. H. Brun, a Danish Red Cross representative in Tashkent, demanded that the local government execute the order, Kolesov, chairman of the Turkestan Council of People's Commissars, told him, "The order is nothing but

with the support of Red Guard detachments organized by the soviet of the New City of Kokand, surrounded the Old City and four days later breached its walls. More than 14,000 persons perished in the massacre that followed.[32]

The Soviet government, fearful that the news of the sack of Kokand would provoke a general Moslem rebellion, tried to minimize the atrocities that were being committed. On March 1 the Regional Congress of Soviets ordered "the Military Revolutionary Committee to refrain from active appearances in order to forestall a declaration of war by Moslems throughout the whole region." [33] On the following day the Soviet Military Revolutionary Committee appealed to the population of Fergana not to believe rumors "spread by the enemies of the people" that Red forces would bombard Kokand and shoot its inhabitants.[34] But the news could not be suppressed, and the worst was confirmed when soldiers began to appear in the bazaars of other towns offering for sale the plunder taken in the Old City of Kokand.[35] Moreover, the Soviet government visited its own punishment upon the Moslem population by commandeering stocks of food in the area and halting further imports of grain. In the ensuing famine, an estimated 25 to 50 percent of the entire population of the Kokand region perished.[36]

The short-lived Kokand Autonomous Government was significant not only because it offered the first organized native

a scrap of paper in our eyes." See Captain A. H. Brun, *Troublous Times: Experiences in Bolshevik Russia and Turkestan* (London, 1931), pp. 78–79.

[32] Colonel P. T. Etherton, *In the Heart of Asia* (London, 1925), p. 154. Even the semiofficial *History of the Civil War in the U.S.S.R.*, edited by the highest Party officials, was obliged to admit in reference to the sack of Kokand that "many of the local Bolsheviks distorted the policy of the Bolshevik Party on the national question and committed gross mistakes in their dealings with the native population." See M. Gorkii, V. Molotov, K. Voroshilov, S. Kirov, and J. Stalin (eds.), *The History of the Civil War in the U.S.S.R.* (New York, 1938), I, 217.

[33] *Novyi Turkestan*, March 2, 1918.

[34] *Ibid.*, March 3, 1918.

[35] Brun, *Troublous Times: Experiences in Bolshevik Russia and Turkestan*, p. 79. Three weeks after the fall of Kokand reports were still arriving in Tashkent of continued pillaging and anarchy which the Kokand Soviet could not stop. *Novyi Turkestan*, March 20, 1918.

[36] Colonel P. T. Etherton, who was serving as British consul in Chinese Turkestan at the time, reported that 900,000 persons died in the famine and that other thousands fled into Chinese Turkestan. Etherton, *In the Heart of Asia*, p. 154.

opposition to the Soviet regime or because it ignited the spark of a later general Moslem rebellion. National in form, its essence was the rise of the native middle class and intelligentsia to leadership within the Moslem community.[37] The events of 1917 had actually set in motion two revolutions in Turkestan: a proletarian revolution of the European workers and soldiers in Tashkent and a bourgeois-national revolution of the native middle class. That the two were mutually exclusive was apparent from the beginning; either one or the other had to eliminate its opponent. Yet the mood of the people was not decisive. The outcome hinged rather on the fact that the Tashkent Soviet had arms and soldiers while the Kokand government did not. Thus the Kokand government perished though it undoubtedly enjoyed far wider popularity than the Tashkent Soviet.

THE REVOLUTION EXPANDS: INCIDENTS IN
TRANSCASPIA AND BOKHARA

Following the liquidation of dual authority in Fergana, the Soviet regime embarked on a similar venture in Transcaspia. There, as in eastern Turkestan, the dichotomy between native aspirations and the reality of Soviet control led, after the October Revolution, to the formation of two sources of authority, one representing the European population and the other the Turcoman tribesmen. The essential difference resided in the inability of the natives to organize their forces and in their failure to form an independent government.

Even before the October events, a nationalist movement, championed by Turcoman intellectuals and centered around the Turcoman officer corps, had begun to form in Transcaspia. October was the catalyst which gave it an organizational profile. In counterweight to the local Soviet regime, the native nationalists convoked their own Regional Turcoman Congress and at it elected an Executive Committee, headed by Colonel Oraz Sirdar, a prominent Turcoman officer. Although the committee

---

[37] It was not, as one Soviet authority has insisted, a movement whose content was counterrevolutionary, aimed solely at the overthrow of the Soviet regime, and which chose a national form only because " 'Autonomy of Turkestan' was the most advantageous slogan for the conditions of the time." Alekseenkov, "Kokandskaia Avtonomiia," in Istpart Sredazbiuro Ts.K., V.K.P. (b), *Revoliutsiia v Srednei Azii*, I, 29.

announced that it desired only to aid native famine victims and to assist the regional soviet in supplying goods to Turcoman villages, it fell immediately under the suspicion of the Soviet government.[38] These suspicions were confirmed when a representative of the Turcomans was included in the Kokand Autonomous Government.[39]

Nevertheless, the Soviet regime took no immediate steps to disband the organization. Instead, it called an All-Turcoman Peasant Congress and created a Turcoman section within the regional soviet. The congress protested the existence of the Turcoman National Committee, raised the question of agrarian revolution in the auls (villages), and demanded the organization of soviets in the auls and of Turcoman sections in the city soviets. After the congress, the Soviet government undertook the formation of Turcoman Red Guard detachments and sent agitators into the auls to enlist peasant support for the social revolution.[40]

The National Committee countered with an agitational campaign for the formation of "parallel power." [41] Let the Russians run the cities, it argued, but power in the auls must belong to the Turcomans. Not only did this argument prove far more effective among the peasants than the agitation of the Ashkhabad Soviet, but the National Committee dared to begin construction of an independent power position. In February, 1918, it undertook to found a Turcoman National Army on the basis of the Turcoman Cavalry Squadron, a relic of Tsarist times which was billeted near Ashkhabad. At this point, an appeal from the Ashkhabad Soviet brought Kolesov from Tashkent with a detachment of troops. The Turcoman squadron, which was not yet prepared to fight, was quickly disarmed and the national revolution crushed before it had gotten underway.[42]

The destruction of Kokand autonomy and the disarming of

[38] E. L. Shteinberg, *Ocherki istorii Turkmenii* (Moscow, 1934), pp. 71–72.

[39] V. Karpych, "Revoliutsionnyi put' Turkmenistana (i o nepravil'nom tolkovanii 'Turkmenii i Revoliutsiia')," *Turkmenovedenie*, No. 1 (5) (January, 1928), p. 13.

[40] Shteinberg, *Ocherki istorii Turkmenii*, pp. 71–72.

[41] Karpych, "Revoliutsionnyi put' Turkmenistana," *Turkmenovedenie*, No. 1 (5) (January, 1928), p. 14.

[42] Z. I. Mindlin, "Interventsiia v Zakaspii," in Z. Mirkin (ed.), *K desiatiletiiu interventsii: sbornik statei* (Moscow, 1929), p. 166.

the Turcoman Cavalry Squadron ended the period of dual power in Turkestan and left the Tashkent Soviet in unchallenged control. The next step—and the Soviet wasted no time in taking it—was the extension of the revolution into new areas. The first target was the khanate of Bokhara, the stronghold of Islam in Central Asia and a Russian protectorate since 1868. Initially the problem of overthrowing the Emir of Bokhara and substituting a friendly regime appeared to be considerably easier to solve than had that of liquidating Kokand autonomy. Not only was the Emir without an effective military force, but a native revolutionary movement led by a Young Bokharan Party had begun to take form in Bokhara. Being unable to overthrow the Emir by its own efforts, this group had sent representatives to Tashkent in January, 1918, to negotiate for Soviet help.

The revolutionary movement in Bokhara had emerged in the inspirational glow of the fires of the 1905 Revolution and the Young Turk rebellion of 1908. Led by Uzbek intellectuals and representatives of the rising commercial class, it appeared first as an extension of the Jadid movement, which among Russia's Islamic peoples was the counterpart of Eastern Slavdom's own Westernizing movement. Its program looked forward to a modernization of the country, broader opportunity for the development of commerce and industry, and an end to the despotism of the ruling dynasty. But the movement and its Young Bokharan Party, which expressed the aspirations of a tiny minority in Bokhara's overwhelmingly peasant population, had no deep roots in the native soil and no opportunity to win popular support for its program. Until the events of 1917 in Russia and their repercussions in Turkestan made radicalism more popular, it remained feeble and ineffectual. Even then the Young Bokharans failed to enlist the support of any substantial element in Bokhara's population. Hence, in January, 1918, after several members of the Party had been chastised publicly for staging a demonstration in the streets of Old Bokhara, they dispatched a delegation to Tashkent to seek Soviet assistance in overthrowing the Emir. The Soviet government, anxious to get rid of what it considered to be the principal remaining center of counterrevolution in Central Asia and to lay hold of the

Emir's large store of grain reserves, quickly fell in with the plan.[43]

Consequently, Kolesov appeared at the railroad town of Kagan on the outskirts of Old Bokhara on March 1, 1918, in the company of 200 Young Bokharans and a detachment of 80 Red Guards armed with cannon and machine guns. There he staged a protest demonstration against the despotism of the Emir and upon its conclusion summoned the ruler of Bokhara to meet him in Kagan.[44] The Emir refused to come in person but, alarmed at the show of military force, sent his Chairman of Ministers and the kadi (Moslem judge) of Bokhara to represent him. To these Kolesov presented for the Emir's signature a manifesto which granted freedom of speech and freedom of the press in Bokhara, dismissed the Emir's counselors and replaced them with members of the Young Bokharan Party, did away with the death sentence and corporal punishment, and abolished certain taxes.[45] When the Emir refused to sign, Kolesov delivered an ultimatum, accompanied by the threat of force. Even then the Emir signed only on condition that there be no publication of the manifesto; that no demonstrations be organized; that no Russian troops be brought into the city of Old Bokhara; and that the proposed reforms be promulgated not immediately but only as they became possible. Meanwhile, he sent for reinforcements, and the mullahs of Old Bokhara stirred up a mob against the Russians and the traitorous Young Bokharans. In the face of the fanatical crowd and after a short battle, the Red Guard retired, ending the first Soviet attempt at the overthrow of the khanate of Bokhara.

[43] Faizulla Khodzhaev, *K istorii revoliutsii v Bukhare* (Tashkent, 1926), p. 45.

[44] Kolesov's plan of action, according to his own testimony, was as follows. He was to begin conversations with the Emir. If the latter refused to meet Kolesov's demands, the Young Bokharans were to start a revolt inside the fortress of Old Bokhara. Should difficulties be encountered, the Red Army would come immediately to their aid. On the eve of the expected meeting with the Emir, the plan was altered. According to the new arrangement, a failure in the negotiations with the Emir was to be followed by an assault by a detachment of Young Bokharans, supported by all Red Army forces, on Old Bokhara. Simultaneously, a rebellion was to break out within the fortress. In order to prevent the Emir from concentrating his own forces to meet the attack, diversionary rebellions were to be engineered also in the Kerki fortress and in the Charjui district. See M. Gorkii, Vs. Ivanov, I. Mints, and F. Kolesov (eds.), *Voina v peskakh: Grazhdanskaia Voina v Srednei Azii* (Moscow, 1935), p. 241.

[45] "Sobytiia v Bukhare," *Novyi Turkestan*, March 31, 1918.

As a result, Soviet Turkestan found itself obliged to conclude a treaty with the Emir by which it not only recognized the independence of Bokhara but also engaged to retrocede to the latter all the territories which Russia had taken from it in the previous hundred years. Furthermore, the Soviet government promised to furnish munitions to the government of Bokhara, a promise which was partially fulfilled by the delivery of six artillery pieces.[46]

Kolesov's abortive attempt to break the Emir's power did not pass without repercussions in Bokhara. Said Alim Khan became from that date an implacable enemy of Bolshevism. Within his own domains he visited a reign of terror upon "subversives" and to prevent Bolshevik use of the railroad for a second invasion he ordered the tracks connecting Bokhara and Turkestan torn up.[47] These were temporary measures. With an eye to the future, the Emir increased his army to 20,000 and concluded agreements with Persia and Afghanistan for the delivery of arms and munitions. Through the intercession of the Emir of Afghanistan, he attempted to secure from Great Britain official recognition of his independence, and failing this, he established contact with the British intelligence service at Meshad, in northeastern Persia.

EUROPEAN RESISTANCE MOVEMENTS IN CENTRAL ASIA

The activities of the Emir of Bokhara did not pass without notice in Tashkent, but a new and more formidable danger in the form of a rising counterrevolutionary movement had meanwhile diverted the attention of the Soviet regime from Bokhara. Strangely enough the first real outburst—it took place in Transcaspia—was proletarian in character. It resulted, not from an effort to restore the old Russia, but from a general revulsion against the excesses of a commissar, Frolov, whom the Tashkent

[46] The guns were useless, however, since the Soviet government supplied no ammunition for them. From the account of the former Emir of Bokhara on the March, 1918, events in Bokhara; Said Alim Khan, *La Voix de la Boukharie opprimée* (Paris, 1929), p. 20.

[47] Khodzhaev, *K istorii revoliutsii v Bukhare*, p. 52; Safarov, *Kolonial'naia revoliutsiia: opyt Turkestana*, pp. 82–83. The Emir has charged the destruction of the railroad bed to "Mensheviks." Said Alim Khan, *La Voix de la Boukharie opprimée*, p. 21.

Soviet had sent into the region to "disarm the counterrevolution." [48] The chain of events which led to the overthrow of Bolshevik authority in Transcaspia began early in June, 1918. The issue which provoked the first unrest was an order of the Ashkhabad Soviet for a census of all males capable of bearing arms. Fear of a general mobilization spread quickly and on the morning of June 17, the day on which registration was to begin, a mob gathered in the town center. A stormy protest meeting took place during which the crowd, whipped to a fever pitch by a series of inflammatory speeches, dragged the War Commissar, Kopilov, from the platform which he had mounted to explain the census, and beat him severely.[49]

From the center, disorders spread throughout the city. On the insistence of the crowd, the magazine was opened. Firing spread rapidly and both the dissidents, who were led by Social Revolutionaries, and the Bolshevik-dominated Ashkhabad Revolutionary Committee summoned reinforcements. On the following day, the troops arrived and a second turbulent meeting took place at which the outnumbered Bolsheviks were forced to promise elections to a new soviet based on universal, direct, and secret ballot.[50]

Frolov, who had hastened from Tashkent, arrived in Ashkhabad on June 24 and immediately set about to undo the damage to Bolshevik prestige. As a first step he altered the election procedure in order to assure Bolshevik and Left Social Revolutionary domination of the new soviet. As a second, he unleashed a "Red Terror" which aroused the opposition of the whole population. Communist authors, referring to the loathing which Frolov engendered in the people, speak of his "personal shortcomings," [51] his lack of patience and "misuse of spirituous liquors." [52] General Malleson, the British commander whose

[48] Mindlin, "Interventsiia v Zakaspii," in Mirkin, *K desiatiletiiu interventsii,* p. 167.

[49] "The Struggle for Soviet Ashkhabad. The Beginning of the Civil War in Transcaspia" (translated from *Turkmenovedenie,* October, 1930) , *Journal of the Royal Central Asian Society,* XVIII (1931) , 620–21.

[50] *Ibid.,* pp. 621–22.

[51] Mindlin, "Interventsiia v Zakaspii," in Mirkin, *K desiatiletiiu interventsii,* p. 167.

[52] "The Struggle for Soviet Ashkhabad," *Journal of the Royal Central Asian Society,* XVIII (1931) , 622.

troops later became involved in the Transcaspian affair, gives a more detailed description of Ashkhabad during his rule:

Many prominent local people, and hundreds of lesser note, were shot down without trial and there was much looting. Frolov used to drive around the streets of Ashkhabad with a rifle in his hands and shoot at anyone he saw.[53]

Nevertheless, a deceptive quiet fell over the city and in early July Frolov felt free to go to Kizil Arvat to put down unrest. His departure was the signal for a second rising in Ashkhabad which, after three days' fighting, saw the fall of the Soviet regime. Frolov, too, fared no better in Kizil Arvat. His trusted Armenian militia revolted and, joining forces with the local railway workers, attacked and killed the commissar and his supporters. With these victories, Bolshevik rule in Transcaspia came to an end.

The government which emerged after the downfall of the Bolshevik Soviet was eminently proletarian in character. Of its members only the Minister of Foreign Affairs, Zimin, a schoolteacher and orientalist by profession, possessed a formal education. Its program, like that of nearly every other anti-Bolshevik group in Russia which opposed a restoration of the monarchy, was based on the future convocation of an All-Russian Constituent Assembly. For Turkestan it demanded the calling of a constituent assembly whose members would be elected on the basis of free and general suffrage. These demands were laid before the Soviet regime as conditions of peace. In the event of their acceptance, and until the proposed Turkestan Constituent Assembly had convened, Turkestan was to be governed by a coalition of the two governments.[54] Tashkent responded by declaring the Transcaspian government outside the law.[55]

[53] From Major General Sir W. Malleson's article, "The Twenty-six Commissars," in *Fortnightly Review*, March, 1933; quoted in William Henry Chamberlin, *The Russian Revolution, 1917–1921* (New York, 1935), II, 421.

[54] Text of document in S. Piontkovskii, *Grazhdanskaia Voina v Rossii (1918–1921 gg.): khrestomatiia* (Moscow, 1925), p. 653.

[55] Immediate action to destroy the Transcaspian rebels, however, was not contemplated. Instead the Tashkent government dispatched a special commission, headed by the Commissar of Labor, Poltoratskii, to Ashkhabad to investigate the activities of Frolov and to achieve a "bloodless settlement" of the dispute. The commission never reached its destination; it was massacred en route. Mindlin, "Interventsiia v Zakaspii," in Mirkin, *K desiatiletiiu interventsii*, p. 168.

Then, in anticipation of an invasion from Tashkent, the Transcaspian government appealed for assistance to General Malleson's headquarters at Meshad, Persia. The British command, whose task was to ward off a possible Turco-German invasion into the Middle East, sent a small detachment of Indian troops into the region in return for the right to mine the harbor of Krasnovodsk and to destroy the usefulness of the Trans-Caspian Railway. Assistance was sought also from the native population, whose hatred of Bolshevism went back to the disarming of the Turcoman Cavalry Squadron in February. With the approval of the Transcaspian government an All-Turcoman Congress met, formed an Executive Committee, and declared its support of the new regime.[56] The government, for its part, appointed Colonel Oraz Sirdar to general command of the front.[57] In addition, it promised to improve the economic situation in the region and to get some foodstuffs into the famine-ridden auls.[58]

War and revolution doomed these efforts to failure. The grain which was so desperately needed could not be obtained and conditions in the villages worsened steadily. Moreover, the regular visits of the tax collectors to the villages and a ceaseless stream of requisitions in the midst of the famine infuriated the peasantry. The village of Azis-Khan revolted.[59] Elsewhere, peasant unrest became so general that the Transcaspian government lost all control of the villages. Grudzinskii, the Transcaspian Minister of Internal Affairs, finally admitted at the beginning of 1919 that "in many places the Turcoman population with the greatest impunity has ceased completely to execute the decrees of the administration." [60]

Yet the Bolsheviks paid little heed to this fertile field for agitation. They placed their main effort rather on preparing unrest and mutiny among Transcaspian troops and on organizing

[56] Karpych, "Revoliutsionnyi put' Turkmenistana," *Turkmenovedenie*, No. 1 (5) (January, 1928), p. 14.

[57] Mindlin, "Interventsiia v Zakaspii," in Mirkin, *K desiatiletiiu interventsii*, p. 168.

[58] *Ibid.*, p. 195.

[59] *Ibid.*, p. 196.

[60] Shteinberg, *Ocherki istorii Turkmenii*, p. 82.

underground cells in the cities of the region.[61] Time, in any case, was on Tashkent's side. In the spring of 1919 the Red Army took the offensive and by the end of May had captured Merv. In June the British force in Transcaspia withdrew to Persia. This broke the morale of the Transcaspian troops and, despite the later arrival of reinforcements from General Denikin's army, they never recovered. In July they were driven out of Ashkhabad; in October Kizil Arvat fell; and finally in February, 1920, Red troops took the last Transcaspian stronghold, Krasnovodsk, by storm. The Transcaspian episode was finished.

With the destruction of the Transcaspian government, the Soviet regime in Turkestan had eliminated its most dangerous competitor in Central Asia. Yet the Transcaspian regime had at no time possessed military resources sufficient to threaten the Tashkent government seriously. It is true that Soviet Turkestan was cut off almost continuously from communication with Central Russia by Dutov's Cossack army in the Orenburg region and nearly surrounded by hostile territory. But it is equally true that it was spared the threat of attack from a major counterrevolutionary army by its very location in the backwash of the main revolutionary and counterrevolutionary tides. Hence the pressure of external enemies never became strong enough during the two years of isolation to imperil the existence of the Soviet center at Tashkent. Its closest brush with disaster came from within. In January, 1919, the War Commissar, Osipov, nearly unseated the Soviet regime in a surprise putsch. This revolt, ostensibly the work of a mere adventurer, was actually the result of considerable planning and was connected intimately with a widespread conspiracy among former Tsarist officers to overthrow Soviet rule in Turkestan.

The events which culminated in the January uprising had begun in December, 1917, when a Cossack division which had been stationed in Persia, Khiva, and the Iomud Steppe collected in Charjui (Leninsk) on the way home. Two governments, one a Russian "provisional" government and the other a native government, sprang up around the Cossack troops and one Colonel Zaitsev assumed command of the military units in

[61] *Ibid.*, pp. 81–82.

Charjui. His first action was to disperse the soviet governments which had emerged in the district. His second was to order an attack on Samarkand. But the Cossacks refused to fight, and Zaitsev and the two Charjui governments were forced to flee.[62] After this defeat, the leaders of the Charjui venture undertook the establishment of a conspiratorial Turkestan Military Organization and encouraged the formation of underground centers of counterrevolution throughout Turkestan. From its center in Tashkent, the Organization began preparations early in 1918 to overthrow the Soviet government. As one step in the plan of revolt, a liaison was formed with the anti-Soviet Moslem guerrilla forces in Fergana. By an agreement between the Organization and the Basmachi chieftains, Irgash and Ishmat, the latter agreed to put their forces at the disposal of the Turkestan Military Organization in return for the delivery of foodstuffs. A second step was completed in May when a representative of the Organization, in conversations at Krasnovodsk, obtained a British promise to aid the new government after the Military Organization had driven out the Bolsheviks.[63]

The next and most intricate stage in the plan entailed persuading disgruntled members of the Soviet government to cast their lot with the insurgents. This portion of the design was facilitated by frictions which had developed within the Soviet camp. For one thing, the uneasy Bolshevik-Left Social Revolutionary coalition was strained severely by the divergence of the goals and methods of the two parties. Locally, conflicts had

---

[62] M. P[okrovskii], "Ocherk kontr-revoliutsionnogo dvizheniia v Turkestane," *Pravda*, November 10, 1922.

[63] S. Bolotov, "Iz istorii 'Osipovskogo' miatezha v Turkestane (s predisloviem G. Lelivicha)," *Proletarskaia Revoliutsiia*, No. 6 (53) (June, 1926), p. 116. According to M. P[okrovskii]'s account, which has never been verified, the agreement consisted of three points. The British pledged to aid the Organization in its struggle against Bolshevism with money, arms, technical equipment, and in special cases with manpower. After the overthrow of the Soviet regime, an autonomous Turkestan regime was to be formed under the exclusive influence of Great Britain. Moreover, Turkestan was promised as a British protectorate for a period of 55 years. In addition, P[okrovskii], and most other Soviet writers, accuse Colonel F. M. Bailey, the British trade representative in Tashkent at the time, of complicity in the plot, but Colonel Bailey records in his memoirs that the events of January, 1919, took him by surprise. M. P[okrovskii], "Ocherk kontr-revoliutsionnogo dvizheniia v Turkestane," *Pravda*, November 10, 1922; Lt. Col. F. M. Bailey, *Mission to Tashkent* (London, 1946), pp. 118–20.

arisen repeatedly out of Social Revolutionary opposition to the more drastic Bolshevik proposals and especially to measures which were directed against the interests of the immigrant European peasantry. Moreover, the dissolution of the Social Revolutionary-Bolshevik alliance and the rapid development of enmity between the two parties at the Russian center had had serious repercussions in the local arena.[64] Even the Bolsheviks themselves were not immune to internal dissension, which became especially intense in the autumn of 1918 after a number of Bolsheviks arrived in Turkestan from Central Russia. The "old Bolsheviks," fearing that their positions were being endangered, began an agitational campaign which came to an end only with their arrest in December.[65] In this atmosphere of suspicion and discontent, the Military Organization was able to persuade Osipov and Krushinin, the commandant of the city of Tashkent, to join in the plot against the government.

At this point, chance intervened. By an accident the Bolsheviks discovered the headquarters of the Turkestan Military Organization and dissolved the organization by shooting the majority of its members. Notwithstanding the sharp reversal in their fortunes, the remaining leaders decided to go ahead, and in January, 1919, the coup was put into action. On the pretext that unrest had broken out in the barracks of the Second Turkestan Regiment, a trusted Bolshevik troop unit which became involved in the mutiny through its commander, Koluvaiev, Osipov called upon the government center to send a delegation to talk to the men. Fourteen prominent local Communists, including Figel'skii, chairman of the Tashkent Council of People's Commissars; Voitintsev, president of the Turkestan Central Executive Committee; and Shumilov, president of the Tashkent Soviet, responded to the appeal. Osipov shot the lot of them, announced that the Bolshevik regime was ended, and,

[64] A clear indication of their "unreliability," according to Bolotov, was an attempt by the Social Revolutionaries to hinder the execution of a Red Terror in Turkestan in retaliation for the attempt on Lenin's life by Fanya Kaplan in Moscow. Bolotov, "Iz istorii 'Osipovskogo' miatezha v Turkestane," *Proletarskaia Revoliutsiia*, No. 6 (53) (June, 1926), p. 121.

[65] *Ibid.*, pp. 122–23.

according to Colonel F. M. Bailey, a British officer who was in Tashkent at the time, "proceeded to get drunk." [66]

Osipov's rebellion almost succeeded. The suddenness of the coup demoralized the Soviet government. But with the support of a detachment of Magyar war prisoners who held the city fort, it was able to rally sufficiently to prevent the fall of Tashkent. In addition, Koluvaiev broke with Osipov after an argument and went over to the Soviet side. This blow was enough to crush the whole revolt. Osipov, having lost his principal military support, was driven from the city.[67] In the course of the Red Terror which accompanied the return of the Bolsheviks to power, some 4,000 persons perished. "It was sufficient," writes Colonel Bailey, "to wear a collar to be classed as bourgeois and be arrested." [68] Arrest meant death before the firing squads. However, the Terror served its purpose; it put an end to the whole counterrevolutionary movement in the Tashkent region.

The Osipov mutiny and the counterrevolution in Transcaspia were the only major attempts made by Europeans to overthrow the Soviet regime in Turkestan. Other minor revolts flared up from time to time but none was well organized or of long duration. In December, 1918, an uprising in Belovodsk in which "even the poorest peasantry participated" [69] was suppressed by the First Pishpek Regiment of the Red Army. At Vernyi (Alma Ata) Red Army units, later celebrated in Dmitri Furmanov's novel *Miatezh'*, mutinied after an order arrived to move the troops to the Fergana front. The mutineers demanded revocation of the order, abolition of the grain monopoly, dissolution of the Army Cheka and Revolutionary Tribunals, and a ban on the formation of Moslem troop units. This, as well as another rebellion which was spearheaded by a "Peasant Army" under the command of one Monstrov, was broken

[66] Bailey, *Mission to Tashkent*, p. 119.
[67] With two hundred men he escaped to Persia. Bolotov, "Iz istorii 'Osipovskogo' miatezha v Turkestane," *Proletarskaia Revoliutsiia*, No. 6 (53) (June, 1926), p. 136.
[68] Bailey, *Mission to Tashkent*, p. 121.
[69] Turar R. Ryskulov, *Kirgizstan* (Moscow, 1935), p. 65.

in the autumn of 1919. None of these uprisings reached dangerous proportions, but they did reflect the attitude of the local
European population toward their "Bolshevik liberators." All
of them bore the seed of counterrevolution, but lacking organization, effective leadership, and armed force they could not
rise above their local character.

THE RISE OF BASMACHISM

The opposition of the European population of Turkestan to
the Soviet regime had its counterpart among Moslems in the
Basmachi or anti-Soviet guerrilla movement which originated
in Fergana and quickly spread throughout Soviet Central Asia.[70]
Its causes were the thwarted desire of the native peoples to
exercise the promised right of self-determination, the repressive
and irresponsible policies of the Soviet government, and the
steadily deepening famine and economic crisis. Its origin
stemmed from Tashkent's initial exclusion of Moslems from
governmental posts and its later extermination of the Kokand
Autonomous Government. Even these acts might not have engendered the rise of a movement as elemental as Basmachism
had the Soviet regime not pursued its policies with a savagery
and callousness which drove nearly all natives first into opposition and later into armed defense of their lives and property.

Political discrimination against the Moslem population was
evident from the very outset of Soviet rule. The Third Regional Congress of Soviets had refused to allow the Moslems a
single seat on the Regional Council of People's Commissars
and had limited their representation in the Regional Executive
Committee to two seats and in the Regional Council to four
seats.[71] In sessions of the Executive Committee, moreover, representatives of the old cities were often ordered to absent themselves when crucial questions were discussed. It is true that a
Moslem Soviet of Deputies was formed, but its members en-

---

[70] Among Turkestani nationalists, the Basmachi movement is known as the
Bek or freemen's movement (Beklar Hareketi). The word Basmachi is derived
from the Turkic verb *basmak*, "to tread on, to oppress," and was applied in
Central Asia to bandits and highwaymen.

[71] Castagné, "Le Turkestan depuis la révolution russe," *Revue du Monde
Musulman*, L (June, 1922), 45.

joyed neither authority nor influence, and its tasks were confined to agitation.

Later, pressure from Moscow compelled local Soviet authorities to admit the right of the Moslem population to participate
in Soviet work,[72] but the admission was always grudging and
hedged with provisos. Typical was the policy decision of the
Fourth Turkestan Congress of the Communist Party (September, 1919). Moslems, it stated, must participate in the work of
the government. To implement this decision, the Party ordered
that "the principle of proportional representation [of the na-
tives] in the Soviet organs of the republic shall be applied under the general leadership of the central or local committee of
the Russian Communist Party in accordance with the regulations of the Soviet constitution." But the congress then proceeded to nullify the effect of its declaration by restricting application of the provision to instances "in which the regional
or local congress of soviets desires this form of representation."
Moreover, the candidacy of natives standing for election was
subject to veto by the Moslem Bureau and the committees of
the Russian Communist Party.[73]

Still harsher discrimination prevailed in the social and economic policies of the Soviet regime toward the Moslem population. In the Kirghiz (Kazakh) areas especially, Russian immigrants, aided and abetted by local soviets, continued without
abatement the prerevolutionary policy of banishing the Kirghiz
to the less fertile regions in order to provide more land for settlement by the immigrant peasantry. In places the immigrants
set up beehives along the nomads' routes of march in order that
they might invoke the right to requisition the nomads' cattle in
the event of "trespass" through the area. Moreover, a system
resembling slavery actually emerged in Semirechie. According

[72] In July, 1919, the Bolshevik Party Central Committee in a telegram to the
Tashkent government pointed out the necessity of "drawing the native Turkestan population into governmental work on a broad proportional basis." Text in
Lenin, Sochineniia (2d ed.), XXIV, 811. The message was received with consternation since the reservation of 95 percent of the administrative posts would
have meant—as Colonel Bailey writes—"an end of the Bolshevik government."
Bailey, Mission to Tashkent, pp. 190–91.

[73] Document reprinted in S. Muraveiskii (V. Lopukhin), Ocherki po istorii
revoliutsionnogo dvizheniia v Srednei Azii (Tashkent, 1926), pp. 27–28.

to an anti-Soviet engineer, Nazarov, who visited the district during his flight from Turkestan, the local soviet organization mobilized the Kirghiz for agricultural labor, distributed them among the Russian peasants, and decreed the death penalty for those who refused or deserted.[74] While the Tashkent government itself did not sponsor these acts, it did assume an attitude of indifference to them; and one prominent Bolshevik commissar, Tobolin, remarked at a session of the Turkestan Central Executive Committee that the Kirghiz were "weakest from the Marxist point of view [and] must die out anyway." [75]

The Tashkent Soviet was hardly more sympathetic toward Moslems in other parts of Turkestan. Within the cities, the government satisfied its financial hunger by repeatedly demanding contributions of money and property from the Moslem population, by conducting house-to-house raids, and by the wholesale confiscation of goods and chattels. Still more terrifying was the method of assessing taxes, which Captain Brun describes as follows:

[The commissar] sent for some eight or ten of the most influential men in the city and addressed them as follows: "I must have one million rubles before the week is out. I leave it to your own judgment how best to assess the taxes. If the sum is not paid me within the fixed period, I shall confiscate a certain amount at my pleasure." And, having spoken, he settled himself right in the center of the gateway, with two soldiers standing beside him, armed to the teeth. He uttered no further word, but left it to the others to fight it out.[76]

[74] P. S. Nazarov, *Hunted through Central Asia* (London, 1932), p. 168. The findings of this violently anti-Soviet account are confirmed in this instance by a Soviet writer. See Turar R. Ryskulov, *Revoliutsiia i korennoe naselenie Turkestana* (Tashkent, 1925), p. 84.

[75] Quoted in Chokaiev, "Turkestan and the Soviet Regime," *Journal of the Royal Central Asian Society,* XVIII (1931), 409–10. Safarov summed up the consequences of this policy at the Tenth Congress of the Communist Party in 1921. "Since the establishment of the Soviet power," he said, "Russian land-ownership has increased in Semirechie province from 35 percent to 70 percent while the number of Kirghiz exterminated is estimated at 35.5 percent." *Protokoly s'ezdov i konferentsii Vsesoiuznoi Kommunisticheskoi Partii (b): Desiatyi S'ezd R.K.P.(b), mart 1921 g.* (Moscow, 1933), p. 197.

[76] Brun, *Troublous Times: Experiences in Bolshevik Russia and Turkestan,* pp. 88–89; Colonel Etherton describes an especially gruesome procedure that was adopted to instill fear in those natives who were delinquent in tax payments. He writes: "If pleading inability to comply with the demands [of the Soviet tax collectors, the natives] were collected in a body and taken to the requisitioning

In the countryside, outlawry and violence were commonplace. Gangs of felons, often composed of Red Army men and sometimes including members of the Communist Party, raided the kishlaks (native villages), killing and robbing the population. Appeals for help not only brought no response, but Tashkent actually ordered the disarming of native Party *druzhinas* (bodyguards) which were formed in some localities for self-defense.[77] So desperate did the condition become that entire villages fled into the mountains and native Communists complained without avail that the situation was "worse than it was in the time of Nicholas the Bloody. . . . Under the pretext of pillaging the rich, everyone has been pillaged." [78]

War and revolution visited still another plague, famine, upon the people of Turkestan. Initially it arose from the isolation of Turkestan from the grain-producing regions of Central Russia, upon which Turkestan depended for its foodstuffs. Prior to the war, agriculture in Turkestan had been converted largely to cotton growing, which was more profitable to the peasant but which also put an end to the area's self-sufficiency in food. Even during the war, the region had felt the first pinch of famine. Transportation had begun to break down as early as 1914–15 and grain shipments which normally entered Turkestan were diverted to meet military needs. With the coming of the October Revolution, the inflow of food had ceased entirely.

Even then the crisis might have been alleviated had the cotton growers reverted to grain production. The price structure became favorable to the change since the market value of grains soared while the price of cotton, which was soon overflowing warehouses because it could not be exported, fell abruptly. In point of fact, cotton growing virtually ceased in Central Asia, but grain production decreased almost as precipitously. The Soviet government stepped into the picture and began fixing

headquarters, one or two of their number being then removed a short distance out of sight. Presently a shot would ring out, the remainder of the delinquents interpreting this as an execution, with the result that they paid up, or gave all they possessed in the world to satisfy the levy." Etherton, *In the Heart of Asia*, pp. 156–57.

[77] Ryskulov, *Revoliutsiia i korennoe naselenie Turkestana*, pp. 99–100.

[78] From a statement by a Moslem delegate before the Third Congress of the Communist Party of Turkestan in June, 1919. Quoted in *ibid.*, pp. 100–101.

prices artificially. When this stopped the flow of goods to the markets, it sent raiding parties to the countryside to requisition grain and other commodities. This policy succeeded temporarily, but its long-run effects were disastrous. Peasants, fearing Soviet confiscation of the fruits of their labors, curtailed production.

The extension of the civil war throughout Turkestan and its attendant lawlessness also drove increasing numbers of peasants off the land. Gangs of felons roved the countryside unimpeded, pillaging defenseless villages and bringing productive life to a standstill. The irrigation network which furnished the life blood of Central Asiatic agriculture fell into disrepair and crops burned out under the desert sun. The planted area under food crops dropped to one half of its prerevolutionary extent. (See Table 1.) The area under wheat alone decreased from 4,732,384 acres in 1917 to 1,290,430 acres in 1919, a decline of

TABLE 1

DECLINE OF PLANTED AREA IN TURKESTAN DURING
THE PERIOD 1917–19
(*Irrigated Area Only Considered*)

	PLANTED AREA IN ACRES		GROWTH (+) OR DECLINE (−)	
CROP	*1917*	*1919*	*In Acres*	*In Percent*
Wheat, winter	1,479,964	608,815	−871,149	−58.9
Wheat, summer	3,252,420	681,615	−2,570,805	−79.0
Rye, winter	2,776	2,794	+18	+0.7
Rye, spring	11,861	6,159	−5,702	−48.1
Barley	933,401	213,238	−720,163	−77.2
Millet	426,805	309,558	−117,247	−27.5
Maize	144,920	177,120	+32,200	+22.2
Sorghum	164,408	213,970	+49,561	+30.1
Rice	419,302	304,676	−114,626	−27.3
Other grains	424,300	173,745	−250,555	−59.0
Melons and garden vegetables	135,081	130,421	−4,660	−3.4
Total	7,395,238	2,822,111	−4,573,127	−61.9

Source: Adapted from data in I. B. Aleksandrov, "Narodnoe khoziaistvo Turkestana i ego vosstanovlenie," *Khlopkovoe Delo*, Nos. 1–2 (January–February, 1922), p. 24.

3,441,954 acres. During the same period the planting of all other grains declined from 2,527,772 acres to 1,671,259 acres, a loss of 856,513 acres. Only maize and sorghum showed an increase, but this was more than offset by the great losses sustained by other groups.

Statistical compilations in no way can record the plight of the Moslems who lived and died in the famine. Travelers in the area reported battles over crumbs of bread thrown from train windows, the abandonment of children on the steppe, and the sale of wives and children in the market places.[79] Even the weather conspired against the hapless people, and during the exceptionally cold winter of 1919 a commission detailed to investigate and combat the famine reported that "the exhausted people collapse from the cold and die like flies." [80] The exact extent of the famine was never estimated but it was reckoned in 1919 that one half of the population was starving, and Ryskulov later calculated that "about one third of the population must have died." [81]

Nor was the policy of the Soviet government of Turkestan designed to relieve the famine. Tobolin's view that it could be liquidated best by allowing the Kirghiz, who were "economically weakest from the Marxist point of view," to die out and that it was "far more important to devote available resources to the maintenance of the front rather than expending them on famine" [82] typified Tashkent's attitude toward the entire Moslem population. At the same time, projects for increasing the tax burden of the European population to raise funds to fight the famine were rejected on the ground that such taxation constituted a "form of repression" which might "augment the number of the [government's] enemies." [83] And the government responded to a Moscow order to reduce the food tax on Moslems in Fergana 50 percent by overcollecting the tax by 20

---

[79] Bolotov, "Iz istorii 'Osipovskogo' miatezha v Turkestane," *Proletarskaia Revoliutsiia*, No. 6 (53) (June, 1926), p. 119. Captain Brun reported two cases of cannibalism in Tashkent itself. They were traced, he writes, to the camps of the Kirghiz in the vicinity. Brun, *Troublous Times: Experiences in Bolshevik Russia and Turkestan*, p. 167.

[80] Ryskulov, *Revoliutsiia i korennoe naselenie Turkestana*, p. 212.

[81] Chokaiev, "Turkestan and the Soviet Regime," *Journal of the Royal Central Asian Society*, XVIII (1931), 410.

[82] Ryskulov, *Revoliutsiia i korennoe naselenie Turkestana*, p. xii.

[83] Chokaiev, "Turkestan and the Soviet Regime," *Journal of the Royal Central Asian Society*, XVIII (1931), 410.

percent. Moreover, the Red Army, given the right of self-provisioning, raided native villages with merciless regularity.

Among Moslems everywhere in Turkestan the calculated callousness of the Soviet regime stirred revulsion, hatred, and despair. "Will the Russian freedom never come to an end?" became a whispered question in every native village and town.[84] The dichotomy between the old and new cities, between the Moslem countryside and the Russian town, sharpened into open hostility and burst into armed opposition, into the native guerrilla warfare which became known as Basmachism. Its defensive character gave it an appeal that transcended class and tribal boundaries among the Moslem population. It emerged directly from the regime of violence, from the ceaseless requisitions, the mass arrests, the degradation of the native population which the Soviet regime in Turkestan had made its policy. Its content was nationalism and the bones of Kokand autonomy were its foundation. The sense of indignation and the nationalism which fathered the movement are clearly expressed in the following complaint which a group of Moslems registered soon after the sack of Kokand:

Under the Red banner, dark deeds are now being perpetrated in Russia. The old rude force which dominated [us] before the revolution has now been strengthened again and has declared open war on the "small" nationalities who strive to embody in life one of the great achievements of the revolution, the idea of self-determination. It [the Soviet government] has spilled rivers of human blood on the lands of these peoples, has abolished their governments, and by its cruelties toward the weak and defenseless has outdone the old [regime]. Recently it sprinkled the streets of Kokand with human blood, razed the Old City which is populated by Moslems, destroyed the lives of thousands of innocent, defenseless Moslems, and looted all their property.[85]

The leadership of the Basmachi movement came predominantly from nationalist groups which had participated in the formation of Kokand autonomy, and its first rallying cries, "Turkestan for the Natives" and "Turkestan without Oppres-

[84] Safarov, *Kolonial'naia revoliutsiia: opyt Turkestana*, pp. 81–82.
[85] *Novyi Turkestan*, March 7, 1918.

sors," showed clearly the orientation toward nationalism.[86] Ideologically, the movement found expression in religious terms. Its struggle, it proclaimed, was waged for the defense of Islam. And its task, according to its leading theorist, Khodji Sami-bey, was "to strengthen in the East tendencies which conform to the structure of the East; working together with the Moslem people, to liberate them . . . and to give Eastern affairs into the hands of organizations possessing real vitality in the East." [87]

In the struggle against Bolshevism, the Basmachi nonetheless did not eschew alliances with European enemies of the Soviet regime. In 1918 Irgash and Ishmat had agreed to support the Turkestan Military Organization but Bolshevik discovery of the central headquarters of the organization in Tashkent ended the alliance before it could bear fruit. A year later the leader of the Peasant Army, Monstrov, joined forces with Madamin Bek on the basis of a common struggle for freedom of labor, trade, education, speech, and press, abolition of Chekas and political commissars, and liquidation of the grain monopoly. This alliance, too, dissolved when the Peasant Army was defeated decisively near Andijan in September.

Outside counterrevolutionary support, in any case, was not a decisive factor in the vitality of the Basmachi movement. Its strength derived from the elemental response which it evoked in the Moslem population. Peasant support was general, and Basmachi bands roved the countryside at will, swooping down from mountain strongholds in repeated forays on Red Army outposts and supply trains. Likewise, a peasant warning system prevented Soviet punitive expeditions from ever contacting the main body of the Basmachi forces.

Soon all Fergana, except the cities and the railway line, was under the control of the guerrilla forces, and in the autumn of 1919 Basmachi leaders felt strong enough to undertake the convocation of a "constituent assembly" and the creation of a Fergana Provisional Government. Aid was sought from Great Britain and Afghanistan. The former, on the advice of Colonel

---

[86] Ginzberg, "Basmachestvo v Fergane," *Novyi Vostok*, Nos. 10–11 (1925), pp. 185–86.

[87] Quoted in M. N., "Pod znakom Islama," *Novyi Vostok*, No. 4 (1923), p. 95.

Etherton, hesitated,[88] but Madamin Bek in a visit to the Afghan delegation in Turkestan in November obtained a promise of support from the latter.[89] The plan bore no fruit, however. Internal bickering, which was later to destroy the strength and cohesion of Basmachism, prevented the achievement of final agreement.

Such was the situation in eastern Turkestan when the long-interrupted connection between Turkestan and Central Russia was restored in the fall of 1919. In September, Red troops in pursuit of Kolchak's retreating army made contact with the Turkestan Red Army at Bor-Chogur. A month later Red forces captured Ashkhabad on the Transcaspian Front and opened the route across the Caspian Sea. In November a special Turkestan Commission, which the central Soviet government had created in order to restore good relations between the European immigrants and the native population of Turkestan,[90] arrived in Tashkent. As a first step in the struggle against Basmachism, the Commission—under the leadership of Frunze, its military member—summoned reinforcements to augment the Red Army garrisons in the Basmachi regions. This reduced somewhat the freedom of Basmachi operations but it did not reduce Moslem sympathy for the movement. As yet, neither the central government for which the Turkestan Commission spoke nor the Soviet government of Turkestan was prepared to relax the harsh policies of War Communism or to institute reforms which might have reconciled at least a part of the Moslem population to the Soviet regime. Hence, 1920 became a year of stalemate in the Soviet struggle against Basmachism.

THE SOVIETIZATION OF KHIVA AND BOKHARA

Meanwhile, the Bolsheviks turned their energies to the task of rounding out the conquests of the October Revolution in Central Asia. For two years the native principalities of Bokhara and Khiva, which formed a deep territorial wedge in Russian Cen-

[88] Etherton, *In the Heart of Asia*, p. 230.

[89] Ginzberg, "Basmachestvo v Fergane," *Novyi Vostok*, Nos. 10–11 (1925), p. 190.

[90] The text of the decree which created the Turkestan Commission appears in Lenin, *Sochineniia* (2d ed.), XXIV, 810–11.

tral Asia, had maintained a precarious hold on independence. Soviet policy in 1920 addressed itself to the installation of friendly regimes in these states and the re-creation under Soviet auspices of their prerevolutionary status of dependency. Khiva was the first to fall before the guns of Red Army units. Here the attack occurred at a time when the danger of resistance based on Moslem fanaticism was at a minimum. An intertribal struggle was raging in Khiva and the intervention which appeared to favor one of the contending sides was supported by a considerable section of the population.

Khiva had long been divided internally by bitter rivalry between the city-dwelling and agricultural Uzbek population and the nomadic Turcoman tribesmen. Prior to the revolution, the Uzbek town dwellers with the support of their Russian protectors had dominated the political and social scene. In the countryside the best agricultural lands and the upper sections of the irrigation canals were in the possession of the sedentary Uzbek farmers while Turcomans, who had settled the land later, had had to be content with less desirable shares.

The hostility bred by this inequality erupted into open conflict when Russian troops evacuated Khiva at the beginning of 1918 and left its Uzbek ruler to his own devices. For the struggle which ensued, the militant Turcoman tribes were infinitely better prepared than the more civilized but poorly armed Uzbek townsmen. Under the leadership of Junaid Khan, a Turcoman brigand who had distinguished himself by capturing and holding the city of Khiva for a short time in 1916, they began a career of raids and lootings which culminated in the capture of Khiva and the execution of the Khan as an accomplice of the Russians and oppressor of the Turcomans. After this, the pillage of the Uzbek population was systematized. The Turcomans preempted water rights and instituted a reign of terror under which the Uzbeks were robbed indiscriminately of their livestock, harvests, and even their household goods and their women.[91]

Among the prostrate Uzbek population there was only one

[91] G. Skalov, "Revoliutsiia v Khive 1920 goda," *Novyi Vostok*, No. 3 (1923), p. 248.

organized group, the Young Khivan Party, which was able to oppose the policies of Junaid. Like its counterpart in Bokhara, the Young Khivan Party had emerged under the influence of the Jadid movement after the Revolution of 1905 and was composed principally of members of the young intelligentsia and the merchant class. This party, which advocated political freedom, private enterprise, and the removal of hindrances to the development of capitalism, did not represent any prominent section of the population before the advent of Turcoman domination. But its opposition to Junaid quickly rallied the Uzbek population to it. In November, 1919, the Young Khivans petitioned for assistance from the Soviet government, and in January, 1920, a Red Army force of 800 men accompanied by a detachment of Young Khivans crossed the Amu-Daria river, drove Junaid into the Kara Kum, and within a month had broken the last Turcoman resistance. In June, Khiva was proclaimed a people's republic under Khiva's ancient name, the Khorezmian People's Soviet Republic.

Although the new regime adopted the soviet form and was in fact at the mercy of the Red forces whose bayonets had put it into power, it was at first by no means socialist in character. The Young Khivans were advocates not only of political freedom but also of private ownership of land and of industrial enterprise. Moreover, they were not inclined to extremism. The puppet khan was retained but was forced to sanction the convocation of a *mejlis* or parliament and to transfer all power to the temporary revolutionary government. Even armed with this legitimization of its authority, the new government did not undertake to liquidate the old ruling class; only the war minister and prime minister of the Junaid regime were shot. And punitive action against the Turcomans was prevented by the Bolsheviks, who were able to compel the inclusion of members of the major tribal units in the government.[92]

The expulsion of Junaid from Khiva and the subsequent establishment of the Khorezmian People's Republic left Said Alim Khan, the Emir of Bokhara, as the principal opponent of Bolshevism in Central Asia. After the failure of the Kolesov

[92] *Ibid.*, p. 254.

adventure in 1918, the Soviet government of Turkestan had watched anxiously as the Emir pursued increasingly reactionary policies and formed open associations with counterrevolutionaries, Basmachi sheikhs, and British military personnel. Nevertheless, Tashkent's hand was stayed by the lack of sufficient military forces to renew the intervention and fear lest new aggressive moves against Bokhara unite all the Moslems of Turkestan in a holy war against Bolshevism.[93] The Soviet government, however, did not abandon its hope of liquidating the Emir's government eventually. As early as June, 1918—only four months after Kolesov's retreat from Bokhara—a proposal had been introduced at one of the sessions of the Turkestan Central Executive Committee to include Bokhara and Khiva in the territory of Turkestan,[94] and the view found approval in the Soviet center. Articles published during 1919 in the columns of *Zhizn' Natsional'nostei,* the official newspaper of the All-Russian Commissariat for National Affairs, not only argued the importance of Soviet control of Bokhara to the extension of the revolution into the Middle East and India[95] but rejected as "unimportant" the treaty commitment of Soviet Turkestan to recognize the independence of the principality.[96]

The Soviet design of intervention itself was facilitated by the presence of the remnants of the Young Bokharan Party on the territory of Soviet Turkestan. Following the collapse of the abortive revolution of 1918, between 150 and 200 members of the Party had settled in Tashkent and Samarkand where they had established political centers. But internal conflicts, arising from prolonged exposure to the Turkestanian manifestations of the social revolution, had produced sharp cleavages within the movement. In the moderate wing of the Young Bokharan Party, fear that the Bolsheviks would compel the Party to adopt a "socialist" program led to numerous defections. The more radical members split into two factions. One clung stubbornly to the original ideals of the Young Bokharan movement while

---

[93] Turkestanets, "K polozheniiu v Turkestane," *Izvestiia,* July 16, 1918.
[94] *Izvestiia,* August 1, 1918.
[95] "Bukhara," *Zhizn' Natsional'nostei,* No. 6 (14) (February 23, 1919).
[96] "Rossiia i Afganistan," *Zhizn' Natsional'nostei,* No. 27 (35) (July 20, 1919).

the other turned for its inspiration to the principles of the Russian Revolution.

One attempt at reconciliation was made in 1919 when the Party was reorganized and given a new name, the Revolutionary Young Bokharan Party. The reorganized party did come a little way toward acceptance of a radical program but not nearly enough to satisfy its militant left wing. Its program, which included liquidation of enmity among the various tribes of Bokhara and concentration of their forces under one center, the establishment of democracy in the country, and freedom from foreign interference in internal affairs, did not foresee the creation of a socialist state. Although demanding the abolition of the emirate and the creation of a people's republic in its place, the Party desired to have nearly all groups in the country, except the Emir and feudal landlords, participate in government. As a concession to the peasants, the program advocated confiscation and redistribution of the land of "oppressors" and promised the adoption of special measures for improvement of the irrigation network.[97]

Among Turkestanian Bolsheviks and those radical Young Bokharans who had accepted the new teaching, the objectives of the reorganized party were manifestly unsatisfactory. Not only did they object to the atmosphere of "petit-bourgeois reformism" that surrounded the Party but they suspected, and even accused, it of pan-Islamism. This antagonism between the moderate and extremist elements led ultimately to a new breakdown. The moderates, unwilling to be driven further leftward, rallied tightly around the new party. The Young Bokharan Bolsheviks, having no program of their own, entered the Russian party in a body[98] and undertook a campaign to "capture" the Bokharan revolution. To strengthen their position they began to organize cells composed principally of share croppers, small peasants, agricultural workers, and petty shopkeepers and by 1919 had established forty-three organizations with a claimed membership of 5,000.[99] Using the organization as a basis for

[97] Khodzhaev, *K istorii revoliutsii v Bukhare*, pp. 63–65.
[98] *Ibid.*, p. 74.
[99] A. Mashitskii, "K istorii revoliutsii v Bukhare," *Vestnik Narodnogo Komissariata Inostrannykh Del*, Nos. 5–6 (July, 1921), pp. 73–74.

asserting that the revolution had outgrown the democratic stage, the Bokharan Bolsheviks then demanded abolition of the central Turkestan Bureau, the directing agency of the Revolutionary Young Bokharan Party, and the submission of all revolutionary groups to the authority of the Bolshevik Central Committee. At that point, the Turkestan Commission intervened in an effort to restore unity to the badly splintered Young Bokharan movement. At the very least, Bolshevik strategy required that the intended revolution in Bokhara bear the outward signs of a national rebellion by the Bokharan people against the oppression of its own ruling class. It was still more important that a projected appeal for Red Army support should appear to have issued from all the native revolutionary forces in Bokhara. These considerations dominated the decision of the Turkestan Commission in the spring of 1920 to reunify the Young Bokharan movement. The invocation of Party discipline quickly quelled opposition within the ranks of Bokharan Bolshevism and a combination of appeasement and threat of exclusion from a share in the fruits of victory eventually brought the moderate Young Bokharans into line.

The reconciliation took place formally at a conference of the two parties in the summer of 1920 and was achieved on the basis of a resolution introduced by representatives of the Russian Communist Party. In the period of preparation for the revolution, the resolution argued, the Young Bokharan Party was a "progressive factor" which would facilitate the "overthrow of the despotic power of the Emir and the *beks* [public officials]." And during the revolution itself, all revolutionary forces, "including the Young Bokharans who are relatively richer culturally than the Bokharan Communists," had to be utilized. In the next breath, however, the resolution relegated the non-Communists to a minority position in the anticipated revolutionary government and actually forecast the eventual extinction of the Young Bokharan Party.[100]

Meanwhile, in Bokhara itself an atmosphere favorable to re-

[100] Text in A. Mashitskii, "Materialy po istorii Bukharskoi Revoliutsii," *Vestnik Narodnogo Komissariata Inostrannykh Del*, Nos. 4–5 (April–May, 1922), pp. 124–25.

bellion had been spreading. Unrest, arising partly from the repressive policies of the Emir and partly from the increasing tax burden that maintenance of his large but poorly armed and poorly trained army required, was becoming general. To exploit it the propaganda mill in Tashkent was turning out appeals to revolt and broadcasting them throughout the country. Agitation in the army was especially fruitful and many of the Emir's soldiers deserted with their equipment to the side of the Young Bokharans. In the countryside, peasant revolts flared up in several districts and cases were reported in which angry mobs attacked officials of the Emir's government.[101]

By late summer of 1920 the campaign against the Emir had reached a high pitch. On August 23, revolutionaries in the railroad town of Charjui seized the New City and murdered thirty-six of the Emir's officials.[102] Immediately, the Young Bokharan Party met in congress in the city, the site having been chosen previously precisely because it was "filled with a revolutionary atmosphere." [103] On August 29, Old Charjui fell to the revolutionaries and revolts broke out in Kermin and Shakhriziab. On September 1 an appeal for aid was sent to the Red Army.[104] The response was more than immediate. Four days earlier Frunze, in his order of the day, already had proclaimed the revolutionary outbreak in Bokhara. Declaring that "the hour of the decisive battle of the overwhelming and enslaved toiling masses of Bokhara against the blood thirsty government of the Emir and the *beks* has struck," he had ordered the Red Army to march against Bokhara.[105] On August 30 the Red Army attack on Bokhara began[106] and in Tashkent Kuibyshev ordered the

[101] Mashitskii, "K istorii revoliutsii v Bukhare," *Vestnik Narodnogo Komissariata Inostrannykh Del*, Nos. 5–6 (July, 1921), p. 74.

[102] I. Kolychevskii, "Bukhara," *Voennaia Mysl'*, No. 1 (September, 1920), pp. 306–7.

[103] Khodzhaev, *K istorii revoliutsii v Bukhare*, p. 75.

[104] *Ibid.*, p. 76.

[105] From the text of the order as reproduced in "M. V. Frunze na Turkestanskom Fronte (vvodnaia stat'ia Komdiva F. Novitskogo)," *Krasnyi Arkhiv*, No. 3 (100) (1940), pp. 74–75. As further evidence of the careful planning that characterized the operation, Frunze's biographer writes that "many sleepless nights" went into the preparation of the campaign. P. Berezov, *Mikhail Vasilevich Frunze: kratkii biograficheskii ocherk* (Moscow, 1947), p. 77.

[106] "M. V. Frunze na Turkestanskom Fronte," *Krasnyi Arkhiv*, No. 3 (100) (1940), p. 75.

Young Bokharans to arrest the Bokharan Consul.[107] After a three-day battle, the fortress of Old Bokhara fell and "the Red banner of world revolution streamed victoriously over the Registan." [108]

In spite of the fact that leftist elements had been prominent in the Bokharan revolutionary movement prior to the overthrow of the Emir, the revolutionary government was no more radical than the one which had appeared in Khiva. At the First Congress of the Toilers of Bokhara which met a month later, representation was given not only to the peasants and the "city poor" but also to the small and middle "bourgeoisie." Only the richest merchants and ex-officials of the Emir's government were excluded. Nor did the decisions of the congress reveal extreme revolutionary tendencies. Confiscatory enactments were limited in application to the property of the Emir and his retainers; the formation of a coalition government was authorized.[109] Actually, moderate Young Bokharans dominated both the eighty-five-member Central Executive Committee and the seven-member presidium of the new government. The former body contained only eight radicals and the latter one.[110]

THE DEFEAT OF BASMACHISM

After the liquidation of the independent khanates of Khiva and Bokhara, the only enemy actively opposing the Soviet order in Russian Central Asia was Basmachism. The revolutions in these two countries as well as the general consolidation of the Soviet regime in Turkestan were not without effect on this movement which, although it had not yet reached its apogee, was already doomed. Territorially, Basmachism expanded into the captive khanates. Numerically, it was strengthened by an influx

[107] Telephone conversation between Frunze and Kuibyshev, August 31, 1920. *Ibid.*, pp. 76–77.

[108] Frunze to Lenin, September 2, 1920. *Ibid.*, p. 77. Emir Said Alim Khan, who had fled to eastern Bokhara, established a headquarters at Dushembe (Stalinabad) and remained there among the Basmachis until the spring of 1921. He then withdrew to Afghanistan.

[109] D. Soloveichik, "Revoliutsionnaia Bukhara," *Novyi Vostok*, No. 2 (1922), p. 272.

[110] Joseph Castagné, "Le Bolchévisme et l'Islam: les organisations soviétiques de la Russie musulmane," *Revue du Monde Musulman*, LI (October, 1922), 225.

of new adherents from the ruined peasantry, from the ruling classes which had been driven from their places of power by the revolution, and from former revolutionaries who had grown dissatisfied with the new order. But the new recruits in addition to augmenting the size of the Basmachi bands began to alter the whole character of the movement. Not only did internal dissension develop which led to a schism along tribal lines and the rise of a struggle between the Kirghiz and Uzbek Basmachi, but the original nationalistic leaders found themselves displaced by more conservative elements.[111]

According to Skalov, a Soviet authority on the revolutionary movement in Central Asia, the return to a natural economy during the famine transformed the nationalistic bourgeoisie, under whose aegis the movement had at first developed, into a parasitic class serving no useful function and deprived it of the chance to lead the struggle.[112] The peasants, whom ruin and degradation had involved in the Basmachi movement and who formed its basic cadres, had little comprehension of the meaning of the political liberalism which the nationalists advocated. They wanted a return to the old ways and were far more susceptible to propaganda which stressed a religious theme than to appeals for the formation of a democratic republic. Thus they allied themselves to the cause of the conservative faction for whom a return to the past meant a return to power. The changes wrought by the influx of these recruits and the growing hegemony of conservative ideals found their reflection in the Basmachi program. The old nationalistic battlecries gave way to religious ones, and the former undertone of Islamism became the predominant theme. In place of such appeals as "Turkestan for the Natives," the slogans of the movement began to call the faithful to "Struggle against the Unbelieving Jadids" and to "Defend the Shariat." [113]

---

[111] Ginzberg, "Basmachestvo v Fergane," *Novyi Vostok*, Nos. 10–11 (1925), p. 197; G. Skalov, "Sotsial'naia priroda Basmachestva v Turkestane," *Zhizn' Natsional'nostei*, Nos. 3–4 (1923), p. 58.

[112] Skalov, "Sotsial'naia priroda Basmachestva v Turkestane," *Zhizn' Natsional'nostei*, Nos. 3–4 (1923), p. 59.

[113] Vasilevskii, "Fazy Basmacheskogo dvizheniia v Srednei Azii," *Novyi Vostok*, No. 29 (1930), p. 134.

As yet Basmachism lacked coordination. Having grown spontaneously, it had wanted in unity from the beginning. Moreover, internal jealousy, petty bickering, and the refusal of individual Basmachi sheikhs to relinquish their prerogatives even for the sake of effective opposition to Bolshevism prevented the achievement of a unified direction. Real leadership did not arrive until 1921. It came then in the person of Enver Pasha, a Young Turk who, having failed to gain Bolshevik support for his schemes to overthrow Mustapha Kemal, appeared in Bokhara in November.[114] His prestige enabled him to unite the various Basmachi leaders and he succeeded in attracting even members of the Young Bokharan Party to his side.[115] Rallying the discontented with semireligious battle cries, such as "The Unification of All the Moslems" and "The Creation of a Great Central Asiatic Moslem State," he began to marshal his forces for a campaign to oust the Bolsheviks from Central Asia.[116] In May, 1922, he signified his readiness by dispatching an ultimatum to Moscow demanding Russian evacuation of Khiva, Bokhara, and Turkestan and the release of political prisoners.[117]

The unification of the Basmachi under Enver Pasha confronted the Soviet regime dramatically with the real seriousness of Basmachism. Moreover, it forced an abrupt change in the customary methods of the local authorities in dealing with the problem of native opposition to Bolshevik rule. The old tactic of sending out punitive expeditions, of which "every Red Guard

[114] According to Agabekov, Enver Pasha had been sent to Central Asia by Lenin with the mission of persuading the Basmachi to make their peace with the Soviet regime. After that, he was to unite all the Basmachi bands into a single revolutionary fighting army and to lead this army in a revolutionary invasion of India through Afghanistan. Enver did succeed in uniting the Basmachi but he directed this army against the Bolsheviks, not the British colonial regime. Georges Agabekov, *OGPU, the Russian Secret Terror* (New York, 1931), p. 16.

[115] Enver's influence spread as well into Turkestan. In 1921 Janzakov, the chairman of the Turkestan Central Executive Committee, and Mullah Sadreddin-Khan, an influential member of the people's court, deserted to the Basmachi; Joseph Castagné, *Les Basmatchis: le mouvement national des indigènes d'Asie Centrale* (Paris, 1925), p. 15.

[116] Soloveichik, "Revoliutsionnaia Bukhara," *Novyi Vostok*, No. 2 (1922), p. 283.

[117] Text in Castagné, "Le Bolchévisme et l'Islam," *Revue du Monde Musulman*, LI (October, 1922), 229–30.

detachment considered it a duty 'to intimidate' [and] 'to suppress' the inhabitants suspected of sympathy to the Basmachi," [118] had proved its bankruptcy. Instead of crushing the enemy, these expeditions had succeeded only in intensifying the hostility of the Moslem population and in inciting new recruits to join actively in the struggle against Bolshevism. The principle of using force to meet force was not abandoned—in fact, Red Army garrisons in Turkestan, Khorezm, and Bokhara were reinforced heavily—but measures were taken to eliminate from Soviet military action the character of a war of Europeans against natives, of infidels against the faithful.

Even before the arrival of Enver Pasha in Central Asia, the Volga Tatar Brigade of the Red Army had been summoned to join the struggle against Basmachism. The appearance of these Moslem Red Army men in Turkestan had had a considerable psychological effect on the natives. The move was followed in 1921 by an unsuccessful attempt to mobilize former Basmachi and to send them against their erstwhile comrades-in-arms. The activities of Enver Pasha hastened the process of introducing natives into the Soviet armed forces. Conscription was decreed in many areas—in Khorezm failure to respond to a draft summons was made punishable by death[119]—and organization was begun of a native Red Militia composed principally of poor peasants who, according to a Soviet account, "were beginning to recognize their friends and foes." [120]

It was evident, however, that forcible suppression, even if it were accomplished with the aid of Moslem soldiers, would not put an end to the idea and the popularity of Basmachism. Only a policy of conciliation, designed to bring Soviet rule into conformity with the mental attitudes of the people and to satisfy basic needs, could win sympathy for the new regime. The need for concessions could not be overlooked. Already, delegates to the Congress of the Peoples of the East, held at Baku in Sep-

---

[118] Ginzberg, "Basmachestvo v Fergane," *Novyi Vostok*, Nos. 10–11 (1925), p. 185.

[119] Castagné, "Le Bolchévisme et l'Islam," *Revue du Monde Musulman*, LI (October, 1922), 215.

[120] Ginzberg, "Basmachestvo v Fergane," *Novyi Vostok*, Nos. 10–11 (1925), p. 196.

tember, 1920, had complained of the arbitrary actions of local soviet governments. And Stalin in an article in *Pravda* (October 10, 1920) had warned Communists in backward areas against pursuing policies that would alienate native populations and had cautioned specifically against "cavalry raids with the object of 'immediately communizing' the backward masses." [121]

In Central Asia it had become apparent that without the sympathy of a considerable portion of the native population "the Soviet authority could not develop and strengthen itself" and the revolution could not be brought to a victorious conclusion.[122] Immediate political measures for soliciting Moslem support took the form of congresses and conferences of various national groups and peasant rallies at which prominent native members of the Soviet administration harangued the delegates with revolutionary slogans and wooed them with promises of a land reform.[123] Moreover, the New Economic Policy, which now came into force throughout Russia, permitted the local government to carry its policy of conciliation into the economic sphere. "Military political expeditions" were dispatched to the more remote regions to explain the principles of the soviet system and, more important, to offer the peasantry aid through agricultural credit, farm inventory, and seed.[124] The grain requisition gave way to the *prodnalog* (tax in kind) and this not only relieved the unbearable burden on the peasant but removed a principal source of rural dissatisfaction and unrest. The flow of trade between Turkestan and Central Russia was resumed, and grain and industrial goods began to appear on the local market. Bazaars, which had been closed during the civil war, were permitted to reopen, and private trading was encouraged. The property rights even of the rich were scrupulously respected.[125]

[121] Stalin, *Sochineniia*, IV, 362.

[122] S. Muraveiskii (P. Lopukhin), "V bor'be za kadry v Srednei Azii," *Kommunisticheskaia Revoliutsiia*, No. 17 (September, 1926), pp. 62–63.

[123] Ll–ov, "K polozheniiu v Bukhare," *Izvestiia*, July 15, 1922.

[124] Vaselevskii, "Fazy Basmacheskogo dvizheniia v Srednei Azii," *Novyi Vostok*, No. 29 (1930), p. 135.

[125] Soloveichik, "Revoliutsionnaia Bukhara," *Novyi Vostok*, No. 2 (1922), p. 286; also P. Baranov, "Polozhenie Turkestanskoi Respubliki i reorganizatsiia Krasnoi Armii," *Voennaia Mysl'*, No. 2 (May–July, 1921), pp. 88–89.

A special effort was made to win the neutrality, if not the support, of the Moslem clergy by sparing religious sensibilities. Mosques which had been seized by the state were returned to their congregations; the remaining religious establishments were left strictly alone; and no interference with the right of worship was tolerated. Shariat justice, which Tashkent had abolished in 1918, was reintroduced for believers. Endowment property (wakf), which had been confiscated during the revolution, was restored to its trustees, and old-style schools operated by Moslem teachers were reopened.[126] Even criticism of mullahs stopped.

In this way the Soviet regime won for itself an increasing amount of native support. Enver Pasha's star began to wane. Hampered by dwindling popular sympathy for his movement and operating with a poorly equipped army that had no artillery, he was compelled to take the field against a Red Army special force armed with modern weapons. On June 15, 1922, Red forces defeated him decisively at the battle of Kafrun and on August 8 he was killed during an attack on a Soviet patrol. Basmachism did not perish with Enver Pasha, but with his defeat the political backbone of the movement was broken,[127] and the uneasy coalition of liberal Jadidists, conservative Moslem leaders, and independent mountain tribesmen, which the magic of Enver's name had inspired, disintegrated. At year's end only 2,000 Basmachi remained in Fergana and in 1923 this number dwindled to a handful.[128] By 1924 the movement had been liquidated in Turkmenia. In the eastern mountainous regions of Uzbekistan and Tajikistan, it was able, with aid from Afghanistan, to persist for many years. But nowhere did it attain more than a local character.

The destruction of the army of Enver Pasha brought the period of revolution and civil war in Central Asia to a close.

[126] Igor M. Reisner, *Afganistan* (Moscow, 1929), p. 203.

[127] The story of Enver Pasha's adventures in Soviet Turkestan is told by a participant in the Basmachi movement in A. Zeki Velidi Togan, *Bügünkü Türkili (Türkistan) ve yakin tarihi* (Istanbul, 1942–47), pp. 434–60. For a summary account which relies principally on this source, see Olaf K. Caroe, *Soviet Empire: The Turks of Central Asia and Stalinism* (London, 1953), pp. 122–27.

[128] Vasilevskii, "Fazy Basmacheskogo dvizheniia v Srednei Azii," *Novyi Vostok,* No. 29 (1930), p. 135.

In its fires, the soviet system—for the most part with neither the consent nor the support of the population—had emerged and consolidated itself. But the right of national self-determination, which Lenin had promised so categorically in his appeal for peace at the Second All-Russian Congress of Soviets, had played no part in the process. In Turkestan, the European proletarian minority which had seized power at the outset of the revolution found justification for its rule in Stalin's formula of self-determination for the toilers. But the necessity of maintaining themselves in power compelled the Turkestanian Bolsheviks to put a peculiar construction even on that narrow formula. Throughout the two-year period of isolation, fear and distrust of the native population led them to reject all Moslem aspirations for a share in shaping Turkestan's future, whether those aspirations were expressed by native sympathizers of the new regime, by middle-class revolutionaries who wanted political democracy, or by representatives of the customary ruling classes. If self-determination there was in any form, it was the self-determination of the big battalions—of the Russian railway workers who possessed the preponderance of weapons and enjoyed the support of numerous European prisoners-of-war. Hence the real purpose behind Bolshevik inclusion of the right of self-determination in the Party program—the fostering of mutual trust between peoples and the removal of obstacles to the voluntary merging of nations—was frustrated.

After the reunification of Central Asia with the main body of the Soviet state, the position of the native population in Turkestan improved appreciably and some of the worst aspects of Tashkent's system of "Great Russian imperialism," which even Lenin had condemned,[129] were eliminated. Moslems who had been permitted no more than nominal participation in government under the Tashkent regime began to appear more frequently in positions of responsibility in the government and Party apparatus. And efforts were undertaken—under the aegis of Moscow—to win the support or neutrality of substantial segments of the native population.

[129] From a letter written by Lenin in 1919 to "Communist comrades in Turkestan." Text in Lenin, *Sochineniia* (2d ed.), XXIV, 531.

Moscow permitted no retreat from the commanding heights of power which the proletariat of Turkestan had won in the revolution. As early as November, 1917, the Russian workers had proclaimed a socialist regime in Turkestan and Moscow desired no retrogression from that position later. The October Revolution, so the argument ran, had crushed Tsarist imperialism "not at all for the purpose of giving to the Turkestan national bourgeoisie the opportunity to exploit the Turkestanian workers and peasants but for the purpose of abolishing all exploitation of the national bourgeoisie."[130] This was ground enough to justify the "overleaping" of the national stage of the revolution in Turkestan. On April 11, 1921, Soviet Turkestan, by decree of the All-Russian Central Executive Committee, entered the family of soviet and socialist republics which composed the RSFSR.

In Khiva and Bokhara, the revolution had followed a pattern which was more readily identifiable with the formula of self-determination which the Bolshevik Party had adopted at its Eighth Congress in March, 1919.[131] In these countries, revolutionary parties, which were more representative of bourgeois than proletarian aspirations, had come into power and their governments—although soviet in form—were by no means socialist in content. The emergence of soviet and people's republics on the territories of the two khanates was perhaps—as Kamenev asserted at the Eighth All-Russian Congress of Soviets in December, 1920—"proof of the fact that the ideas and principles of the Soviet authority are attainable and immediately realizable not only in industrially developed countries, not only with such a social bulwark as the proletariat, but also on a peas-

---

[130] Alekseenkov, "Kokandskaia Avtonomiia," in Istpart Sredazbiuro Ts.K., V.K.P.(b), *Revoliutsiia v Srednei Azii*, I, 23.

[131] At its Eighth Congress, the Party had rejected Stalin's narrow formula of "self-determination for the working masses" in favor of the more flexible "historical class viewpoint." This formula, which was written into the Party program, required the Bolsheviks to base the decision on which class expressed the will of a nation on the stage of social development which the nation had reached, i.e., on whether the nation was "evolving from medievalism to bourgeois democracy or from bourgeois democracy to soviet or proletarian democracy, etc." Text in *VIII S'ezd Rossiiskoi Kommunisticheskoi Partii (bol'shevikov), 18–28 marta, 1919* (Moscow, 1919), pp. 343–44.

ant basis." [132] It is nevertheless true that a toiling-class dictatorship. which was the embodiment of the soviet idea, was not introduced directly in either country. The causes of this hesitancy arose from the manner in which the revolution had been carried out and from the special position which these countries had occupied in the Russian Empire.

Unlike Turkestan, Khiva and Bokhara had not been incorporated into the Empire before 1917. The old rulers, although subordinated to Russia through Russian Residents in their capital cities, had remained in power, and internal administration had been left largely in their hands. Thus the advent of revolution found neither railway workers to seize power in these countries nor a ready-made European administrative apparatus, such as the Tsarist government had established in Turkestan, which could be turned to the uses of a proletarian dictatorship. The revolution was thus unable to proceed in Khiva and Bokhara on the same basis as it had in Turkestan.

The emergence of the Jadidist revolutionaries and their appeals to the Soviet regime for aid had provided the solution to the initial problem of sovietizing these countries. In the post-revolutionary period, these same revolutionaries also provided convenient instruments for political rule during the transition to a socialist form of government. But the Soviet government also took care to establish and to consolidate its own superintendency over the course of future development in the new republics through the medium of treaties by which the latter agreed to employ "soviet experts" in all their important government departments and agencies.[133] Through these experts, the Soviet government extended its control rapidly but quietly throughout the administrative and political system of each republic. Thus the people's governments of Bokhara and Khorezm, which outwardly were independent, popular, and non-

---

[132] From Kamenev's report on the international situation at the Eighth All-Russian Congress of Soviets. See *Vos'moi Vserossiiskii S'ezd Sovetov Rabochikh, Krest'ianskikh, Krasnoarmeiskikh i Kazach'ikh Deputatov (23–29 dekabria 1920 goda): stenograficheskii otchet* (Moscow, 1921), p. 11.

[133] For further details, see below, pp. 71–72.

socialistic, were in truth merely agents of a social revolution whose course was charted in Moscow.

Except for the fact that the regimes in Bokhara and Khorezm rested on somewhat broader political foundations, there was nothing in their content to distinguish them from the soviet and socialist order which had been established in Turkestan. The Bolsheviks themselves did not claim for Turkestan a basically higher level of cultural or economic development than that achieved by these other nations. Rather, they regarded it as a proving ground on which principles, useful for the guidance of other oppressed peoples in the transformation of their societies from precapitalistic backwardness to proletarian progressiveness, could be worked out in detail. Implicit in this conclusion was the recognition that the establishment of the new system, far from signaling the completion of the great revolution, had denoted only its real beginning. For Turkestan as well as for Bokhara and Khorezm, the path of noncapitalist development which Lenin had pointed out at the Second Comintern Congress still lay ahead.

II

THE POLITICAL
UNIFICATION
OF CENTRAL ASIA

◆

BY THE END of 1920 the Soviet government had repudiated, in fact if not in principle, its early promise to the nations of Russia of the right to self-determination up to and including secession. In Central Asia as in numerous other parts of the Tsarist Empire, Stalin's 1918 formula of "self-determination for the toilers" had furnished the practical basis on which the Soviet government supported or opposed the claims of national groups for self rule, and the Red Army had become the real instrument of "self-determination." But doctrine had also evolved toward a new conception of self-determination as a demand not for separation from Russia but for national equality within the socialist order. And this in turn had given rise to a further notion of the socialist state in Russia as a hierarchically organized union of autonomous and federated national soviet republics. In the course of the revolution and civil war, Bolshevism thus adopted the idea of a federal socialist commonwealth both as a counterpoise to non-Russian tendencies toward separation and as a device for guaranteeing those national rights which the Soviet regime had pledged itself to honor.

Although the Soviet federal system did not achieve its ultimate structural delineation until the USSR was formed in 1923, its evolution began in the chaos and disintegration which attended the Bolshevik ascent to power in November, 1917. The Bolsheviks had entered the period of revolution with a long record of opposition to federalism in Russia and with a nationalities program which envisaged the creation of autonomous national regions under a rigidly centralized system of government.[1] But the rapid evaporation of central authority in the non-Russian peripheries of the Empire soon compelled them to revise their attitude. As Stalin confessed later, the vigor of the national movements was greater and the path toward reassembling the various nationalities was more complicated than prerevolutionary doctrine had anticipated. Under the circumstances, federation became an appropriate transitional device for recruiting the scattered nations to the Soviet regime.[2] As early as December, 1917, the Soviet government announced its intention to support the formation of a "United States of Russia" if the workers and peasants desired it.[3] At the end of January, 1918, the Third Congress of Soviets announced that the Soviet Russian Republic was constituted on the basis of a free union of free nations, as a federation of national soviet republics.[4]

Neither declaration attempted to define the exact form of the projected federation; and the succeeding three years of crisis, which witnessed the consolidation of Bolshevik rule and the extension of Soviet authority to the outlying territories of the Russian Empire, did not permit the establishment of a precise institutional framework around the principle. In the constitu-

---

[1] For a brief examination of prerevolutionary Bolshevik views on federalism, see E. H. Carr, *The Bolshevik Revolution, 1917–1923* (New York, 1951), I, 135–38; also, V. I. Lenin, *State and Revolution* (New York, 1932), pp. 60–62. The nationalities program which the Bolsheviks carried into the November revolution had been adopted at the Seventh Party Conference in April, 1917. The resolution on the subject demanded "wide regional autonomy, the abolition of tutelage from above, the abolition of a compulsory state language, and the determination of the boundaries of self-governing and autonomous regions by the local population itself based on economic and social conditions, the national composition of the population, etc." See *Vse-Soiuznaia Kommunisticheskaia Partiia (b) v rezoliutsiiakh i resheniiakh s'ezdov, soveshchaniei i plenumov Tsentral'nogo Komiteta (1898–1932)* (4th ed., Moscow, 1932), I, 271–72.

[2] J. V. Stalin, *Sochineniia* (Moscow, 1946—), III, 30–31.

[3] *Pravda*, December 26, 1917.

[4] From the Declaration of the Rights of the Toiling and Exploited People. Text in *Izvestiia*, January 17, 1918.

tion of the RSFSR, adopted by the Fifth Congress of Soviets in July, 1918, the regime returned in large measure to the pre-revolutionary Bolshevik formula of regional autonomy. Article 11 of that document granted to regions "distinguished by a special mode of life and national composition" the right to unite into "autonomous regional unions" which could enter the RSFSR "on a federal basis." [5] Some of the Tsarist territories, reclaimed by Soviet forces during the civil war, were incorporated into the RSFSR and recreated on the basis of this article as autonomous republics and regions. "Constitutions," subsequently drafted and promulgated by the central agencies of the Soviet government, granted to these formations limited forms of local self-government whose principal ingredient was the right to organize local political, administrative, and judicial institutions "with a guarantee of plenary rights of the local language native to the laboring masses of the region." [6]

In other cases, notably the Ukraine, Belorussia, and the Transcaucasus, nominally independent soviet republics were established; these were subsequently incorporated into the administrative system of the RSFSR through treaties of military and economic alliance which each of them concluded with the Russian republic. Typical of such arrangements was the treaty concluded with the Ukrainian SSR on December 28, 1920. By this agreement the commissariats of military and naval affairs, foreign trade, finances, national economy, communications, labor, and posts and telegraphs in both republics were merged and redesignated as "unified commissariats." These agencies thenceforth formed part of the Council of People's Commissars of the RSFSR.[7] Similar bilateral agreements concluded between

[5] From the text of the first constitution of the RSFSR. See G. S. Gurvich, *Osnovy Sovetskoi Konstitutsii* (2d ed., Moscow, 1922), pp. 143, 150–51.

[6] From Stalin's definition of Soviet autonomy as given in his "Appeal to the Soviets of Kazan, Ufa, Orenburg, and Ekaterinburg" on April 9, 1918. Stalin, *Sochineniia*, IV, 75.

[7] Text in *Sbornik deistvuiushchikh dogovorov, soglashenii i konventsii, zakliuchennykh RSFSR s inostrannymi gosudarstvami* (Moscow, 1921–23), I, 15–16. The treaty also provided that the "unified commissariats" be represented in the Council of People's Commissars of the Ukrainian SSR by plenipotentiaries "who shall be confirmed and directed by the Ukrainian Central Executive Committee and Congress of Soviets." Moreover, the treaty made provisions for Ukrainian representation in the All-Russian Congress of Soviets and Central Executive Committee on the basis of a separate directive.

the RSFSR and the soviet socialist republics of Belorussia, Azerbaijan, Armenia, and Georgia in 1920 and 1921 conformed
fundamentally to this pattern.[8] By the end of 1921 only the
Central Asiatic republics of Bokhara and Khorezm remained
outside the framework of administrative unification although
they too had bound themselves to the RSFSR through treaties
of military and economic alliance.

The end of the civil war thus found the several "treaty republics" in various degrees of union with the Great Russian
center. All of them were joined to the RSFSR through the unification of administrative agencies, but the unified branches
of administration were not the same in every case. Moreover,
the establishment of orderly relations was further impeded by
the absence of a clear division of authority between the center
and these borderlands and the lack of a common legislative and
judicial system. The formal summons to regularize the existing
arrangements and to complete the edifice of unification was
given at the Tenth Party Congress in March, 1921. Representatives of the Ukrainian and Belorussian republics had already
been brought into the All-Russian Congress of Soviets and the
Central Executive Committee through treaty arrangements.[9]
And delegations from all five treaty republics were seated without protest at the Ninth All-Russian Congress of Soviets in December, 1921.

Meanwhile, preparations went forward to shift the initiative
in the unification movement from the center to the national republics. Discussion groups were organized throughout the soviet
republics, and a deluge of resolutions, adopted by local Party
and public organizations, began to pour into Moscow. In mid-
December, 1922, congresses of soviets meeting in the Ukraine,
Belorussia, and the Transcaucasus ordered delegations to be sent
to a Congress of Soviet Socialist Republics and empowered
them to subscribe to a compact of union. On December 26, the

[8] The texts of these agreements appear in *ibid.* as follows: Belorussia, I, 13–
14; Azerbaijan, I, 1–2; Georgia, III, 18–19; and Armenia, II, 3–4. The Armenian
treaty related only to financial matters.

[9] The treaty with Georgia, which was concluded on May 21, 1921, after the
Tenth Party Congress had dissolved, also provided for republican representation
in the Russian Congress of Soviets and Central Executive Committee. *Ibid.*, III,
18–19.

Tenth All-Russian Congress of Soviets added its approval. Four days later, the delegations of the four republics, who had reconstituted themselves as the First Congress of Soviets of the USSR, adopted a draft "Declaration" and a "Compact Concerning the Formation of the USSR." Sovereignty at length passed from the four independent republics to the newly created union on July 6, 1923, after a draft constitution had been approved by the All-Union Central Executive Committee.

The phases of reunion outlined here were common to all the regions and territories of the Russian Empire which Soviet forces reclaimed during the revolution and civil war. In individual regions, however, the pace and pattern of unification were not uniform and the forms which Soviet state building followed were in no wise rigidly standardized. In Central Asia, as in other borderlands, the Bolsheviks keyed their tactics to the opportunities of the moment. At the outset, Moscow's effort to introduce its own brand of autonomy into that region was forestalled by the physical isolation of Turkestan from the Soviet center. And it was later complicated by the resistance of the regional soviet regime to central encroachments upon its prerogatives. After the incorporation of Turkestan into the RSFSR, the people's republics of Bokhara and Khorezm still remained on the fringes of the Soviet federal system. In these republics the absence of an experienced hard core of native Communists, coupled with a Soviet compulsion to respect their prerevolutionary status of quasi-independence, had necessitated the temporary establishment of soviet, but not socialist, regimes. These special circumstances did not prevent the Central Asiatic republics from participating in the general unification movement of soviet republics but they delayed the evolution toward "Bolshevik" forms of national autonomy. Bokhara and Khorezm were admitted into the USSR more than two years after the signing of the Compact of Union.

SOVIET AUTONOMY IN TURKESTAN: A PROBLEM IN ADJUSTMENT

Despite the late amalgamation of Central Asia into the Soviet federal system, the advance toward reunion began in the region soon after the Bolshevik advent to power in Petrograd. The

very fact that the Tashkent Soviet had seized power in Turkestan early in November, 1917, and that it had organized a
socialist regime shortly thereafter, constituted the first step.
These acts determined that, whatever the ultimate form of the
connection between Turkestan and the center, its content
would be socialist and soviet. This does not mean that the question of Turkestan's place in the Soviet state arose in the Tashkent Soviet at this time. In point of fact, the Soviet regime in
Turkestan was less concerned initially with advancing claims to
autonomy or independence than with consolidating its authority in the face of an unfriendly native population.

To the Moslem population, Turkestan's future status was
the crucial question of the Russian Revolution. From the fall
of the monarchy, native leaders had been active in seeking to
establish some form of Moslem self-government and local independence. The unsympathetic attitude of the Provisional
Government, however, had frustrated their early hopes. In
April, 1917, it had vetoed "full political autonomy" for the
region and had proposed in its place "self-government on the
model of the English and French colonies." [10] In September
the Second All-Moslem Congress demanded the reorganization
of Turkestan as an autonomous territorial federation within
the Russian republic and the installation of a Moslem government. After the October events in Tashkent, the Moslems took
decisive action. Repelled by the prospect of "social revolution"
and angered at Tashkent's policy of excluding natives from
governmental posts, the Moslem leaders betook themselves to
Kokand and there proclaimed the autonomy of Turkestan.

This action and the subsequent decisions of the Third All-
Russian Congress of Soviets, establishing the principles of federation and the self-determination of the toilers, brought the
question of autonomy to the forefront. In the waning days of
January, 1918, the Fourth Regional Congress of Soviets met in
Tashkent and went on record for the establishment of a "soviet
autonomy" in Turkestan. But the congress described no bound-

[10] *Turkestanskii Kur'er*, April 28, 1917. Quoted in S. Radzhapov, "Etapy razvitiia sovetskogo gosudarstvennogo stroia v Srednei Azii," *Sovetskoe Gosudarstvo
i Pravo*, No. 11 (November, 1948), p. 61.

aries to the relationship and did not ask the approval of the center. Action in these areas had to await the elimination of the anti-Soviet national center in Kokand and the summoning in April of the Fifth Regional Congress of Soviets.

Even before the congress convened, Stalin, in his "Appeal to the Soviets of Kazan, Ufa, Orenburg, and Ekaterinburg," promised autonomy for the region "on the basis of recognition of the soviets of volost's (rural districts), counties, and towns." [11] Armed with this approval, the Fifth Congress adopted a "Statute on the Autonomy of the Turkestan Soviet Socialist Republic" and, having elected a Central Executive Committee and a Council of People's Commissars, proclaimed the autonomy of the "Turkestan Soviet Federal Republic" within the Russian republic.[12] Confirmation was immediately forthcoming from Moscow. In a telegram, dispatched on April 22 over the signatures of Lenin and Stalin, the center pledged itself to "support the autonomy [of Turkestan] on Soviet principles." [13]

By virtue of this act the Turkestan Soviet Republic became the first autonomous national unit, actually in being, to receive recognition from the central regime. Nonetheless, formal admission to the federation was withheld pending agreement upon the division of power between Moscow and Tashkent. The central government in its telegram of recognition referred to this problem and requested the Turkestan government to dispatch a commission to Moscow for the "joint elaboration" of the relationship of the regional government to the All-Russian Council of People's Commissars. The local authorities accordingly drew up a constitution for the Turkestan republic and in midsummer of 1918 a delegation arrived in Moscow with the document. There it became clear that the interpretation of "autonomy" in Tashkent differed markedly from that of the center. In the settlement of federal affairs the Bolsheviks of Turkestan demanded a position approaching equality with the government of the RSFSR, and in local affairs they expected to tolerate no interference by the center.

[11] Stalin, *Sochineniia*, IV, 76.
[12] G. Nepesov, "Vozniknovenie i razvitie Turkmenskoi Sovetskoi Sotsialisticheskoi Respubliki," *Voprosy Istorii*, No. 2 (February, 1950), p. 6.
[13] Text in Stalin, *Sochineniia*, IV, 81.

The draft constitution of the Turkestan delegation adhered closely to the norms of statehood promulgated in Moscow, such as the "Declaration of the Rights of the Toiling and Exploited Peoples" and the "General Regulations of the Constitution of the RSFSR." [14] But the Turkestan draft reserved to the regional Soviet government the right of legislation and administration in Turkestan and even gave it the right to challenge the appointment of federal officials assigned to Turkestan and to supervise them in the execution of their duties.[15] Moreover, no federal decree could enter into force in Turkestan until it had been confirmed by the Turkestan Central Executive Committee or the Regional Congress of Soviets. In some cases, particularly those in which the decree affected the constitutional regime, only the Regional Congress of Soviets could grant confirmation.[16] In addition, the Regional Congress of Soviets, the Turkestan Central Executive Committee, and the Council of People's Commissars possessed "the right to introduce into federal decrees those changes which they recognize as necessary for their more successful application in the region." [17]

Even the extent to which federal legislation could function in Turkestan was limited. The Turkestan government reserved to itself exclusive jurisdiction over the lands, waters, and mineral resources of the region, the enactment of labor legislation, the establishment of taxes and duties (except those instituted by the central government), the fixing of legal norms, and the determination of the judicial structure and procedure. Within Turkestan the government had the right to establish and alter the territorial borders and the competence of regional and national units which formed a part of the Turkestan Soviet Socialist Republic, and the right of arbitration of disputes between these entities. Moreover, the establishment of the administrative divisions of the territories of the republic was made a

[14] A. Turubiner, "Konstitutsii Turkestana, Kryma, Dagestana," *Vlast' Sovetov,* No. 1 (April, 1924), p. 133.

[15] I. Poliukaitis, "Oblast' ili respublika," *Zhizn' Natsional'nostei,* No. 23 (31) (June 22, 1919).

[16] A. G. Goikhbarg, "O Turkestanskoi konstitutsii," *Proletarskaia Revoliutsiia i Pravo,* Nos. 8–10 (November 15–December 15, 1918), p. 24.

[17] *Ibid.,* p. 25.

matter of local concern. Turkestan reserved the right of partial and general pardon and amnesty within the republic. The budget of Turkestan was to be determined locally, although provision was made for subsequent confirmation by the All-Russian Central Executive Committee.[18]

In regard to relations with the central government the Turkestan constitution anticipated a special position for the republic. It provided not only for permanent Turkestanian representation at the federal center but reserved to the Turkestan delegation the right of decisive vote on all matters concerning Turkestan.[19] The document specified no procedure for registering the vote, but it did stipulate that disagreements between Turkestan and the central government were to be resolved at arbitral sessions of the permanent Turkestan delegation and the All-Russian Central Executive Committee. At such meetings both sides were to be accorded equal representation.[20]

These reservations of power and the special status which Turkestan sought to obtain within the federation did not meet with approval in Moscow. Notwithstanding the repeated protestations of Soviet leaders and the categorical statement of the constitution of the RSFSR that the Soviet state was a voluntary union of equal peoples, no such equality was ever conceded to the federating parts. Soviet autonomy did not mean political equality. It was merely a recognition that local peculiarities prevented a standardized application of the policies, administrative regimen, and legal norms of the center to all peoples and that these should be altered, in so far as was consistent with the accomplishment of their purpose, to fit local conditions. But the alteration of central legislation and administrative procedures was not a matter for local decision; this was within the province of a federal agency, the People's Commissariat for National Affairs.

Some months earlier Stalin had condemned precisely the type of autonomy proposed by the Turkestanian draft constitu-

---

[18] Turubiner, "Konstitutsii Turkestana, Kryma, Dagestana," *Vlast' Sovetov,* No. 1 (April, 1924), pp. 134–35.

[19] Goikhbarg, "O Turkestanskoi konstitutsii," *Proletarskaia Revoliutsiia i Pravo,* Nos. 8–10 (November 15–December 15, 1918), pp. 26–27.

[20] *Ibid.,* pp. 28–29.

tion. In a speech on May 10, 1918, before delegates to the conference on the convocation of the constituent congress of the Tataro-Bashkir Soviet Republic, he had insisted that preservation of the conquests of the revolution, the demands of economic rehabilitation, and the tasks of socialist construction required the establishment of a strongly centralized state. He had then warned of the consequences of insistence upon local independence:

The creation of local and regional sovereign organs parallel with the central authority would mean, in fact, a breakdown of all power and a return to capitalism. Precisely on this account, we must leave in the hands of the central authority all functions of importance to the whole country and offer to regional organs mainly administrative-political and cultural functions of a purely regional character.[21]

Harsh criticism of the projected Turkestanian constitutional regime notwithstanding, Moscow was not in a position in those desperate times to compel alterations in it. The interests of a united struggle against the internal and external enemies of the Soviet order required postponement of a settlement until happier circumstances should permit the center to enforce its will without endangering the revolution. Hence, Moscow did not protest overtly when the Turkestan Extraordinary Sixth Regional Congress of Soviets adopted the constitution in October without substantial change. It confined expression of its displeasure to a refusal to grant the Turkestan republic a formal charter of autonomy in the RSFSR.

The dispute remained at this impasse until the autumn of 1919 when the Red Army broke the Dutov barricade and reunited Turkestan with Central Russia. Even then the central authorities did not abrogate the Turkestan constitution of 1918; instead they embarked upon a fundamental solution of the Turkestan problem. Frunze, the commander of Red Army troops in Central Asia, summoned trusted divisions from the center and proceeded to disband the Turkestan garrison, thus breaking up this possible center of resistance. The Turkestan Commission, which had been sent into the region from Moscow

[21] Stalin, *Sochineniia*, IV, 89.

with instructions to effect a "Leninist solution" [22] to the nationality question, then proceeded to a "thorough reorganization of the whole soviet apparatus." [23] While this campaign was in progress, the Commission also busied itself with preparations for the convocation of the Ninth Regional Congress of Soviets and for the revision at this congress of the constitutional regime of the republic. In September, 1920, the congress convened in Tashkent and adopted a new constitution which corresponded in all details to Moscow's concept of autonomy. The new constitution not only entertained no pretension to equality with the RSFSR but, in the words of L. M. Kaganovich, a member of the Turkestan Commission who was later to rise to prominence in the Politburo of the Communist Party, it "indicated a further development [than the previous constitution] . . . relative to the practical application of power in the localities." [24] In this latter respect, it both formulated the class character of state power in the republic precisely and reserved this power to the native masses as well as to the European workers.

After the adoption of the 1920 constitution the objections of Bolshevik leadership to formal inclusion of Turkestan in the RSFSR disappeared. On April 11, 1921, the All-Russian Central Executive Committee adopted a decree proclaiming the formation of the Turkestan Soviet Socialist Republic including the Syr-Daria, Semirechie, Fergana, Samarkand, Transcaspia, and Amu-Daria regions. Gone were the objectionable features of the first constitution. State power, according to the decree, was organized "in conformity with the constitution of the RSFSR." Control of foreign affairs, foreign trade, and military affairs fell within the exclusive jurisdiction of the federal government. The Commissars of Communications, Posts and Telegraph, and Finance were to be appointed on the basis of agreement between the Turkestan Central Executive Committee and the corresponding people's commissariats to which they were subordinated, and all decrees of the federal government relating

[22] Georgii Safarov, *Kolonial'naia revoliutsiia: opyt Turkestana* (Moscow, 1921), p. 59.

[23] *Ibid.*, p. 104.

[24] Radzhapov, "Etapy razvitiia sovetskogo gosudarstvennogo stroia v Srednei Azii," *Sovetskoe Gosudarstvo i Pravo*, No. 11 (November, 1948), p. 65.

to these commissariats were to be extended to the Turkestan
SSR. In addition, the Central Council of National Economy
and the People's Commissariat of Supply were obliged to operate in conformity with plans established by the All-Russian
Council of National Economy and the Federal Commissariat of
Supply, and the chairmen of these commissariats were appointed in agreement with their federal counterparts. The residue of administrative power in the republic was left within
the competence of the Turkestan Central Executive Committee
and the Council of People's Commissars.[25] The promulgation
of the 1921 decree thus introduced Turkestan into the RSFSR
and brought the relationship between Turkestan and the central government into line with the Bolshevik concept of autonomy.

THE POLITICAL TRANSFORMATION OF KHIVA AND BOKHARA

In the case of Turkestan, the cement which united the Soviet
center with the national locality was a grant of political autonomy within the framework of the RSFSR. Relations between
the RSFSR and the soviet republics of Bokhara and Khorezm
were on a treaty basis. Politically, both republics were bound to
Moscow by treaties of alliance[26] which in their preambles and
early articles bestowed upon them political independence but
in the body of the texts robbed them of its practical consequences. On the one hand, these agreements abolished all previous agreements between former Russian governments and
these khanates and nullified all the rights which Russians had
formerly enjoyed in them. They transferred to the "people's

[25] Text of decree in I. Lozovskii and I. Bibin (eds.), *Sovetskaia Politika za 10
let po natsional'nomu voprosu v RSFSR: sistematicheskii sbornik deistvuiushchikh aktov pravitel'stv Soiuza SSR i RSFSR po delam natsional'nostei RSFSR
(oktiabr' 1917 g.–noiabr' 1927 g.)* (Moscow, 1928), pp. 114–15.
[26] The treaties are strikingly similar both in their terminology and in the
relationships which they established between the republics of Bokhara and
Khorezm and the RSFSR. For the texts of the treaties, see A. V. Sabanin (ed.),
*Sbornik deistvuiushchikh dogovorov, soglashenii i konventsii zakliuchennykh
s inostrannymi gosudarstvami* (Moscow, 1924–28), I, 42–46 (Bokhara), 184–88
(Khorezm). The treaties are reproduced in English in Leonard Shapiro (ed.),
*Soviet Treaty Series: A Collection of Bilateral Treaties, Agreements and Con-
ventions, etc., Concluded between the Soviet Union and Foreign Powers* (Wash-
ington, 1950), I, 59–60 (Khorezm), 98–100 (Bokhara).

republics" title to all properties in these countries which had belonged to the Russian republic and Russian state institutions. They voided all concessions and rights to land and water granted previously to Russian citizens, societies, and institutions, and they bestowed all Russian-owned private businesses in Bokhara and Khorezm in full property to these governments.[27]

On the other hand, the Soviet government reserved for itself a broad range of privileges—on a mutual basis—that opened the way to penetration into every sphere of life in the republics. Citizens of the RSFSR who belonged "to the working class or to the peasantry (nonexploiting, nonemployer)" and who took up residence in Bokhara and Khorezm for purposes of work were accorded the same rights and privileges as the indigenous citizens.[28] The RSFSR undertook to supply these republics with instructors, teachers, literature, printing presses, and supplies[29] and in the case of Khorezm, the sum of 500,000,000 rubles.[30] The military forces of both republics were, for practical purposes, incorporated into the Red Army since both treaties provided for the "establishment of a common plan, common direction and training of forces" for defense. The details of these articles were to be worked out in military-political agreements concluded simultaneously with the alliance treaties.[31] In the case of Bokhara, the RSFSR undertook in a later agreement the "armed protection" of the Bokharan-Afghan customs frontier and subordinated the border guards to the Turkestan Military District.[32] To prevent Khorezm and Bokhara from succumbing to capitalistic penetration, both republics undertook to refuse economic concessions to other than soviet republics and to sub-

[27] In treaty with Khorezm, Articles 1–5; in treaty with Bokhara, Preamble and Articles 1, 7, 9.

[28] In treaty with Khorezm, Articles 13, 15; in treaty with Bokhara, Articles 11, 12.

[29] In treaty with Khorezm, Article 18; in treaty with Bokhara, Article 14.

[30] Article 19.

[31] In treaty with Khorezm, Article 17; in treaty with Bokhara, Article 2.

[32] Article 8 of Customs Agreement between RSFSR and the Bokharan People's Soviet Republic concluded in Moscow on May 31, 1923. Text in *Sobranie uzakonenii i rasporiazhenii Rabochego i Krest'ianskogo Pravitel'stva RSFSR* (Moscow, 1923), I, 961–64. English translation in Shapiro, *Soviet Treaty Series*, I, 216–17.

ordinate themselves to the economic plans of the RSFSR.[23]

These two treaties were basically different in character from
the agreements concluded between Moscow and independent
soviet socialist republics, such as the Ukraine and Belorussia.
The latter provided for a unification of the most important people's commissariats, whereas the treaties with Bokhara and
Khorezm merely promised "concerted action" in the formulation and execution of policy in the military and economic
spheres. The absence of administrative unification in no wise
endangered the application of Soviet policy to Bokhara and
Khorezm. The alliances were in themselves formal guarantees
of Soviet political supremacy. And their effect was reinforced
by the presence of a network of officials and agencies which
were put in control of the most strategic positions in government, but whose allegiance was to Moscow and to Communism.
In both countries Communist Parties emerged and their members, who were under the disciplinary control of the Communist International, were brought to the center of political
life while moderate native leaders and politicians were removed
from office on one pretext or another. One method of accom-
plishing this and of forestalling organized opposition was the
utilization of an implied threat deriving from the presence of
Red Army garrisons in the country. Another was the introduction of seasoned Bolsheviks, usually Moslems from the more
highly developed Tatar regions, into inconspicuous but highly
strategic positions in the government, the police system, and
the native militia.

The policy of the Soviet government in establishing a monopoly of control in Bokhara and Khorezm included economic
as well as political life. In this region, however, the deftness
which had distinguished Bolshevik political activity almost
from the moment of the overthrow of khanate government was
absent at the beginning. And the first attempts of Communists
to interfere in local economic life and to tie these countries
into the Soviet economic system aroused the anger and opposi-

[23] In alliance treaty with Khorezm, Articles 20, 21; in alliance treaty with
Bokhara, Article 5.

tion of the natives. Two examples illustrate the clumsiness of these early methods.

In the case of Khiva, the Turkestan Commission, responding to an appeal from the revolutionary government, dispatched an "Extraordinary Representation of the RSFSR and the Amu-Daria Division" to Khiva in March, 1920, to bring order out of the local economic chaos. The expedition was well supplied with money and technical equipment, but apparently included no economists among its more than 200 members. Its major achievement was financial. In the hope of creating a monetary crisis in Bokhara, which at the time was still ruled by Said Alim Khan, the commission depreciated the currency of Khiva. This maneuver succeeded not in undermining the economy of Bo-khara—the money market in Khiva was regulated by Bokhara and Afghanistan—but in angering the population of Khiva, in-creasing suffering in the country, and destroying the confidence of the Khivan people in their currency.[34]

The same ineptness characterized the early economic rela-tions of the Soviet regime with the Bokharan People's Republic. In September, 1920, after the overthrow of the Emir, Russia and Bokhara made arrangements for a planned commodity ex-change. In return for Russian cloth, manufactures, dry goods, matches, pottery, and kerosene, the Bokharan government guar-anteed to supply Russia with its entire production of cotton, wool, and karakul beyond internal consumption requirements. But the agreement, which was designed to drive European goods off the local market and to orient the Bokharan economy to-ward Russia, provided no basis for determining the value of goods being exchanged; and each side soon felt that it had been cheated. The Bokharan government attempted to negotiate trade contracts in Europe. Moscow quickly put a stop to this but in doing so it lost good will in Bokhara.[35]

The lessons of these early attempts to regulate the economic

[34] K. Khromykh, "Sozdanie fronta revoliutsii v Srednei Azii: Khorezmskaia Respublika," *Voennaia Mysl'*, No. 1 (September, 1920), pp. 292–93.

[35] Ter-Pogos-Avetisov, "Nashi ekonomicheskie vzaimootnosheniia s Bukharoi v proshlom i nastoiashchem," *Voennaia Mysl'*, No. 2 (May–July, 1921), p. 235.

life of Bokhara and Khorezm were not ignored in Russia. There was, of course, no question but that Moscow, by the use of non-economic means, could have integrated these states into the economic system of the RSFSR and prevented the formation in them of independent economic centers either public or private. Aware that native hostility would reduce the flow of commodities and hinder economic recovery, the Bolsheviks sought a different solution, one which would guarantee Russian domination of local economic life without discouraging native cooperation. This formula of economic control called for (1) a uniform production plan; (2) a single commodity fund and a uniform import-export plan; (3) a uniform structure and uniform guidance by operating agencies in the conduct of economic relations with non-Soviet states; (4) Soviet support for the development of local industry; and (5) concerted opposition to the foreign bourgeoisie and to the influx of foreign industrial capital.[36]

This formula became the basis of a series of economic agreements concluded between the RSFSR and the two republics.[37] By their terms Bokhara and Khorezm entered the customs area of the RSFSR, and in the case of Bokhara, Russia took over the administration of the customs frontier with Afghanistan. Both republics agreed to conduct trade with the RSFSR on the basis of a planned interchange of commodities, and with third states

[36] S. Iranskii, "Tendentsii v razvitii organizatsionnykh form torgovli SSSR so stranami Vostoka," *Torgovlia Rossii s Vostokom,* Nos. 1–2 (January–February, 1925), p. 4. An interesting comparison can be drawn between these principles which were applied to Bokhara and Khorezm and those that were adopted by the Soviet government in relation to the bordering Eastern states, Turkey, Persia, Afghanistan, Sinkiang, Tannu Tuva, and Outer Mongolia. For an analysis of this policy, see Violet Conolly, *Soviet Economic Policy in the East* (London, 1933).

[37] The texts of these agreements may be found in *Sbornik deistvuiushchikh dogovorov* as follows: between the RSFSR and the Bokharan People's Soviet Republic: an economic agreement concluded on March 4, 1921, at Moscow, II, 12–14; an economic agreement superseding the agreement of March 4, 1921, concluded on August 9, 1922, at Moscow, IV, 9–10. Between the RSFSR and the Khorezmian People's Soviet Republic: an economic agreement concluded on September 13, 1920, at Moscow, I, 23–26; an economic agreement superseding the agreement of September 13, 1920, signed at Tashkent on June 29, 1922, IV, 13–14. In addition, two agreements were concluded between the RSFSR and both republics jointly in 1921 and 1923. Text of latter agreement is reproduced in *ibid.,* V, 5.

on the basis of a mutually established uniform import-export plan. In the latter instance, the republics relinquished their right to enter into trade relations with non-Soviet states except under the supervision and guidance of representatives of the RSFSR. They were obliged, moreover, to oppose the influx into their territories of "predatory industrial capital and of elements of the foreign bourgeoisie." Concessions to foreigners, if they were contemplated, had to be proffered preferentially to the RSFSR. Even if the RSFSR declined, its prior consent was required before the republics could offer the proposed concessions abroad.

By these treaty provisions the RSFSR was able to quarantine Bokhara and Khorezm economically from the non-Soviet world. At the same time, the Soviet government sought to offset the harmful consequences of their economic isolation by offering assistance in the reconstruction of agriculture and local irrigation networks and by taking steps to develop local industry. The services of trained technical personnel were made available to both states; needed machinery was promised; financial support was offered; and in the case of Khorezm, the RSFSR undertook to supply "the necessary personnel for organizing an apparatus of supply and for conducting supply 'campaigns.' " [38]

The system of Russian guidance and control which these agreements established over the economic life of Bokhara and Khorezm satisfied the Soviet claim to ascendancy without effecting an actual unification of governmental agencies. But the treaties did not establish any institutional method for cooperation between the two people's republics and the Turkestan ASSR in solving mutual problems of reconstruction in Central Asia. At first Moscow was reluctant to propose measures leading to unification of all of Central Asia. In part it hoped to encourage among non-Soviet Asian peoples the myth that the republics of Bokhara and Khorezm were genuinely independent. In part it was hampered by the fiction that even a local administrative unification was unsuitable as a form of connection between "people's republics" and socialist regimes.

[38] Article 4, economic agreement between Khorezmian People's Soviet Republic and RSFSR, concluded at Moscow, September 13, 1920. *Ibid.*, I, 23–26.

Until the autumn of 1922, the Soviet government not only acted on these premises but allowed them to obscure the fact that all of Soviet Central Asia formed a single economic and geographic unit and that a planned economic recovery, to be effective, had to rest on this unity. However, the existence of major regional problems, revolving primarily around the rehabilitation and development of the communications network, the reconstruction and expansion of irrigation systems, the planned utilization of water resources, and the restoration of cotton production, soon demonstrated the necessity for close and continuous cooperation among the three republics.

In late November, 1922, the Soviet regime took a first step toward reversing its former position. The Second Turkestan Conference, meeting in Tashkent, adopted a decision advocating creation of a Central Asiatic Economic Council composed of representatives of the three Central Asian soviet republics and competent to regulate their economic relations.[39] This act was followed by the First Conference of Central Asian Republics, held in March, 1923, which agreed to unite the republics "on the principles of unity of economic policy and planning" through the establishment of a Central Asiatic Economic Council. The republics of Bokhara and Khorezm agreed moreover to adopt the monetary system of the USSR, to integrate their transportation systems under the USSR Commissariat of Communications, and to merge their post and telegraph systems with that of Turkestan. The conference also undertook to unify the administration of foreign trade, to eliminate "mutual competition on the internal market," and to maintain close contact in regard to all measures dealing with statistical affairs, state trading, cooperatives, agriculture, and irrigation. In the case of agriculture and irrigation, the three republics agreed further to adopt a unified plan, utilizing in this the "cultural and technical forces and experience" of Turkestan, and in the case of cotton production they contracted to adopt the same legislation.[40]

[39] G. Nepesov, "Vozniknovenie i razvitie Turkmenskoi Sovetskoi Sotsialisticheskoi Respubliki," *Voprosy Istorii,* No. 2 (February, 1950), p. 7.

[40] G. Skalov, "Ekonomicheskoe ob'edinenie Sredne-Aziatskikh respublik kak faktor natsional'noi politiki," *Zhizn' Natsional'nostei,* No. 4 (1923), p. 41.

The economic unification of Central Asia was in practice equivalent to an indirect incorporation of Bokhara and Khorezm into the administrative system of the USSR, and in this respect it served a double function. It subordinated these republics to the administrative regimen of the center through their connection with the Turkestan Autonomous Republic; and on the other hand, it preserved the distinctive relationships of Bokhara and Khorezm to the USSR as a whole, while advancing them one step further toward eventual admission into the Soviet Union. On political as well as economic grounds Communist observers hailed the agreement as a new stage in the transition of Bokhara and Khorezm onto a socialist path of development, under the guidance of the advanced proletariat of Russia, and in preparing for their ultimate incorporation into the Soviet federation.[41]

From the inception of "popular" government in Bokhara and Khorezm the Russian Bolsheviks had manifested a determination to tolerate no other objective in their political evolution. This was confirmed officially by Stalin in his report on the formation of the Union of Soviet Socialist Republics (December 23, 1922) at the Tenth All-Russian Congress of Soviets. Making note of the exceptional relationship of Bokhara and Khorezm to Soviet Russia, he told the assembly:

Two independent soviet republics, Khorezm and Bokhara—being people's soviet, but not socialist, republics—remain for the present outside the framework of this union solely and exclusively because they are not yet socialist. I have no doubt [he prophesied]—and I hope you too have no doubt—that, in proportion to their internal development toward socialism, they likewise will enter the structure of the Union state now being formed.[42]

Thus, while proclaiming the freedom of these two states, the Soviet government was making ready to absorb them. Such was the application to Central Asia of the Leninist contention that

[41] Turar Ryskulov, "Ekonomicheskoe ob'edinenie Sredne-Aziatskikh respublik," *Izvestiia*, March 28, 1923; I. Liubimov, "Ekonomicheskoe ob'edinenie Sredne-Aziatskikh respublik," *Pravda*, April 1, 1923.

[42] *Desiatyi Vserossiiskii S'ezd Sovetov Rabochikh, Krest'ianskikh, Krasnoarmeiskikh i Kazach'ikh Deputatov. 23–27 dekabria 1922 goda* (Moscow, 1923), p. 187.

peoples who had been given full freedom of separation would gladly forsake it for the benefits to be obtained from membership in a great socialist state.

The faith of the Bolshevik leaders that, upon fulfillment of the preconditions of a grant of liberty and of guidance on the part of experienced Bolsheviks, backward countries would evolve easily and naturally toward socialism, was not confirmed in Bokhara and Khorezm by reality. In Khorezm, the revolution had brought to power the Young Khivan Party, a group whose aims were hardly compatible with those of the Soviet government. From the very beginning of its rule this party resisted the efforts of Soviet advisers and technicians to introduce measures which would pave the way for the "further development" of the revolution. Nevertheless, the Bolsheviks were not able to dispense with its leaders immediately. Because of its opposition to Junaid Khan, the party had won a large following, and the Soviet regime felt itself obliged to undermine the prestige of the Young Khivans before it could drive them from power. Moreover, the ideas of the Soviet system were completely unknown to the peasantry. Until propagandists could acquaint the masses with the benefits of Communism, recruit Party followers, and organize at least the semblance of a mass movement, no second revolution was possible. This work of preparation was carried on for more than a year after the overthrow of Junaid Khan.

In the meantime the administration of the country remained in the hands of the Young Khivans. In April, 1920, the First Kuraltai or Congress of Khiva, in which 150 delegates from all districts in the khanate had participated, had given this party popular sanction and had installed a temporary government, headed by an Uzbek, Iusupov, and consisting of five persons who represented the large and middle "bourgeoisie," the clergy, and the Turcomans.[43] From the Soviet point of view, this was hardly a promising composition for a revolutionary government, and Soviet suspicions of its unsatisfactory character were soon confirmed. Not only did it fail to wage an energetic strug-

---

[43] I. Maiskii, *Vneshniaia politika RSFSR, 1917–1922* (Moscow, 1922), pp. 149–50. Khromykh, "Sozdanie fronta revoliutsii v Srednei Azii," *Voennaia Mysl'*, No. 1 (September, 1920), pp. 295–96.

gle against the underlings of the deposed khan, but it was suspected of opposing the establishment of an administration
friendly to the Soviets. Certainly, it was a lethargic government.
It made no effort to introduce administrative order in the
country but left this work entirely in the hands of Soviet advisers. The "Extraordinary Representation of the RSFSR and
the Amu-Daria Division," which had earlier caused the financial crisis in 1920 in Khorezm, undertook to create an administrative apparatus. It established administrative procedures and
created commissariats, a supreme revolutionary tribunal, and
people's courts. In the villages of Khorezm no revolutionary
power had come into existence, and the commission set about
to create one. In addition, it worked out a procedure for elections to local soviets and carried on political work to attract
mass support for the Communist Party of Khiva and for the
cause of social revolution.[44]

It was intertribal enmity rather than class struggle which led
to the overthrow of the first government of Khorezm. In September, 1920, after Iusupov had ordered the execution of eighty
Turcoman leaders, the Turcoman tribes revolted. The Soviet
representatives seized the opportunity. While mediating the
quarrel in order to prevent the outbreak of a tribal war, they
also took steps to exploit the friction. In January, 1921, Safonov, the Soviet plenipotentiary in Khiva, called an All-Turcoman Congress in the town of Porsa. By promising to hasten
the creation of Red Turcoman troop units and to support a
redistribution of irrigational waters in the Turcoman districts,
he won Turcoman backing in his dealings with the government
of Khorezm.[45]

This support put Safonov in a position to challenge the authority of Iusupov's government. As elections to the Second
Kuraltai approached, Safonov demanded that the nonlaboring
elements of the Khorezmian population be disenfranchised.[46]
When Iusupov refused, Safonov initiated a mass outbreak. On
the ground that the government was spreading false rumors to

[44] Khromykh, "Sozdanie fronta revoliutsii v Srednei Azii," *Voennaia Mysl'*,
No. 1 (September, 1920), pp. 295–96.
[45] Maiskii, *Vneshniaia politika RSFSR*, pp. 149–50.
[46] *Ibid.*, p. 150.

the effect that the Russians and Tatars serving in the Khorezmian Red Army were planning to massacre the local population, he called a mass meeting on March 4. The assembled mob
adopted resolutions on the trust of the people to all Red Army
men and on their distrust toward the Khorezmian government.
Iusupov responded by dismissing the Central Electoral Bureau
and postponing indefinitely the elections to the Kuraltai. On
the following day, the Red Army garrison, supported by a mob,
marched on the government offices and, after a disorderly demonstration, declared the Iusupov government overthrown. A
revolutionary committee of the Khorezmian republic, consisting of two Uzbeks, a Turcoman, a Kirghiz, and "a member of
the Komsomol," was chosen on the spot, and an announcement
was made that the elections to the Second Kuraltai would proceed as soon as possible.[47] "Thus," writes the Soviet chronicler
of this episode, "the Khivan people were liberated from the
power of the beys (large landowners), from the compromising
government of the Young Khivans." [48]

The Second Kuraltai met in May, 1921, and devoted most of
its attention to eliminating the major sources of Turcoman-
Uzbek friction. It established a special Turcoman division with
seven members under the Khorezmian Central Executive Committee, declared an amnesty for all Turcomans who had opposed the people's government, and dispatched an appeal to
Turcomans who had fled into the desert to return to the oases
and settle in peace with the Uzbek population. Reviewing these
achievements, Maiskii, who was later to become Soviet ambassa-
dor to the Court of St. James's, called the meeting of the Second Kuraltai a turning point in internal Khivan relations.[49]
Khorezm nevertheless remained constitutionally a people's soviet, but not socialist, government. Private ownership of land
and of the tools of production was guaranteed, and the congress
ignored Safonov's demand for a restricted franchise. The con-

[47] N. Chekalin, "Sobytiia v Khorezmskoi Respublike," *Voennaia Mysl'*, No. 1
(January–April, 1921), pp. 228–29.
[48] *Ibid.*, p. 229.
[49] Maiskii, *Vneshniaia politika RSFSR*, pp. 150–51; also A. Vinogradova,
"Khorezmskaia Sovetskaia Narodnaia Respublika," *Zhizn' Natsional'nostei*, No.
1 (January, 1923), p. 187.

stitution guaranteed the right to elect and be elected to all citizens of the republic over 18 years of age, irrespective of their class status or religion. It disenfranchised only known opponents of the Soviet people's government, officials of the prerevolutionary regime, convicted criminals, and the insane.[50]

The expulsion of the Young Khivan Party, nevertheless, paved the way for a series of steps that led ultimately to the establishment of a "dictatorship of the toiling classes" in Khorezm. The first act in the transition took place in October, 1921. Several members of the Khorezmian government were arrested for participation in a "counterrevolutionary" movement; a number of them were executed and the rest sentenced to long prison terms.[51] The year 1922 witnessed a widespread purge of allegedly hostile elements in the government and in the Communist Party of Khorezm. Finally, in October, 1923, the Fourth Khorezmian Kuraltai altered the constitution to deprive nontoiling elements of the franchise and transformed the Khorezmian People's Republic into the Khorezmian Soviet Socialist Republic.[52]

The "further development" of the revolution in Bokhara followed much the same pattern as in Khorezm. Initially the Young Bokharan Party shared the governing of the Bokharan People's Republic with the Communist Party of Bokhara, which had been organized during the exile of the Bokharan revolutionaries in Turkestan. While these two parties represented diverse political aspirations, the new Bokharan regime was, nevertheless, considerably more progressive from the Soviet viewpoint than its counterpart in Khorezm. This was due

[50] Pavel V. Gidulianov, *Otdelenie tserkvi ot gosudarstva v SSSR* (Moscow, 1926), p. 288; also Prof. I. I. Kryl'tsov, "Publichnopravovaia storona natsional'nogo razmezhevaniia," *Vsia Sredniaia Aziia; spravochnaia kniga na 1926 khoziaistvennyi god* (Tashkent, 1926), p. 15.

[51] Maiskii, *Vneshniaia politika RSFSR*, p. 151.

[52] *Izvestiia*, October 23, 1923. According to Agabekov, a former OGPU agent who may not be an entirely reliable witness, Byk, the Russian plenipotentiary in Khorezm, engineered the declaration of socialism. As the Fourth Kuraltai met in session, this gentleman surrounded the building with Red Army troops, then demanded of the delegates, "Do you recognize the Soviet power or do you not?" The delegates, hearing the clatter of arms in the street, voted unanimously for the Soviet power. Georges Agabekov, *OGPU, the Russian Secret Terror* (New York, 1931), p. 17.

principally to the organized strength of the local Communist center and to the zealous pursuit of a "soviet" policy by the leader of the native Communist Party, Faizulla Khodzhaev. Moreover, this government sought to apply "Bolshevik" solutions to pressing social and political problems.

One of the first acts of the All-Bokharan Revolutionary Committee, which came into power after the downfall of Said Alim Khan, was an attempt to introduce Soviet principles into the solution of the agrarian question. It nationalized all lands, waters, and mineral resources of Bokhara and forbade the sale, purchase, mortgage, or rental of land or water—a violation being considered a crime against the state—or the use of hired labor. It also decreed the confiscation of all landed endowment properties and the landholdings of former emirate officials and beys, together with their livestock and equipment, and ordered them distributed among the small and landless peasantry.[53] Although the First Congress of Toilers of Bokhara endorsed the decree, it never actually came into force. It alienated too many influential sections of the native population before the radical forces had established a base of internal support for their policies. However, at the Second Kuraltai, the new regime declared the equality of all ethnic groups in the Bokharan People's Soviet Republic and guaranteed them equal rights to participate in local and central organs of power, to receive education in schools using the local languages, and to use their native tongues in the courts.[54]

In spite of these progressive policies, the early government in Bokhara was not at all reliable from the Soviet point of view. Of the eighty-five-member Central Executive Committee, five represented rightist tendencies, eight leftist ones, and the remainder the center. The seven-member presidium of this body contained two conservatives and one progressive.[55] In these

[53] Text in A. Mashitskii, "Materialy po istorii Bukharskoi Revoliutsii," *Vestnik Narodnogo Komissariata Inostrannykh Del*, Nos. 4–5 (April–May, 1922), pp. 127–28.

[54] Dervish, "Bukharskaia Sovetskaia Narodnaia Respublika," *Zhizn' Natsional'nostei*, No. 1 (January, 1923), pp. 197–98.

[55] Joseph Castagné, "Le Bolchévisme et l'Islam: les organisations soviétiques de la Russie musulmane," *Revue du Monde Musulman*, LI (October, 1922), 225.

bodies the Young Bokharans, who desired no advance beyond the stage of political democracy, had the preponderant weight of representation. Even former officials of the prerevolutionary regime were able to exert conservative pressure. Although they were excluded from the central policy-making bodies, many of them continued to function in administrative posts, particularly in more remote districts. The new ruling class, handicapped by the general illiteracy and its own lack of training and experience in government, was unable to replace or even to supervise them.[56]

The weight of these forces found expression in the constitutional regime of the republic. Compounded of a mixture of traditional values and democratic concepts of government stretched over a soviet framework, the basic principle of the constitution of the Bokharan People's Soviet Republic was that of popular sovereignty. The document made no reference to a dictatorship of the toiling masses. On the contrary, it declared that, in consequence of the collapse of the emirate and its despotism, the administration of the country had passed "into the hands of the Bokharan people itself" and stated categorically that "state power in the Bokharan republic throughout its territory, both in the center and in the localities, henceforth belongs entirely to the representatives of the whole Bokharan people, organized in Soviets of People's Deputies." [57] Later articles which elaborated this definition of sovereignty and enumerated the rights of the people left no question concerning the democratic and "petit-bourgeois" character of the Bokharan republic.

The document contained no provisions abolishing private ownership of land or providing for the nationalization of large-scale industry, and it failed to place any limitation on the ownership or disposition of private property. Citizens of the republic were guaranteed (Article 5) "the unlimited right to use and dispose of their own movable and immovable property" and the privilege of "private ownership and disposition of capi-

[56] D. Soloveichik, "Revoliutsionnaia Bukhara," *Novyi Vostok*, No. 2 (1922), pp. 273–74.

[57] N. B. Arkhipov, "Bukharskaia Narodnaia Sovetskaia Respublika," *Sovetskoe Pravo*, No. 1 (4) (1923), p. 134.

tal in any amount." In addition, the constitution sought to
defend the entire population against the danger of arbitrary
action by the government. In a three-article Bill of Rights
(Articles 7 to 9), it guaranteed to all citizens freedom of conscience, freedom of speech, press, assembly, and association, and
inviolability of the person and the home. Moreover, the popular character of governing agencies was assured by the extension
of the franchise (Article 58) to "all citizens of the Bokharan
People's Soviet Republic of both sexes who have reached 18
years of age." The constitution, however, included certain limitations of the franchise which pointed away from democracy
and toward class rule. Article 59 disenfranchised not only persons who had served the prerevolutionary regime in responsible
posts and all "state officials of the emir" but also "large landowners and capitalists." [58] But this limitation was hardly
enough to weaken the democratic structure of the regime or to
compromise the principle of popular sovereignty.

Even the institutionalization of administration differed
sharply from the usual soviet forms. Although a hierarchy of
soviets leading up to the All-Bokharan Congress of Soviets was
established, the system varied in important respects from that
created in other soviet republics. On the local level, the governing agency was defined as the kishlak or village assembly of
electors and the executive function was delegated to an *aksakal*
(elder) elected for a period of one year.[59] This was a master
stroke in bringing the soviet system into conformity with tradition. What it actually amounted to was a pronouncement of a
new legal sanction of a system of local administration that had
existed in the villages of Bokhara long before their peace had
been disturbed by civil war and revolution. Nor did the provision of election threaten the authority of customary local leaders; it merely obligated them to submit annually to a process of
popular acclaim.

While the central governmental agencies adopted names and
forms associated with the soviet structure, they bore no more
than a casual resemblance to their counterparts in Soviet Rus-

[58] *Ibid.*, pp. 134–35.
[59] *Ibid.*, p. 137.

sia. The All-Bokharan Congress of Soviets, unlike the Congress
of Soviets in Russia, was the decisive legislative body, but it
was not, as in the case of the RSFSR, the highest organ of power.
Supremacy was reserved for the constitution itself.[60] Actually
the Bokharan Congress of Soviets had considerably more constitutional authority than similar bodies in Russia. It alone
could ratify peace treaties and, more important, it alone could
promulgate changes or additions to the constitution. Since Article 26 declared that "no published laws of the republic may
contradict the foundations of Islam," [61] the Congress of Soviets
in this latter capacity also became the defender of the faith in
Bokhara.

The executive organ of the Bokharan republic was defined
constitutionally as the Central Executive Committee. Elected
by the Congress of Soviets and functioning in the interim between congresses, it not only held the supreme power of decision over all matters except those reserved for the Congress
of Soviets but it also possessed (Article 25) "the exclusive right
of confirmation and publication of all laws in all branches of
the state administration of the country." [62] The delegation of
this authority to the Central Executive Committee left little
power indeed to the Council of People's Commissars, which the
constitution reduced to little more than a routine administrative agency. It had the right to enact decrees but such of its
edicts as the Central Executive Committee determined to be in
contradiction to established laws lost their obligatory force.[63]

By Bokharan standards the regime instituted by this constitution was extremely radical; as a matter of fact, it represented
too great an innovation to be understood by any except the
most cultivated groups of the population. But by Soviet standards—and these standards were decisive because they could be
implemented by force—it was no more than a temporary expedient. Even before the Red Army had installed the Young
Bokharans in power, the Bolsheviks had decided to compel
Bokhara to adopt eventually a socialist form of government.

[60] *Ibid.*
[61] *Ibid.*, pp. 136–37.
[62] *Ibid.*, pp. 135–36.
[63] *Ibid.*, pp. 136–37.

But native unrest and the danger of the growth of Basmachism prevented the immediate institution of a "Bolshevik" policy. Not until the new regime had been in power for more than a year did circumstances permit the Bolsheviks to take aggressive action against the non-Communist forces in the government. At this time, they initiated efforts to tighten their control of the governmental apparatus and to remove from office those elements which opposed Bolshevik policies.

In a measure, the Bolshevik-Young Bokharan coalition dissolved of itself. Many of the old officials who had been retained and some members of the Young Bokharan Party went over to the Basmachi. In 1922 the campaign to institute a "Bolshevik" policy was stepped up and a great purge carried through both in the government and in the Party. Even this cleansing did not have the desired effect. In June, 1923, at the Fourth Conference with Responsible Workers of the National Republics and Regions, Stalin pointed to the fact that the Bokharan Council of Nazirs (Commissars) contained eight merchants, two members of the intelligentsia, and one mullah, but no peasants. He accused the government of catering to the well-to-do and charged that there was "nothing either popular or soviet" in its activities.[64]

This was the signal for a new and even more sweeping purge. Charging that "a group of merchants had seized the apparatus of state power" and "were using [it] for their own private ends and in the interests of the wealthy classes," the Central Committee of the Communist Party of Bokhara dismissed the Nazirs of Foreign Affairs, Education, and Finances and other prominent members of the Central Executive Committee, and satisfied Stalin's complaint by establishing a new Council of Nazirs consisting of "representatives of the workers and peasants." The long broom of the Party extended to the *vilayet* or provincial agencies of power; scores of officials were dismissed and many arrests were made.

The Bolsheviks forced through other measures to bring the policy of the government into line with Stalin's conception of a properly functioning Soviet regime. Agricultural credit was

[64] Stalin, *Sochineniia*, V, 332.

extended to the peasantry and funds were appropriated for the establishment of credit cooperatives. In order to eliminate Turcoman-Uzbek friction, which plagued Bokhara as well as Khorezm, districts populated by Turcomans were separated into autonomous regions.[65] Two months later an extraordinary session of the Bokharan Kuraltai disenfranchised members of the old bureaucracy, usurers, merchants, and large-scale traders and, at the same time, increased the representation of trade-union members in the government. A year later in September, 1924, the Kuraltai proclaimed Bokhara a socialist republic.

Quantitatively, the changes wrought by the transformation of Bokhara and Khorezm from popular soviet to soviet socialist republics were not great. In neither case did the adoption of the socialist form of government bespeak accomplishments in the economic or cultural fields. Politically, however, the change was significant. By it, three small but important social groups—the feudal lords, the "bourgeoisie," and the intellectuals who supported them—were legally eliminated from political life. The disenfranchisement of these groups by no means broke their power or removed them as a threat to the new regime. Over a year later, complaints were reaching Bokhara that the "beys, ishans,[66] mullahs, and emirate officials" were still in power in the localities.[67] In Khorezm, it was charged, serfdom still existed and in one district feudal landowners continued to maintain armed *druzhinas*.[68] Nevertheless, the disenfranchisement of these elements diminished their ability to influence the population and to oppose further "deepening" of the revolution.

THE NATIONAL DELIMITATION OF CENTRAL ASIA

In the relationship of Bokhara and Khorezm to the USSR, the adoption of a socialist state structure marked the opening of a new phase of development. Having debarred "nontoiling"

[65] O. Galustian, "Smena pravitel'stva v Bukhare," *Izvestiia*, July 11, 1923.

[66] The term *ishan*, as used in Turkestan, denotes a teacher or guide. An ishan usually lives in a monastery or other holy place whence he emerges from time to time to conduct religious work among the population at large.

[67] A. Shutemov, "Itogi i perspektivy Sovetskogo stroitel'stva v Turkmenistane," *Vlast' Sovetov*, IX, No. 13 (March 28, 1926), 6.

[68] "Pervyi uchreditel'nyi s'ezd sovetov Turkmenskoi SSR," *Vlast' Sovetov*, VIII, No. 12 (March 22, 1925), 17.

elements from participation in government, the two republics placed themselves on the same path of development as the more advanced soviet republics. Moreover, they eliminated the obstacles which Stalin, in his report to the Tenth Congress of Soviets, had put in the way of their admission into the USSR. By this time Bolsheviks both in Moscow and in Central Asia had reached the conclusion that the Central Asian republics must be reorganized and rid of their multitribal nature before they would be eligible for membership in the Soviet federation.

Unlike other republics and regions of the USSR, the republics of Central Asia in 1924 were highly heterogeneous in national composition. Turkestan, Bokhara, and Khorezm represented a tribal mélange second only to the Caucasus. Uzbeks and Turcomans inhabited all three republics; Kazakhs and Kara-Kalpaks were settled in Turkestan and Khorezm; and Tajik communities existed in Turkestan and Khorezm. These were tribal, not racial, divisions. With the exception of the Tajiks, an Iranian ethnic strain which was concentrated in the piedmont of the Pamirs, the various tribes were all Turkic in origin.

In economic development, the region represented considerably more range of diversity. Most numerous and sedentary in character, the Uzbeks formed the bulk of the agricultural popu-

TABLE 2

THE NATIONAL STRUCTURE OF CENTRAL ASIA
PRIOR TO THE NATIONAL DELIMITATION
(*In Percentages*)

				NATIONALITY				
REPUBLIC	*Uz-beks*	*Ka-zakhs*	*Kir-ghiz*	*Turco-mans*	*Kara-Kalpaks*	*Ta-jiks*	*Rus-sians*	*Others*
Turkestan ASSR	41.4	19.4	10.7	4.7	1.4	7.7	9.5	2.6
Bokhara PSR	45.1			7.5		40.0	1.5	5.9
Khorezm PSR	64.7	3.4		26.8	3.8			1.3

Source: Adapted from data in M. Nemchenko, "Natsional'noe Razmezhevanie Srednei Azii," *Mezhdunarodnaia Zhizn'*, Nos. 4–5 (1924), p. 86.

lation of Central Asia, dominating the oases and providing the strongest class of merchants, traders, and usurers. Of the other major tribal groups, the Kirghiz and Kazakhs were in a transitional stage between nomadism and agriculture. Tribal ties, though still important, were slowly disintegrating as the organizational discipline, required by periodic migrations, gave way to the greater independence of the farming community. Among the Turcomans, who were predominantly nomadic, tribal organization was strongest. Even when they settled on the land, the Turcomans often settled as tribal units and retained the old political organization.

Out of these differences—tribal and socioeconomic—arose conditions which Bolsheviks considered prejudicial to a healthy development toward socialism. The traditional dichotomy between the nomadic tribes of the desert and the settled peoples of the oases had created "national" frictions which, in consequence of Tsarist exploitation, Bolsheviks contended, had given rise to mutual hostility and to recurrent outbreaks of violence. Such an atmosphere of disunity and hostility was unsuited to the process of soviet construction. Within Central Asia, it left to the "local bourgeoisie, the khans, and the emirs" opportunities to subvert and to harass the soviet order. From the outside the imperialist powers could take advantage of internal frictions, exploit them, encourage intertribal warfare, and debilitate, if not finally destroy, soviet rule.

Even in the absence of the threats of internal disunity and external provocation, the conditions imposed by the task of peaceful construction required a national reorganization of Central Asia. So great were the social, economic, and customary differentiations between the various peoples that the Soviet regime felt unable to establish norms of social development and administrative procedure. This did not mean that Bolsheviks considered Central Asia doomed to backwardness so long as the national question remained unsolved. Rather it signified, as Khodzhaev told the Second Session of the All-Union Central Executive Committee, that the peoples of the region "would achieve less in the struggle with their own adversities than they could achieve with unification along national and economic lines." [69] In a soviet society, based on maximum development of

[69] SSSR Tsentral'nyi Ispolnitel'nyi Komitet Vtorogo Sozyva, *Vtoraia Sessiia Ts. I.K.: stenograficheskii otchet* (Moscow, 1924), p. 545.

social and economic forces through planning, such an "artificial" barrier to progress was intolerable.

There is no question that the cultural heterogeneity of the peoples of Central Asia created complex problems for soviet planners. In the area of economic development, uniform policies which required mass popular support could not be pursued. A single cooperative policy which would attract the support of both the cotton-producing *dekhkan* (peasant) and the stock-raising nomad could not be formulated. The same conditions applied to other areas of soviet construction. The same judicial standards could not be established for sedentary and nomadic districts nor could cultural development proceed along the same lines. In the words of one Soviet writer, "National development on soviet principles demands the unification of the toiling strata of nations into unified soviet countries in order to strengthen economic and political uplift and to deepen national-cultural construction." [70]

The Bolsheviks also insisted that the formation of national states in the region would at last give satisfaction to the "elemental" longing for national recognition which had, they felt, been at the root of intertribal frictions. A delegate from Turkestan, Islamov, stressed this aspect of the proposed national delimitation in his report to the All-Russian Central Executive Committee. "We are striving to strengthen the soviet order in Central Asia," he said. "We seek to create clearer, simpler international relations among the peoples of Central Asia. We are striving to establish an even more durable, even more stable national peace." [71] The Bolsheviks also believed that reorganization into national territories would strike a death blow to "banditry" by removing the source of its strength, the disunited "national strips," and by organizing the toiling masses of the various tribal units for the presentation of a united opposition.

The movement which led finally to the national delimitation of Central Asia began soon after the close of the civil war, not as an effort to replace the traditional units by national state

[70] F. Ksenofontov, *Uzbekistan i Turkmenistan: k voprosu ob ikh vkhozhdenii v SSSR* (Moscow, 1925), p. 32.

[71] *Vserossiiskii Tsentral'nyi Ispolnitel'nyi Komitet XI Sozyva: Vtoraia Sessiia: stenograficheskii otchet* (Moscow, 1924), p. 313.

formations, but rather as an attempt to satisfy demands for local autonomy within the then existing republic boundaries.[72] Each of the three republics was left to solve its own problem, and only Khorezm failed to make some arrangement for the autonomy of its national minorities. Even there a division of the country into Turcoman and Uzbek regions had been proposed in 1921 as a means of eliminating intertribal friction. But the Turkestan Commission, to which the problem was referred for solution, took no action. After the establishment of a socialist form of government in the republic, no attempt was made to establish autonomous national regions. In Bokhara, on the contrary, the purge of 1923 was followed closely by the establishment of autonomous Turcoman, but not Tajik, regions.

Among the Central Asian republics, Soviet Turkestan took the lead in forming autonomous regions. In the summer of 1921, upon petition of a Transcaspian Regional Congress of Soviets, the Tashkent government decreed the reorganization of the Transcaspian region into a Turcoman autonomous region. During the following spring (April 22, 1922) the Turkestan Central Executive Committee, again upon petition of the inhabitants, created a special mountain region, consisting of several districts of the Jetysuisk and Syr-Daria regions, for the Kirghiz.[73] The creation of these national regions for the Turcomans and the Kirghiz led inevitably to demands from the representatives of other sections of Turkestan for autonomy. At the Thirteenth Turkestanian Congress of Soviets in 1924, a "Declaration of Thirty Fergana Delegates" demanded the autonomous separation of Fergana from Turkestan and its direct attachment to the RSFSR. Representatives of the Kirghiz and Kazakhs introduced similar resolutions.[74]

---

[72] Lenin himself took an early interest in the problem. In June, 1920, he instructed the Turkestan Commission to draw up a map of Turkestan with "subdivisions into Uzbekia, Kirghizia, and Turkmenia" and to uncover "in detail the conditions of merging or separating" the three parts. *Leninskii Sbornik* (2d ed., Moscow, 1925—), XXXIV, 326.

[73] I. Khodorov, "Natsional'noe razmezhevanie Srednei Azii," *Novyi Vostok*, Nos. 8–9 (1925), p. 66.

[74] The congress took no action on the requests. V. Karpych, "K istorii vozniknoveniia Turkmenskoi SSR," *Turkmenovedenie*, Nos. 10–11 (14–15) (October–November, 1928), p. 45.

These demands for recognition together with actions already taken by the Central Asian republics to form tribal autonomies laid the foundation for the national delimitation. But another factor, the Sultan-Galiev "deviation," which Stalin exposed at the Fourth Conference with Responsible Workers in June, 1923, was probably decisive in determining the timing of the campaign to reorganize the state structure of the region. Sultan-Galiev's alleged crime was to have formed a conspiratorial organization in the North Caucasus and to have sought, with the aid of Moslem and Turkish nationalists, to form a Pan-Turanian Eastern International. His movement apparently had sympathizers in Central Asia. He was reportedly in correspondence with Ryskulov, the Kirghiz Communist leader, and, through an intermediary, with Velidov, a former Communist and Basmachi leader.[75] Moreover, Sultan-Galiev's idea of a Pan-Turanian Union was in direct lineal descent from the unsuccessful attempt of the "Mussulman Communists" in 1919 and 1920 to unify all the Turkish tribes around the nucleus of a soviet Turkestan. Such a unification, difficult to control and probably more nationalistic than soviet in content, was not in Moscow's plans.[76]

After the Fourth Conference with Responsible Workers the campaign for a national delimitation of Central Asia gained momentum. Before the year was out, congresses of national minorities had met in Bokhara and Turkestan and issued resolutions urging the formation of national states. Thus, according to one Soviet publicist, the question of the national delimitation "acquired reality." [77] The problem then became the concern of the Central Asian Communist Parties. In February and March, 1924, the central committees of the Communist Parties of Bokhara, Khorezm, and Turkestan adopted decisions favoring the delimitation and on April 13, 1924, the Central Asiatic

[75] Stalin, *Sochineniia*, V, 301–6.

[76] Chokaiev, the one-time president of Kokand autonomy, went so far as to say that "it was as a counterpoise exactly to this attempt . . . that the plan of 'the division of Turkestan into the tribal states' was invented." Mustapha Chokaiev, "Turkestan and the Soviet Regime," *Journal of the Royal Central Asian Society*, XVIII (1930), 414.

[77] Khodorov, "Natsional'noe razmezhevanie Srednei Azii," *Novyi Vostok*, Nos. 8–9 (1925), p. 66.

Bureau of the Central Committee of the Russian Communist
Party gave its approval to these resolutions.

The decision to reorganize the state boundaries of Central
Asia touched off a major debate among the peoples of the region. Some charged that it was an attempt to "parcellize" the
traditional territories of the East. In Bokhara, conservative elements insisted that Bokhara remain independent as a Moslem
state. Khorezmians argued that Khorezm, because of its special
peculiarities, should exist as a federated republic with an extension of its territories to include the Uzbek populations of
Turkestan and Kara-Kalpakia. Others saw in the delimitation
an opportunity to carve tribal empires out of Central Asia.
Kazakh nationalists urged the formation of a "great Kazakhstan" with territories stretching from Siberia and the Bokharan
steppe to the Volga, while Kirghiz and Uzbek groups countered
with plans for the establishment of a "great Kirghizia" and a
"great Uzbekistan." Still others offered projects for the creation
of "separate autonomies," "unions of free tribes," "independent
cities," and other unworkable state structures.[78]

The Bolshevik leadership rejected all of these projects. Moreover, it dismissed the subjective desires of the population of the
various districts of Central Asia to enter one or another of the
proposed republics. Its own plan called for the definition of the
boundaries of the future state formations according to objec-
tively determined nationality and economic geography. To collect the necessary data, national bureaus and commissions, composed of prominent Central Asian Bolsheviks, political leaders,
and experts, were created. These bodies conducted socioeconomic studies of each individual district in order to discover its
language and cultural patterns, its economic profile, and its
economic relationship with other districts. Out of these studies
was to emerge the concrete basis for delimitation.[79]

The very determination of nationality and the boundaries of
nationalities proved to be no easy task. With the exception of

[78] Radzhapov, "Etapy razvitiia sovetskogo gosudarstvennogo stroia v Srednei
Azii," *Sovetskoe Gosudarstvo i Pravo*, No. 11 (November, 1948), p. 66.
[79] E. L. Shteinberg, *Ocherki istorii Turkmenii* (Moscow, 1934), p. 110; also
Khodorov, "Natsional'noe razmezhevanie Srednei Azii," *Novyi Vostok*, Nos. 8–9
(1925), p. 66.

the Tajiks, all were of Turkic origin and in many cases tribal lines were difficult to determine. The Kazakhs, the Kirghiz, and the Kara-Kalpaks, although related, could be distinguished by differences in physique, language, and cultural pattern, and the major tribal units of the Turcomans—the Tekkes, the Yamuts, the Salors, and the Ersaris—could be ascertained. But the Uzbeks presented a special problem. Divided into about eighty tribes with various branches, having over 150 different names, they were uniform in neither physical type nor language pattern. Physically, they represented in many cases admixtures of Tajik, Sart,[80] Persian, Afghan, Mongol, and Turk. Moreover, they spoke numerous dialects, some of which were not easy to relate to the major dialectal strains. Nor could the investigators always rely on the testimony of the inhabitants of the localities to determine nationality. A subsequent investigation undertaken in 1926 in Bokhara showed that in many areas the peasants did not know whether they were Uzbek or Kirghiz.[81]

Even after the national bureaus and commissions had determined national boundaries, the problem of defining the political boundaries of the new states remained. National boundaries seldom coincided with economic ones, and the Communists were forced to choose between the principles involved. They could consider the national principles to be decisive and fix boundaries according to the ethnic composition of the population without regard to the economic unity of the territory it inhabited, or they could give predominance to economic factors. In the latter case, the borders of the republic would be drawn to take into account regional economic interests, lines

[80] The term Sart was dropped from the Soviet vocabulary in the early 1920's. In its original use, it referred to merchants as opposed to nomads. Later, it came to designate an Iranian-Turkish tribe which resides in Fergana and Syr-Daria. It is notable that the Soviet regime ignored this people completely in the national delimitation. This may have arisen from the fact that the term Sart was in general use among Europeans in Central Asia as a designation—and not always a complimentary one—for all the native peoples of Turkestan. Soviet abandonment of the term appears to have been motivated primarily by a desire to promote good will toward the Soviet regime. As a sidelight to this, Stalin's reference to "Sarts" in his article, "Nashi zadachi na Vostoke," *Pravda*, March 2, 1919, has been altered to read "Turcomans" in his *Collected Works*. See Stalin, *Sochineniia*, IV, 236.

[81] E. Zel'kina, "Zemel'naia reforma v Srednei Azii," *Revoliutsionnyi Vostok*, No. 3 (1927), p. 134.

of communications, irrigation systems, and other conditions. In the end a compromise was effected, and it was agreed that the national principle should serve as the basis of the delimitation—that it should be decisive in questionable cases—but that in special circumstances the economic principle would take precedence.[82]

Even so, the fact that two principles were involved in the delimitation led to a number of controversies over the placing of boundary lines. The most important of these centered around the disposition of the Tashkent district. In terms of population the city of Tashkent itself was Uzbek but the rest of the district was predominantly Kazakh. The Kazakh commissioners therefore insisted that the whole district be included in Kazakhstan. The demand was rejected on the ground that it violated the nationality principle. The district as a whole was 46 percent Uzbek and 26 percent Kazakh in population.[83] The Kazakhs then entered a claim for three volost's (rural districts) of the district. But the second proposal was also unacceptable, this time for economic reasons. It was rejected on two counts: (1) that the headwaters of the Boz-su and Salara canals which served the city of Tashkent would be in Kazakh territory while their lower courses would be in Uzbekistan; and (2) that the Central Asiatic Railway which terminated in Tashkent would be cut by a wedge of Kazakh territory eleven miles south of the city.

Under pressure the Kazakhs were forced to yield "temporarily and conditionally" to a compromise solution which placed most of the Tashkent district in Uzbek territory.[84] This did not end the dispute. In the fall of 1924, the Kazakhs appealed their case to the All-Russian Central Executive Committee. In a bitter denunciation of the settlement, the Kazakh delegate charged that the very purpose of the delimitation would be defeated if the ethnic principle were not strictly adhered to. He

[82] Khodorov, "Natsional'noe razmezhevanie Srednei Azii," *Novyi Vostok*, Nos. 8–9 (1925), p. 68.

[83] M. A. Nemchenko, "Natsional'noe razmezhevanie Srednei Azii," *Mezhdunarodnaia Zhizn'*, Nos. 4–5 (1924), p. 86.

[84] Khodorov, "Natsional'noe razmezhevanie Srednei Azii," *Novyi Vostok*, Nos. 8–9 (1925), pp. 68–69.

was ruled out of order.[85] And in the final settlement, Tashkent and its environs were included in Uzbekistan.

The preparatory work lasted through the summer of 1924 and provided a detailed plan of territorial redivision. The territory of the Turcoman republic was to include the Turcoman region of Turkestan and the western parts of Bokhara and Khorezm. Uzbekistan was to include eastern Bokhara, southern Khorezm, and portions of Samarkand, Fergana, Amu-Daria, and the Syr-Daria regions of Turkestan. The Kirghiz Autonomous Region was to be established in northeastern Turkestan. Kara-Kalpakia was to include northeastern Khorezm and a portion of the Amu-Daria region, and the Kazakh ASSR was to take control of parts of the Syr-Daria and Jetysuisk regions.

Territorial questions settled, the next step in the process of delimitation was the dissolution of the existing republics and their replacement by the new national states. On September 20, 1924, the Fifth All-Bokharan Kuraltai declared its support of a national state unification of the peoples of Central Asia.[86] The Khorezmian Central Executive Committee followed suit. In Turkestan, an extraordinary session of the Central Executive Committee adopted a similar decree but in addition specified that the delimitation be completed not later than the end of the year.[87] The question was then referred to the center, first to the government of the RSFSR, whose compliance was necessary before the Turkestan ASSR could dissolve itself, and later to the government of the USSR. In the former case, the Central Executive Committee gave its consent in a decree (October 14, 1924) which affirmed the delimitation as a triumph for the Soviet nationality policy and a "fulfillment of the expressed . . . will" of the toilers of Turkestan.[88] The decree was adopted unanimously but not, however, until the session had been disturbed by the attempt of representatives of dissatisfied

[85] *Vserossiiskii Tsentral'nyi Ispolnitel'nyi Komitet XI Sozyva: vtoraia sessiia*, pp. 317–19.

[86] Text of decree in Ksenofontov, *Uzbekistan i Turkmenistan: k voprosu ob ikh vkhozhdenii v SSSR*, pp. 31–33.

[87] Text in *ibid.*, pp. 29–30; see also *Vserossiiskii Tsentral'nyi Ispolnitel'nyi Komitet XI Sozyva: vtoraia sessiia*, pp. 320–22.

[88] Text of decree in Lozovskii and Bibin, *Sovetskaia Politika za 10 let po natsional'nomu voprosu v RSFSR*, p. 113.

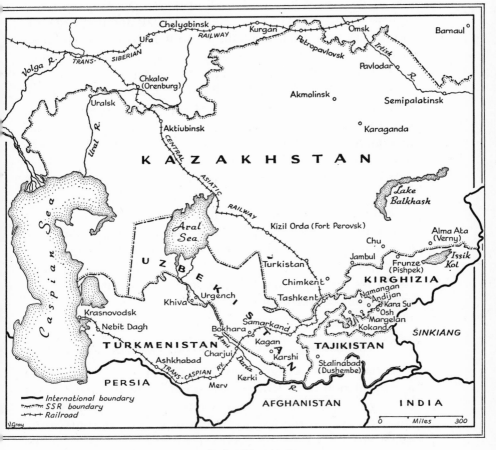

SOVIET CENTRAL ASIA

nationalities to introduce boundary questions into the debate and by the complaint of a Kara-Kalpak delegate that the Kara-Kalpak people had not been consulted at all about the delimitation.[89] At the meeting of the Central Executive Committee of the USSR, there were no such distractions. After a report by Khodzhaev, the Central Executive Committee (October 27, 1924) voted the dissolution of Bokhara, Khorezm, and Turkestan and their reconstitution as the Uzbek and Turcoman SSR's, the Tajik ASSR, and the Kirghiz Autonomous Region, and incorporated into the Kazakh ASSR the Kazakh territories of Turkestan.[90]

In December, national revolutionary committees were formed in Central Asia to establish central organs of government for the new republics, to prepare and carry out elections to constituent congresses of soviets, and to exercise temporary government authority. In February, 1925, the first congresses of soviets met in the newly formed republics. The regimes established by these congresses all fit into the format of state organization as worked out in the RSFSR and other union republics.

THE CONSEQUENCES OF NATIONAL REORGANIZATION

Essentially, the new regimes in Central Asia represented merely a reaffirmation of the soviet and socialist principles which had already been in force in the previously existing republics. The shift also opened the way for the incorporation of Turkmenia and Uzbekistan into the USSR. Two years previously, at the First All-Union Congress of Soviets, the governments of Bokhara and Khorezm had signified their desire for eventual admission into the Union. At their first congresses of soviets, the republics of Uzbekistan and Turkmenia, which replaced them, again adopted resolutions seeking inclusion in the USSR. But this time the applications were a formality. The actual decision had already been taken by the All-Union Central Executive Committee in October, 1924, and in May, 1925, the Third All-

[89] *Vserossiiskii Tsentral'nyi Ispolnitel'nyi Komitet XI Sozyva: vtoraia sessiia,* p. 322.

[90] Text of decree in Lozovskii and Bibin, *Sovetskaia Politika za 10 let po natsional'nomu voprosu v RSFSR,* p. 19.

Union Congress of Soviets accepted the Turkmen and Uzbek republics into the USSR.[91] A month later Foreign Commissar Chicherin notified the world officially that Bokhara and Khorezm had ceased to exist.[92]

In Central Asia the consequences of delimitation were more than political in scope. The reorganization of state boundaries was accompanied by the redistribution of economic wealth. Territorially, the Uzbek SSR, if the Tajik area is included, came into control of the largest, and economically the most profitable, area of the region. Over 187,180 square miles (see Table 3) of the most fertile land fell under the domain of this

TABLE 3

TERRITORY, POPULATION, AND PLANTED AREA OF
CENTRAL ASIAN REPUBLICS

REPUBLIC	TERRITORY IN SQUARE MILES	POPULATION[a]		TOTAL PLANTED AREA	
		1923–24	1926	In Acres	Percentage of Total Planted Area
Uzbek SSR	153,790	3,963,285	4,445,600	3,762,299	53.81
Tajik ASSR	33,394	739,503	827,200	1,735,136	24.82
Turcoman SSR	161,598	855,114	900,000	602,996	8.62
Kirghiz AO	70,304	714,648	993,000	665,593	9.52
Disputed Districts	...	170,682	...	225,723	3.23
Total	419,086	6,443,232	7,165,800	6,991,747	100.00

Source: Adapted from figures in N. Baranskii, *Economicheskaia Geografiia Sovetskogo Soiuza: obzor po oblastiam gosplana* (Moscow, 1926), pp. 268–69.

[a] Population figures for 1923–24 are unreliable. At the time, no census data at all had been collected for Bokhara and Khorezm. Census data for Turkestan were inaccurate. In many cases, figures were arrived at by vote rather than by actual count of the population. I. Khodorov, "Natsional'noe Razmezhevanie Srednei Azii," *Novyi Vostok*, Nos. 8–9 (1925), p. 70. For comparison, figures from the 1926 census are reproduced here. See Gleb N. Cherdantsev, *Sredne-Aziatskie Respubliki* (Moscow, 1928), p. 55.

republic (including Tajikistan) as against 161,598 square miles for Turkmenia and 70,304 square miles for the Kirghiz Autonomous Region. In terms of the populations which inhabited the various republics, the disparity was even greater. Uzbekistan

[91] Text of decree in *Tret'ii S'ezd Sovetov Soiuza Sovetskikh Sotsialisticheskikh Respublik. Postanovleniia* (Moscow, 1925), p. 3.

[92] B. L. Rozenblium, "O rasprostranenii deistviia mezhdunarodnykh dogovorov, zakliuchennykh Soiuzom SSR i otdel'nymi respublikami vnov' vstupaiushchie v SSSR Respubliki," *Sovetskoe Pravo*, No. 5 (29) (1927), p. 98.

(including Tajikistan), with an estimated population of 4,702,-788, had about six times as many inhabitants as either of the other republics, a situation traceable largely to the early Uzbek transition from nomadism to agriculture. Moreover, the urbanization of the Uzbek population had advanced considerably beyond the limits reached in Turkmenia and Kirghizia. Estimates based on the 1923–24 census placed the city population of Uzbekistan proper at 18.1 percent of the population, while the estimates for the other republics ranged between 3.3 and 10.9 percent.[93]

The higher level of development of the Uzbeks was decisive in the redistribution of the wealth of Central Asia, which accompanied the national delimitation. Measured in terms of property valuation, the national reorganization showed a disparity even greater than that in population. While approximately one half of the population of the region resided in Uzbekistan, about two thirds of the total wealth accrued to the republic. In terms of state property, the Uzbek SSR, excluding Tajikistan, received a valuation of 45.8 million rubles, or 60.8 percent of the total. The shares allotted to the Turcoman and Kirghiz republics were 10.4 million rubles (13.8 percent) and 3.6 million rubles (4.7 percent) respectively. The railway network was distributed almost equally between Turkmenia and Uzbekistan, the former taking control of 47.5 percent of the total and the latter receiving 49.8 percent. The remaining 2.7 percent was in Kirghiz territory.[94]

In agriculture, the most important source of wealth of the region, Uzbekistan was likewise far in the lead. Data collected for the 1923–24 planting year (see Table 4) show that Uzbekistan received 80 percent (R 316,915,000) of the gross agricultural income of Central Asia while Kirghizia and Turkmenia received only 7.7 percent (R 30,525,000) and 7.1 per-

[93] Khodorov, "Natsional'noe razmezhevanie Srednei Azii," *Novyi Vostok*, Nos. 8–9 (1925), p. 71. The real disparity in the urbanization of the Central Asian republics can be seen in the distribution of town population among them. Uzbekistan had 79 percent of the urban population; Turkmenia, 9.8 percent; Kirghizia, 8.6 percent; and Tajikistan, only 2.6 percent. See Gleb N. Cherdantsev, *Sredne-Aziatskie Respubliki* (Moscow, 1928), pp. 152, 155, 159, 161.

[94] I. Khodorov, "Sredne-Aziatskoe razmezhevanie," *Planovoe Khoziaistvo*, No. 4 (April, 1925), p. 258.

TABLE 4

DISTRIBUTION OF AGRICULTURE AND AGRICULTURAL INCOME IN CENTRAL ASIA AT THE TIME OF NATIONAL DELIMITATION

(Data for 1923–24)

A. COTTON

REPUBLIC	PLANTED ACREAGE[a]			GROSS INCOME[b]		
	In Acres	Percentage of Total Cotton Acreage in Central Asia	Percentage of Total Cultivated Area by Republic	In 1,000 Rubles	Percentage of Total Cotton Income in Central Asia	Percentage of Total Agricultural Income by Republic
Uzbek SSR	638,169	72.5	17.0	60,759	83.4	19.2
Tajik ASSR	...	...	...	309	0.4	1.5
Turcoman SSR	128,493	14.5	21.3	11,041	15.2	39.1
Kirghiz AO	35,810	4.0	5.3	726	1.0	2.4
Disputed Districts	77,917	9.0	34.5	...	...	...
Central Asia	880,389	100.0	12.6	72,835	100.0	18.4

TABLE 4 (Continued)

B. Principal Field Crops (Except Cotton)

REPUBLIC	PLANTED ACREAGE[a]			GROSS INCOME[b]		
	In Acres	Percentage of Total Crop Acreage in Central Asia	Percentage of Total Cultivated Area by Republic	In 1,000 Rubles	Percentage of Total Crop Income in Central Asia	Percentage of Total Agricultural Income by Republic
Uzbek SSR						
Cereals	2,715,494	49.4	72.2	⎱		
Lucerne	275,635	65.1	7.3	⎰ 194,696	80.3	61.5
Tobacco	5,511	86.7	0.1			
Tajik ASSR						
Cereals	1,696,045	30.9	97.8	⎱		
Lucerne	16,333	3.9	0.9	⎰ 15,307	6.3	75.1
Tobacco	81	1.3	0.0			
Turcoman SSR						
Cereals	393,188	7.1	65.2	⎱		
Lucerne	53,738	12.7	8.9	⎰ 11,617	4.8	41.1
Tobacco	59	0.9	0.0			
Kirghiz AO						
Cereals	573,820	10.5	86.2	⎱		
Lucerne	51,624	12.2	7.8	⎰ 20,712	8.6	67.9
Tobacco	516	8.1	0.1			
Disputed Districts						
Cereals	113,673	2.1	50.4	⎱		
Lucerne	25,977	6.1	11.5	⎰ ...	...	...
Tobacco	192	3.0	0.1			
Central Asia						
Cereals	5,492,220	100.0	78.5	⎱		
Lucerne	423,307	100.0	6.1	⎰ 242,332	100.0	61.2
Tobacco	6,359	100.0	0.1			

C. ORCHARDS AND VINEYARDS

	PLANTED ACREAGE[a]			GROSS INCOME[b]		
REPUBLIC	In Acres	Percentage of Total Orchard and Vineyard Acreage in Central Asia	Percentage of Total Cultivated Area by Republic	In 1,000 Rubles	Percentage of Total Orchard and Vineyard Income in Central Asia	Percentage of Total Agricultural Income by Republic
Uzbek SSR	127,491	67.3	3.4	35,016	86.3	11.0
Tajik ASSR	22,677	12.0	1.3	3,128	7.7	15.3
Turcoman SSR	27,518	14.5	4.6	1,212	3.0	4.4
Kirghiz AO	3,823	2.0	0.6	1,199	3.0	3.9
Disputed Districts	7,965	4.2	3.5	...	...	...
Central Asia	189,474	100.0	2.7	40,555	100.0	10.2

D. LIVESTOCK

	LIVESTOCK[a]		GROSS INCOME[b]		
REPUBLIC	Number of Head	Percentage of All Livestock	In 1,000 Rubles	Percentage of Total Livestock Income in Central Asia	Percentage of Total Livestock Income by Republic
Uzbek SSR	2,589,063	35.0	26,444	65.6	8.3
Tajik ASSR	862,054	13.0	1,659	4.1	8.1
Turcoman SSR	1,701,100	23.0	4,350	10.8	15.4
Kirghiz AO	1,881,658	25.4	7,888	19.5	25.8
Disputed Districts	269,010	3.6	...	...	...
All Central Asia	7,402,885	100.0	40,341	100.0	10.2

TABLE 4 (Continued)

E. SUMMARY DISTRIBUTION

	PLANTED ACREAGE (ALL CROPS)[a]		TOTAL GROSS INCOME (INCLUDING LIVESTOCK INCOME)[b]	
REPUBLIC	In Acres	Percentage of Total Cultivated Area	In 1,000 Rubles	Percentage of Total Agricultural Income
Uzbek SSR	3,762,300	53.8	316,915	80.0
Tajik ASSR	1,735,136	24.8	20,403	5.2
Turcoman SSR	602,996	8.6	28,220	7.1
Kirghiz AO	665,593	9.5	30,525	7.7
Disputed Districts	227,724	3.3	...	...
All Central Asia	6,993,749	100.0	396,063	100.0

[a] Adapted from data in N. Baranskii, *Ekonomicheskaia geografia Sovetskogo Soiuza: Obzor po oblastiam Gosplana* (Moscow, 1926), pp. 268–69, and S. K. Kondrashov, "Sredne-Aziatskoe razmezhevanie," *Planovoe Khoziaistvo*, No. 4 (April, 1925), pp. 256–57.

[b] Adapted from data in N. I. Balashev, *Uzbekistan i sopredel'nye respubliki i oblasti: geograficheskii i ekonomicheskii ocherk* (Tashkent, 1925), p. 93.

cent (₽ 28,220,000) respectively. The gross income from Uzbek cotton alone (₽ 60,759,000) was greater than the combined incomes of the two other republics even though this crop accounted for slightly less than one fifth of the total agricultural income and occupied only one sixth of the planted area of Uzbekistan.

The causes of the disparity in agricultural wealth grew out of the social structures which predominated in the various republics. The largely nomadic populations of Turkmenia and Kirghizia subsisted mainly from herding, an occupation which not only was less profitable than farming but which had suffered an especially serious depletion of stock during the civil war. Recovery was by its nature a slower process among the nomads than among the farmers. While farms that had been abandoned during the most troubled period could often be returned to production in a relatively short time, the depleted herds required a longer period before they could be replenished. Moreover, the scarcity of irrigated land prevented these people from shifting to sedentary forms of agriculture. Central Asiatic conditions required that the major share of agricultural land be irrigated before it could produce, but the irrigation network was concentrated in Uzbekistan, which at the time of the delimitation had over five times as much artificially watered land as Turkmenia.

The disproportion in the distribution of industry among the new republics ran even more strongly in favor of Uzbekistan. Of the 132 cotton ginning mills located in Central Asia, 110 were situated in this republic. Over 50 percent of the region's fuel industry was situated in Uzbekistan as compared with 22 percent in Kirghizia and 19 percent in Turkmenia.[95] In terms of gross production of industry, the Uzbek position was even better. During the 1924–25 productive year, Uzbek enterprises employed 75 percent (8,657 employees) of the total active labor force of the three republics and supplied 83 percent (106,863,-000 *chervonetz* rubles) of the total industrial production. By comparison the Turkmenian republic employed 17 percent

[95] Khodorov, "Natsional'noe razmezhevanie Srednei Azii," *Novyi Vostok,* Nos. 8–9 (1925), pp. 74–75.

(1,934 employees) of the labor force and produced 16 percent (20,779,600 *chervonetz* rubles) of the total value of production, while Kirghizia with 887 industrial employees (8 percent) produced only 1 percent (775,200 *chervonetz* rubles) of the industrial value.[96]

It is clear even from these sketchy data that Uzbekistan emerged from the delimitation as the strongest and most advanced of the new state formations in Central Asia. The very nature of the delimitation—its emphasis on a national reorganization—had rendered this inevitable. The Uzbeks, who had traditionally dominated oasis life, were in occupation of the best agricultural lands. They had monopolized trade and other native commercial activities. Since the Uzbek tribes were settled in the heart of the cotton region, the industry of Central Asia, based as it was mainly on the processing of this commodity, was concentrated in Uzbekistan.

The economic inequality among the new state formations of Central Asia in no way frustrated the purposes of the reform. On the contrary, the idea of equalizing the distribution of the wealth of the region had not been under consideration. The conductors of the reform had sought primarily to separate the major tribal units of Central Asia territorially in so far as possible. Although they were not completely successful in achieving their objective of forming uninational states—the population strength of the major nationalities varied between 74.7 percent in Uzbekistan and 66.6 percent in Kirghizia[97]—they considered the reform as a whole to be eminently successful. Islamov, a leading Turkestanian Communist, told the All-Russian Central Executive Committee that the delimitation represented "one of the biggest steps toward the practical realization of the principles of national policy proclaimed by the October Revolution and its brilliant leader, V. I. Lenin." [98]

[96] Tsentral'noe Statisticheskoe Upravlenie SSSR, *Fabrichno-zavodskaia promyshlennost' SSSR v 1925/26 gody* (Moscow, 1927), pp. 125, 132.

[97] Cherdantsev, *Sredne-Aziatskie Respubliki*, p. 55. The national minority groups left within the Central Asian republics were formed into small national-autonomous districts.

[98] *Vserossiiskii Tsentral'nyi Ispolnitel'nyi Komitet XI Sozyva: vtoraia sessiia*, p. 309.

On the level of practical Soviet policy, the national delimitation also removed the last obstacle to the incorporation of all of
Soviet Central Asia into the USSR, thereby bringing to a conclusion the process of soviet unification in that region.

The evolution of soviet forms of statehood had shown two
distinct lines of development within the general movement.
One of them, which affected national minorities residing within
independent soviet republics, led to the establishment of a soviet form of national autonomy. The other terminated in the
unification of these independent republics into a single union
of soviet socialist republics. In Central Asia, the process of state
building followed the same pattern and was part of it. On the
one hand, the procedure by which Soviet autonomy, as defined
in Moscow, was introduced into Turkestan formed part of the
general process of bringing local governmental structures into
conformity with centrally determined principles. On the other
hand, the people's republics of Bokhara and Khorezm, although
they were not parties to the "Compact of Union" and had no
part in the establishment of the constitutional regime of the
USSR, were involved directly in all other stages of the general
unification movement, passing through the phases of military-
economic unification, diplomatic unification, and finally economic unification.[99] Only in its final phases did the course of
unification differ from the general process; and the entrance of
Bokhara and Khorezm into the Soviet "family of nations" was
delayed until these states had been transformed into soviet socialist republics and had submitted along with the Turkestan
ASSR to a national territorial reorganization. But while fulfillment of these additional requirements for admission into the
USSR had prolonged and complicated the process of unification
in Central Asia, it did nothing to alter the content or consequences of the process.

It must be noted too that the campaign to bring Bokhara
and Khorezm into the "socialist" stage was conducted almost

[99] As a consequence, these republics from the end of 1922 until their dissolution were in what one Soviet jurist has called "confederative relationships" with
the USSR. Konst. Arkhippov, "Tipy sovetskoi avtonomii," *Vlast' Sovetov*, Nos.
8–9 (August–September, 1923), p. 33.

exclusively on the political level. The internal changes in government which occurred in Bokhara and Khorezm were not accompanied by alterations in the social and economic structures of the societies. Industry did not develop significantly nor did a class of industrial workers emerge. In point of fact, Soviet figures for 1924–25, the year of the delimitation, show that all industries (283 enterprises) in Kirghizia, Uzbekistan, and Turkmenia employed only 10,596 workers.[100] Agricultural relationships also remained largely unchanged. No important sector of socialized agriculture emerged to change the economic base of society. Socially and culturally, the new regime had made little effort to replace the traditional institutions of society with new forms of social organization. On the contrary, the Bolsheviks walked softly and concentrated their attention in consolidating and strengthening their political position.

This was the essence of the transition from the "people's republic" to the "socialist" republic. The transformation expressed primarily a change in the correlation of political forces in the governmental centers of the republics. It signified in practice a step-by-step elimination of non-Communist political leaders from participation in the governments of their respective countries. And the final act of this campaign—the establishment of a socialist government—was the external manifestation of the establishment of a Bolshevik monopoly of power. Such also was the essential meaning of the term "socialist" in relation to the Turkestan republic and in relation to the new state formations which emerged from the national delimitation. The Bolsheviks themselves made no other claims.

[100] Tsentral'noe Statisticheskoe Upravlenie SSSR, *Fabrichno-zavodskaia promyshlennost' SSSR v 1925/26 gody*, pp. 125, 132.

III

THE STRUCTURE
OF POLITICAL
GUIDANCE

◆

THE "ROOTING" of the Soviet state apparatus in the backward national areas involved more than the formulation of a theoretical basis for sovietizing these regions. It presumed as well the continuous leadership of trained Bolsheviks and strict centralization and coordination in the making and execution of policy. These principles were crucial to Bolshevik doctrine respecting the nationality question.

The leadership principle in Bolshevik doctrine is a direct outgrowth of Lenin's conception of the relationship between the Party and the masses. Prior to his time, Marxists had tended, as a rule, to identify the Party and the masses as a unity. Lenin treated them as a dichotomy. Influenced by the lack of mass support for left-wing Social Democracy in Russia, Lenin had concluded early in his career that the working class was constitutionally unable to develop real revolutionary consciousness. The workers, he argued, might form trade unions and engage in economic struggle, but the most they would demand was the enactment of labor legislation. They could never achieve a program of revolutionary political action. Implicit in this conviction was a recognition of differences between the self-determined goals of the working class as a whole and those of the Social Democratic Party which presumed to represent and to lead it. Class consciousness—a revolutionary social-democratic

consciousness—Lenin claimed, could not develop in the working class itself but "could only be brought to [it] from without." [1] In Lenin's view, the only organization capable of
performing this function and of supplying the organizational
talent and the leadership for a successful revolution was the
Bolshevik faction of the Social Democratic Labor Party.

This concept did not fall into eclipse after the Bolshevik
revolution; in Stalin's words, it was "even more necessary after
the seizure of power." [2] Two fundamental assumptions, one of
them military in nature, were employed to justify this conclusion. The first grew out of the state of undeclared war which
existed between the Soviet Union and the capitalist world.
"Dictatorship," Lenin pointed out, "is a state of acute war"
which, he prophesied, would continue until the final issue in
the struggle against world capitalism had been decided. "À la
guerre comme à la guerre," he wrote, "we do not promise any
freedom or any democracy." [3] The second assumption concerned the education of the masses for participation in a socialist society. Until the last vestiges of the past had vanished and
the new type of man whom Engels had predicted [4] emerged, the
argument ran, the Party was obliged to wage a prolonged struggle against habits and attitudes inherited from the old regime.
And the Soviet power was visualized as a gigantic "school of
Communism" in which the toilers, guided and supervised by
the Party, could prepare themselves eventually to rule.

The principle of centralism[5] is closely related to the theory

[1] V. I. Lenin, *Selected Works* (New York, n.d.), II, 53.

[2] Joseph Stalin, *Leninism* (New York, 1932–33), I, 170.

[3] V. I. Lenin, *Sochineniia* (1st ed., Moscow, 1919—), XVIII, 336.

[4] For the best statement, see Friedrich Engels, *The Origin of the Family,
Private Property and the State* (New York, 1942), pp. 61–73.

[5] The use of the term "democratic centralism," which represents an elaboration
of centralism, does not appear in the annals of the Bolshevik Party until the
Tammerfors Conference in 1905 nor does it occur in Lenin's writings until
1906. Before the Revolution of 1905, it would appear that Lenin was in opposition to the use of the word "democratic" to the extent that it should apply to
Social-Democratic party organization in Russia. For a brief examination of the
question, see Barrington Moore Jr., *Soviet Politics—the Dilemma of Power*
(Cambridge, 1950), pp. 64–71. It would appear also from the record of Lenin's
political life that he championed democracy when he was in the minority and
demanded strict centralism when he was in the majority. See Bertram D. Wolfe,
Three Who Made a Revolution (New York, 1948), especially Chapters IX, XIII,
XV, XVII.

of the relationship between the Party and the masses and in some respects represents an extension of that theory to the Party itself. The most complete early expression appears in Lenin's pamphlet *What Is to Be Done?* written in 1902. Throughout most of his life Lenin was frankly interested in a system of "proletarian discipline" within a rigorously centralized revolutionary party in which the center would issue commands and the local organizations would carry them out. Discussion in the lower echelons would be limited to how best to execute centrally determined policies. The center would draw people out of local work for its own purposes and would have the power to approve or reject the personnel of leading committees in the localities.

This schema, which provided the organizational basis of the Bolshevik Party, was transferred after the October Revolution to the state and public institutions of the Soviet republic. In operation this meant an upward stream of political intelligence, suggestion, and accounting from lower organs and a downward stream of laws, decrees, and instructions from central agencies. Lenin was nonetheless careful to emphasize a broad interpretation of the principle of democratic centralism and warned repeatedly against rigidities which would eventually be self-defeating. "Unity in the fundamental, the cardinal, the essential is not violated," he argued, "but is secured by variation in particulars, in local peculiarities, in modes of approach to the thing, in methods of effectuating control." [6]

It was this approach which left the door open to Soviet autonomy and to the principle of federalism. From the Leninist point of view the admission of local initiative in a local sphere entailed no sacrifice of the concepts of central leadership and of the responsibility of local agencies to superior ones. It was, in fact, necessary to the proper and efficient operation of the Soviet system. In one definition of the boundaries of centralism Lenin made this point quite clear:

Just as democratic centralism by no means excludes autonomy and federation, so it by no means excludes—to the contrary, it presup-

[6] V. I. Lenin, *Sochineniia* (2d ed., Moscow, 1926–32), XXII, 166; also Andrei Y. Vyshinsky, *The Law of the Soviet State,* tr. by Hugh W. Babb (New York, 1948), pp. 230–31.

poses—that different localities, and even different communities of the state, are completely and utterly free in working out varying forms of state, social, and economic life. Nothing is more fallacious than to confuse democratic centralism with a stereotyped bureaucracy.[7]

Centralism on the state level, from the Bolshevik viewpoint, was at least as beneficial to the national groupings as to the state as a whole. On the one hand, it promoted the development and strengthening of autonomous and federated units, increased their actual independence, and gave them instruments of self-help. On the other hand, it permitted the center to render systematic assistance to the nationalities. The strengthening of central leadership and of the role of central agencies, instead of restricting the rights of national state units, provided the best guarantee of "hastening the process of liquidating actual inequality." [8] Centralism, the argument ran, eliminated contradictions between individual parts of the state, unified all the parts in the accomplishment of common tasks and the satisfaction of common interests, and permitted as well the development of local initiative in the solution of local problems. Hence, it opened the way to the most expeditious political, economic, and social development both of the Soviet Union and of its individual parts.[9]

The principle, moreover, had peculiar application to the backward nationalities. These peoples, Bolshevik theorists claimed, were not only the least able to promote their own development but the most likely to fall under imperialistic domination if denied the protection of the Soviet state. Lenin, in his theses introducing the concept of noncapitalistic development, had insisted upon Western (Russian) proletarian leadership and the rendition of aid "by all means at their disposal" by soviet governments as prerequisites to the achievement of

[7] Lenin, *Sochineniia* (2d ed.), XXII, 416. The comparison made here is with what Vyshinsky calls the "bureaucratic centralism of the capitalistic states" and which he claims is "employed to crush the weak nations." Vyshinsky, *The Law of the Soviet State*, pp. 230–31.

[8] A. Alymov and S. Studenikin, "Sovetskii federalizm i demokraticheskii tsentralizm," *Sovetskoe Gosudarstvo*, Nos. 1–2 (1933), p. 18.

[9] Vyshinsky, *The Law of the Soviet State*, pp. 230–31, 269–70.

socialism by underdeveloped nationalities.[10] Stalin was equally
determined that the Russian center take the lead in a crusade
"to elevate the [backward] masses to the Soviet power." [11] This,
he indicated, included not only grants of local political autonomy on a soviet basis but the conduct of concentrated and centrally guided campaigns to raise the economic and cultural levels
of minor nationalities. The Russian Communists, in Lenin's
words, had to assume the "mantle of leadership" and to learn
how to apply the principles of scientific socialism to the primitive conditions that existed in the East.

More than a year before Lenin had given his blessing to the
idea that underdeveloped nations might by-pass the stage of
capitalism with proletarian help, Stalin, as Commissar for National Affairs, had marked out in broad terms the policy through
which the Soviet regime expected to achieve this end. In an
article in *Pravda* (March 2, 1919) he had outlined three major
duties of the Soviet government: to raise the cultural level of
the backward peoples, to enlist the masses of the East in the
building-up of the Soviet state, and to strike off every limitation retarding the development of the backward peoples toward
higher forms of social organization. Stalin's further demand that
Party and Soviet workers transform Turkestan into an "ex-
emplary republic, into an advanced post of the revolutioniza-
tion of the Orient," [12] made the application of this policy to
Soviet Central Asia specific and urgent.

In that region, moreover, the absence of experienced native
Bolsheviks and the lack of a revolutionary heritage served to
redouble the emphasis on central control and guidance. Even
the native intellectual class was so small that Stalin was moved
to comment that its size was a "serious hindrance . . . to the
realization of soviet autonomy," and he demanded special
efforts to involve intellectuals who were "revolutionary-demo-
cratic or even simply loyal to Soviet rule" in soviet work.[13]
Here again close central supervision became necessary both to

[10] Lenin, *Sochineniia* (1st ed.), XIX, 246.
[11] J. V. Stalin, *Sochineniia* (Moscow, 1946—), IV, 75.
[12] *Ibid.*, V, 329.
[13] *Ibid.*, IV, 360.

prevent unintentional deviations from a Bolshevik line of action and to check the conscious attempts of hostile elements to hinder the realization of Bolshevik goals.

Implementation of the central control which the Party program envisaged proceeded on three levels: through governmental agencies, through the Party, and through national and local mass organizations. On the governmental level, leadership and guidance were exercised not only through usual channels —the soviet system, the federal administrative system, and, until 1923, the Commissariat for National Affairs—but also through dispatch of the Turkestan Commission to the region. The Party maintained control through its network of local organizations, culminating in Central Asia in the Central Asiatic Bureau, through the local organs of the Komsomol, which the Party supervised directly, and for a short period through a special Moslem Bureau of the Party Central Committee. At the mass level, policy was executed mainly through trade unions and in Central Asia through a peculiar peasant organization, the Koshchi, which corresponded in some respects to the Committees of the Poor that had sprung up in Central Russia at the height of the revolution. On each level these agencies had special functions, but centrally determined Party policies served to coordinate the activities of all.

GOVERNMENTAL AGENCIES FOR SUPERVISION AND CONTROL

Until 1923 the governmental agency most directly concerned with the problems of non-Russian peoples within the Soviet state was the People's Commissariat for National Affairs. Throughout this period it served as the principal link between the central government and the nationalities and was the forerunner of the second chamber in the All-Union Central Executive Committee. Its function was not limited, however, to providing a medium for the expression of the needs, desires, and opinions of representatives of the non-Russian nationalities. During the period of revolution and civil war, it acted as the central agency for combating counterrevolutionary activity among the non-Russian peoples, for establishing autonomous state units, and for organizing nuclei of native Communists and sympathizers to take power in the national regions.[14]

In later years the function of the commissariat was broadened to include authority to resolve disputes between different nationalities and to study and implement measures designed to protect the interests of national minorities and to guarantee the fraternal collaboration of the peoples and tribes of the RSFSR.[15] A decree of May 26, 1921, spelled out these duties and, in view of the expanded operating areas of the commissariat, extended their application to friendly Soviet republics. The commissariat was given twelve specific tasks: (1) to elaborate projected legislative enactments (bills) in the area of national policy and to lay them before the Central Executive Committee or the Council of People's Commissars as appropriate; (2) to unify and guide the work of the national delegations from individual autonomous republics, regions, and communes within the RSFSR; (3) to protect the rights of national minorities; (4) to aid autonomous units in their relations with federal institutions; (5) to review the draft decrees and enactments of the various people's commissariats which involved autonomous and treaty republics; (6) to supervise the fulfillment of the articles of the constitution and of decrees, statutes, and treaties which affected the nationalities; (7) to establish its own representation in autonomous units and treaty republics; (8) to conduct negotiations with representatives of the various nationalities and to propose to the Central Executive Committee and the Council of People's Commissars the formation of new autonomous units; (9) to comment on material and financial changes presented by autonomous units; (10) to gather and study materials concerning the life of nationalities within and outside the RSFSR and to publish informational tracts; (11) to organize special scholarly societies and schools for the study of the life of

[14] For an analysis of the work of the Commissariat for National Affairs by a current Soviet writer, see N. Mansvetov, "Velikaia Oktiabr'skaia Sotsialisticheskaia Revoliutsiia i sozdanie Narodnogo Komissariata po Delam Natsional'nostei," *Voprosy Istorii*, No. 8 (August, 1949), pp. 9–29.

[15] Text in Narodnyi Komissariat po Delam Natsional'nostei RSFSR, *Politika Sovetskoi Vlasti po natsional'nomu voprosu za tri goda, 1917–xi–1920* (Moscow, 1920), p. 147.

the nationalities and for the training of cadres of non-Russian political workers; and (12) to publish its own newspaper and to guide the publication of the national press of the delegations and divisions under the Commissariat for National Affairs.[16] A later decree of August, 1921, further defined the duties of the commissariat, calling upon it to apply federal regulations, decrees, and other enactments to local situations, to represent the interests of the nationalities in budgetary matters, and to coordinate the activities of local and federal agencies.[17]

The catalogue of responsibilities which the Central Executive Committee imposed upon the Commissariat for National Affairs was paralleled by a bestowal of almost absolute power in its dealings with the non-Russian peoples. Decrees of October and November, 1920, transformed the commissariat into the primary legal channel of contact between the nationalities and the government of the RSFSR.[18] A later decree (July 27, 1922), which abolished the federal committees operating under various people's commissariats and recreated these committees under the Commissariat for National Affairs, eliminated all access by the nationalities to the center in economic and cultural matters except through the medium of the commissariat.[19] Equally important to the concentration of power in the commissariat were the rights which it exercised in relation to legislation affecting the nationalities. The commissariat had no right to legislate itself, but no law regarding national units could pass without its opinion. All departments were obliged to acquiesce in projects dealing with the nationalities which the commissariat introduced.[20]

The task of directly supervising the activities of soviet governments in minority regions fell to "national commissariats" which the Commissariat for National Affairs had organized at the beginning of 1918. These commissariats—originally seven

[16] Text in *Spravochnik Narodnogo Komissariata po Delam Natsional'nostei* (Moscow, 1921), pp. 5–9.

[17] Text in *Izvestiia*, August 12, 1922.

[18] Texts in Narodnyi Komissariat po Delam Natsional'nostei RSFSR, *Politika Sovetskoi Vlasti po natsional'nomu voprosu za tri goda*, pp. 150–51.

[19] V. I. Ignat'ev, *Sovet Natsional'nostei Tsentral'nogo Ispolnitel'nogo Komiteta SSSR* (Moscow, 1926), p. 10.

[20] *Ibid.*, p. 11.

existed, Polish, Lithuanian, Jewish, Armenian, Moslem, Belorussian, and Latvian[21]—were actually small national cells of Bolsheviks and were designed to function as instruments for the promulgation of Soviet nationality policy among the non-Russian populations.[22] In practice, they became coordinating agencies for the activities of the center and during the civil war period took under their charge the solution of problems relating to economic development, supply, culture and education, the establishment of national troop formations, labor, and social security. To the nationalities which they claimed to represent, the national commissariats became in effect super-commissariats which sought to concentrate in their own hands a monopoly of power.[23]

On the local level, the national commissariats conducted their operations through national divisions which were attached to local soviets of deputies and enjoyed equal status with other local governmental agencies. These divisions were subordinated in their operations to local central executive committees, but provision was also made for referring disputes between the latter and the national divisions to the Commissariat for National Affairs. The national divisions were responsible for promoting the principles of Soviet nationality policy among local national groups, for executing the decrees of the Commissariat for National Affairs, for taking steps to elevate class consciousness and the cultural level of the native toilers, and for conducting the struggle against "counterrevolution and its national

[21] Similar agencies were created later for Estonia, the Ukraine, the Czechs, and others, but their autonomy was restricted. Moreover, they were denominated "national divisions," not "commissariats." Eighteen of these agencies together with the names of their chiefs are listed in *Zhizn' Natsional'nostei*, No. 1 (November 9, 1918).

[22] In an organizational meeting which took place on February 15, 1918, the chairmen (commissars) of the national commissariats, meeting in committee once a week, were constituted as the College of the Commissariat, the true forerunner of the Council of Nationalities. The meeting also organized the work of the commissariat functionally by creating six desks which dealt respectively with (1) agitation and propaganda of the Soviet power, (2) communications of national committees, (3) editing, (4) preparation of general decrees, (5) communications with abroad, and (6) statistics. Mansvetov, "Velikaia Oktiabr'skaia Sotsialisticheskaia Revoliutsiia i sozdanie Narodnogo Komissariata po Delam Natsional'nostei," *Voprosy Istorii*, No. 8 (August, 1949), pp. 15–17.

[23] *Ibid.*, pp. 18–19.

manifestations." [24] In the performance of these functions, they not only conducted propaganda and agitation for the Soviet government but took advantage of class divisions on the local level to break down the solidarity of hostile groups and to foster pro-Soviet attitudes among non-Russian workers and peasants. They acted also as the eyes and ears of the central government, reporting regularly on the moods of the various localities and on the "needs of the population." [25]

Contact between the national commissariats and the local divisions was maintained by emissaries who were dispatched to the localities to establish relations with the native toiling classes and to aid in the organization of national divisions. Throughout the period of civil war these emissaries constituted, in the words of one national commissar, "the only intermediary link of the impulse of the life of the center to the periphery." [26] Consequently, they wielded especially broad powers. Not only did they exercise control over local national organizations and institutions, but they served as the principal agents for local execution of the enactments of the national commissariats, for the establishment of liaison with the localities, for the conduct of propaganda, and for channeling information to the center.

Almost from the first, these emissaries encountered opposition, noncooperation, and even sabotage from local soviets which resented central interference in their affairs. It reached such proportions that Stalin found it necessary to order local soviets "to render every assistance to the emissaries." [27] Nevertheless, the commissariat also took steps to appease the localities, and the termination of the civil war saw a sharp reduction of the authority of the emissaries. In the spring of 1921 their function was limited to supervising the execution of Soviet nationality policy in the localities, assisting in the establishment of correct relations between the agencies of the RSFSR and auton-

---

[24] Text in *Zhizn' Natsional'nostei*, December 15, 1918.

[25] Text in Narodnyi Komissariat po Delam Natsional'nostei RSFSR, *Politika Sovetskoi Vlasti po natsional'nomu voprosu za tri goda*, pp. 148–49.

[26] Mansvetov, "Velikaia Oktiabr'skaia Sotsialisticheskaia Revoliutsiia i sozdanie Narodnogo Komissariata po Delam Natsional'nostei," *Voprosy Istorii*, No. 8 (August, 1949), p. 24.

[27] *Ibid.*, p. 25.

omous units, and reporting twice monthly to the Commissariat for National Affairs on local conditions.[28] That the old power of the emissaries was gone was made completely clear by *Izvestiia* in August, 1922. The emissary, the newspaper pointed out, did "not act as an administrative representative but as a political and diplomatic agent, informing us [the center] and acting as the medium for the transmittal of the general ordinances of the central government." [29]

Within the Commissariat for National Affairs, the Commissariat for Moslem Affairs was the body which dealt originally with the problems of Central Asia.[30] Organized in January, 1918, it was authorized not only to conduct propaganda among Moslems throughout Russia but to participate actively in the unionization of Moslem workers, the organization of soviet schools in the Eastern borderlands, the application of social security measures to peasant conditions, and the collection of statistical data. At the center, it took part in the dissolution, and took over the assets, of the anti-Soviet All-Russian Moslem Council.[31] Shortly thereafter, it began to extend its activities to the Moslem regions of Russia. The initial impetus sprang from a decree of January 27, 1918, of the Commissariat for National Affairs, instructing soviets in Moslem districts to create Moslem divisions with sections for labor, the peasantry, military affairs, and culture and education.[32] Following this the Moslem Commissariat established divisions in Kazan, Ufa, Orenburg, and Astrakhan. After a later decree (June 30, 1918) had ordered the formation of divisions at the county (*uezd*) and provincial levels,[33] it organized agencies in Central Asia in Semipalatinsk, Vernyi (Alma Ata), and Tashkent.

[28] Text of instruction dated April 28, 1921, in *Spravochnik Narodnogo Komissariata po Delam Natsional'nostei,* pp. 25–26.

[29] A. Volkov, "Novye zadachi Komissariata Natsional'nostei," *Izvestiia,* August 16, 1922.

[30] The first director of the commissariat was Mullah Nur-Vakhitov, a former delegate to the Constituent Assembly from Kazan. His assistants were Galimzian Ibrahimov and Sharif Manatov. For the decree of appointment, see Narodnyi Komissariat po Delam Natsional'nostei RSFSR, *Politika Sovetskoi Vlasti po natsional'nomu voprosu za tri goda,* p. 79.

[31] Text in *ibid.,* p. 81.

[32] Text in *ibid.,* pp. 79–80.

[33] Text in *ibid.,* p. 81.

The direct influence of these agencies never became as great in Central Asia as in other Moslem regions of the RSFSR. Before the Commissariat for National Affairs could assert its authority in the region, Dutov's army had cut the link between Central Asia and Russia proper. And the Soviet government of Turkestan, which was not disposed to permit central interference in Turkestanian affairs, frustrated the subsequent efforts of local Moslem divisions and of the Commissariat for National Affairs to take the leadership in Soviet relations with the native community. In point of fact, the Turkestan republic in November, 1918, established its own Commissariat for National Affairs, but it also carefully limited the functions of that agency to the conduct of propaganda in the languages of the region and the publication of *Ishtrakiun,* a triweekly newspaper with a circulation of 3,000 copies.[34]

The reunification of Turkestan with Russia in November, 1919, did not bring the Commissariat for National Affairs and its agencies to the fore as the primary instruments for the implementation of Soviet nationality policy in Central Asia. The task of overcoming the native hatreds, engendered by the policies of the Turkestan government, required the institution of extraordinary measures. On October 3, 1919, the Central Executive Committee and the Council of People's Commissars of the RSFSR created a Commission for Turkestanian Affairs and empowered it to represent the central Soviet government and to act in its name both in Turkestan and in neighboring states. The mandate of the commission was set forth clearly in the resolution which created it.

The self-determination of the peoples of Turkestan [it read in part] and the abolition of all national inequality and all privileges of

[34] Organizationally, the Turkestanian Commissariat followed closely the pattern which had been established in the All-Russian Commissariat for National Affairs. Like the parent body, the Turkestanian Commissariat created divisions and sections for the principal nationalities of the regions. Four divisions were created which dealt with affairs of the Uzbeks, Turcomans, Kirghiz, and national minorities. In the case of national minorities, special sections for the Tajiks, Dungans, Russians, Armenians, Jews, and others were established within the division. For a brief description of the commissariat and its activities, see "Iz deiatel'nosti Turkestanskogo komissariata po natsional'nym delam," *Zhizn' Natsional'nostei,* No. 20 (28) (June 1, 1919).

one national group over another constitute the foundations of the entire policy of the Soviet government of Russia and serve as a guiding principle in all the work of its organs. . . . It is only through such work that the mistrust of the native toiling masses of Turkestan for the workers and peasants of Russia, bred by many years' domination of Russian Tsarism, can finally be overcome.[35]

The commission was ordered to put the principle of self-determination into effect in Turkestan, to abolish national inequality, and to enlist the native population in soviet work. Lenin himself took a special interest in the commission and, in a letter of November 13, 1919, appealed to the Communists of Turkestan "to treat our Turkestan Commission with the greatest trust and observe its directives exactly." [36]

Upon arrival in Tashkent, the Turkestan Commission immediately put a "Leninist" policy into effect. With the help of imported troops it disarmed and disbanded the local garrison, initiated a purge of "kulaks, colonizers, and adventurers" and set about reorganizing the entire soviet apparatus. These activities both alienated Russian Bolsheviks and non-Bolsheviks who were stripped of their authority and privileges and incurred the wrath of those native Bolsheviks who had expected to assume real power after central control had been established. The Turkestan Central Executive Committee even sent a delegation to Moscow to seek dissolution of the commission and to suggest that "the unification of Turkestan with the center can in no way be interpreted as the conquest of Turkestan by central troops."[37]

The mission failed, and with it the government it represented. Initially, the Turkestan Commission had attempted to work through the existing Turkestanian government, especially through native representatives in it. After the dispatch of the delegation to Moscow, it swept away nearly the whole of the old apparatus and demoted, dismissed, or exiled its personnel.

[35] Text of resolution in Lenin, *Sochineniia* (2d ed.), pp. 810–11. The members of the commission included Boky, Eliava, Frunze, Kuibyshev, Goloshchekin, and Rudzutak. Georgii Safarov, *Kolonial'naia revoliutsiia: opyt Turkestana* (Moscow, 1921), p. 105.

[36] Lenin, *Sochineniia* (2d ed.), p. 531.

[37] Safarov, *Kolonial'naia revoliutsiia: opyt Turkestana*, pp. 119–20.

Under the guidance of the commission, the 1918 constitution of Turkestan was scrapped and a new constitution was promulgated by the Ninth Regional Congress of Soviets. The commission did not disband even then but stayed on in the region until the national delimitation had been carried out, guiding the policies of the governments of Turkestan, Khorezm, and Bokhara and continuing as the chief agent of the RSFSR in Central Asia.

Nevertheless, the adoption of the 1920 constitution in Turkestan and the subsequent decree of the All-Russian Central Executive Committee "On the Formation of a Turkestan SSR" (April 11, 1921) brought into operation the federal administrative system in Turkestan and subjected the most important agencies of local government to the daily supervision and control of central organs. The Turkestanian commissariats of foreign affairs, foreign trade, and military affairs were eliminated. Under the principle of dual subordination the commissariats of posts and telegraph, communications, and finance were made responsible both to the Turkestan Central Executive Committee and to their federal counterparts; and the appointment of their commissars required confirmation from the federal commissariat. Similarly the local Council of National Economy and Commissariat of Supply were required to operate in conformity with plans elaborated by the federal commissariats with the same names, which also confirmed the appointment of republican commissars.[38]

The extension of direct federal administrative control to Bokhara and Khorezm occurred in March, 1923, after the formation of the Central Asiatic Economic Council.[39] But this control did not become complete until the republics of Uzbekistan and Turkmenia, which were formed in the national delimitation, entered the USSR. After this latter act, the full force of the All-Union administrative apparatus was brought to bear. The dissolution in 1923 of the Commissariat for National Affairs had eliminated the control which that agency had exercised—

[38] Text in I. Lozovskii and I. Bibin, *Sovetskaia Politika za 10 let po natsional'nomu voprosu v RSFSR* (Moscow, 1928), pp. 114–15.
[39] See above, pp. 76–77.

directly through its own delegates in Central Asia and indirectly through its control over legislation affecting the nationalities— and with the consolidation of the Soviet regime in the region, the Turkestan Commission had completed its assignment. After the dissolution of these two agencies, the federal administrative apparatus remained the sole operating arm of the central government, the arm which maintained daily direct control of the execution of its acts and instructions.

Upon the entrance of Uzbekistan and Turkmenia into the USSR, all activities in these republics relating to foreign affairs, military and naval affairs, foreign trade, communications, and posts and telegraph fell within the jurisdiction of the All-Union commissariats bearing these names. Locally, these commissariats conducted their affairs through "representatives" [40] who were empowered to promulgate and to supervise the execution of the ordinances of their parent commissariats as well as to report the adoption of local legislation which contradicted the laws and decrees of central organs.[41] This provided one aspect of the subordination of local organs of power to the policies of the central administrative system.

Another avenue of central administrative supervision and control was through the unified commissariats.[42] In these commissariats—the Supreme Council for National Economy and the commissariats of food supply, labor, finance, and worker-peasant inspection—the principle of dual subordination was enforced. On the one hand, the republican executive committee was completely autonomous in selecting and dismissing the personnel of these commissariats in the republic and in supervising their activities. On the other hand, the republican commissariats were required to execute the directives of their federal

[40] These representatives could be proposed either by the All-Union commissariat which they represented or by the Central Executive Committee of the republic to which they were assigned. In both cases, confirmation of appointments was made by the Council of People's Commissars of the USSR. The union republics had one check on the appointment of these representatives. Their Central Executive Committees possessed the right to challenge the appointment of a given representative but they could not prevent it. See I. N. Ananov, *Ocherki federal'nogo upravleniia SSSR* (Moscow, 1925), pp. 46–47.

[41] *Ibid.*, pp. 35–36, 46–47.

[42] Unified commissariats were those which existed in both the USSR and the union republics and which, on both levels, bore the same name.

counterparts and to submit to annulment of their own ordinances if these contravened federal legislation or the directives of the All-Union commissariat concerned. There was one exception to this rule. An All-Union commissariat could not abolish a decree of a republican commissariat of the same name if that decree was "based on a precise order of the Council of People's Commissars of the republic concerned." [43]

THE COMMUNIST PARTY: AGENT OF TUTELAGE

The federal institutions and their local agencies provided one channel through which Moscow was able to exercise guidance and supervision over the administration and execution of its policies and laws in Central Asia. But the crucial agency of control and centralization was the All-Russian Communist Party (bolshevik). Like the governmental institutions and their agencies, the local Party organization was an instrument which translated central policies into daily local practice. In this respect the central Party organization faced special difficulties in Central Asia during the early years of Soviet rule. One problem concerned the advancement of local Party bodies to the center of power and the consolidation and reinforcement of their control in local governmental and public organizations. Another arose from the need to create a trustworthy regional Party apparatus which represented the native laboring classes as well as Russian immigrants. Still a third involved the purification of a regional Party organization which was young, irresponsible, and, at the time of Turkestan's reunification with the center, infiltrated with unreliable elements.

Prior to the February Revolution, no Social Democratic Party organization had existed in Central Asia, and no Bolshevik organization emerged until after the October events.[44] During the first half of 1918, Party cells sprang up in Charjui, Perovsk, Ashkhabad, Merv, Tashkent, Samarkand, Kokand, Khodjent, Cherniaevsk, Kushka, Aktiubinsk, and in other small localities and districts. But with the exception of the Charjui organiza-

---

[43] Ananov, *Ocherki federal'nogo upravleniia SSSR*, pp. 47–49.
[44] I. Vrachev, "K ocherednomu s'ezde K.P.T(urkestana)," *Pravda*, July 12, 1922; see also Safarov, *Kolonial'naia revoliutsiia: opyt Turkestana*, p. 71.

tion, which boasted a hundred members, and the Tashkent organization, which increased its membership from 64 in December, 1917, to 261 in June, 1918, most of them were insignificant.[45] Sparseness of numbers, however, was the least of the Party's weaknesses. Having sprung up in Turkestan's European community after power in Russia proper had passed into Bolshevik hands, it tended not only to assume the characteristics of an "official" party but to carry attitudes of European superiority forward into the period of revolution.

The Tashkent organization alone made efforts to recruit Moslems during the early months of Soviet rule, and by June, 1918, it counted twenty-eight native members (mostly Uzbeks) and claimed 125 additional "Party followers" in the Old City of Tashkent.[46] At its first regional congress in June, moreover, the Party solemnly resolved that the "Moslem proletariat must be the main bulwark of the Soviet power in Turkestan" and recommended action along the following lines: (1) to declare the "Turkic language" as well as Russian to be a state language; (2) to establish commissariats for national affairs under all provincial, regional, and county soviets; (3) to publish all official organs in the "Turkic" tongue and to organize courses to prepare Party workers from the indigenous nationalities; (4) to establish a Moslem Red Army; and (5) to start publishing Party literature in the "Turkic" language.[47]

For practical purposes this resolution remained a dead letter until after the arrival of the Turkestan Commission in Central Asia in the autumn of 1919. While a Turkestan Commissariat for National Affairs was formed in November, 1918, and fitful attempts were made to elicit native support for Party and Soviet objectives, the Turkestanian Bolsheviks made no serious effort to enlist the indigenous population in Party or Soviet work. One hindrance was the traditional dichotomy between the Russian townsman and the native peasant which developed into armed conflict during the course of the civil war. Another was

[45] P. Antropov, "Pervyi S'ezd Kommunisticheskoi Partii Turkestana," in Istpart Sredazbiuro Ts.K., V.K.P. (b), *Revoliutsiia v Srednei Azii* (Tashkent, 1928), I, 11–12.

[46] *Ibid.*, p. 11.

[47] *Ibid.*, pp. 13–14.

the colonial heritage which had developed an attitude of superiority among the Russian workingmen in Turkestan.[48] Still a third grew out of the infiltration into the Party and the government of persons who were unsympathetic with the Bolshevik program in general and hostile to its nationality policy in particular.

While the Communist Party in Turkestan hesitated, Moscow went forward with its own program for attracting Moslem support for the Communist Party. In November, 1918, a Congress of Moslem Communists in Moscow, at which Stalin played a leading role, created a Central Bureau of Moslem Organizations of the Russian Communist Party—the Moslem Bureau— as a special agency of the Party Central Committee and authorized it to supervise the activities of all Moslem Communist organizations in the Soviet state.[49] Although the principal function of this agency was to organize and promote pro-Soviet propaganda among Moslems in Russia and abroad,[50] it did take the initiative in forming Moslem Communist cells in the Tur-

[48] The accordance of special rights and privileges to Russians by the Soviet government of Turkestan was especially embittering to the native population. Acts such as the removal of all cases concerning Communists from the jurisdiction of the regular courts to the Party court (see G. I. Broido, "Turkestanskie Problemy," *Zhizn' Natsional'nostei,* No. 23 [80] [July 18, 1920]) and the confiscation of the property of natives while that of Europeans was untouched contributed to growing hatred and distrust. At the Third Congress of the Communist Party of Turkestan in June, 1919, a native bitterly remarked, "The representatives of the Soviet power protect only the Russians. These are given good footwear and these decorate their homes with silks and precious textiles— stolen from others [Moslems]. And what is done for us Moslems? Are we fed? Is footwear distributed to us? No. Were it so, our poor would not be going about with naked feet. If we had been given food, thousands, tens of thousands of us would not have died of starvation. What remains in our houses? There remains only old pieces of bedcovers. Nothing else." G. Macartney, "Chez les Soviets en Asie Centrale," *Journal of the Central Asian Society,* XVI (1929), 99–100.

[49] *Zhizn' Natsional'nostei,* No. 3 (November 24, 1918). The report of Stalin's speech before the congress has not been included in his *Sochineniia.*

[50] The Moslem Bureau concentrated its attention on organizing propaganda for the Soviet system and promoting the slogans of the Moscow government among Moslems in Russia and abroad. Divisions were established to carry out propaganda work among the Arabs, Persians, Turks, Azerbaijanians, Sarts (Turkestan), Kirghiz, Mountain Caucasians, Kalmyks, Chinese, and Tatars. Propaganda brochures, designed to appeal to each nationality, were published and distributed, presses were established in the localities, and organizers were sent out. *Vos'moi S'ezd Rossiiskoi Kommunisticheskoi Partii (b)* (Moscow, 1919), pp. 384–85.

kestan region, and in May, 1919, it sponsored the First Regional
Conference of Moslem Organizations at Tashkent. This was
a beginning but it was hardly a promising one. Even while the
conference was meeting, the Tashkent Soviet was actively promoting its campaign of suppression against the native population of Turkestan, and the conference found itself obliged to
provide its members with special certificates exempting them
from search and arrest without the consent of the conference
presidium.[51] In spite of this, the conference published two appeals, one to the natives of Turkestan to desert the Basmachi,
and the other to "the oppressed laboring brethren of India,
Afghanistan, Persia, China, Asia Minor, and Eastern Asia" to
support the Russian Communist Party in its struggle against
imperialism.[52]

The conference also adopted a resolution looking forward
to the formation of a "Unified Turkestan Soviet Republic"
composed of all the Turkic tribes of Russia from Azerbaijan
and the Volga to Turkestan. The Soviet government became
alarmed. Although it had supported the organizational centralization of Party work among the Moslems, it had no intention
of forming a unified Turkic republic. At the Fifth Congress of
the Turkestan Communist Party, a resolution was passed which
condemned "native chauvinism" as well as "colonizers." [53] Communist commentators complained that "the organization of the
local masses followed the unhealthy path of the utilization of
the Soviet power by the nationalistic intelligentsia for purposes
of national self-determination." [54]

In Turkestan and elsewhere the deviation toward nationalism
became pronounced in the Moslem Communist organizations.
These bodies nevertheless aided in the extension of Soviet control to new areas during the civil war and nothing was done
then to limit their activities. But the return of peaceful conditions in Russia brought their usefulness to an end; in January,

[51] Safarov, *Kolonial'naia revoliutsiia: opyt Turkestana,* pp. 96–97.

[52] Mustapha Chokaiev, "Turkestan and the Soviet Regime," *Journal of the Royal Central Asian Society,* XVIII (1931), 412–13.

[53] Vrachev, "K ocherednomu s'ezde K.P.T(urkestana)," *Pravda,* July 12, 1922.

[54] S. Muraveiskii, *Ocherki po istorii revoliutsionnogo dvizheniia v Srednei Azii* (Tashkent, 1926), p. 26.

1921, a conference of the Turkic peoples of Russia obediently voted to reorganize and rename the Moslem Bureau as the Central Bureau of Agitation and Propaganda among the Turkic Peoples of the RSFSR.[55] After this, it quietly disappeared from the scene.

Despite its short existence, the Moslem Bureau played an important part in the early development of native Communist cadres in the Eastern republics of the RSFSR. Through the intervention of its Central Bureau, native forces in many regions were first introduced into Communist Party work. In Central Asia, moreover, the district Moslem Bureau became a rallying point of opposition to many of the excesses of the Tashkent Soviet and its agents, and after the arrival of the Turkestan Commission in Tashkent, it became the primary instrument through which that body advertised its appeals to the native population.

The reunification of Turkestan to Russia marked the actual beginning of the growth of a native section in the Communist Party of Turkestan. Hitherto, native Communists had played only a minor role in the making and execution of Party policy and their numbers had been insignificant. The reestablishment of central control brought an abrupt change in Party attitudes. In the summer of 1920 a letter from the Moscow Central Committee ordered removal of "all the Turkestanian Communists who are contaminated with colonizing fever and Great Russian nationalism" and called upon the Turkestan Party to "gather under its banner all the best proletarian, semiproletarian, and laboring elements." [56] Thereafter, the Turkestan Party organization began to take in natives and to place them in conspicuous Party positions. By 1921 it not only had swelled its ranks to 65,000[57] but at the Sixth Regional Congress, which convened

---

[55] Stalin, *Sochineniia*, V, 402.

[56] From a letter of the Central Committee of the Russian Communist Party to the Communist Party of Turkestan, June 29, 1920. Safarov, *Kolonial'naia revoliutsiia: opyt Turkestana*, pp. 121, 134.

[57] Joseph Castagné, "Russie Slave et Russie Turque: les chances d'une politique islamique allemande," *Revue du Monde Musulman*, LVI (December, 1923), 181.

in the late summer, over half of the delegates were Moslems.[58]

A similar growth took place in the Party organizations of other parts of Central Asia. In Bokhara and Khorezm, Party bodies with thousands of members were established. The Kirghiz Party, which had emerged in the Pishpek (Frunze) district in late 1918 and which had approximately 8,500 members in July, 1919, increased its membership to well over 11,000 after a drive to enlist natives in 1919 and 1920.[59] Many of the new members, however, did not understand the Party's aims or methods or were unsympathetic to them but hoped to use their membership to promote personal careers or to alter the Party outlook. Complaints to the center increased and at the Tenth All-Russian Party Congress in March, 1921, Safarov charged that the ranks of the Party in Central Asia were "polluted" with "Communist fathers, Russian police, and Semirechian kulaks." [60]

Moscow called a halt. In a circular letter to the Communist Party of Turkestan (January 11, 1922) the Central Committee directed the local organization to harden its native cadres and to rid itself of "colonizers."[61] The letter touched off the first of a series of Party purges which lasted into mid-1923 and shook all of the Central Asian Party organizations to their foundations. The Turkestanian Party was the first to be stricken. By the meeting of its Eleventh Party Congress in March, 1922, 10,036 members had been expelled, 3,229 had been demoted to candidacy, and 1,758 had resigned.[62] This was only the first blow. In successive waves, the purge engulfed the Party organization on the lower levels. In Semirechie, one half of the Party mem-

---

[58] Of the total delegation of 231 members, 178 were Moslems, including 71 Uzbeks, 64 Kirghiz, 20 Tatars, 6 Turcomans, 6 Tajiks, 2 Azerbaijanians, 1 Persian, and 9 others. *Zhizn' National'nostei*, No. 18 (116) (September 16, 1921).

[59] A. N. Zorin, *Revoliutsionnoe dvizhenie Kirgizii (severnaia chast')* (Frunze, 1931), pp. 29–33; Turar R. Ryskulov, *Kirgizstan* (Moscow, 1935), pp. 158–63.

[60] *Protokoly s'ezdov i konferentsii Vsesoiuznoi Kommunisticheskoi Partii (b): Desiatyi S'ezd R.K.P.(b), mart, 1921 g.* (Moscow, 1933), p. 195.

[61] From a circular letter of the Central Committee of the Russian Communist Party to the Communist Party of Turkestan (January 11, 1922). Text in *Zhizn' Natsional'nostei*, No. 3 (132) (January 26, 1922).

[62] *Protokoly s'ezdov i konferentsii Vsesoiuznoi Kommunisticheskoi Partii (b): Odinnadtsatyi S'ezd R.K.P. (b)* (Moscow, 1936), p. 396.

bers were dismissed[63] and the Turcoman organization was reduced from 4,132 members to 1,700. Of the remainder, in the latter case, 70 percent were Russian and 15 percent Turcomans.[64] A report in *Pravda* on August 2, 1923, indicated that Party membership in Turkestan stood at 13,156 members and 4,000 candidates, a bare one fourth of the 1921 figure.

Communist Parties in Kirghizia, Bokhara, and Khorezm shared the same fate. The Kirghiz Party dropped in strength to 2,957 but 2,254 of the remainder were Kirghiz.[65] In the purge in Bokhara, 16,000 Party members were expelled, and Stalin reported in June, 1923, that membership in the Khorezmian section would probably be reduced to a hundred persons after the current purge there had been completed.[66]

The purge represented the destructive facet of a concentrated campaign to strengthen and tighten up the Communist organizations in the borderland republics. On the constructive side, Party headquarters insisted on the development of strong national Party sections, based upon a tempered core of reliable native Communists. This facet received its clearest expression at the Fourth Conference with Responsible Workers in June, 1923. In a directive concerning the backward nationalities, the conference emphasized that "a fundamental task of the Party is to rear and develop young Communist organizations in the national republics and regions, consisting of proletarian elements of the local population, to help them stand on their feet, to give them a real Communist education, and to create truly internationalist cadres, however few they may be." [67] The conference insisted, in accordance with the resolutions of the Twelfth Party Congress, on the need to form Party circles of local Party workers, to create instructor cadres of local workers, and to develop Marxist and mass Party literature in native languages, and demanded in addition the institution of non-Party conferences of workers and peasants and the utilization of se-

[63] *Izvestiia*, February 14, 1923.
[64] "V Turkestane," *Zhizn' Natsional'nostei*, No. 2 (1923), pp. 138–39.
[65] Zorin, *Revoliutsionnoe dvizhenie Kirgizii*, p. 46.
[66] Stalin, *Sochineniia*, V, 330.
[67] *Ibid.*, V, 293.

lected native Communists for work in the central agencies of the Russian Communist Party.[68]

The primary emphasis in recruiting was placed on drawing native industrial workers into Party work. But these were so few in number that the Party was forced to expand its range. Stalin, for one, insisted that loyal elements in the native intellectual class had to be drawn into Party and Soviet work. "There are so few intellectuals," he said, "so few thinking people, even so few literate people generally in the eastern republics and regions that one can count them on one's fingers. How can one help setting store by them?" [69] Even after the Sultan-Galiev episode, he still maintained that reliable "bourgeois-democratic" elements should be utilized and the Party continued its policy of receiving repentant nationalists into the Soviet fold.

The main field for Party recruitment necessarily became the peasantry in the border regions. In these areas, even the native industrial workers were almost exclusively of peasant origin and the Party reached the conclusion that entrance qualifications had to be relaxed so that stable national sections could be built. Zinoviev gave the justification in 1924 when he pointed out that "a workers' party in a peasant country must have among its members a certain percentage of peasants." [70] Nonetheless, the Communist Party did not intend to permit peasant Communists to dominate even the most backward regions. It still based its policy, Zinoviev was careful to explain, on "the pick of its members, on the workers." [71] These were expected to provide proper guidance for the more backward elements.

At the same time, the Party undertook intensive training programs among the non-Russian Communists to fit them for active Party work in their communities and for responsible positions in government and economic work. Indeed, the low

[68] *Ibid.*, V, 297, 300; also *Vse-Soiuznaia Kommunisticheskaia Partiia v rezoliutiiakh i resheniiakh s'ezdov, soveshchaniei i plenumov Tsentral'nogo Komiteta (1898–1932)* (4th ed., Moscow, 1932), I, 595–96.

[69] Stalin, *Sochineniia*, V, 303.

[70] L. Kamenev, J. V. Stalin, and G. E. Zinoviev, *Leninism or Trotskyism* (Chicago, 1925), p. 21.

[71] *Ibid.*

level of education and training presented a real obstacle to the attainment of positions of responsibility by native Communists in Party and public bodies. In the Moslem community in Central Asia illiteracy was universal during the early years of Soviet rule; inevitably it found reflection in the native sections of the Party organizations. Of the indigenous nationalities, only the Uzbeks furnished Party cadres that were not almost entirely unlettered. Reports of literacy in the Turcoman section in 1923 showed that barely more than 1 percent of the native members were able to read and write;[72] three years later 70 percent of all Party members in the Turcoman SSR were classified as "technically illiterate." [73] The condition of the Kirghiz Party was no more favorable. A census of Party members taken at the Kirghiz capital city in 1923 showed less than 7 percent literacy.[74]

The problem of eliminating illiteracy in Party circles and of training strong cadres of native Party workers was a matter of real concern to the central leadership. During the civil war— while the question was discussed in the central organs of the Communist Party and in the columns of *Zhizn' Natsional'nostei* —measures to cure the disease could not be implemented. As soon as peaceful conditions returned steps were taken to help the non-Russian Party organizations "to stand on their own feet" and to achieve a "real Communist education."[75] These educational activities were contrived to satisfy the Party's needs on two distinct levels. The program, on the first level, was designed to increase literacy among the rank-and-file Party members and to provide them with a basic training in Marxist-Leninist dogma. It was supplemented by a second program of superior training which purposed to prepare native Communists for responsible positions in the Party and government and for duty as trained instructors and propagandists in local Party organizations.

[72] Only 15 percent of the members of the Turcoman Party organization were Turcomans and nearly all of these were illiterate. See "V Turkestane," *Zhizn' Natsional'nostei,* No. 2 (1923), pp. 138–39.

[73] G. Beichek, "Shkoly-peredvizhki v Srednei Azii," *Kommunisticheskaia Revoliutsiia,* No. 8 (April, 1926), p. 67.

[74] *Izvestiia,* August 3, 1923.

[75] From a resolution of the Twelfth Congress of the Russian Communist Party. Quoted in N. N. Popov, *Natsional'naia politika Sovetskoi Vlasti* (Moscow, 1927), p. 101.

On the primary level, school programs of three descriptions —each of which corresponded to a different level of literacy— were undertaken. Illiterate Communists were required to attend classes at Illiteracy Liquidation Points, which were operated under the supervision of the All-Russian Extraordinary Commission for the Liquidation of Illiteracy. These schools, whose classes were open to all illiterates, enjoyed a rapid—though inadequate—expansion after the civil war. In 1923, fifty-seven such schools with an enrollment of 2,662 were operating in Turkestan, and by the end of 1926 almost 46,000 pupils were attending 1,497 of them in Uzbekistan and Turkmenistan.[76] For barely literate and politically uneducated Communists of the rural areas, the Party established in Central Asia a network of traveling schools (shkoly-peredvizhki). Moving from place to place, these schools—one Communist called them the primary instrument for the liquidation of political illiteracy in the village[77]—offered simple abbreviated courses in Communist dogma. The training of lower-level Party workers and functionaries was the task of the Party training school, the third in the triumvirate of primary Party educational institutions. These schools, which offered a basic course in Party training to literate Communists, were put into operation in the major administrative centers of Central Asia. In 1923, five schools with a total attendance of 532 were offering courses, and this number had been increased to eleven schools with an enrollment of 1,038 by December, 1926.[78]

During the same period, Party training of a superior type, designed to prepare Party workers for positions of high responsi-

[76] Central Statistical Board, USSR, Ten Years of Soviet Power in Figures, 1917–1927 (Moscow, 1927), pp. 84–85; Tsentral'noe Statisticheskoe Upravlenie, Narodnoe khoziaistvo Soiuza SSR v tsifrakh: kratkii spravochnik (Moscow, 1924), p. 44.

[77] From a speech by a delegate, Syrtsov, at the Fourteenth Conference of the Russian Communist Party. Chetyrnadtsataia Konferentsiia Rossiiskoi Kommunisticheskoi Partii (b): stenograficheskii otchet (Moscow, 1925), pp. 32–33.

[78] Central Statistical Board, USSR, Ten Years of Soviet Power in Figures, pp. 84–85; Tsentral'noe Statisticheskoe Upravlenie, Narodnoe khoziaistvo Soiuza SSR v tsifrakh, p. 44. According to another reporter there were only eight Party training schools in Soviet Central Asia in 1926. See S. Muraveiskii, "V bor'be za kadry v Srednei Azii," Kommunisticheskaia Revoliutsiia, No. 17 (September, 1926), p. 65.

bility, was offered to carefully selected native Communists in Communist universities. A number of these universities catering to various national groupings were established at the beginning of the 1920's in Central Russia and in the outlying republics and regions of the Soviet state. Of them, three—the Central Institute of Living Eastern Languages at Leningrad, the Communist University of the Toilers of the East at Moscow, and the Lenin University at Tashkent—had special facilities for training students from the eastern republics and regions.

Easily the most advanced was the Central Institute for Living Eastern Languages, whose goal was the training of personnel for "practical activities" in the East in every sphere.[79] The bulk of its student body was of Russian origin but it enrolled students who were native to Central Asia. In 1927 there were in attendance 27 representatives of the Turkic nationalities of the USSR. Its course of study extended over a period of three years, two of which were spent in attendance at the university and one of which was devoted to work in the field. The study of Turkology was an important phase of the program of course work, with heavy emphasis given to the study of the Turkic languages (Osmanli, Uzbek, Kazakh, Turkmenian, Kirghiz, and Uigur) and the historical, political, economic, and cultural background of the Turkic peoples. According to Vel'tman (Pavlovich), the Central Institute performed distinguished service in the "preparation of qualified workers for our Eastern republics." [80]

While the course work of the Central Institute was designed primarily to prepare Russian students for careers in the eastern republics, the Communist University of the Toilers of the East[81] concentrated its attention on training native Party members for "political work" in their own republics. Specifically it was established for the purpose of preparing cadres of Com-

[79] From a decree (November 25, 1920) of the Central Executive Committee of the RSFSR on the formation of the Central Institute of Living Eastern Languages. Text in Narodnyi Komissariat po Delam Natsional'nostei RSFSR, *Politika Sovetskoi Vlasti po natsional'nomu voprosu za tri goda*, pp. 161–62.

[80] M. Pavlovich, *Revoliutsionnyi Vostok* (Moscow, 1927), I, 109.

[81] The Communist University of the Toilers of the East was organized under the Commissariat for National Affairs by decree of the Central Executive Committee of the RSFSR on April 21, 1921. Text in Lozovskii and Bibin, *Sovetskaia politika za 10 let po natsional'nomu voprosu v RSFSR*, pp. 277–78.

munist agitators and instructors for Party schools, for training functionaries for responsible service in the soviet and Party apparatus, and for satisfying the cultural needs of the Eastern peoples of the Soviet state.[82] The university had two faculties, one of natural sciences and the other of social science. The former offered courses in physics, chemistry, geography, and biology,[83] while the latter, after grounding its students in Communist theory for four months, trained them as specialists in various areas of Party and soviet work.[84]

After the founding of the university in 1921, the student body, due in part to a policy of compulsory recruitment, grew quickly. In 1921, over 600 students, representing 44 nationalities, were in attendance, and this number increased in 1922 to 700 students and in 1923 to 933.[85] Students from the Central Asian republics were in attendance from the beginning. In the fall of 1921, there were sixty-two Uzbeks, thirty-two Turcomans, and six Kirghiz in the student body.[86] By 1926, more than 500 students from Central Asia had been graduated from the school and over 300 others were currently in attendance.[87]

The only Communist university in Central Asia itself was

---

[82] G. I. Broido, "Kommunisticheskii Universitet Trudiashchikhsia Vostoka," in Narodnyi Komissariat po Delam Natsional'nostei RSFSR, *Natsional'nyi vopros i Sovetskaia Rossiia* (Moscow, 1921), p. 86. The author of this article, a prominent Central Asian Communist, was the first chancellor of the university.

[83] *Zhizn' Natsional'nostei*, No. 3 (9) (March 14, 1922), p. 13.

[84] All students in the social science area were required to take the four-month theoretical course. This included natural science (the study of evolution); the history of human society and the essence of the historical process; the theory and development of capitalism; the history of the struggle of the proletariat for Communism; the history of the revolutionary movement in Russia and of the Russian Communist Party; the program and by-laws of the Russian Communist Party; the economic geography of the world and of the RSFSR; the national-colonial question; and Eastern learning and the history of the social and revolutionary movements in the countries of the East. Upon completion of the theoretical course, the students entered upon a two-month course of specialization. This course included offerings in production, supply, agriculture, cooperatives, administration, labor and labor unions, education, agitation, and Party organization. See Broido, "Kommunisticheskii Universitet Trudiashchikhsia Vostoka," in Narodnyi Komissariat po Delam Natsional'nostei RSFSR, *Natsional'nyi vopros i Sovetskaia Rossiia*, pp. 84–90.

[85] *Pravda*, July 25, 1922; V. Viktorov, "Kommunisticheskii Universitet Trudiashchikhsia Vostoka," *Zhizn' Natsional'nostei*, No. 1 (January, 1923), pp. 263–65.

[86] I. P. Trainin, *SSSR i natsional'naia problema: po natsional'nym respublikam i oblastiam Sovetskogo Soiuza* (Moscow, 1924), p. 46.

[87] Pavlovich, *Revoliutsionnyi Vostok*, I, 109.

the Communist Worker-Peasant University of Turkestan.[88] Founded in 1922 through a merger of the Central Turkic School of Soviet and Party Work and the European Soviet Party School, the Lenin School operated under the guidance of the Central Committee of the Communist Party of Turkestan. It offered a one-year course of instruction divided into four three-month periods, during which students were trained in Communist theory and in Soviet and Party work.[89] The student body was recruited primarily from the indigenous nationalities, although Russians were admitted, and the instruction itself was given in Russian "because of the huge number of nationalities." [90] Enrollment, which was small at the beginning (225 students, 150 of whom were natives),[91] climbed steadily; in 1925 there were 381 students enrolled and by the fall of 1926 over 650 were in attendance.[92]

Through this educational program, the Communist Party sought to prepare its native members in Central Asia to assume command of their own Party organizations and to open the way to an increase in native members in them. Nevertheless, the Communist Party organizations in Central Asia continued to draw their primary strength from a hard core of Russian Communists, recruited mainly from the railroad shops. According to a 1922 Party census, there were only 2,043 Uzbeks, 197 Turcomans, and 2,254 Kirghiz in the Party and the majority (3,549) were peasants. The emphasis placed upon "nationalization" of the non-Russian Party organizations brought about a rapid increase in the sections in Turkmenia and Uzbekistan (1,410 and 562 percent respectively between 1922 and 1927), but in both Party sections the primary nationality remained in the minority

[88] After the national delimitation, the name was changed to Central Asiatic Communist University. The university was commonly referred to as the Lenin School, having been named originally in his honor.

[89] V. Rozner, "Vysshaia partiinaia shkola v Turkestane," *Kommunisticheskaia Revoliutsiia*, Nos. 11–12 (35–36) (October 1, 1922), pp. 182–83.

[90] Muraveiskii, "V bor'be za kadry v Srednei Azii," *Kommunisticheskaia Revoliutsiia*, No. 17 (September, 1926), p. 69.

[91] Rozner, "Vysshaia partiinaia shkola v Turkestane," *Kommunisticheskaia Revoliutsiia*, Nos. 11–12 (35–36) (October 1, 1922), pp. 182–83.

[92] Central Statistical Board, USSR, *Ten Years of Soviet Power in Figures*, pp. 84–85.

(see Table 5). The Kirghiz section alone had and maintained a native majority.

Although the number of workers as compared with the number of peasants increased gradually between 1922 and 1927, the

TABLE 5

NATIVE MEMBERSHIP IN REPUBLICAN COMMUNIST
ORGANIZATIONS

REPUBLIC	1922		1927	
	All Party Members and Candidates	Party Members of Primary Nationality	All Party Members and Candidates	Party Members of Primary Nationality
Uzbekistan				
Total	no data	2,043[a]	26,819[d]	11,488[d]
Workers		597	13,005	4,399
Peasants		1,036	6,256	4,538
Employees		204	6,340	1,953
Others		206	1,218	598
Turkmenia				
Total	no data	1,000[a,b]	8,024[d]	2,779[d]
Workers		110	3,491	422
Peasants		836	2,659	2,073
Employees		21	1,709	245
Others		33	165	39
Kirghizia				
Total	2,957[c]	2,254[c]	4,273[d]	2,159[d]
Workers	no data	295[a]	1,068	233
Peasants		1,677	2,231	1,744
Employees		92	833	143
Others		190	141	39

[a] I. P. Trainin, *SSSR i natsional'naia problema: po natsional'nym respublikam i oblastiam Sovetskogo Soiuza* (Moscow, 1924), pp. 26–27.

[b] Broken down as follows: Taranches, 530; Turcomans, 197; Kuramichi, 153; Karakles, 71; Dungans, 37.

[c] A. N. Zorin, *Revoliutsionnoe dvizhenie Kirgizii (severnaia chast')* (Frunze, 1931), p. 46.

[d] Central Statistical Board, *Ten Years of Soviet Power in Figures, 1917–1927* (Moscow, 1927), p. 21; Statisticheskii Otdel Tsentral'nyi Komitet, V.K.P.(b), *Sotsial'nyi i natsional'nyi Sostav V.K.P.(b)* (Moscow, 1928), pp. 124, 126.

native element in all three Parties remained heavily peasant, and natives classified as workers were largely of peasant origin. The strength of these organizations in Party workers was correspondingly weak. Figures, compiled in 1927, showed only 2,054 Uzbeks, 269 Turcomans, and 58 Kirghiz in this category. Of these, 664 Uzbeks, 73 Turcomans, and only one Kirghiz were classified as qualified.[93] The meaning was clear. The European element, supported by Turkic Communists, who had been imported from the Tatar republic, continued to dominate the Central Asiatic Communist organizations. Being concentrated in the most important political and administrative centers, they were able to supervise closely the execution of Party policy and to check native deviations before they became serious. Moreover, their strategic position enabled them to exercise close and unremitting guidance and control over local governmental agencies and mass organizations. Through the Central Asiatic Bureau of the Communist Party, an agency whose purpose was to centralize, coordinate, and supervise the activities of all the Central Asiatic Party organizations, the European group had in addition a direct channel to the highest Party agencies.

The actual enforcement of Party policy within Central Asia was performed indirectly. Except in its conduct of agitation and propaganda and its activity as a supervising agency which reported on local conditions generally and on the fulfillment by Party and public organizations of Party policies specifically, the Communist Party in Central Asia did not exercise its power directly. Instead it conducted its operations—exercised its monopoly of power—through Bolshevik fractions in Soviet and public organizations. Bound by the iron discipline of the Party and obligated under Party rules to perform to the letter Party decisions and instructions, these fractions, whose members occupied strategic positions in all governmental and public agencies, were the actual instruments through which the Party realized its dictatorship.

THE MASSES ORGANIZED: THE YOUTH LEAGUE
AND THE TRADE UNIONS

The soviet system itself was not the only vehicle of mass activity and control which emerged in Central Asia from the revolution. Equally significant were the numerous mass organizations which also sprang up during the same period. The soviets themselves were one arena of mass activity, one instrument through

[93] Statisticheskii Otdel, Tsentral'nyi Komitet V.K.P.(b), *Sotsial'nyi i natsional'-nyi sostav V.K.P.(b)* (Moscow, 1928), p. 134.

which the changing moods of the masses could be gauged and their voices could be skillfully converted into a chorus of approval of Party policy.[94] Outside the direct chain of government of which the soviets formed a part, the Party encouraged the formation of, and assumed leadership in, mass public organizations. In them the Party found a medium to influence and to guide the thought and action of the masses in areas which could not be reached satisfactorily through direct Party and government channels. By means of them, the Party acted to deepen the class struggle, to encourage "spontaneous" mass activity on the lowest level, to involve the masses in the process of Soviet rule, to activate them to accomplish Party and Soviet purposes, and to furnish daily proof of the efficacy and correctness of the Party line.

Each of the mass organizations was directed at a special population group—workers, peasants, women, the youth—and had as its purpose both the common objective of indoctrinating its members—and through them, the whole community—with a soviet spirit and special objectives which related specifically to the particular groups. In Central Asia, the most important of these were the Komsomol (League of Communist Youth), the trade unions, and the Koshchi. The last-named organization, which was peculiar to Central Asia, was designed to win the cooperation and support of the native peasantry for the Soviet regime. Special efforts were also made in Central Asia to organize native women, to break down the barriers which custom and Moslem law had placed in the way of their participation in community activities, and to introduce them into public life. None of these was notably successful during the first ten years of Soviet rule.

Of the mass organizations, only the Komsomol occupied a dual place in Soviet thinking. On the one hand, it was defined as a mass "non-Party organization," and on the other it was denominated as "the assistant of the Communist Party and its reserve." [95] The Komsomol thus performed two functions. As

[94] See below, pp. 190–200.

[95] See Julian Towster, *Political Power in the USSR, 1917–1947* (New York, 1948), pp. 137–44; also Samuel N. Harper, *Civic Training in Soviet Russia* (Chicago, 1929), pp. 42–60.

a quasi-Party organization, patterned structurally and organizationally after the Party, it was required to master the teachings of Marxism-Leninism, to assist the Party in the execution of its program and directives, and to train the future cadres from which the Party would replenish its ranks. As a mass organization, its task was the organization of Soviet youth and the education of the latter in the spirit of Communism and of service to the Soviet regime.

The performance of these disparate functions, in the official viewpoint, created no internal antagonisms which would impair the vitality of the organization. Stalin, in a declaration "On Contradictions in the Komsomol," made in April, 1924, made this clear:

What is the League—a reserve [of the Party] or an instrument? It is both. . . . The Communist League of Youth is a reserve, a reserve of peasants and workers, whence the Party draws replenishment. But, in addition, it is an instrument, an instrument in the hands of the Party which subjects the masses of the youth to its [the Party's] influence. It would be more specific to say that the League is an instrument of the Party, a subsidiary weapon of the Party in the sense that the active personnel of the Komsomol is an instrument of the Party for influencing the youth which remains outside the League. These concepts do not and cannot contradict one another.[96]

The growth of the Komsomol in Central Asia was uneven during the early years of Soviet rule. Only after the middle twenties did it succeed in recruiting large numbers of the native youth. Serious efforts at recruitment did not begin until 1920–21 when Communist youth congresses met in Tashkent. At the second congress, which convened in January, 1921, delegates from 310 organizations with a membership of more than 20,000 were present.[97] The membership, however, was by no means solidly native in composition. Despite demands from the center to expand and build up native youth organizations, the size of the indigenous component of the Komsomol increased slowly. Figures for 1925 showed only 13,368 Uzbek, 3,010

[96] Stalin, *Sochineniia*, VI, 65–66.
[97] Joseph Castagné, "Le Turkestan depuis la révolution russe," *Revue du Monde Musulman*, L (June, 1922), 69.

Kirghiz, and 1,633 Turcoman members in the organization.[98] One hindrance to large-scale native participation grew out of the leading position which Europeans had taken. Another flowed from the language barrier—a highly important one, since the majority of local cells conducted their business in Russian. Cognizance was taken of these impediments in 1926 and led both to a demand for the formation of "national cells using the native language" and to official discouragement of the practice of leaving native youths ignorant of Russian on the fringe of Russian organizations.[99]

Demands for the creation of national units on the primary level also brought to the fore two other difficult problems, one of which involved recruitment. In many localities, especially in the "national" village, there was no youth movement. As early as its Third Congress in October, 1920, the Komsomol had resolved to "influence" rural youth and to offer it "a full opportunity to develop politically and culturally and to escape . . . the isolationism" of village life.[100] But branch organizations in the non-Russian regions did not undertake serious campaigns to bring the movement to the "national" villages until the middle twenties. Then renewed pressure from the highest levels compelled republican and regional bodies to increase the number of primary organizations and to strengthen the membership of existing cells by increasing the number of agricultural workers and poor peasants in them. Simultaneously, an educational campaign got under way to fit members for leadership in their communities. In the towns, the practice was initiated of requiring attendance at *politgramota*[101] classes conducted in the native tongue. In the villages, where illiteracy was general, Komsomol members were required to attend "traveling schools." [102] These recruiting and educational drives did have a

[98] Komissia po Izucheniiu Natsional'nogo Voprosa, Kommunisticheskaia Akademiia, *Natsional'naia politika V.K.P.(b) v tsifrakh* (Moscow, 1930), p. 159.

[99] Ia. Mushpert and E. Fainberg, *Komsomol i molodezh' natsional'nykh men'shinstv* (Moscow, 1926), pp. 16–17.

[100] From a resolution of the Third Congress of the All-Russian Communist League of Youth. Quoted in *ibid.,* p. 15.

[101] A course of instruction in which rudimentary political, economic, and social subjects were taught in accordance with the current Communist Party viewpoint.

[102] Mushpert and Fainberg, *Komsomol i molodezh' natsional'nykh men'shinstv,* pp. 25–26.

considerable effect. By mid-1927, the number of Uzbek Komsomol members had reached 36,131; of Kirghiz, 10,107; and of Turcomans, 7,048.[103] And the influence of the organization as an instrument of mass control had grown correspondingly.

Among the general population the Komsomol pursued familiar goals: agitation, organization, and education. Through agitation and propaganda it sought to combat the growth of native nationalism, to promote the development of the soviet system and the principles of "revolutionary legality" in rural areas, to popularize the Red Army and Fleet[104] among village youth, to encourage the development of cooperatives, and to "liberate" the poor and middle peasants and agricultural workers from the influence of the kulaks. In its organizational work the Komsomol sought to rally the poorest classes for struggle against forces hostile to the soviet order and to encourage them to enter the trade unions, cooperatives, and associations of the poor. The Komsomol also played a leading role in the process of mass education. It took active part in the campaign against illiteracy, established reading huts in the rural areas, encouraged the poor to attend lecture and study courses, and introduced political education on the lowest level.[105]

The second major channel of mass organization and control was the trade union movement and its branches in Central Asia. In industry the labor unions were concerned mainly with increasing production, enforcing labor discipline, acting as watchdogs for the central authorities over the activities of managerial staffs, and satisfying the cultural needs of their members. Since the unions were the special organizations of the wage earners and represented the class upon which the Communist Party based its dictatorship, it was natural that the Party should also seek both to expand them into the non-Russian regions of the Soviet state and to encourage them and their members to

[103] Komissia po Izucheniiu Natsional'nogo Voprosa, Kommunisticheskaia Akademiia, Natsional'naia politika V.K.P.(b) v tsifrakh, p. 159.

[104] In October, 1922, the Komsomol assumed the role of patron of the Soviet Navy. In this capacity it organized welfare activities for the Navy, encouraged its members to enter that branch of service, and in other ways took a particular interest in it.

[105] Mushpert and Fainberg, Komsomol i molodezh' natsional'nykh men'shinstv, pp. 42–55, 85–86.

participate actively in public life. Through them the Party expected "to knit the thin stratum of the native working class closely together and to indoctrinate it with a really proletarian ideology." [106] Hence the responsibilities of these organizations extended beyond the workbench and into the major areas of political and social life. Not only were they assigned industrial tasks but they were expected to assist in the liquidation of survivals of patriarchal-feudal relationships, in the development and strengthening of Soviet statehood, in the establishment of a judicial and administrative system conducting business in native languages, and in the development of a press, school, theater, and other cultural institutions using local languages.[107]

Supervision and guidance over the activities of republican and lower-echelon trade unions took place through two main channels. The trade union structure, rising hierarchically from the factory and local committee through regional committees and republican committees to the central union organization and the All-Union Central Council of Trade Unions, provided one chain of command for orders, directives, and instructions from the center to the lowest body. In addition, Communist Party members occupied strategic positions on all levels of the trade union organization and on the upper levels monopolized power. Figures for 1925, which are typical for trade unions in Central Asia during the twenties, show that all members of the presidiums of the republican trade union councils in Uzbekistan, Turkmenia, and Kirghizia were Party members. In the central administrations, and in the regional division in Kirghizia, two thirds or more of the members were Bolsheviks. Only in factory and local committees was the Party in a minority position.[108]

At the time of the revolution, trade union work in Central Asia was in an embryonic stage of growth and centered around the railroad shops. The membership was almost exclusively

---

[106] Z. Yefanov, "Professional'noe dvizhenie," in *Vsia Sredniaia Aziia: spravochnaia kniga na 1926 khoziaistvennyi god* (Tashkent, 1926), p. 327.

[107] *Professional'nye soiuzy v Srednei Azii 24–25 god: otchet Sr.-Aziatskogo Biuro V.Ts.S.P.S. k Pervoi Sredne-Aziatskoi Konferentsii Profsoiuzov* (Tashkent, 1925), p. 4.

[108] *Ibid.*, p. 49.

Russian and remained so throughout most of the civil war. No attempt was made to recruit native laborers until after Turkestan had been reunited with Central Russia in 1919. Even then it was the center, rather than local trade unions, which took the initiative. Through the political division of the "agit-train" *Red Orient,* the first native kustar' workers, employed by the state or co-ops, were drawn into trade union work.[109] The policy of recruiting kustar's as well as native industrial workers continued until the end of 1922. At that time native union membership had reached 34,752 in Turkestan and 11,088 in Bokhara, but an order from the All-Russian Central Council of Trade Unions to dismiss kustar's reduced the number to 11,697 in Turkestan and to less than a thousand in Bokhara. After the purge had been completed, the remaining native trade unionists composed less than 15 percent of the 64,000 organized workers in Central Asia.[110]

A new membership campaign in 1924 brought total trade union strength in Central Asia up to 112,853 and the strength of the native contingent up to 31,516. Among the unions the Agricultural and Forestry Workers' union (Rabzemles) received the greatest influx of native workers, increasing its native strength from 481 to 9,051. Of the other unions, only mining, leather working, food industry, building trades, textiles, railways, motor transport, education, and soviet workers had a thousand or more native members.[111] During the following years, labor union strength developed rapidly and 238,029 union members were counted in the 1927 census. Of these, 78,906 members were natives of Central Asia (67,120 Uzbeks, 5,564 Turcomans, and 6,222 Kirghiz). In spite of this increase, native workers still occupied a minority position—a situation attributable more to the small numbers of native industrial workers than to a lack of zeal in recruitment. Only in the

---

[109] Safarov, *Kolonial'naia revoliutsiia: opyt Turkestana,* pp. 114–15.

[110] Turkestanskoe Biuro, V.Ts.S.P.S., *Rabota profsoiuzov Turkestana v novykh usloviiakh; otchet Turkbiuro V.Ts.S.P.S. IV Kraevoi Turkestanskoi Konferentsii Professional'nykh Soiuzov za vremia: aprel' 1922 g.-dekabr' 1923 g.* (Tashkent, 1923), pp. 4, 13, 15; Sredne-Aziatskoe Biuro, V.Ts.S.P.S., *Professional'nye soiuzy v Srednei Azii 24–25 god,* p. 45.

[111] Sredne-Aziatskoe Biuro, V.Ts.S.P.S., *Professional'nye soiuzy v Srednei Azii 24–25 god,* pp. 16, 21.

Rabzemles, where they outnumbered Europeans 33,478 to 17,-304,[112] did they form a majority.

Real efforts were nevertheless made to bring natives to the center of labor union activities. As early as 1923 they occupied 223 positions in the trade union apparatus in Turkestan. One was a member of the presidium of the Turkestan Bureau of the All-Russian Central Council of Trade Unions and thirteen sat on the presidiums of regional trade union councils.[113] Two years later, native trade unionists were occupying 632 positions—sixty-two of them in republican trade union councils—in the union apparatus of Turkmenia, Uzbekistan, and Kirghizia,[114] and by 1927 natives held 43.5 percent of the elective positions in the trade unions of Uzbekistan.[115]

The object behind the increase of native membership in the administrative and deliberative agencies of the trade unions was not merely to achieve "nationalization." It was designed rather to increase the influence of the unions—and through them the influence of the Communist Party—over native workers and the native population generally. The trade unions, as previously noted, had political as well as industrial tasks to perform; their effectiveness in the former capacity depended upon the trust which they were able to inspire in their members and in the whole society. Even with the wooing of native workers, the trade unions, as instruments through which the Soviet authority sought to organize close contact with the masses, operated under the burden of serious limitations. Except in the case of the Rabzemles, their role was limited to the towns. But even there the paucity of native proletarians and the restricted influence of trade unions suggested that trade unions did not provide a good base for the Soviet power in Central Asia.[116]

[112] Komissia po Izucheniiu Natsional'nogo Voprosa, Kommunisticheskaia Akademiia, *Natsional'naia politika V.K.P.(b) v tsifrakh*, p. 170; Mustapha Chokai-Ogly (Chokaiev), *Turkestan pod vlast'iu Sovetov* (Paris, 1935), pp. 28–29.
[113] Turkestanskoe Biuro, V.Ts.S.P.S., *Rabota profsoiuzov Turkestana v novykh usloviiakh*, p. 14.
[114] Sredne-Aziatskoe Biuro, V.Ts.S.P.S., *Professional'nye soiuzy v Srednei Azii 24–25 god*, p. 19.
[115] Mikhail Katsenelenbogen, "Ob 'uklonakh' v natsional'noi politike V.K.P.(b)," *Bol'shevik*, No. 22 (November 30, 1927), p. 26.
[116] G. Skalov, "Opyt klassovogo rassloeniia v usloviiakh Turkestana (soiuz 'Koshchi')," *Zhizn' Natsional'nostei*, No. 2 (1923), pp. 36–37.

THE PEASANT IN UNION: GROWTH AND DECLINE
OF THE KOSHCHI

The answer to the problem of mass organization in Central Asia lay in the rural areas and necessarily turned on the peasant, not the worker. The organization of regional branches of the Rab-zemles represented one approach, but the restriction of membership in that union to agricultural workers (hired laborers) limited its ability to influence the mass of the peasantry. The real solution to the problem was found through the formation of the Koshchi, a mixture of rural trade union and cooperative with a predominantly political character, which included landless and small peasants, agricultural workers, tenant farmers, share croppers, and village kustar's.

As a political tool of the Soviet authority, the Koshchi came to the fore only during the latter part of 1922. The original movement whence it sprang had apparently grown out of a disorganized ferment in the native villages of Central Asia. During the course of the civil war, peasant organizations such as the "Union of Kirghiz Poor and Agricultural Workers" in Jety-suisk, the "Union of Landless and Small Peasants and Share Croppers" in Syr-Daria, and "Unions of the Poorest Peasantry" in other localities had appeared in many parts of Turkestan,[117] only to be ignored by the Tashkent Soviet. After the reunification of Turkestan with Central Russia, Moscow quickly recognized their influence. In September, 1920, shortly after the Fifth Congress of the Communist Party of Turkestan, the plenum of the central committee decreed the formation of a "Union of Toiling Peasants," the Koshchi, and directed it to organize the rural proletarian and semiproletarian masses for the purpose of "promoting class stratification in the village, kishlak, and aul." [118]

The Tenth Congress of Soviets of Turkestan, which met in

[117] A. Chanyshev, "O soiuzakh 'Koshchi,'" Sovetskoe Stroitel'stvo, Nos. 4–5 (1926), p. 124.

[118] Ilias Alkin, Sredniaia Aziia: ekonomiko-geograficheskii ocherk Kara-Kalpakstana, Kirgizstana, Tadzhikistana, Turkmenistana i Uzbekistana (Moscow, 1931), I, 355–56.

October, 1921, also took cognizance of the Koshchi, defining it as a "special type of trade union in the kishlaks and auls" and calling upon it "to effect the political organization of the native semiproletarian masses . . . and to pave the way for their conscious transition to Communist construction." [119] Although the congress cautioned the Koshchi against "assuming functions of state power," it specifically enjoined it to guard against the infiltration of hostile elements into Soviet agencies and "to render assistance to the soviets in the execution of all ordinary tasks and enactments." To enable the Koshchi to fulfill these functions, the congress bound it closely to the Soviet apparatus. All members of the kishlak soviets and executive committees were required to join the Koshchi. It was given the right to recommend the appointment of "responsible workers" on the aul, volost', and district levels. The Commissariat of Agriculture was instructed to invite members of Koshchi administrative boards to participate in the work of its institutions and enterprises and to include the chairmen of central, regional, and county Koshchi boards as members of the boards of its agencies on these levels. The congress also ordered the inclusion of "the most reliable and experienced members" of the Koshchi in punitive judicial agencies.[120]

Curiously, the Koshchi had not yet been formally organized when these instructions were issued. In fact, the congress itself suggested the convocation of a congress of Koshchi and the formation of a central organ.[121] At the end of 1921, jointly with the meeting of a congress of the agencies of the Commissariat of Agriculture, the first Koshchi Congress met and elected a central committee, consisting of eighteen members and seven candidates.[122] In March, 1922, the government of Turkestan ac-

[119] From a resolution of the Tenth Congress of Soviets of Turkestan on unions of the poor. Text reproduced in *Zhizn' Natsional'nostei*, No. 21 (119) (October 10, 1921).

[120] *Ibid.;* also S. Itsyna, "Bedniatskie organizatsii na Sovetskom Vostoke i ikh zadachi," *Sovetskoe Stroitel'stvo*, Nos. 2–3 (1925), pp. 220–21.

[121] Itsyna, "Bedniatskie organizatsii na Sovetskom Vostoke i ikh zadachi," *Sovetskoe Stroitel'stvo*, Nos. 2–3 (1925), p. 221.

[122] Chanyshev, "O soiuzakh 'Koshchi,'" *Sovetskoe Stroitel'stvo*, Nos. 4–5 (1926), pp. 124–25.

corded the Koshchi official status through the promulgation of a special charter of organization.[123] This identified the Koshchi as a "professional-political organization" of the rural proletariat and charged it with promoting class differentiation in the villages, indoctrinating the rural masses politically, encouraging friendly relations between the native and European poor, and eliminating the dichotomy between the urban proletariat and the village poor. The charter accorded the union special privileges in its relationship with the government and assigned it quasi-administrative duties. It guaranteed the Koshchi representation in the colleges of the Republic Central Council of National Economy, Commissariat of Agriculture, and Commissariat of Supply, and, where necessary, in other central agencies. It gave the union the right of consultative voice in the Council of People's Commissars and the Economic Council in matters concerning the Koshchi. In the localities, the Koshchi was bound to assist economic agencies in the promulgation of governmental enactments, particularly when these dealt with agrarian law, water distribution, and produce taxes.

The charter also fixed the terms of membership, opening the union to small and landless peasants, small herders, rural hired laborers, kustar's and rural semiproletarians, and to members of collective farms which had not adopted a regular charter. Expressly debarred were hirers of labor, rentiers, private traders and commercial middlemen, mystics and employees of religious cults, and persons who had worked as foremen on the estates of beys. The charter failed to establish an explicit organizational framework for the Koshchi and one emerged only with the convocation of the Second Congress of Koshchi in February, 1924. This congress established a hierarchical structure, parallel to the soviet and Communist Party edifice, from the village committee through district and regional committees to an All-Turkestan Central Committee. In addition, the congress effected a close and continual working arrangement with the Party and the government by offering membership to the chairman of the

[123] "Polozhenie o Koshchi." Decree No. 27 of the Turkestan Central Executive Committee, dated May 14, 1922. *Sobranie Uzakonenii i rasporiazhenii Turkestanskoi Respubliki,* May 15, 1922.

soviet and the secretary of the Party committee in the Koshchi committee on each level.[124]

The authority of the Koshchi grew as a quasi-administrative and political organ of Soviet control in the villages. By the spring of 1924 it had gained control over the committees of peasant mutual aid and had extended its influence to the co-operative movement in Central Asia. In the former instance, the Central Executive Committee and the Council of People's Commissars of Turkestan in December, 1923, transferred all committees of peasant and socialized mutual aid with their funds from the jurisdiction of the Commissariat of Social Security to that of the Koshchi.[125] Acting on the basis of this decree, the Koshchi established mutual aid divisions. Membership in them was independent of membership in the Koshchi, but the division chairmen were required to join the Koshchi and the sections were compelled to present their acts to the Koshchi for confirmation.[126]

Both these grants of quasi-administrative and political power to the Koshchi and the official encouragement of the extension of Koshchi activity into every important aspect of rural life were aimed at one specific goal—preparation of the Central Asiatic countryside for a sweeping land reform and for a complete reversal of traditional agrarian relationships.[127] It is noteworthy in this connection that the Communist Party manifested its greatest interest in the Koshchi on two occasions. The first was in 1920–21, the period immediately prior to and during the land reform in Semirechie. The second was in 1924–26, when preparations were going forward for the great land reform in Central Asia. In both cases the Soviet government utilized the Koshchi as the primary instrumentality to weaken the traditional bonds of village unity and to drive a wedge between the customary leaders and the masses. After the land reform the Koshchi was shorn of its powers and stripped of much of its

[124] Chanyshev, "O soiuzakh 'Koshchi,'" *Sovetskoe Stroitel'stvo*, Nos. 4–5 (1926), p. 126.

[125] *Ibid.*, p. 125.

[126] Itsyna, "Bedniatskie organizatsii na Sovetskom Vostoke i ikh zadachi," *Sovetskoe Stroitel'stvo*, Nos. 2–3 (1925), p. 225.

[127] See below, pp. 330–32.

membership; prior to that time it had received a large measure of support from the government and the Party.

This was illustrated clearly in the Party handling of a controversy in 1924–25 between the Koshchi and the Rabzemles over jurisdiction in the recruitment of agricultural workers. The dispute arose during a drive in 1924 by the Turkestan Bureau of the Central Council of Trade Unions to strengthen the Rabzemles and to expand its influence over farm laborers. Originally, the Rabzemles had paid little attention to organizing the rural proletariat and comprised merely employees of the Commissariat of Agriculture and scattered employees of state farms.[128] The Koshchi, on the other hand, had made intensive efforts to recruit these workers and had established a special organizational division to deal with their problems.

As soon as the success of the Koshchi movement among the farm hands became apparent, the Central Council of Trade Unions called a conference of Koshchi and Rabzemles leaders and arranged for the transfer of leadership in the division to the Rabzemles. It was agreed that the chairman of the Rabzemles on each administrative level should take over the chairmanship of the Koshchi farm laborer division on that level and should exercise the right of decisive vote on all questions concerning agricultural workers which might arise in the committees of the Koshchi. As one result of this agreement, membership in the Rabzemles increased from 3,676 to 16,520 in six months' time (January–October, 1924).[129]

Another result was the development of a backstage struggle over control of the farm hands which finally drew the criticism of *Pravda Vostoka* (April 15, 1925) that it "complicates and sometimes directly hampers the work of the Rabzemles." The central point of the dispute was a Rabzemles effort—on the ground that farm hands had peculiar class interests which were distinct from, and frequently quite the opposite of, those of the peasantry as a whole—to eliminate the Koshchi as an organizing

[128] Turkestanskoe Biuro, V.Ts.S.P.S., *Rabota profsoiuzov Turkestana v novykh usloviiakh*, p. 15.

[129] Sredne-Aziatskoe Biuro, V.Ts.S.P.S., *Professional'nye soiuzy v Srednei Azii 24–25 god*, pp. 12–13.

medium for agricultural workers. Only the intervention of the Central Committee of the Party in Turkestan defeated the attempt. Demanding that the agricultural worker maintain membership in both organizations, the Central Committee insisted that the Soviet authority would fail in the village "if the most revolutionary stratum is removed from the sphere of struggle." But the Party did not close the door completely. With an eye to a future time when it might be expedient to stress differences of interest between the farm hands and small peasant landowners, it added cryptically, "Inasmuch as political tasks have not yet been solved, the question of the withdrawal of the agricultural workers from the Koshchi cannot be raised." [130]

The Koshchi was much too important a tool of class struggle for the Party to entertain proposals which would ultimately destroy the organization. The dispute had arisen, moreover, on the eve of the Central Asiatic land reform. At this time practical Soviet policy required achievement of the utmost solidarity among all ranks of the peasantry in preparation for the forthcoming struggle to dispossess the beys and kulaks. Nonetheless, Bolshevik insistence that the integrity of the Koshchi be maintained was not tantamount to a vote of confidence in the organization. The Party was never wholly satisfied with it and repeatedly complained that it was infiltrated with "hostile elements" and interfered in regular administrative and Party work. The former charge became a constant refrain throughout the life of the organization, but the Party reserved its criticism on the latter account until the land reform was well under way and the usefulness of the Koshchi as a political weapon was nearing an end.

There appears to be little question that infiltration presented a major problem for the Koshchi. It arose largely from the rapid growth of the organization. In Semirechie alone, membership in the Koshchi climbed from 40,000 to 80,000 between the autumn of 1921 and the summer of 1922. By autumn, 1922, six regional, thirty-two county, over 200 volost', and approximately 2,000 kishlak and aul organs were operating, with a membership

[130] Itsyna, "Bedniatskie organizatsii na Sovetskom Vostoke i ikh zadachi," *Sovetskoe Stroitel'stvo,* Nos. 2–3 (1925), pp. 228–29.

of 260,000.[131] The rapid increase in membership had two unwelcome features, which led to a rising clamor of protest in the Communist Party. The majority of the new members were small and middle peasants who were able to "capture" many local organs on the strength of their numbers alone. This evoked the criticism that the Koshchi had ceased to "represent the interests of the agricultural proletariat" [132] and was no longer a truly revolutionary force in the village. Secondly, "class enemies" of the rural poor were able to infiltrate Koshchi organs and, according to Communist charges, seized control of them in many instances.[133] In Kirghizia, the influence of beys and manaps (tribal leaders) became so widespread that the Party ordered the Koshchi there disbanded, and even after a reorganization in March, 1926, the Party claimed that one fifth of the members were "hangers-on." [134]

As soon as the land reform was well under way, a storm of Party criticism also arose over the political activities of the Koshchi. Critics charged that Koshchi committees were replacing the soviets as organs of power in many localities, that they had taken "command" of the economic council and the cooperatives, and that the Koshchi was seeking to become a "supreme organ." Everywhere, a resolution of the Fourth Plenum of the Central Committee of the Uzbek Communist Party declared, "the Koshchi is interfering in Party work." [135] At the same time, the complaint was voiced that the Koshchi had lost its significance and that it had become separated from its mass base. According to one critic, the Koshchi had fulfilled its assignments.

[131] This figure is probably excessive. That falsification of registration records was not uncommon is attested to by Skalov's complaint that the rolls of some of the organizations included a "huge percentage of dead souls." See Skalov, "Opyt klassovogo rassloeniia v usloviiakh Turkestana (soiuz 'Koshchi')," *Zhizn' Natsional'nostei,* No. 2 (1923), p. 37.

[132] Itsyna, "Bedniatskie organizatsii na Sovetskom Vostoke i ikh zadachi," *Sovetskoe Stroitel'stvo,* Nos. 2–3 (1925), p. 222.

[133] From a report of Ikramov, "Itogi i ocherednye zadachi," before the Second Plenum of the Central Committee of the Communist Party of Uzbekistan (February, 1926). Reproduced in I. S. Kraskin (ed.), *Zemel'no-vodnaia reforma v Srednei Azii: sbornik materialov* (Moscow, 1927), p. 46.

[134] P. Kushner (Knyshev), *Gornaia Kirgiziia (sotsiologicheskaia razvedka)* (Moscow, 1929), pp. 110–11.

[135] S. Itsyna, "Organizatsiia krest'ianskoi bednoty v natsional'nykh respublikakh," *Vlast' Sovetov,* IX, No. 3 (January 17, 1926), 10.

It had organized the poor and middle peasants and farm hands against the beys and paved the way for the land reform, and it had assisted in the establishment of a local soviet apparatus. Now, he said, the Koshchi should become a "social organization." [136]

The same view prevailed in the Central Asiatic Bureau of the Communist Party, which in a resolution of its Twelfth Plenum (January, 1927) declared that the "state-administrative functions [of the Koshchi] have become a hindrance to further development." Repeating the charge that the Koshchi had overstepped the limits of its authority and had entered into competition with the soviet apparatus, the Central Asiatic Bureau stripped it of all administrative functions and transformed it into a "voluntary social organization." It still maintained the task of protecting the "interests of the small and landless peasantry" but its political activity was limited to the struggle against "bureaucratism." [137] This resolution put an end to the Koshchi as an effective political force in the Central Asiatic village. However, the Koshchi was not disbanded (it was still in existence in 1933);[138] it had merely ceased to be important in the political life of Soviet Central Asia.

It was through all the organizations examined here—Party, state, and public—that the Soviet authority promulgated its national policy in Central Asia. The Party, as the leading organ, made policy and drew up the strategical and tactical plans of operation. Governmental agencies, the soviets and the administrative agencies, translated Party policy into law. The mass organizations encouraged public cooperation in the fulfillment of Soviet goals and on special occasions initiated "spontaneous" activity in favor of important innovations or created the "elemental" demand for change which often preceded the promulgation of important legislation.

[136] E. Cherniavskii, *Sailaular-saili: prazdnik vyborov* (Tashkent, 1927), pp. 33–34.

[137] Text of resolution on reorganization of the Koshchi in Sredne-Aziatskoe Biuro Ts.K. V.K.P.(b), *Rezoliutsii i Postanovleniia XII Plenuma (24–27 ianvaria 1927 g.)* (Tashkent, n.d.), pp. 23–26.

[138] An explanatory note in the protocols of the Tenth Congress of the Communist Party, which were published in 1933, refers to the Koshchi as a still active organization. *Desiatyi S'ezd R.K.P.(b)*, p. 859.

The hierarchical structure of all these organizations and the extreme centralism under which they operated brought them under the close guidance and supervision of the center and facilitated coordination of their operations. Uniformity, growing out of this central control, characterized their activity. This was precisely what the Communist Party had envisioned. Using these organizations as instrumentalities to manipulate and coerce the masses according to plan, the Party was able to promote a consistent and undeviating advance toward achievement of its own objective in Central Asia—the fashioning of a classless society out of the clay of backward, semifeudal political, social, and economic relationships.

IV

POLITICAL EQUALITY: THE "NATIONALIZATION" OF ADMINISTRATION

◆

THE PRINCIPAL objective of the Communist Party in Central Asia during the postrevolutionary period was the construction of a solid footing of mass native support under the superstructure of Soviet rule. Neither the initial seizure of power nor the later extension of central control to the region had established this foundation.

Broadly speaking, Bolshevik doctrine regarded the fulfillment of three conditions—the overthrow of "exploiting" classes, the establishment of a proletarian dictatorship, and the implantation of the soviet form of government—as essential to the solution of the political aspect of the nationality question. During the revolution and civil war the Bolsheviks had installed their dictatorship in Central Asia. But they had not succeeded in removing anti-Soviet elements from all places of authority and influence, nor had they drawn significant numbers of the indigenous nationalities into soviet or Bolshevik Party work. If anything, the policies of the Tashkent Soviet had tended to unite Moslems of all ranks against the new regime and its agencies. Even those native governments which Soviet troops had brought into power in the principalities of Khiva and Bokhara resisted Bolshevik demands for extension of the soviet system and elimination of survivals of the old political order. Hence, it fell to central Soviet and Party agencies in the 1920's to work out a practical policy stern enough to permit the removal of hostile elements, whether Moslem or European, from places of influence, yet conciliatory enough to win native support for the Soviet regime.

Stalin drew the outlines of this policy in an article for *Zhizn' Natsional'nostei* of October, 1920. "In order to liquidate mistrust," he reasoned, "we must first of all help the population of the borderlands to liberate itself from survivals of the feudal-patriarchal yoke." Administrative measures alone, Stalin argued, would not suffice to establish the kind of society which Bolshevik doctrine envisioned or to enlist the cooperation of the non-Russian "toiling masses." Success depended upon the ability of the Soviet government to give the common people "a taste of the material good of the revolution." [1] While Stalin's formula indicated a growing concern in high Party circles over the course of events in the minority republics and regions of the Soviet state, it did not represent new thinking or presage a new policy toward the non-Russian peoples. The same concept expressed in different terms had been implicit in the Declaration of the Rights of the Peoples of Russia, the Appeal to the Working Moslems of Russia and the Near East, and other early acts of the Soviet government. And Stalin, in a previous Appeal to the Soviets of Kazan, Ufa, Orenburg, and Ekaterinburg, had stressed the importance of involving the toilers of the borderlands in "the process of revolutionary development" so that the soviet form of government would become "popular" and the laboring masses "socialist." [2]

Disregard of this counsel had constituted the principal transgression of the original Soviet government in Turkestan. From 1917 the Bolsheviks in Central Asia had striven to extend and consolidate the Soviet order in the region, but their interpretation of the principle was colored by the social atmosphere in which they operated. Existing as tiny European islands amid an alien sea of Turkic peoples, fearful lest these peoples unite to destroy them, they were inclined at the outset to interpret the

[1] J. V. Stalin, *Sochineniia* (Moscow, 1946—), IV, 357.
[2] *Ibid.*, IV, 75.

class struggle as a conflict between Moslem and European and to minimize class differences within the European community for the sake of solidarity against the greater danger.

The emergence of a competing native government in Kokand and the later rise of Basmachism convinced the Tashkent government that the price of survival was a ruthless campaign to wipe out every vestige of native opposition. And this campaign only served to enhance the native distrust and hatred of Russians, which half a century of Russian mastery and exploitation had ingrained into the non-Russian community, and to focus this enmity upon the Soviet system. Moslems of all classes—including groups which were potentially friendly to the ideals of the October Revolution—rallied to the standards of the most active and resolute enemies of the regime. Even Communist-sponsored conferences of Moslems passed resolutions condemning the excesses of the Tashkent government and protesting against Soviet "colonialism." At the Congress of the Peoples of the East in the summer of 1920, the delegation from Turkestan embarrassed Zinoviev and the Soviet government by complaining that depredations committed by Russians in Central Asia were "alienating the laboring masses from the Soviet authority" and demanding that the principles of freedom, equality, and brotherhood be put into practice.[3]

THE WAR AGAINST NATIONALISM

Prior to the Russian Revolution the spirit of nationalism in the non-Russian community of Central Asia had been confined to a small and uninfluential group of intellectuals. But the disappointments of the revolution and the spoliations committed and permitted by Soviet officials and the Red Guard in the region gave the ideal the nourishment it required, and it soon permeated the ranks of important segments of the Moslem population. Not only was nationalism the cornerstone of the Kokand Autonomous Government and a binding force of the Basmachi movement, but it lay at the root of the revolutionary

---

[3] See especially the speech of the Turkestanian delegate, Narbutabekov, in *Pervyi S'ezd Narodov Vostoka. Baku, 1–8 sent. 1920 g. stenograficheskie otchety* (Petrograd, 1920), pp. 87–89.

movements in Bokhara and Khiva. Among educated Moslems it
was a dominant motivating force after the revolution. Through
Bolshevik members of this group—many of whom had participated in the Jadid or Westernizing movement among the
Turkic peoples—nationalism penetrated the native sections of
the Party.

During the initial period of revolution and civil war, the
Bolsheviks were too deeply involved in the crusade to destroy
the "national councils" and other anti-Soviet nationalist movements to concern themselves seriously with manifestations of
nationalism within Party ranks. But, when the tide of battle
had turned in favor of the Soviet regime, they began a new
campaign to purify borderland Party organizations of this influence. Stalin opened the attack at a Congress of Turkic Communists in January, 1921, and continued at the Tenth and
Twelfth Party Congresses, the Fourth Conference with Responsible Workers, and at other public occasions to warn against the
"national deviation." [4] At its Tenth Congress, the Communist
Party itself adopted a strong resolution condemning "native
Communist deviations," but the resolution seems not to have
cured the disease. Frequent complaints that Jadidists were "con-
taminating [the Party] with a petit-bourgeois psychology" [5] and
that local Party organizations, in their rush to increase membership, were admitting "philistine nationalistic elements" and
"careerists" [6] indicate that the borderland Party organizations
hesitated to eliminate "deviationists" from their ranks. At the
Fourth Conference of the Central Committee of the Russian
Communist Party with Responsible Workers in 1923, Stalin
again demanded the institution of a "decisive struggle against
nationalism in the Party." [7] A flurry of local activity followed
in which avowed nationalists were driven out of the Party. But
Stalin's renewed warning in 1925 to students of the Communist
University of the Toilers of the East against "hidden national-

[4] Stalin, *Sochineniia*, V, 2, 40, 188–90, 192–93, 248–52, 266–68, 301–12.

[5] S. Muraveiskii, "V bor'be za kadry v Srednei Azii," *Kommunisticheskoe
Revoliutsiia*, No. 17 (September, 1926), pp. 64–65.

[6] Stalin, *Sochineniia*, V, 28–29.

[7] *Ibid.*, V, 310.

ism" [8] shows that the deviation persisted in the Party. And, in fact, the charge of nationalism still figured prominently in the trials of leading Central Asian Bolsheviks during the Great Purge in the mid-thirties.[9]

Outside the Party, nationalism developed in two directions, both of which were antithetical to the aims and principles of the Soviet state. On the one hand, nationalism appeared to Communists to encourage the growth of local particularism, all kinds of opposition to central interference in local affairs, and, in its worst form, the development of what Stalin called "local chauvinism." In essence, these were held to be manifestations not only of the traditional distrust of Russians but of the "clashing interests of the bourgeoisie" of competing national groups.[10] Although local nationalism was considered initially to be of minor significance—the native bourgeoisie, it was claimed, was weak and without influence—it began to draw the attention of high Party officials after the promulgation of the New Economic Policy. At the Twelfth Party Congress, Stalin insisted that the "tendency" be "nipped in the bud." [11] It was, he said, a major disruptive force within the national republics and especially within those republics with a mixed population. Referring specifically to Turkestan, Bokhara, and Khorezm, he charged that "national" discrimination was leading to internal conflicts

[8] *Ibid.*, VII, 143.

[9] If the revelations of defendants in these trials are true, nationalism extended even into the highest Party ranks in the borderland regions. Khodzhaev, who had been president of the Council of Nazirs of the Bokharan People's Republic, chairman of the Council of People's Commissars of the Uzbek SSR, and a leader in the Communist Party in Central Asia, confessed membership in "Milli Ittikhad" (National Alliance), a nationalist organization in Bokhara, and a "Group of Eighteen," which, he declared, consisted of prominent Uzbek government officials who opposed the land reform in Central Asia. Through these organizations principally, he admitted supporting a course of action aimed at eventual dismemberment of the USSR along national-territorial lines. See People's Commissariat of Justice of the USSR, *Report of Court Proceedings in the Case of the Anti-Soviet "Bloc of Rights and Trotskyites." Verbatim Report* (Moscow, 1938), pp. 212–16. It is noteworthy that nothing of these "counter-revolutionary organizations" reached public print in the Soviet press during or immediately after the period of their alleged activity.

[10] G. Broido, "Turkestanskie Problemy," *Zhizn' Natsional'nostei*, No. 23 (80) (July 18, 1920).

[11] *Dvenadtsatyi S'ezd Rossiiskoi Kommunisticheskoi Partii (bol'shevikov), 17–25 aprelia 1923 g.* (Moscow, 1923), p. 447.

which weakened the Soviet regime and threatened to undermine the bonds of internationalism created by the revolution.[12]

That friction among the various tribal units inhabiting Central Asia hindered Bolshevik efforts to consolidate the Soviet system in the region is a matter of record. But it is doubtful that intertribal animosities expressed nationalistic ambitions or the conflict of interests of competing "bourgeois" elements. They seem rather to have sprung from three sources: the historical conflicts between the nomadic tribes and the agricultural peoples, the traditional intertribal struggle for control of the oases, and the inequality of land tenure which emerged from the historical sequence of tribal settlement on the land. Thus, the Uzbek peoples who had turned to agriculture earliest had preempted the best lands and seized control of the oases. The Uzbeks, moreover, had nurtured a class of traders, merchants, and usurers who preyed on the less cultivated Turcomans, Tajiks, and Kirghiz. Nationalism, which, after all, is expressive of the desire to form a national state, appears to have been of minor importance in the intertribal disputes which periodically marred the peace of Central Asia.

In point of fact, nationalism in Central Asia had developed and manifested itself primarily in the Pan-Turanian movement, which was the direct antithesis of tribal exclusiveness. Unlike the local nationalism which Stalin complained of at the Twelfth Party Congress, Central Asian nationalism sought the unification of the Turkic peoples and the formation of a single Turkic state which would gather together the scattered Turkic tribes from Tataria and Transcaucasia to the Altai mountains. Based on the premise that Central Asia was divided into two natural tribal divisions—the Turks and the Tajiks (an Iranian people) —the Pan-Turanian movement in effect opposed a racial or linguistic internationalism to the class internationalism of the Communist Party. And this ideal appealed more to the native intelligentsia and to the mass of the native population than did the theory of working class unity—a theory which, in the absence of a native working class, could hardly expect to win mass support on its own merits. Moreover, although Pan-Turkism

[12] *Ibid.*, pp. 441–47, 596–98.

was essentially secular in its approach to tribal unification,[13] its close association with the Pan-Moslem movement after the October Revolution won it the support of influential members of the Moslem religious community and the traditional ruling class.

Historically, the movement had developed in Turkey as an outgrowth of the Ottoman defeat in the Balkan wars. The Young Turks, aware that the Empire was doomed, had replaced the ideal of Ottoman unity with that of the establishment of a homogeneous Turkic state which eventually would unify all the Turkic peoples of the Near East and Central Asia. Adherents of the Jadid movement were mainly responsible for the introduction of the idea into Central Asia. Turkish prisoners-of-war interned in Turkestan during World War I gave further impetus to the movement.[14] But it was confined to a relatively small group of native intellectuals until the revolutionary events of 1917 inspired the Turkic peoples with the hope of liberation from the Russian colonial yoke. Between the February and October Revolutions, the Pan-Turanian movement, which expressed itself in the demand for national cultural autonomy within the Russian state, gained wide support among influential native groups in Turkestan.

After the Bolshevik Revolution, the Pan-Turanian movement acquired greater momentum. Two new factors inspired native nationalist groups to translate their demands for national recognition into a program of action. Unlike the February Revolution, which had promised to respect the national rights of the non-Russian peoples and to refrain from interfering with the structure of native society, the Bolshevik Revolution sought to eliminate existing social, economic, and political institutions and to replace them with socialist institutions. The very threat of social revolution was enough to arouse the hostility of nearly the whole of the indigenous population, which either did not

[13] It should be noted, however, that the tribal division corresponded to a religious division. The Turkic tribes universally accepted the Sunni doctrine while the Tajiks had brought Shiah sectarianism with them on their migration from Persia.

[14] S. Radzhapov, "Etapy razvitiia Sovetskogo gosudarstvennogo stroia v Srednei Azii," Sovetskoe Gosudarstvo i Pravo, No. 11 (November, 1948), pp. 63–64.

understand the revolution or feared its consequences, and to rally it behind those forces which sought separation from the Russian state. In addition, Soviet Russia's repeated promises to respect the right of the non-Russian peoples to self-determination—promises which conflicted with the obvious reluctance of the Soviet government in Turkestan to honor the pledge—gave further momentum to the Turkic nationalist movement.

From this time forward the ideal of Turkic unification lay at the root of every anti-Soviet native movement in Central Asia. It found expression in the Kokand Autonomous Government, which not only claimed to represent all the peoples of Turkestan but was in fact constituted by and composed of delegates of all the major tribal units of the region. Although the Tashkent Soviet dispersed this government in March, 1918, the Pan-Turanian movement did not crumble but actually succeeded in expressing itself with greater vigor in the Basmachi movement. With the arrival of Enver Pasha in Central Asia in 1921 and his assumption of command of the Basmachi forces, Pan-Turkism achieved its greatest popularity and succeeded in winning recruits not only from groups in opposition to the Soviet regime but from native members of the Soviet government and the Communist Party as well.[15]

At the outset, the Communist Party viewed the nationalism of Central Asia and other borderland regions largely as a consequence of "Great Russian chauvinism" and of the careless attitude of Russian officials and Party workers toward peculiarities in the customary, cultural, and social life of less developed peoples. Toward destroying this tendency, which Bolsheviks re-

---

[15] In 1919, a conference of Moslem Communists had opposed the division of the Turkic tribes into "small individual republics" and supported the formation of a unified "Turkic Soviet Republic." Georgii Safarov, *Kolonial'naia revoliutsiia: opyt Turkestana* (Moscow, 1921), p. 110. A number of natives who occupied positions of trust in the Soviet government and the Communist Party deserted outright to the Basmachi. Others established contact with the Basmachi and began to use their offices to sabotage the Soviet regime and to conduct espionage against the Red Army. Georges Agabekov, *OGPU, the Russian Secret Terror* (New York, 1931), p. 20. A third group, led by Sultan-Galiev, attempted secretly to divert the revolutionary movement in Central Asia into nationalistic channels by plotting the establishment of an Eastern International aimed at unification of the Turkic peoples within and without the Soviet state. Stalin, *Sochineniia*, V, 301–6.

garded as an evil heritage from the past, the Party first turned its attention. As early as the Eighth Party Congress, Lenin had warned against Communist attempts to erase national distinctions by force,[16] and Stalin took up the struggle at later Party congresses and conferences.[17]

After 1919 the accusation of Great Russian chauvinism did become the basis for the dismissal of numerous Soviet and Party officials in the borderlands. But the initial effort to stamp out this deviation failed. At the Twelfth Party Congress, Stalin, demanding a vigorous campaign to eliminate it, declared that Great Russian chauvinism was increasing, not diminishing. Unless this "rankest kind of nationalism which strives to obliterate all that is not Russian, to gather all the threads of administration into the hands of Russians, and to crush everything that is not Russian" were overcome, he said, the Russian proletariat might forfeit the confidence which it had inspired among the non-Russian peoples during the revolution.[18]

Although the congress adopted a resolution condemning Russian chauvinism and demanding a "decisive struggle" against it,[19] effective measures to eliminate the chauvinistic elements from places of authority in the borderland regions appear not to have been taken. At the Fourth National Conference with Responsible Workers in June, 1923, Khodzhanov and Ikramov, two prominent Central Asian Bolsheviks, protested that Turkestan still remained in colonial subjugation.[20] And throughout the twenties, complaints against the highhandedness of Russian officials, against affronts to the national dignity of the Central Asian peoples, and against the outright plundering of the native population were voiced regularly in the press and in the debates of the soviets of the region.[21]

---

[16] V. I. Lenin, *Sochineniia* (1st ed., Moscow, 1919—), XIX, 234–35.

[17] Stalin, *Sochineniia*, V, 27, 189–90, 238–39.

[18] It is of note that Stalin ascribed the growth of chauvinism to the New Economic Policy, to the growth of trade, to the partial revival of capitalism, and to a growing petit-bourgeois psychology. See *ibid.*, V, 239, 245.

[19] *Vse-Soiuznaia Kommunisticheskaia Partiia v rezoliutsiiakh i resheniiakh s'ezdov, soveshchaniei i plenumov Tsentral'nogo Komiteta, 1898–1932* (4th ed., Moscow, 1932), I, 591.

[20] Stalin, *Sochineniia*, V, 306–7.

[21] For specific examples, see Agabekov, *OGPU, the Russian Secret Terror*, pp. 23–24; Mustapha Chokaiev, "Turkestan and the Soviet Regime," *Journal of the*

The failure of the central authorities to put a quick end to
Russian chauvinism in the borderlands can be ascribed largely
to their primary reliance upon administrative measures rather
than upon an effective educational program aimed at reorient-
ing Russian thinking in regard to the nationalities. During the
frequent purges of Party and Soviet officialdom in Central Asia,
the Bolsheviks did succeed in removing some of the worst
offenders from positions of authority. But the effect of these acts
was largely vitiated by Moscow's persistence in replacing them
with Russian administrative and military personnel who were
unacquainted with, and often contemptuous of, local customs
and peculiarities. It is noteworthy, moreover, that the Party in
later years became less insistent in its belief that Great Russian
chauvinism was the primary hindrance to solution of the nationality question.[22]

The original Party position had been based on the assump-

Royal Central Asian Society, XVIII (1931), 419; Mustapha Chokaiev, *Turkestan
pod Vlast'iu Sovetov* (Paris, 1935), pp. 16–17. The inability of the Soviet regime
to check manifestations of the Russian chauvinism in the border republics led
in 1927 to accusations that the decisions of the Twelfth Party Congress and the
Fourth National Conference were being ignored and that Russian "bureaucratism" had succeeded in damaging good relations between the center and the
borderlands. Mikh. Katsenelenbogen, "Ob 'uklonakh' v natsional'noi politike
V.K.P.(b)," *Bol'shevik,* No. 22 (November 30, 1927), p. 19. The Trotskyist opposition made these accusations, to be sure, but they were also confirmed in a
resolution of the Twelfth Plenum of the Central Asiatic Bureau of the Communist Party, which criticized the failure of local Party bodies to struggle consistently against the deviation. Sredne-Aziatskoe Biuro, Ts.K., V.K.P.(b), *Rezoliutsii i Postanovleniia XII Plenum (24–27 ianvaria 1927 g.)* (Tashkent, n.d.),
p. 6. Moreover, the question came up at the Fifteenth Party Congress and
became the subject of condemnatory resolutions at this and later congresses.
*Piatnadtsatyi S'ezd Vsesoiuznoi Kommunisticheskoi Partii (b), 2–19 dekabria
1927 g. stenograficheskii otchet* (Moscow, 1928), pp. 146–47. See also *Shestnadtsatyi
S'ezd Vsesoiuznoi Kommunisticheskoi Partii (b), 26 iunia–18 iulia 1930 g.* (Moscow, 1931), pp. 105, 430–32; *Semnadtsatyi S'ezd Vsesoiuznoi Kommunisticheskoi
Partii (b), 26 ianvaria–10 fevralia 1934 g. stenograficheskii otchet* (Moscow,
1934), pp. 70–72, 141.

[22] Stalin in the thirties turned against the application of "mechanical"
formulae to national problems and in 1934 laid down the rule that "the question of which is the major danger (Great Russian chauvinism or local nationalism) in the sphere of the national question is determined not by futile and
formal controversies, but by a Marxist analysis of the situation at the given
moment, and by a study of the mistakes that have been committed in this
sphere." Stalin, *Marxism and the National and Colonial Question* (New York,
n.d.), pp. 267–68.

tion that nationalism in the non-Russian regions was essentially
a reaction to Great Russian chauvinism and that it would cease
to be popular as soon as Russian oppression and activities associated with it had been eliminated. Experience, however,
forced the Bolsheviks to modify this belief, and, at the Twelfth
Party Congress in 1923, Stalin insisted, over the objections of
Bukharin and Rakovskii, that the Party take resolute action directly against nationalism. Local nationalism, although "in the
long run" a form of defense against Great Russian nationalism,
he said, was developing in some republics into "aggressive nationalism" and was beginning to pose a real threat to the friendship and unity of the Soviet peoples. Nor, he pointed out in
reply to an objection by Bukharin, could the Russians hope to
win the confidence of the non-Russian peoples by ignoring local
nationalism and by placing themselves artificially "in an inferior
position" in relation to other nationalities.

We cannot but wage a struggle on two fronts [he warned] because
only by struggle on two fronts—with Great Russian chauvinism,
on the one hand . . . and with local chauvinism, on the other—
can we achieve success; because without this two-sided struggle no
union of the Russian and non-Russian workers and peasants can
be secured.[23]

This interchange marked the first full-scale debate at an All-
Russian Party Congress on the means to be employed in overcoming local nationalism. But at a much earlier date the Soviet
government had adopted a program aimed principally at abat-
ing the nationalistic spirit in the borderlands and at diverting
the constructive aspects of local nationalism into channels useful
to the Soviet regime. From the October Revolution forward, the
Bolsheviks, both at the center and at the localities, had employed military measures to eliminate "bourgeois nationalists"
who openly opposed the Communist dictatorship. But as soon
as they had consolidated themselves in power, Soviet leaders had
supplemented military action with a program of conciliation
designed to wean the non-Russian masses away from their cus-

[23] *Dvenadtsatyi S'ezd Rossiiskoi Kommunisticheskoi Partii (b)*, pp. 446–47,
596–98.

tomary leaders, to develop a pro-Soviet current within the ranks of the native intellectual group,[24] and to replace the symbols of national struggle with those of class struggle and Communist internationalism.[25]

Early indications of this policy appeared during 1919 when a series of warnings were dispatched from Moscow demanding an end to the reckless policy of requisition and oppression which the Tashkent Soviet had adopted in regard to Moslems in Turkestan. By 1920 the policy had become precise. In a Circular Letter of the Russian Communist Party of June 29, 1920, to the Communist Party of Turkestan, the center demanded that local Bolsheviks exercise the "greatest prudence" in dealing with the native peoples and that they base their policies upon a recognition that "outlived prejudices are overcome by the toiling masses in the course of practical Soviet construction." [26] That this dictum was meant to apply generally to all the non-Russian regions of the Soviet state became immediately clear. Speaking at the Second Congress of the Comintern, Lenin insisted that Bolsheviks should treat "with special caution and special attention" survivals of national sentiment among oppressed peoples and suggested the advisability of "certain concessions with a view to rapidly removing" national distrust and prejudices.[27] Stalin, writing in *Pravda* shortly thereafter, demanded an end to "cavalry raids with the object of 'immediately communizing' the backward masses" and their replacement with a "cautious

[24] As early as 1920, Stalin advocated a policy of involving native intellectuals in industrial, agricultural, provisioning, and other soviet work. "For it will hardly be maintained," he wrote, "that these intellectual groups are less reliable than, let us say, the counterrevolutionary military experts who, their counterrevolution notwithstanding, were appointed to work at important posts and were subsequently sovietized." Stalin, *Sochineniia,* IV, 360–61. Hesitation on the part of local soviet governments to make a serious attempt to put the policy into effect led to renewal of this demand at the Fourth Conference with Responsible Workers in 1923. *Ibid.,* V, 294, 310.

[25] The most notable maneuver in this phase of the campaign to overcome nationalism was the national delimitation of Central Asia. For details, see above, pp. 88–99.

[26] From the text of a Circular Letter of the Russian Communist Party (b) to the Communist Party of Turkestan, dated June 29, 1920, as reproduced in Safarov, *Kolonial'naia Revoliutsiia: opyt Turkestana,* p. 134.

[27] Lenin, *Sochineniia* (1st ed.), XIX, 240–41.

and well-conceived policy of gradually drawing these masses into the general stream of soviet development." [28]

Military conditions prevented immediate application of the new policy to Central Asia, but toward the end of 1921 a series of political concessions—aimed primarily at weakening the Basmachi but designed as well to weaken nationalism—were introduced. In an effort to appease Moslem sentiment generally, Moslem schools were allowed to reopen, shariat justice was reintroduced, subject to certain limitations, and endowment property which had been confiscated by the Tashkent Soviet was returned to its owners. Moreover, special expeditions of agitators were dispatched to those regions in which Basmachism was endemic to expound the principles of the Soviet order and to distribute free seed and supplies to the peasants.

The general retreat of the Soviet regime to the New Economic Policy gave added impetus to the campaign to mollify the Moslem population. Restrictions against private trading were lifted. The bazaars were allowed to reopen. The policy of forced requisitions by the state was dropped, and efforts were made to start a flow of industrial goods into the region. In consequence, long-absent commodities began to appear on the market and Central Asia entered upon a period of slow recovery from the effects of seven years of war and revolution. Viewed as one phase of the campaign to lessen the hatred of the Moslem community toward the Soviet regime and to attenuate the bond between the masses and native opponents of Communism, these reforms produced auspicious results. The passing of the atmosphere of terror, which War Communism had inspired, and the decrease of Soviet interference in native affairs was followed by a rapid diminution of peasant support of nationalism and by a dwindling of the ranks of active opponents of the Soviet regime. Basmachism declined rapidly and by 1925 it had retreated to its last strongholds in eastern Bokhara.[29]

[28] Stalin, *Sochineniia*, IV, 362. See also the resolution of the Twelfth Party Congress in *Vse-Soiuznaia Kommunisticheskaia Partiia (b) v rezoliutsiiakh*, I, 589–90.
[29] I. M. Reisner, *Afganistan* (Moscow, 1929), p. 203; also Vasilevskii, "Fazy Basmacheskogo dvizheniia v Srednei Azii," *Novyi Vostok*, No. 29 (1930), p. 135.

The effectiveness of the policy of caution and conciliation, which owed much of its success to the fact that it was put into effect during the period of general retreat from the rigors of War Communism, did not alter its temporary and essentially negative character. The policy did moderate the widespread popular antagonism toward the Soviet government. It accomplished the isolation of Bolshevism's most obdurate enemies and the neutralization of the urban and rural middle groups (small merchants and traders, kustar' workers, and middle peasants). And although it did not undermine directly the traditional social order, the policy created a more favorable atmosphere for Bolshevik promotion of the major objectives of emphasizing class division and class struggle within the Moslem community.

DIVISION AND CONQUEST: THE POLICY
OF CLASS STRATIFICATION

Even when the policy of conciliation had been introduced, the Bolsheviks took pains to differentiate between concessions to the general population and the stimulation of class conflicts. Safarov made precisely this point at the Tenth Party Congress in 1921. Although agreeing that prudence was a "good point," and that Communism should develop a "special approach in order to unchain the toiling masses," he insisted that caution should not apply in the promotion of a policy of class stratification.[30] Safarov's warning was in part a reflection of his own experience in Turkestan, and it constituted an oblique criticism of Bolshevik behavior in that region. Between the arrival of troops of the central government in Turkestan and the dissolution of the Tashkent government, the Bolsheviks had minimized the principle of class struggle among the natives. Rather, they had concentrated their energies on a campaign to drive out Russian kulaks and colonizers and actually had encouraged friction between Moslems and Russians in the guise of class struggle. This policy culminated in the Semirechie land reform of 1921 during which the lands and equipment of Russian colonists, but not of Moslem landlords, were expropriated.

[30] Protokoly s'ezdov i konferentsii Vsesoiuznoi Kommunisticheskoi Partii (b): Desiatyi S'ezd RKP(b), mart, 1921 g. (Moscow, 1933), pp. 201–2.

Emboldened by this policy, elements within the Moslem section of the Communist Party actively resisted measures designed to promote class conflicts within the native community. Many questioned the expediency of such a course on the ground that an indestructible bond existed between the leaders and the tribe in regions where the tribal structure was strong.[31] Others carried their opposition a step further, insisting that there was no capitalism and therefore no class differentiation in the tribal units.[32] It followed that no basis existed for a class struggle. The center considered these objections to be serious enough to require a detailed refutation,[33] but it did not hesitate also to brand them simply as manifestations of the deviation toward local nationalism and to overrule them on this ground. The Communist Party had never intended to relinquish its right to spread its influence among the masses and to prepare Central Asia for a "deepening" of the revolution even during the New Economic Policy. Rather, it utilized the decline of counterrevolutionary activity attendant upon relaxation of the restrictions of War Communism to tighten up and purify the apparatus of

[31] V. Vorshev, "Osnovnye etapy razvitiia partorganizatsii Turkmenistana," *Revoliutsiia i Natsional'nosti*, No. 12 (58) (December, 1934), pp. 69–70. Apparently belief in the existence of an indestructible bond between the tribal leaders and the tribe was widespread among Bolsheviks in the border regions. Shteinberg reproduces the text of an "Instruction to Instructors, Inspectors, and All Soviet Workers Sent to the Localities" issued by the Transcaspian Regional Revolutionary Committee in April, 1920—he cites it as characteristic of the thinking in local Soviet organs at the time—which orders Soviet workers to conduct their work through "the most respected and authoritative" persons in the localities. See E. L. Shteinberg, *Ocherki istorii Turkmenii* (Moscow, 1934), pp. 99–100.

[32] Z. Mindlin, "Kirgiz i Revoliutsiia," *Novyi Vostok*, No. 5 (1924), p. 220.

[33] The fundamental thesis of the challengers of the theory of tribal unity revolved around the claim that capitalistic pressures had already broken down tribal bonds and that national consciousness had replaced tribal exclusiveness. For examples, see Mindlin, "Kirgiz i Revoliutsiia," *Novyi Vostok*, No. 5 (1924), pp. 217, 220–21; Safarov, *Kolonial'naia revoliutsiia: opyt Turkestana*, p. 14; Vorshev, "Osnovnye etapy razvitiia partorganizatsii Turkmenistana," *Revoliutsiia i Natsional'nosti*, No. 12 (58) (December, 1934), pp. 69–70; S. Dimanshtein, "Po povodu uchrezhdeniia Narkomnatsa Turkrespubliki," *Zhizn' Natsional'nostei*, No. 28 (126) (December 3, 1921); M. A. Nemchenko, "Agrarnaia reforma v Turkmenii," *Novyi Vostok*, No. 19 (1927), p. 127; M. A. Nemchenko, "Natsional'noe razmezhevanie Srednei Azii," *Mezhdunarodnaia Zhizn'*, Nos. 4–5 (1924), pp. 73–74; P. Prager, "K postanovke voprosa o nekapitalisticheskoi puti razvitiia otstalykh stran," *Proletarskaia Revoliutiia*, No. 5 (100) (May, 1930), p. 59; Georgii Safarov, *Problemy Vostoka* (Petrograd, 1922), p. 24.

government and to sow the seeds of class conflict within the Moslem community.

In calling upon the Party "to help [the laboring masses among the backward nationalities] to liquidate the remnants of patriarchal-feudal relationships," Stalin had indicated this course of action in his theses on the nationality question published on the eve of the Tenth Party Congress.[34] At the congress itself, Safarov elaborated upon the procedure to be pursued in implementing the "policy of class stratification in the East." The Soviet regime, he said, must adopt measures to eliminate the influence of all native exploiting elements upon the masses, to encourage in all Soviet administrative agencies an unrelenting struggle against exploiters, to deprive exploiters of "class privileges," and to improve the economic and political position of the poor at the expense of the rich.[35]

Politically, the application of these measures to Central Asia was tantamount to ordering the removal of the whole customary leadership group from participation in public life. In the initial stage of the execution of this policy, the Communist Party undertook a campaign to drive conservative elements out of the Soviet administrative and governmental apparatus. This campaign took its most spectacular form in the republics of Bokhara and Khorezm, where the Bolsheviks, with the support of the Red Army, expelled the representatives of the Young Bokharan and Young Khivan Parties from posts of authority and in a period of three years replaced the "people's" form of government with a "socialist" form. In Turkestan, the purification of the Soviet government, although accomplished with less fanfare, was considerably more thorough. In the course of the frequent purges which swept through the Party and administrative apparatus, many untrustworthy and oppositional elements were eliminated.

To reinforce and give permanence to these measures, administrative and legal disabilities were brought into force to prevent nonlaboring elements from seeking office or participating in elections. By constitutional provision these groups had been

[34] Stalin, Sochineniia, V, 25.
[35] Desiatyi S'ezd R.K.P.(b), pp. 200–201.

denied the franchise in Turkestan from 1918 onward. But in Bokhara and Khorezm many of them retained the right to vote and to hold public office until the dissolution of the people's regimes in 1923. After the national delimitation these restrictions were reinforced in the constitutions of Uzbekistan and Turkmenia by articles which denied to individuals and groups rights which they utilized to the detriment of the socialist revolution.[36]

While placing these legal disabilities in the way of class enemies of the Soviet regime, the Bolsheviks assiduously encouraged the poorest elements to engage in political activity and promoted the development of schisms within the native community. Native agitators who were intimately acquainted with local conditions were dispatched to the villages to exploit existing frictions and inequalities, to stress the contradictions between the interests of the rich and the poor, and to arouse class consciousness among the masses. Even religious beliefs were utilized to encourage opposition to customary leaders. Appropriate passages were selected from the Shariat and Adat to demonstrate the unjustness of the existing distribution of property and power. At the same time, efforts were made to show that customary practices put special disabilities upon the poor, thereby protecting the power of the rich.[37] On the other hand, the Soviet regime attempted to show its solicitude for the poorest groups by distributing food supplies, seed, and equipment to them and by promising a future redistribution of land and water.

The Soviet authority had undertaken this campaign in order to create exploitable hatreds and antagonisms within the customary social order and to destroy those loyalties and beliefs which were the foundation of the native community. It proposed, moreover, to replace these loyalties with new allegiances to the

[36] F. Ksenofontov, *Uzbekistan i Turkmenistan: k voprosu ob ikh vkhozhdenii v SSSR* (Moscow, 1925), pp. 38–39.

[37] An example of this technique is furnished by Bolshevik agitation against *kalym* or the bride price. Agitators did not fail to point out that the poorest peasants often were unable to pay the bride price and hence were denied the right to utilize the irrigation system to water their land since water rights were allowed only to married persons. See I. I. Kryl'tsov, "Zakonodatel'stvo Sredne-Aziatskikh Sovetskikh Respublik," *Sovetskoe Pravo*, No. 5 (29) (1927), p. 136.

principles advanced by the October Revolution, to the Soviet order, and to the Communist Party. Expressed in terms of the national question, this presumed the establishment of mutual trust between the Russian workers and peasants and the toiling masses of the non-Russian peoples and the institution of a regime based on the "collaboration and brotherly coexistence" of the nationalities of Russia.[38] Therein lay the key, the Bolsheviks believed, to the consolidation of Soviet rule in the East, and this idea appears in nearly every one of Stalin's articles and speeches on the nationality problem.[39]

Soviet publicists have repeated the idea of "collaboration and brotherly cooperation" so often and applied it to such disparate situations that it would seem to have little meaning. Examination of Soviet usage, however, helps to clarify its content. "Mutual trust" was to encourage close and friendly relations between the Great Russian people of the Russian republic and the non-Russian peoples organized in various types of autonomous territories. Within the non-Russian republics "mutual trust" also called for the establishment of a bond between the European population which was concentrated in the urban areas and the native population which dominated the rural areas. Later, Bolsheviks also began to discuss the question of "mutual trust" as one aspect of the problem of alliance or *smychka* between the proletariat and the peasantry.[40] Broido, chancellor of the Communist University of the Toilers of the East, expressed this concept most clearly in an article in *Zhizn' Natsional'nostei* in 1923.

The *smychka* of the town with the village, the strengthening of the alliance of the workers with the small and smallest peasants, translated into the language of our national policy, signifies a *smychka* of the *Russian* town with the *native* backward village, the *Great*

---

[38] Stalin, *Sochineniia*, V, 241.

[39] For example, see *ibid.*, IV, 77, 161, 237; V, 20, 59, 240–41.

[40] The concept of an alliance between the proletariat and the peasantry as one aspect of the nationality problem was introduced by Lenin at the Second Congress of the Communist International in 1920. In his speech on the revolutionary movement in the East, Lenin urged Communists to support the establishment of peasant soviets in the backward countries and to ally these soviets with the revolutionary movement in the advanced capitalistic states.

Russian proletariat with the *Uzbek* peasant, the Kirghiz and Kalmyk nomad, and so on.[41]

At the Twelfth Party Congress, Stalin made a similar allusion, referring to the establishment of trust between the proletariat of the erstwhile ruling (*derzhavnoi*) nation (Russia) and the peasantry of the formerly oppressed nationalities as the "class essence" of the nationality question.[42]

Observed in this light, the alliance of the Russian and non-Russian toilers was not one of equals; instead, the "proletariat," constituting itself as the dominant element in the state, undertook to lead the peasantry to "socialism." But, as the theses of the Fifth Plenum of the Executive Committee of the Communist International on the peasant question indicated, "collaboration with the peasantry never signifies the division of power." [43] Until socialism was achieved, the function of leadership would remain securely in the hands of the Russian proletariat, or rather of the Bolshevik Party.

In Bolshevik eyes, the distrust toward Russia which existed in the borderlands was primarily a heritage of the past, the consequence of Tsarist imperialism. National hatreds, the argument ran, were a by-product of the regime of colonial oppression and Russification which the Imperial government had pursued. The revolution, by destroying the Empire and repudiating its policies, had opened the way to the development of national friendship on the basis of class solidarity.[44]

From the Communist viewpoint, a major factor in dispelling national estrangement had been the early Soviet recognition of the right of national self-determination for the peoples of Rus-

[41] G. I. Broido, "Osnovnye voprosy natsional'noi politike," *Zhizn' Natsional'-nostei*, Nos. 3–4 (1923), p. 5.

[42] Stalin, *Sochineniia*, V, 239–40.

[43] *Rasshirennyi Plenum Ispolkoma Kommunisticheskogo Internatsionala (21 marta–6 aprelia 1925 g.). stenograficheskii otchet* (Moscow, 1925), pp. 536–37.

[44] In this vein Stalin, in an article in *Zhizn' Natsional'nostei* in March, 1919, claimed that the "triumph of the proletarian revolution in Russia and the liberatory policy of the Soviet authority in relation to the oppressed peoples without doubt cleared the atmosphere of national enmity [and] won for the Russian proletariat the trust and respect of the peoples of the East." Stalin, "Nashi zadachi na Vostoke," *Zhizn' Natsional'nostei*, No. 7 (15) (March 2, 1919).

sia. According to Soviet theory, this had reversed the old relationship between the center and the borderlands and had
encouraged the workers and peasants of the borderlands to resist
reactionary and bourgeois demands for separation from the
Russian state. Of equal importance was the nature of the Soviet
authority itself. "The Soviet power," Stalin had pointed out,
"is the power of the workers, the dictatorship of the proletariat,
which, by its nature, disposes the toiling elements of the republics and the peoples entering the union favorably toward one
another." [45] The basis of this assertion is the Marxist postulate
that capitalism and private property inevitably disunite peoples
and cause national oppression while socialism inevitably draws
peoples together. As proof of the contention, the Bolsheviks
pointed to the experience of the October Revolution. "The
establishment of the Soviet order," reads a declaration of the
Tenth Party Congress, "transformed the relationships between
the toiling masses of the nationalities of Russia, smashed the old
national enmity, removed the soil of national oppression, won
for the Russian workers the trust of their national brothers, and
evoked enthusiasm in Europe and Asia." [46]

In order to abolish what Stalin called the "estrangement and
sullenness of the borderlands," [47] the mistrust toward Central
Russia which lingered on even after the revolution, Bolshevism
also required a positive policy, the achievement of "actual equality" for the non-Russian peoples of the Soviet republic. The old
regime, Stalin pointed out, had left a heritage of political, economic, and cultural backwardness in the borderlands, and even
though the Soviet government had eliminated national oppression, it still had to contend with "historically inherited inequality." [48]

The substance of this inequality of nationalities [he said] consists
in the fact that, as a result of historical development, we have received a heritage from the past by virtue of which one nationality,
the Great Russian nationality, is more developed politically and

[45] *Dvenadtsatyi S'ezd Rossiiskoi Kommunisticheskoi Partii (b)*, pp. 443–44.
[46] *Vse-Soiuznaia Kommunisticheskaia Partiia (b) v rezoliutsiiakh*, I, 454.
[47] Stalin, *Sochineniia*, IV, 356.
[48] *Dvenadtsatyi S'ezd Rossiiskoi Kommunisticheskoi Partii (b)*, pp. 445–46.

industrially than the other nationalities. Hence the existence of actual inequality, which cannot be eradicated in one year, but which must be eradicated, and eradicated by economic, political, and cultural assistance being rendered to the backward nationalities.[49]

In the political area, the central government recognized early the importance of convincing the people of the backward regions that the new government was truly their own, and it realized that this could best be accomplished by allowing them to participate in the work of government. As early as April 9, 1918, in an article in *Pravda*, Stalin had emphasized the necessity of attracting the toilers and exploited masses of the borderlands into Soviet work,[50] and in 1920 he elaborated the means by which the task could be accomplished.

The Soviet government must become no less near and dear to the populace of the border regions of Russia. But to do so the Soviet government must be comprehensible to them. It is therefore necessary that all Soviet organs in the border regions—the courts, the administration, the economic bodies, the direct organs of government (as also the organs of the Party)—should as far as possible be recruited from among local people acquainted with the customs, life, habits, and language of the native population; that the best people from among the native masses should be got to participate in these institutions; that the local toiling masses should be drawn to every sphere of the administration of the country, including military formations, in order that the masses may see that the Soviet government and its organs are the products of their own efforts, the embodiment of their aspirations.[51]

As a corollary, Bolshevik policy required the exclusion from participation in soviet work on any level of persons and groups whose class membership rendered them suspect or whose activities, regardless of class, hindered achievement of the aims of the Soviet regime. Political equality in Bolshevik thinking was not divorced from class nor could it be allowed to lead in directions not contemplated by doctrine. In the national, indeed, in all spheres, the Party viewed individuals and groups as a means of achieving its own aspirations. For that reason, rights bestowed

[49] *Desiatyi S'ezd R.K.P.(b)*, pp. 185–86.
[50] Stalin, *Sochineniia*, IV, 75.
[51] *Ibid.*, IV, 358.

upon the nationalities had only a relative value. The Soviet government applied them only to the extent that they did not contradict the aims of Party policy. Similarly, the Party examined each citizen from the viewpoint of his usefulness to the Soviet state and, corresponding to this usefulness or harmfulness, accorded or denied him rights. In this sense—that is, in the sense that various groups of society according to class bore a different relation to the Soviet regime and its objectives—there was no equality.[52]

THE STRUGGLE FOR EQUALITY: MILITARY AND LANGUAGE ASPECTS

Within the limitations set by the class principle, the Soviet government entered upon a course of action designed to achieve political equality for the toilers of all the nationalities. In terms of content, as indicated by Party decisions, this equality was intended to operate primarily in four spheres. The first concerned the training of non-Russian military personnel. The second was the elevation of the minority languages to a basis of equality with the Russian tongue. A third sought encouragement of the pretense of native participation in the administrative apparatus in the national regions, and a fourth, the development of a system of local soviets based upon participation and representation of the masses.[53]

In the sphere of military training, Bolshevik progress during the first decade of Soviet rule was generally unsatisfactory. In Central Asia, the Communist Party had lent its support to the formation of Moslem Red Army detachments as early as June, 1918.[54] But growing opposition to the inclusion of natives in

[52] A. M. Turubiner, *Gosudarstvennyi stroi RSFSR* (Moscow, 1923), p. 7.

[53] All of these rights had been denied to the natives of Central Asia under the Tsarist regime. In Turkestan, as in all other parts of the Empire, the language of the Government-General was Russian, its use being mandatory in all official proceedings. Administration above the volost' level was in the hands of Russian military personnel, while that of the native villages and volost's was conducted by native officials who owed their positions to superior Russian officials. For a succinct description, see Edward Dennis Sokol, *The Revolt of 1916 in Russian Central Asia* (Baltimore, 1954), pp. 44–52. Likewise the tribes of Turkestan were exempted from military service until 1916 when the Tsar ordered the mobilization of all male natives between 19 and 43 years of age for labor service in rear areas. This mobilization decree touched off the revolt of 1916.

[54] P. G. Antropov, *Materialy i dokumenty I S'ezda Kompartii Turkestana* (Tashkent, 1934), pp. 51–52.

the army during the civil war forestalled a positive program. A renewed attempt to develop native military cadres, culminating in a trial mobilization of the native population in 1920, was made after the arrival of Frunze's army in Central Asia in 1919. Again the results were unsatisfactory.[55] At the Tenth Party Congress and the Fourth Conference with Responsible Workers, the central Party authorities tried a new approach, advocating the formation of national militia regiments in the border republics. Two years passed before this plan took concrete form in 1925, when a Turcoman cavalry squadron was activated and later expanded into a cavalry regiment.[56]

By way of comparison, the Uzbek republic did nothing in the military sphere other than to limit to toilers the right to bear arms. At the Second Uzbek Congress of Soviets, Kuz'min, the reporter on military problems, pointed out that only 5 percent of the troops in the Central Asiatic Military District were Uzbeks and that only 37 percent of the officer personnel within this group was Uzbek.[57] The matter of national troop formations in Central Asia also came up at the Fourth All-Union Congress of Soviets. Voroshilov reported that the government was just beginning to put into operation plans for the establishment of local troop formations. He cited two reasons for the previous lack of progress: the absence of a staff of trained native commanders and the lack of military experience resulting from the Tsarist policy of keeping natives out of the army. To repair the deficiency in officers the Soviet government had founded a training school for junior officers in Tashkent, from which the first class was graduated in 1927.[58] As a step toward providing the local population with military experience, the Turcoman government also decreed conscription in 1927. The All-Union Con-

[55] M. Shkliar, "Musulmanskaia bednota i Krasnaia Armiia," *Zhizn' Natsional'-nostei*, No. 32 (89) (October 17, 1920); "M. V. Frunze na Turkestanskom fronte," *Krasnyi Arkhiv*, No. 3 (100) (1940), pp. 57–59, 62, 70, 73–74.

[56] For an examination of the Soviet effort to organize Turcoman military formations, see T. S. Kozlov, *Krasnaia Gvardiia i Krasnaia Armiia v Turkmenii (istoricheskaia spravka ob organizatsii i etapakh bor'by)* (Ashkhabad, 1928).

[57] *Vtoroi Vseuzbekskii S'ezd Sovetov Rabochikh, Dekhkanskikh i Krasnoarmeiskikh Deputatov Uzbekskoi Sovetskoi Sotsialisticheskoi Respubliki. stenograficheskii otchet* (Samarkand, 1927), pp. 72, 131.

[58] *Chetvertyi S'ezd Sovetov: stenograficheskii otchet* (Moscow, 1927), pp. 546, 579.

stitution of 1936, which made military service compulsory for all Soviet citizens, led to the introduction of conscription in Uzbekistan, but the Uzbek republic enacted no conscription law of its own until World War II.

Much greater progress was made in raising the local languages to a status of equality with Russian, formerly the sole official language. Western European Marxists had opposed the establishment of a state language in multinational states on the ground that language under capitalism served as an instrument of national oppression. Although the replacement of the capitalist mode of production by a socialist mode of production would put an end to the struggle for markets, and the state would disappear as an agency of coercion, the interests of national administration in the socialist state would still require the use of official languages. According to Kautsky, the new society would transform language from an instrumentality serving the interests of the ruling classes into a vehicle for the satisfaction of the needs of the masses.[59]

Lenin was inclined to agree with Kautsky's conclusions. He welcomed the growing unity of language, fostered by the requirements of economic relations among peoples, as one portent of the eventual extinction of national differences, but he opposed the use of legal compulsion to hasten the process. In an exchange of correspondence with the Armenian Social Democrat Stephen Shaumian in 1913, Lenin vigorously criticized the tendency among zealously "internationalist" Party members to promote Russian as the general state language because it represented the highest culture and the greatest possibilities for unity. "The Russian language," he wrote, "would be without question of progressive significance for many of the unfortunate and backward nations. But unfortunately, you do not see that it would be of still greater significance if there were no compulsion to use it."[60] While Lenin was opposed to the establishment of Russian by decree as the state language, he did not insist that the

---

[59] See Karl Kautsky, *The Liberation of Nations*, Chapter VIII. Quoted in V. N. Durdenevskii, *Ravnopravie iazykov v Sovetskom Stroe* (Moscow, 1927), p. 18.

[60] V. I. Lenin, *Sochineniia* (2d ed., Moscow, 1926—), XVII, 90.

non-Russian tongues be elevated to a position of equality with Russian by administrative procedure.

The new Soviet government had taken no immediate steps to clarify the right to use non-Russian languages in state institutions. The first official declaration concerning language rights appeared in the decree of March 7, 1918, on the courts.[61] According to Paragraph 7 of the decree (repeated in Paragraph 21 of the decree on the courts of November 30, 1918), "pleadings in the courts of all instances are allowed in all local languages. The establishment of rules concerning which language or languages are to be used in pleadings and legal proceedings is left to the courts in conference with the Soviets of Workers', Soldiers', Peasants', and Cossacks' Deputies." During this early period, the Soviet government published no formal guarantee regarding equality of languages in other spheres of public life. The decree concerning the formation of the first autonomous unit within the RSFSR, the Tataro-Bashkir republic (March 22, 1918), contained no mention of language rights. The question was likewise ignored in the acts which formed the Kirghiz (Kazakh) republic, the separate Tatar and Bashkir republics, the Chuvash, Mari, Kalmyk, and Votiak autonomous regions, and the Karelian Labor Commune during 1919 and 1920.

The right to use the local language in the conduct of official business was nevertheless clearly implied in these and other acts dealing with the formation of autonomous territorial units. In his appeal to the Soviets and Moslem Commissariats of Kazan, Ufa, Orenburg, and Ekaterinburg issued in April, 1918, Stalin had, for practical purposes, equated autonomy with the right to use the native tongue in public institutions. Autonomy he defined as "the organization of the local school, local court, local administration, local organs of power, local socio-political and educational institutions with a guarantee of plenitude of the right of the local language, native to the toiling masses of the region, in all spheres of socio-political work." [62]

[61] Text of decree in *Sobranie uzakonenii i rasporiazhenii Rabochego i Krest'-ianskogo Pravitel'stva RSFSR*, 1918, No. 26, p. 420. This provision is repeated in Paragraph 21 of the decree on the courts of November 30, 1918. Text in *ibid.*, 1918, No. 85, p. 889.

[62] Stalin, "Odna iz ocherednykh zadach," *Izvestiia*, April 11, 1918. He repeated

In Central Asia, where the language barrier between the European and the native population hindered Soviet attempts to influence the indigenous toiling masses, the language problem was first discussed at the First Congress of the Communist Party of Turkestan in June, 1918. After recognizing by resolution that autonomy in Turkestan had failed to develop a class consciousness among the Moslem proletariat and to win its sympathy for the Soviet regime, the congress went on record in support of according the "Turkic language" a place of equality with Russian as the state language, of requiring the publication of all official organs in Turkic and the translation of Party literature into Turkic.[63] In July the Central Executive Committee of the Turkestan government took the first step toward implementing this resolution. It adopted a statute which declared the local customary tongues (Uzbek and Kirghiz) as state languages on a basis of equality with Russian and ordered the distribution of Soviet literature from the center on a broad scale in both the Russian and the native languages.[64]

This decree, however, had no practical consequence. The predominance in administrative positions of Europeans unacquainted with the local speech rendered it impossible to put the law into effect without disrupting the process of government. Moreover, the exigencies of civil war prevented the establishment of Soviet cultural institutions capable of training trustworthy native functionaries. Despite these problems, the Communist Party did not lay aside its plan to give the non-Russian tongues an equal status. At the Tenth Party Congress, it adopted a resolution, offered by Stalin, in favor of helping the nationalities to develop and strengthen a court and administrative system and economic and legislative organs, to establish

the same proposition in his speech at the conference on the convocation of the constituent congress of soviets of the Tataro-Bashkir republic in May, 1918. See Stalin, *Sochineniia*, IV, 89.

[63] P. Antropov, "Pervyi S'ezd Kommunisticheskoi Partii Turkestana," in Istpart Sredazbiuro Ts.K., V.K.P.(b), *Revoliutsiia v Srednei Azii* (Tashkent, 1928), I, 13–14.

[64] Ilias Alkin, *Sredniaia Aziia: ekonomiko-geograficheskii ocherk Kara-Kalpakstana, Kirgizstana, Tadzhikistana, Turkmenistana i Uzbekistana* (Moscow, 1931), I, 348–49.

cultural institutions such as press, schools, theater, and clubs, and to found technical and general educational schools and courses, all functioning in the native languages.[65] Progress toward achievement of these goals was painfully slow and at the Twelfth Party Congress Stalin again urged the "nationalization" of all organs and institutions "so that they will act in a language comprehensible to the masses." [66]

Lack of trained and reliable personnel acquainted with local languages, nevertheless, prevented a rapid transition to the use of these tongues in the borderlands and brought to the fore the need for a program for training cadres of native government functionaries. This was especially true in Turkestan where the overwhelming majority of government officials were recent arrivals from the RSFSR and the Ukraine and, for the most part, unable or disinclined to master the difficult Turkic languages. Despite this difficulty, the Turkestan government decided to go ahead with a planned transfer of government work to the local languages.

On August 27, 1923, the Central Executive Committee of the Turkestan republic ordered local Soviet agencies to adopt the local languages in their public dealings within three months. In the central agencies of the republic, the decree directed establishment of a parallel business correspondence. The decree also ordered the immediate recruitment of cadres of native "practitioners" with a preparation period of six months in courses operated by government departments. This was done in order to strengthen the administrative reserve with persons from the native population and to provide for a transition to the local languages "painlessly without harming the customary course of work of the institutions." [67] The transition was anything but painless and in October, 1923, after efforts to implement the decree had disrupted the routine of government offices, the project was abandoned.

Hasty measures such as the Turkestan decree led to confusion

[65] *Desiatyi S'ezd R.K.P.(b)*, p. 579.
[66] *Dvenadtsatyi S'ezd Rossiiskoi Kommunisticheskoi Partii (b)*, p. 451.
[67] Text in Durdenevskii, *Ravnopravie iazykov v Sovetskom Stroe*, p. 71.

in the administrative apparatus and only added to the burdens of the overworked Soviet officials. In order to overcome the objectionable features of these measures while expediting the adaptation of Soviet institutions to the mode of life in the national regions, the All-Russian Central Executive Committee on April 14, 1923, enacted a decree "Concerning Measures for Translating the Business Correspondence of State Organs of National Regions and Republics into Local Languages." [68] This represented the first systematic approach to the problem. The primary requirement for success, it was now recognized, was preparation of a trained corps of native administrative workers. To that end the decree ordered local Soviet governments to begin immediately to organize training facilities and to recruit probationers, giving preference to persons who were acquainted with the local tongues. In the matter of translating business correspondence, the decree also demanded observance of a "strict sequence, beginning with the translation of business correspondence or the introduction of parallel business correspondence in the local languages of those parts of the state apparatus which dealt directly with the broad masses of the population." At the same time, local governments were cautioned against taking measures which would hinder the work of the central organs of the RSFSR.

The concern evidenced in this document is indicative of the urgency with which the center had come to regard the problem of language equality. It was followed by other guarantees both in the RSFSR and in the borderland republics for the purpose of elevating the non-Russian tongues to an equal position with Russian. The Second Constitution of the RSFSR, adopted by the Twelfth All-Russian Congress of Soviets in 1925, specifically guaranteed to non-Russians the right to receive instruction in the schools in their own languages and the right to use their own languages freely in congresses, in the courts, in administration, and in social life. This not only represented an advance over the

[68] Text in I. Lozovskii and I. Bibin, *Sovetskaia Politika za 10 let po natsional'-nomu voprosu v RSFSR: sistematicheskii sbornik deistvuiushchikh aktov pravitel'stv Soiuza SSR i RSFSR po delam natsional'nostei RSFSR (oktiabr' 1917 g.–noiabr' 1927 g.)* (Moscow, 1928), p. 423.

1918 constitution, which had been silent on the question, but it was hailed at the congress as a guiding principle for other soviet republics.[69]

These provisions were in fact faithfully repeated in constitutional articles and decrees in the Central Asian republics. Typical of acts of these governments was Article 17 of the constitution of the Uzbek SSR, which "recognized for all national minorities of the Uzbek SSR the right of free utilization of the native languages in congresses, in the court, administration, and social life and . . . guaranteed the right to study in the native language in the school." [70] These republics went a step further, declaring by ordinance or constitutional provision that both Russian and the major local tongues be granted equality as state languages and directing the publication of the decrees and other acts of these governments concurrently in these official languages.[71] Moreover, these governments made strenuous efforts to comply with the stipulations of the central decree concerning the "nationalization" of business correspondence. Both the Uzbek and Turcoman SSR's included among their first acts programs designed to introduce the native tongues progressively into local administrative agencies. Business correspondence was to be conducted concurrently in Russian and the native language, although provision was made that correspondence be carried on solely in the local language in regions which had no European population. Special administrations were appointed

---

[69] *Dvenadtsatyi Vserossiiskii S'ezd Sovetov, stenograficheskii otchet* (Moscow, 1925), pp. 142–43.

[70] From the constitution of the Uzbek SSR of March 31–July 11, 1927. See *Sobranie Uzakonenii i Rasporiazhenii Uzbekskoi SSR*, 1927, No. 24, p. 145. Provision repeated in Article 14 of the constitution of the Kirghiz ASSR (see Durdenevskii, *Ravnopravie iazykov v Sovetskom Stroe*, p. 243) and in the constitution of the Turcoman SSR. See speech by Atabaev in *Tretii S'ezd Sovetov Soiuza Sovetskikh Sotsialisticheskikh Respublik, stenograficheskii otchet* (Moscow, 1925), p. 19.

[71] By Article 16 of the constitution of the Kirghiz republic, Kirghiz, Russian, and Uzbek were declared official languages. By an act of the Turcoman SSR of February 20, 1925, Turcoman and Russian were declared the state languages of that republic. For texts, see Durdenevskii, *Ravnopravie iazykov v Sovetskom Stroe*, pp. 143, 243. The Uzbek republic, by decree, declared Russian, Uzbek, and Tajik to be official languages. See *Sobranie Uzakonenii i Rasporiazhenii Uzbekskoi SSR*, 1927, No. 15, p. 83.

to supervise the planned introduction of the program.[72] These measures, however, were not immediately successful and government criticism of the failures was constant but largely without effect.[73]

The lack of success of these efforts to generalize the use of native languages in public institutions in Central Asia could not be attributed to a willful disregard of decrees and ordinances directing their adoption. Essentially, the solution depended upon training cadres of administrative workers capable of utilizing local tongues and dialects in their daily work. The Russians who had dominated the administrative agencies in the region since the October Revolution were seldom acquainted with the native languages, and those Europeans who were recruited in Central Russia and the Ukraine after the civil war to staff government offices were for the most part even less qualified in this respect. The central government attempted to overcome this difficulty by establishing a number of educational institutions designed to train Europeans for work in the national republics and regions. But graduates of these schools were too few in number during the twenties to fill even the most important administrative posts. In an early attempt to remedy the situation, cadres of literate Turks from the Tatar republic and Baku had been introduced into the government apparatus in Turkestan, Bokhara, and Khorezm, but they too had difficulty in mastering the local dialects.[74]

[72] From a decree "On the Obligatory Conduct of Business Correspondence in the Uzbek Language and on the Formation under the Revolutionary Committee of the Uzbek SSR of a Central and, in the Localities, Regional Commissions for the Nationalization of the State Apparatus," dated December 31, 1924. See *Sobranie Uzakonenii i Rasporiazhenii Uzbekskoi SSR*, 1925, No. 1, p. 22; see also a similar decree of the Revolutionary Committee of the Turcoman SSR of January 18, 1925, in *Sobranie Postanovlenii i Rasporiazhenii Raboche-Dekhkanskogo Pravitel'stva Turkmenskoi SSR*, 1925, No. 1, p. 19.

[73] For example, see the circular letter of the Central Executive Committee and the Council of People's Commissars of the Uzbek SSR of March 21, 1925, in *Sobranie Uzakonenii i Rasporiazhenii Uzbekskoi SSR*, 1925, No. 11, p. 123.

[74] As an instance of the results of the language difficulty, the Tatar editor of the newspaper *Kyzyl Bairak* (The Red Standard) permitted the inscription "Vagrants of the World Unite" to be printed on the flag. See Joseph Castagné, "Le Turkestan depuis la révolution russe," *Revue du Monde Musulman*, L (June, 1922), 71.

THE HALFHEARTED CRUSADE: THE CAMPAIGN
FOR ADMINISTRATIVE EQUALITY

The crux of the whole problem was the inability of the indigenous population to furnish qualified personnel for work in the
local administrative apparatus. The almost universal illiteracy
among natives in Central Asia prevented the Bolsheviks from
taking adequate measures to train cadres of local people quickly
to assume responsible positions in government. There did exist
a small group of educated Moslems in the region, but Soviet
leaders hesitated to employ them since the majority came from
politically unreliable classes and many were openly hostile to the
Soviet regime. Moreover, even the most educated native groups
had had little or no experience in public administration. In
Turkestan, the Russians, who in fact had introduced a modern
system of administration, had virtually excluded Moslems from
government posts, and until the elimination of the khanate form
of government both Bokhara and Khiva were devoid of a true
administrative machinery. When the machinery was established,
it was organized on the initiative of Russian technical personnel
who had been sent into the republics under the provisions of
treaties with the RSFSR.

From an early stage of the revolution the leaders of the Communist Party were aware of the importance of training local
personnel to participate in the public life of their regions. At
its Seventh Congress the Party had demanded a concrete program to unify "the most active, conscious parts of the oppressed
classes, their advanced guard, which must prepare the entire
toiling population for independent participation in the administration of the state on a practical, not theoretical, basis." [75] In
Central Asia, however, there is no evidence of any attempt prior
to 1921 to bring Moslems into public life except under limitations so severe as to render it ineffective.

Even after the central government had asserted its authority
in Central Asia there was no immediate change for the better.
A few Tatars and Turcomans were imported in order to make

[75] *Sed'moi S'ezd Rossiiskoi Kommunisticheskoi Partii* (Moscow, 1923), p. 205.

the Soviet regime more palatable to the Moslem population, but no move was made to bring natives into the administrative apparatus. An article in *Zhizn' Natsional'nostei* of mid-1920 reported that Russian immigrants and workers continued to dominate the life of Turkestan and complained that the native toiling masses remained completely in the background. As a result, it pointed out, the administrative machinery did not serve the needs of the native population. The Commissariat of Health, according to the writer, allotted only 5 percent of its budget to the care of native sick and the Commissariat of Education spent about 2 percent of its budget on primary schools for native children while devoting 17 percent to theaters, art schools, and conservatories which did not serve the native population at all.[76]

These revelations coincided with a renewed effort by the central organs of the Communist Party to encourage local soviet governments to introduce natives into all public institutions. In October, 1920, Stalin again emphasized the need to give local peoples responsible positions in the state machinery in order to inculcate loyalty to the Soviet regime among non-Russians,[77] and the Tenth Party Congress called for developing an administrative machinery "constituted of local people who know the mode of life and the psychology of the local population." [78] This demand was repeated at the Twelfth Party Congress and at conferences and congresses of Party and government agencies of all levels.[79]

The first reaction of the Soviet authority in Central Asia was an obvious one. Native Bolsheviks and sympathizers were appointed to the most conspicuous positions in the local administrative apparatus despite the fact that some of them lacked qualifications which would enable them to discharge their offices efficiently or intelligently.[80] Russian experts exercising *de facto*

[76] Broido, "Turkestanskie Problemy," *Zhizn' Natsional'nostei*, No. 23 (80) (July 18, 1920).
[77] Stalin, *Sochineniia*, IV, 358.
[78] *Desiatyi S'ezd R.K.P.(b)*, p. 579.
[79] See speech by Stalin in *Dvenadtsatyi S'ezd Rossiiskoi Kommunisticheskoi Partii (b)*, p. 442; Stalin, *Sochineniia*, V, 297; S. Dimanshtein, "Bor'ba na ideologicheskom fronte v Srednei Azii," *Revoliutsiia i Natsional'nosti*, No. 12 (58) (December, 1934), p. 22.
[80] During the early twenties, Soviet officials took a peculiar pride in putting

control prevented these figureheads from engaging in capricious or harmful activities. In practice, moreover, spectacular measures such as these were indicative of little more than an attempt to mollify the non-Russian peoples and to give some immediate substance to the claim that local soviet governments represented the local population. They were accompanied, however, by a serious program of training whose purpose was the preparation of qualified natives for public service careers on all levels in the various public institutions of Central Asia. One of the principal tasks of the special Communist universities which began to function in 1921–22 was to train members of national minorities as well as Russians for positions of high responsibility in republican and regional administrative offices. A second source for the recruitment of native public servants in Central Asia was provided by Soviet high schools and the Central Asiatic State University. Government agencies also provided courses of in-service training for rank-and-file administrative workers from the indigenous population.[81]

The policy of "rooting" the administrative apparatus was initiated in the face of two major handicaps, which the Soviet regime could not easily overcome. One was the low level of literacy among the Moslem peoples of Central Asia. In comparison with a 35 percent literacy rate among Russians in the region, the indigenous nationalities were in no case more than 5 percent

natives into conspicuous public positions in the localities even though more competent Russian officials had to step aside to create vacancies. At the Fourth Conference with Responsible Workers, Stalin made a special point of the fact that the central government had refused to approve the appointment of Europeans to important local governmental posts. See Stalin, *Sochineniia*, V, 319–20. Other writers, however, have pointed out that natives who were brought to the forefront of local political life during the campaign to "nationalize" the governmental apparatus were often illiterate and universally incompetent. See Chokaiev, "Turkestan and the Soviet Regime," *Journal of the Royal Central Asian Society*, XVIII (1931), 418–19; V. Karpych, "K istorii vozniknoveniia Turkmenskoi SSR," *Turkmenovedenie*, Nos. 10–11 (14–15) (October–November, 1928), p. 41.

[81] See the decree of the All-Union Central Executive Committee on the nationalization of business correspondence, Lozovskii and Bibin, *Sovetskaia Politika za 10 let po natsional'nomu voprosu v RSFSR*, p. 324; also a similar decree of the Turkestan government (August 27, 1923) in Durdenevskii, *Ravnopravie iazykov v Sovetskom Stroe*, p. 71, and a decree of the Revolutionary Committee of the Uzbek SSR (December 31, 1924) in *Sobranie Uzakonenii i Rasporiazhenii Uzbekskoi SSR*, 1925, No. 1, p. 22.

and in one case as little as 0.6 percent literate.[82] In terms of the success of the policy of "rooting," this meant that very few natives possessed sufficient background to enable them to enter government service directly and only a handful were qualified even to begin their training for eventual employment. As late as 1927–28, the peoples of Central Asia—Uzbeks, Turcomans, Tajiks, Kazakhs, and Kirghiz—provided less than 10 percent of the student body of the higher educational institutions of Uzbekistan.[83]

The program of "rooting" was hindered also by the perpetual lack of adequate funds. Indirectly, this handicapped plans for establishing a broad network of schools and courses designed both for the immediate training of native cadres of government workers and for equipping the rising generation for future participation in state service. More directly, it prevented government agencies from purchasing equipment which was necessary in order to permit a transition to the use of the native languages. For example, there were only two native typewriters in Turkestan in 1923.[84] It also forced the government to pay regular employees wages which were too low to make government service attractive and to pay probationers no wage at all. In the latter case, one native official predicted in 1923 that failure to provide salaries would lead to a mass exodus of probationers from government service.[85] Later events bore him out. In 1926 only 358 natives were employed in the government apparatus of Uzbekistan.[86]

By the end of 1927, after ten years of Soviet rule in Central Asia and seven years of effort to bring the machinery of government close to the local population, the policy of "rooting" the

[82] Durdenevskii, *Ravnopravie iazykov v Sovetskom Stroe*, pp. 70–71; see also speech by Khidyr-Aliev before the All-Russian Central Executive Committee in *Tret'iaia Sessiia Vserossiiskogo Tsentral'nogo Ispolnitel'nogo Komiteta X Sozyva (29 oktiabria–23 noiabria 1923 g.) stenograficheskii otchet* (Moscow, 1924), p. 104.

[83] A. Rysakoff, *The National Policy of the Soviet Union* (New York, n.d.), p. 52.

[84] From a speech by Khidyr-Aliev in *Tret'iaia Sessiia Vserossiiskogo Tsentral'nogo Ispolnitel'nogo Komiteta X Sozyva*, pp. 104–5.

[85] *Ibid.*, p. 105.

[86] Korbe, "Sovety Srednei Azii," *Revoliutsiia i Natsional'nosti*, No. 12 (58) (December, 1934), p. 57.

administrative apparatus had not achieved its purpose. The native tongues had not been adopted universally as the language of administration and persons of Russian origin still dominated government offices numerically. In Uzbekistan they filled over 60 percent of the administrative posts, and in other minority republics the percentage was higher still.[87] It should be pointed out, however, that in supporting the program of "nationalization" the central government had never intended that representatives of the non-Russian peoples should exercise unhindered and unsupervised control of the local machinery of administration. Shalva Eliava, an authoritative Bolshevik and erstwhile member of the Turkestan Commission, took this position at the Fourth Session of the Central Executive Committee of the USSR, in reply to charges made by Chokaiev that power in Central Asia was completely in the hands of Moscow agents:

One must not forget that the Uzbekistanian republic is working in the absence of a proletariat. Proletariat in Uzbekistan is a somewhat vague category. The skilled workers from among the Uzbeks do not as yet exist. . . . If there are any skilled workers, they are from among the immigrants—the Russians.[88]

Eliava's statement was both an excuse for the failure of the Soviet regime to prepare adequate cadres of native administrative workers and a justification for the continuation of tight central control over local public institutions though the presence of Russian personnel in all branches of administration. During the 1920's the Soviet government devoted at least as much effort to making Russian administrative workers proficient in the use of the languages of the national minority republics to which they were assigned as it did to the training of natives for government service. This does bespeak an honest attempt to make the language of administration conform to the vernacular of the localities. But it also indicates practical hesitancy to give local administrative responsibility into the hands of local people who might utilize their offices to hinder the accomplishments of

[87] *Izvestiia,* December 11, 1927.
[88] From the stenographic report as reproduced in the Bulletin of the Fourth Session of the Central Executive Committee of the USSR, No. 21, pp. 47–48. Quoted in Chokaiev, "Turkestan and the Soviet Regime," *Journal of the Royal Central Asian Society,* XVIII (1931), 417–18.

centrally determined goals. In the larger sense, it suggests a growing conviction, seldom expressed but nonetheless plainly evident, among Party leaders that the pressure of political realities and the requirements of power rendered it impossible at one stroke either to wipe out all traces of the prerevolutionary system of administration or to adopt a system which would be completely responsive to the needs and desires of the non-Russian masses and in which these masses could participate.[89]

THE SOVIETS: ARENA OF MASS ACTIVITY

Soviets of toilers' deputies offered a more logical and more easily supervised medium for mass participation in government on the local level than did the administrative apparatus. From the standpoint of Bolshevik theory these organs, which had sprung originally from the revolutionary creativeness of the toilers themselves, provided an arena for mass expression and inventiveness. They were also, in theory, immediately responsive to the needs of the masses and subject to their will. Moreover, they constituted under Bolshevik guidance a "school of government for tens and hundreds of thousands of workers and peasants," binding these millions to the Soviet regime and involving them actively in the process of soviet construction. Unlike the normal administrative institutions, they were regarded as mass organs through which the proletarian and semiproletarian element "led" by its vanguard, the Communist Party, exercised "all power" in the soviet state. In this respect, the soviets functioned as schools in which the masses would learn to "rule," as transmission belts for the fulfillment of the general Party line, and, to some extent, as barometers of public sentiment.

As early as 1905 Lenin had regarded the soviets (the factory committees which had emerged spontaneously during the Revolution of 1905) as incipient organs of state power. From that time forward, except for a short period after the failure of the July demonstration in 1917, the Bolsheviks looked upon them as the appropriate state form of the dictatorship of the prole-

[89] Stalin in 1923 stated categorically that "Our government apparatus is bureaucratic and will be bureaucratic for a long time." Stalin, *Sochineniia*, V, 361. For a discussion of the problem, see Barrington Moore, Jr., *Soviet Politics— the Dilemma of Power* (Cambridge, 1950), pp. 169–76.

tariat. In the months immediately following the October Revolution, these ideas found their way into the decrees and enactments of the revolutionary government. The Second Congress of Soviets, which convened on the day following the Bolshevik *coup d'état*, transferred all power in the Russian state to the soviets of workers', soldiers', and peasants' deputies. Later directives of the government and of the Third and Fourth Congresses of Soviets elaborated their functions and powers. The constitution of 1918 proclaimed in its first paragraph that "Russia is a Republic of Soviets of Workers', Soldiers', and Peasants' Deputies," and later declared that "all power belongs to the entire working population of the country, united in city and village soviets."

These acts clearly indicated an intention that the soviets should function as instruments of mass expression and of liberation from the oppression of capital in the non-Russian as well as Russian regions of the republic. As early as the Third Congress of Soviets, the central government made it plain that the only satisfactory solution to the national question in Russia lay in the establishment of autonomous regional unions of soviets representing the native workers and peasants of these regions.[90] Autonomy, Stalin wrote in April, 1918, "must be constructed on the basis of soviets in the localities" in order that the new regime become "popular and dear for the masses." [91] This concept was implicit in Article 11 of the 1918 constitution which gave to the soviets of regions distinguished by a peculiar mode of life and by national structure the right to combine into regional unions and indicated a definite emphasis upon building the soviet structure from the bottom upwards. "Class soviets of deputies as the basis of autonomy; autonomy as the form of expression of these soviets of deputies" was Stalin's definition of soviet autonomy.[92] This definition plainly implied involvement of the non-Russian toiling masses in the process of local government. It was, moreover, an indirect repudiation of the attempts of Russian immigrants and colonists in the national regions to

[90] Stalin, *Sochineniia*, IV, 32–33.
[91] *Ibid.*, IV, 76.
[92] *Ibid.*, IV, 88.

clothe prerevolutionary forms of oppression in soviet garments as a means of maintaining themselves in power.

In their application to Central Asia these declarations were little more than statements of Communist intention. During the revolution and civil war, the Moscow government possessed no means by which to implement them and the Tashkent government chose to ignore them. Although the latter insisted upon rigid adherence by the central government to the principle, elaborated in the "Instruction on the Rights and Obligations of Soviets" of December 24, 1917, that local soviets were completely independent as regards local affairs, it resisted with equal firmness all demands for "nationalization" of the soviet structure in Turkestan. Russian workingmen and soldiers had engineered the revolution in Tashkent without support from the native population and were suspicious of and hostile toward Moslems. During the initial period of revolution there was little contact between the non-Russian masses and the Soviet regime. Only three natives were present at the Third All-Turkestanian Congress of Soviets in November, 1917.[93] Moreover, the network of soviets which emerged in Central Asia after the revolution was limited to "proletarian" (Russian) centers principally along the railroad.[94] A number of peasant soviets did appear in Kirghizia —in May, 1918, there were forty-one volost' soviets, 119 village soviets, and fifty-three aul soviets[95]—but these too were Russian organizations operated by immigrant peasants and colonists.

The Tashkent government did nothing to solicit native cooperation with local soviets until the First Congress of the Communist Party of Turkestan in June, 1918. Then pressure from Moscow forced the local Party organization to condemn past practices and to agree to bring Moslems into the work of the soviets.[96] Shortly thereafter (July 14, 1918) the Turkestan Central Executive Committee directed Soviet officials to begin

---

[93] S. Dimanshtein, "Po povodu uchrezhdeniia narkomnatsa Turkrespubliki," *Zhizn' Natsional'nostei*, No. 28 (126) (December 3, 1921).

[94] From a report by Petrovskii in *Tretii S'ezd Sovetov Soiuza Sovetskikh Sotsialisticheskikh Respublik*, p. 7.

[95] M. Belotskii, *Kirgizskaia Respublika* (Moscow, 1936), p. 30.

[96] Antropov, "Pervyi S'ezd Kommunisticheskoi Partii Turkestana," in Istpart Sredazbiuro Ts.K., V.K.P.(b), *Revoliutsiia v Srednei Azii*, I, 13–14.

organizing the native proletariat, peasantry, and agricultural workers into local soviets.[97] During the ensuing months Moslem sections were formed as an adjunct to existing soviets in some urban areas but their members were denied the right to participate in debates concerning critical questions. A few soviets of Moslem deputies were also established. But the Communist Party exercised such effective and apparently arbitrary control over them that the opportunity for native initiative was quickly extinguished. Their work, in the words of one critic, fell completely into the hands of "Party bosses with generals' habits." [98]

The fact of tight Party control in the local soviets was not in itself alarming to the central leadership of the Party. Although responsible Communist leaders preached the doctrine of broad autonomy of local soviets, a determined Party effort to consolidate its authority characterized the whole period. The Bolsheviks at no time attempted to conceal this goal and in 1919, at the Eighth Party Congress, openly proclaimed their intention to conquer "undivided political dominance in the soviets and actual control over all their work." [99] At the same time the Party encouraged a trend toward a rapid centralization of power. Through a series of decrees promulgated during the civil war, the central government pushed local soviet organizations into the background and progressively concentrated authority in governing centers, in executive committees, their presidiums and their chairmen.[100]

On the other hand, Party leaders repeatedly insisted that regional soviet governments create the formal instrumentalities of local self-government by organizing broad networks of local soviets in the rural areas and by attracting trustworthy natives into the work of regional soviets at every level. As applied to Russia's Eastern borderlands, this demand was strengthened by

[97] Alkin, *Sredniaia Aziia*, I, 348–49.
[98] From an article in *Turkestanskii Kommunist*, No. 45 (June 11, 1919). Quoted in Turar R. Ryskulov, *Revoliutsiia i korennoe naselenie Turkestana* (Tashkent, 1925), pp. 99–100.
[99] *Vse-Soiuznaia Kommunisticheskaia Partiia (b) v rezoliutsiiakh* (4th ed.), I, 314–15.
[100] For an abbreviated orthodox Soviet account of the measures taken, see Andrei Y. Vyshinsky, *The Law of the Soviet State* (New York, 1948), pp. 442–48.

the belief that establishment of "correct" relations with the Moslem masses was exceptionally important to the revolutionizing of the Eastern peoples beyond Russia's borders. This was Stalin's major point in a reminder "To the Soviets of Deputies and Party Organizations of Turkestan" in February, 1919.[101] In an important article in *Zhizn' Natsional'nostei* he again declared it a general Party task "to attract the masses of the toilers of the East into the building of the Soviet state, helping them in every way to create their own volost', district (*uezd*), and other soviets of deputies from people who support the Soviet power and are closely connected with the local population." [102] Neither these appeals nor orders from Moscow in June, 1919, insisting upon the establishment of a system of proportional representation of natives in Soviet organs[103] altered the Turkestan government's policy of maintaining the indigenous population in an inferior status. The Fourth Regional Party Congress, in September, made one concession by directing that the principle of proportional representation be applied "in every instance in which this form of representation is desired by the regional or local congress of soviets." But it also vitiated even the limited effect of this step by requiring approval of all native candidates for office by the Moslem Bureau and by the Communist Party committees.[104]

A system of rural soviets began to emerge in Central Asia only after agents of the central government took command of the regional organs of power at the end of 1919. Under the direction of the Turkestan Commission, a reorganization of the whole soviet apparatus was undertaken and a broad agitational campaign to encourage the development of a rural network of soviets begun.[105] The new Turkestan constitution of 1920, which based all power in the Turkestan republic on the native masses as well as the laboring European population also defined the

[101] Text in *Zhizn' Natsional'nostei*, No. 7 (15) (March 2, 1919).

[102] Stalin, "Nashi zadachi na Vostoke," *Zhizn' Natsional'nostei*, No. 7 (15) (March 2, 1919).

[103] Lenin, *Sochineniia* (2d ed.), XXIV, 811.

[104] S. Muraveiskii, *Ocherki po istorii revoliutsionnogo dvizheniia v Srednei Azii* (Tashkent, 1926), pp. 27–28.

[105] Safarov, *Kolonial'naia revoliutsiia: opyt Turkestana*, p. 104.

functions and composition of local soviets.[106] The rural soviet apparatus was further broadened under the influence of the numerous mass organizations which sprang up in the early twenties. The Koshchi were especially active in promoting the establishment of village soviets and were often almost indistinguishable from them.

These efforts, nevertheless, fell short of the goals advanced by the Communist Party. Frequent criticisms of the local soviet apparatus at public gatherings and in the Soviet press indicated that the Bolsheviks had not succeeded in winning a mass rural following. Too often the peasants insisted upon electing "class enemies" to the local soviets, and Bolshevik-dominated soviets often isolated themselves from the masses. The regime's inability to win mass support was frequently attributed to the lack of qualified cadres of native Party and Soviet workers, to the political and cultural backwardness of the masses, and to the undiminished influence of nationalistic and counterrevolutionary elements.[107]

The extreme centralism which characterized the entire soviet system effectively stifled local interest in these organs. Directives from higher organs tended to take the place of local initiative in the solution of most questions.[108] In matters of purely local concern, the representatives to the soviets were often denied the opportunity to participate in decision making since it was usual for the Communist fraction to arrive at the decisions in previous caucus and to use the general meeting of the soviet merely to ratify them. Instances were reported, moreover, in which meetings of local soviets were dispensed with entirely and their powers concentrated in the hands of their chairmen.

The central authorities had been aware of these problems

---

[106] Radzhapov, "Etapy razvitiia sovetskogo gosudarstvennogo stroia v Srednei Azii," *Sovetskoe Gosudarstvo i Pravo*, No. 11 (November, 1948), p. 65.

[107] Korbe, "Sovety Srednei Azii," *Revoliutsiia i Natsional'nosti*, No. 12 (58) (December, 1934), p. 55.

[108] The Party, moreover, considered extreme centralism to be a virtue rather than a necessary evil. In this vein the *Soviet Encyclopedia of Government and Law*, which was published in 1925, boasted: "Not a single political or organizational question is decided by a single government establishment in our republic without leading directives from the Central Committee of the Party." See Moore, *Soviet Politics—the Dilemma of Power*, p. 131.

since the Kronstadt uprising in 1921, during which the rebels had proclaimed the slogan "Soviets without Communists," and in 1924 they ordered the restoration of "soviet democracy" under the slogan of "Enlivening the Soviets." [109] The announcement of this policy did not foreshadow a relaxation of the Party's monopoly of power on any level of government nor the introduction of any cardinal changes into the soviet system. According to a declaration of the Party Central Committee in July, 1926, the policy was intended to complete "the destruction of the remnants of the influence of bourgeois elements (New Economic Policy men, kulaks, the bourgeois intelligentsia) upon the toiling masses" and to involve the broad masses of the proletariat and the peasantry in the task of strengthening the Soviet state. The declaration, moreover, reaffirmed the directing role of the proletariat.[110] In practice, this signified Party support for a number of surface alterations in the system of command, but no modification of its substance.[111] At the Fourteenth Party Conference, Kaganovich advocated a policy of encouraging an increase in discussion in local soviets without limiting the decision-making power of the Communist fraction.[112] Other general measures included a termination of Party support for local Communist tyrants and severe criticism of the practices of appointing representatives to local soviets in place of holding elections and of reducing elections to a mere ratification of lists of candidates.

These measures were designed to apply to Communist policy in the non-Russian as well as the Russian regions of the USSR. They were supplemented by additional directives aimed specifically at the national minorities. In May, 1925, the Third All-Union Congress of Soviets ordered the Central Executive Committee to bring representatives of the national minorities into elective soviet organs and to establish separate soviets which

[109] See Stalin, *Sochineniia*, VI, 302, 320.

[110] *Vse-Soiuznaia Kommunisticheskaia Partiia (b) v rezoliutsiiakh* (6th ed., Moscow, 1941), II, 104–5.

[111] See Stalin's comments on the danger of a non-Party opposition in his *Sochineniia*, VII, 192–93.

[112] *Chetyrnadtsataia Konferentsiia Rossiiskoi Kommunisticheskoi Partii (b)* (Moscow, 1925), p. 38; also Stalin, *Sochineniia*, VII, 126–27.

would conduct their business in local languages where conditions warranted that.[113] Later directives enjoined lower-level executive committees to establish proportional representation of national minorities in electoral commissions, to sponsor meetings featuring reports by deputies to the soviets during electoral campaigns, to bring representatives of these minorities into the executive committees of soviets, and to encourage Soviet and Party officials to take part in local congresses of soviets and the congresses and conferences of other local public organizations.[114]

The critical evaluation to which the Party leadership had submitted the local soviet apparatus was repeated in the Central Asian republics. Out of the national delimitation the newly formed Uzbek and Turcoman republics had inherited all the evils which Moscow was currently attacking. And in the former territories of Bokhara and Khorezm especially, the new soviet institutions had come into control of a local soviet apparatus which was frequently dominated by "class enemies" of the Soviet regime. At the First Uzbek Congress of Soviets a representative of the Party's Central Asiatic Bureau complained that local soviets often failed either to reflect the general Party and Soviet line or to satisfy the needs of the peasantry. The problem had arisen, he charged, because republic authorities were too little interested in the daily life of the villages.[115] The remedy, according to the resolution of the congress, lay in the establishment of procedures for a strict accountability of local soviets, a systematic dispatch of experienced workers for instruction in the localities, and in investigation of local soviets in order to eliminate enemies of the regime.[116]

The effort to improve the local soviet apparatus in Central Asia met its first test in the elections of 1925–26. In preparation for them, the governments of Uzbekistan and Turkmenia ordered the disenfranchisement of large numbers of suspected

[113] Text in Lozovskii and Bibin, *Sovetskaia Politika za 10 let po natsional'nomu voprosu v RSFSR*, p. 14.

[114] *Ibid.*, pp. 29–31, 42–43.

[115] *Pervyi Vseuzbekskii S'ezd Sovetov Rabochikh, Dekhkanskikh i Krasnoarmeiskikh Deputatov Uzbekskoi Sovetskoi Sotsialisticheskoi Respubliki, fevral' 1925 goda. stenograficheskii otchet* (Tashkent, 1925), pp. 10–11.

[116] *Ibid.*, pp. 90–92.

enemies (in Uzbekistan over 21,000 persons were denied the right to participate in the elections)[117] and organized a broad agitational campaign which included reports by prominent officials before local groups and mass meetings, and demonstrations in the rural areas. These efforts bore fruit but failed to achieve decisive gains in popular support for the soviet system. In Uzbekistan almost 46 percent of the electorate went to the polls, but in Turkmenia something less than 30 percent of the enfranchised population voted.[118] The government registered its greatest successes in the regions affected by the land reform, where the peasants, aroused by rumors that a vote favorable to the beys would lead to a reversal of the land reform policy, took pains to elect representatives of the poorest elements to the soviets.[119] In other regions the government suffered an embarrassing defeat. The peasants not only refused to approve Communist-supported lists of candidates but in some districts elected "bey-mullah" elements to three fourths of the seats.[120] These results, however, were not allowed to stand. Investigative commissions, hurriedly created to "study the soviet apparatus and to correct errors," traveled through the localities affected, nullified the elections, and ordered new ones. Then they jailed a number of local officials for crimes committed in the conduct of local soviet organs.[121]

The election results provided Bolshevik leaders in Central Asia with a clear warning that a continuous program of indoctrination in the rural areas was the prerequisite to winning peasant support. As a first step, the republican governments assigned special cadres to permanent positions in the local soviet apparatus. Following this, the Party opened a sustained agitational campaign designed to acquaint the peasants with their revolutionary rights and to explain the nature and tasks of the

[117] E. Cherniavskii, *Sailaular-saili: prazdnik vyborov* (Tashkent, 1927), p. 64.

[118] *Ibid.*, p. 65; Korbe, "Sovety Srednei Azii," *Revoliutsiia i Natsional'nosti*, No. 12 (58) (December, 1934), p. 56.

[119] A. Gurevich, "Zemel'no-vodnaia reforma v Uzbekskoi SSR (1925–1929)," *Voprosy Istorii*, No. 11 (November, 1948), pp. 65–66.

[120] Korbe, "Sovety Srednei Azii," *Revoliutsiia i Natsional'nosti*, No. 12 (58) (December, 1934), pp. 55–56.

[121] *Ibid.*, p. 56.

Soviet order. The climax was reached in the new electoral campaign of 1926–27, during which the government and the Party sponsored non-Party conferences in all the principal districts of Central Asia, convoked assemblies of the poor in rural areas, and distributed motion pictures depicting the election system, in addition to producing and distributing a flood of poster and pamphlet material.[122] Traveling troops of musicians were even employed to serenade the peasants as they worked in the fields and to drum up the election spirit. In its total effect the Bolsheviks considered the preelection campaign a success, and despite numerous defects in agitation work[123] some 40 percent of the population was believed to have participated in it.[124]

The Party nevertheless failed to rally unanimous support for its candidates. A number of cases were reported in which the peasants objected to the lists of candidates and to individuals proposed by the electoral commissions—in at least one case the opposing peasants were thrown into jail—and many candidates were elected against the will of the voters.[125] Moreover, the intense campaign to increase popular participation in the election was only moderately successful. Some 40 percent of the electorate turned out in Turkmenia, an increase of 10 percent over the 1925–26 vote. But only 46 percent of the Uzbek voters appeared at the polls even though the number of eligible voters had been reduced drastically in the period between the 1925–26 and the 1926–27 elections.[126] Despite Soviet claims that the election proved that the Communists had won over the peasantry and had involved it in a decisive struggle against the beys,[127] it is impossible not to attribute a good share of the stay-at-home

[122] For examples and a discussion see Cherniavskii, *Sailaular-saili: prazdnik vyborov*, pp. 21–24, 26–27, 31–33; P. Zaitsev, "Provedenie izbiratel'noi kampanii v Uzbekistane," *Vlast' Sovetov*, X, No. 9 (February 27, 1927), 10–14.

[123] Because of the widespread illiteracy, posters and pamphlets were not as effective as expected and in some cases gave the peasants the opposite impression from the one intended. Moreover, many of the non-Party conferences failed in their purpose because delegations to them were often composed exclusively of Party members. See Cherniavskii, *Sailaular-saili: prazdnik vyborov*, pp. 23–24, 26–27.

[124] *Ibid.*, p. 23.

[125] *Ibid.*, p. 29.

[126] *Ibid.*, pp. 64–65.

[127] *Ibid.*, p. 53.

vote to the influence of landowners and religious elements who had appealed to the natives to boycott the election.[128]

An examination of the election results in the context of the ten-year history of the soviet system in Central Asia leaves no doubt, however, that the Bolsheviks had successfully encouraged a tremendous increase of mass participation in the election process.[129] But it is questionable that this indicated a growth of "grass roots" democracy. Too many instances were reported in which Party candidates were railroaded into office over the objections of the voters. The Communist Party, moreover, maintained a tight rein on the soviets. Even in the rural soviets, nearly one third of the presidents were Communists or Komsomols, and above the volost' level the Party reserved for its members a majority of seats in all soviet organs.[130] In the higher soviet organs a solid nucleus of Russians exercised further supervision over the conduct of government business. As late as 1927, native deputies were a minority in the highest executive committees in Turkmenia. According to a report in *Sovetskoe Stroitel'stvo*, they filled only 16 percent of the seats in the central apparatus of the republic, 46.2 percent of the seats in the okrug executive committees, and 59.7 percent of the seats in district executive committees.[131]

From the foregoing survey of soviet practice it cannot be said that the Communist Party had successfully promoted the achievement of actual, as opposed to formal and legal, political equality in the Central Asian republics. Ten years after the soviet order had been proclaimed, Europeans still dominated the administrative hierarchy and the key organs of the soviet apparatus. In administrative agencies, natives not only constituted a numerical minority but with few exceptions were

[128] *Ibid.*, p. 40.

[129] In 1929, 60 percent of the eligible voters went to the polls in Uzbekistan and 70 percent in Turkmenia. See Rysakoff, *The National Policy of the Soviet Union*, p. 63.

[130] Communists also dominated volost' executive committees numerically, constituting in 1927 58.9 percent of the total membership in Uzbekistan and 64.4 percent in Turkmenia. Central Statistical Board, USSR, *Ten Years of Soviet Power in Figures, 1917–1927* (Moscow, 1927), pp. 14–15.

[131] "Prezidium Soveta Natsional'nostei," *Sovetskoe Stroitel'stvo*, Nos. 8–9 (13–14) (August–September, 1927), p. 135. No comparative report for Uzbekistan was available.

recruited to fulfill technical functions; in the soviet system, they worked under the direct supervision and surveillance of Europeans who maintained a tight control—often by preempting a majority of the seats—in the superior executive committees. The failure of the Bolsheviks to put into practice the policy of "rooting" the political institutions of the Central Asian republics—a policy which, according to its early enunciation, entailed the transfer of the machinery of government into the hands of the native population—is partially attributable to the scarcity of reliable cadres of educated natives. But the lack of an indigenous proletarian base upon which to build a stable soviet edifice, a residue of suspicion and distrust toward the native population, which persisted among Europeans in Central Asia, and even the vested interests of local European officials in their offices contributed substantially to the hesitant pace at which natives were introduced into posts of command.

Yet, even though the dictatorship of the proletariat in Central Asia was not dissimilar from the predominance of Great Russians, there is much evidence that the Bolsheviks were sincere in their efforts to grant the nationalities an equal status within the soviet order under the same general conditions imposed on all the peoples of the Soviet Union by the Bolshevik dictatorship. It must be remembered that many of the disabilities which operated to hinder the rapid development of a strong native leadership arose from class rather than national distinctions. Moreover, the nature of the soviet system, especially its emphasis on strict centralism, tended to restrict local popular initiative to narrow limits and to promote a spirit of "bureaucratism" among the hosts of appointed officials. Inevitably this encouraged administrators to lose contact with the masses, to stifle even legitimate criticism, often on the ground that it was counterrevolutionary, and to deviate in other ways from the national policy proclaimed by the central government.

A further explanation of many of the practical inconsistencies in the conduct of Soviet policy in the non-Russian republics lies in the constant pressure by the central government upon local officials to achieve a variety of objectives which were contradictory in fact if not in theory. On the one hand, central policy required that Soviet and Party officials work assiduously to bring the soviet system close to the masses and in other ways to encourage a growth of "soviet democracy" on the local level. On the other hand, it required that popular initiative be directed into channels which would promote the fulfillment of Party-assigned goals despite the fact that these goals were often inconsistent with, and sometimes quite opposite to, the self-determined goals of the masses. Faced with this dilemma, local Bolsheviks took measures to stimulate the development of many of the outward manifestations of local self-government but destroyed its essence by transferring the decision-making powers of the soviets to their presidiums, by appointing outsiders to supervise the work of local soviets, by annulling elections in which the local population refused to support Communist lists of candidates, and by similar practices.

While high Party officials and Soviet political writers subjected local officials to unremitting criticism for these and other shortcomings in the local system of government, the ultimate responsibility for providing a solution to these problems lay at the center. If anything, the experiment in "enlivening the soviets" had proved the impossibility of promoting a growth of local democracy while concurrently maintaining a system of strict centralism. By the end of the twenties it had become clear that a choice of goals on the highest Party level was necessary and inevitable. The Party, influenced no doubt by the atmosphere of crisis which attended the execution of the Five-Year Plans, chose to tighten the system of centralized control.

Out of this decision arose the pattern of strict Party control which has become a constant feature of the Soviet order. Local governmental organs were deprived of a large part of their decision-making power. For the most part this power was transferred to higher agencies, in which Party influence was stronger, or to administrative agencies. On the local level, too, it has not been unusual for Party officials to usurp the function of issuing and executing orders and directives without reference to local soviets. The structure of the local soviets and the ideology upon which it rested have nevertheless continued to exist. But the soviets have tended to become increasingly an administrative device of the Party and the principles of popular support and mass activity now find expression principally in carefully managed election campaigns.

V

BOLSHEVISM
AND ISLAM

◆

ISLAM is a syncretic religion revealed in a book, the Koran, and a prophetic tradition, the Sunna. Like Eastern Roman Christianity, it is a collectivistic religion in which truth is envisaged as dwelling in the congregation and is manifested at any given period in Ijma or the consensus of the faithful. Decisions which are reached by agreement between the teachers and the ulema or body of scholars trained in the Moslem religion and law are binding upon orthodox believers—that is, the sunnis who predominate outside of Persia—and are regarded as equal in authority to the Koran.[1]

It is characteristic of Islam to draw no distinction between spiritual and temporal authority. The traditional Moslem state was not merely the sword of Islam; it was an instrument for the enforcement of Moslem law—public, penal, and civil—and a guardian of the mode of social intercourse and private conduct which Islam prescribes for the faithful. Practical considerations of rule, however, long since have formed a division between lay and spiritual power in numerous spheres, a condition which facilitated the establishment of European hegemony in Moslem communities during the decline of the Ottoman Empire. Tsarist

[1] A general consultation is not required for the determination of Ijma. The organization of Islam renders impossible the convocation of synodal assemblies or ecumenical councils at which decisions of this nature could be taken. The decision of a group of ulema becomes authoritative if it meets with the tacit approval of their colleagues. See H. Lammens, *Islam: Beliefs and Institutions* (New York, n.d.), pp. 93–101.

rule in the Moslem regions of the Russian Empire accommodated itself to these conditions. Although Imperial Russia superimposed its own administrative regimen upon the Moslem community and refused recognition to local languages, it maintained the existing Moslem institutions—the shariat courts, civil laws, and customs—and in Bokhara and Khorezm continued the local theocratic rulers in office.

At the passing of the Tsarist regime, European influences had made few inroads into the solidarity of the Moslem community, and the revolution found the Moslem social and economic system in Central Asia firmly entrenched. Among the Kirghiz, Islam rested upon shallow foundations, but elsewhere in the region it was interwoven into the very fabric of social customs and the mode of life of the indigenous population. The existence of an economic system based upon small producers, in which landlord, tenant, and farm hand alike had an interest, and a spirit of religious fellowship which infused relationships between the laity and the Moslem scholars and teachers promoted internal Moslem solidarity and prevented the emergence of class antagonisms.

The nature of Islam, especially its close relationship with the customary social and economic processes in Central Asia and its inherent denial of the idea of class discord, brought it into conflict with the Soviet regime at numerous points. Broadly speaking, the revolution in Central Asia opened the way for a direct collision of two mutually exclusive philosophies of life in which Communist materialism and humanism were pitted against Moslem theism and mysticism for control of the spiritual allegiance of the masses. On the practical level, Islam was a constant hindrance to the realization of the social goals of the revolution. Moslem conservatism, intimately connected with the patriarchal mode of life of the native peoples, was antithetical to Soviet plans for the reorganization of society and struggled for the retention of customary religious and social institutions which Bolshevik theory condemned to extinction.

THE SOVIET STATE AND MOSLEM SENTIMENT

While committed ideologically to the proposition that Islam, in common with all religions, was an opiate blinding the masses to their class destiny, Communist leaders were aware that it had profound roots in social and economic conditions. Engels, echoing the views of Marx, had written in *Anti-Dühring* that religion was "nothing other than the reflection in the minds of men of those external forces which dominate them in their daily life." It would vanish, he believed, only when man had mastered the social process, had seized the means of production, and had systematically converted them to his own use.[2] Lenin agreed completely, and this viewpoint eventually found its way into the program of the Communist Party, Article 13 of which states that the Party "is guided by the conviction that only conscious and deliberate planning of all the social and economic activities of the masses will cause religious prejudices to die out." [3]

Article 13 represents in essence a formal recognition of the long-standing Bolshevik belief that Soviet success in achieving the programmatic goals of the October Revolution, together with a prolonged program of mass education, alone would serve to overcome the religious predilections of the masses. However much the idea of tolerance may have been ignored in the course of daily struggle, the Bolsheviks were united, in theory, in rejecting administrative repression as a means of destroying religion. Their own acquaintance with the consequences of persecution led them to the conclusion that outrages against the religious sentiments of believers would fail to weaken the "social roots" of religion and would even strengthen religious fanaticism. Fundamentally, the Bolsheviks were paying tribute to man's profound involvement in religious experience. In one of his early articles on the national problem, Stalin asserted the right of peoples to religious belief and likened it to the right to nationality.[4] But while recognition of nationalities became a cornerstone of the formal Soviet edifice, religion drew no comfort from the revolution, at best merely cold toleration.

[2] From an excerpt from *Anti-Dühring*, reprinted in G. A. Gurev (ed.), *Anti-religioznaia khrestomatiia: posobie dlia propagandistov, prepodavatelei i uchashchikhsia* (4th ed., Moscow, 1930), pp. 480–81.

[3] From text of Article 13, reprinted in Emelian Yaroslavsky, *Religion in the USSR* (London, 1932), p. 17.

[4] J. V. Stalin, *Sochineniia* (Moscow, 1946—), II, 355.

Notwithstanding its disavowal of persecution or even recognition of a right to religious belief, the policy of the Party—and consequently the policy of the Soviet government—was inherently antireligious. It was designed to facilitate the "dying out" of religion. At the same time it was flexible in that it was readily adaptable both to the varying strength of religious conviction among the diverse peoples of the Soviet state and to the immediate requirements of the international revolutionary movement. The Party did not hesitate to retreat from untenable positions, to offer concessions, or even to compromise its principles temporarily in regions where religion was deeply entrenched. In like manner, the Party offered encouragement to religious movements outside of Russia which were embarrassing to the imperial powers and tempered its internal policy toward religion in order to extend its influence upon these movements.

Nowhere was the flexibility of Bolshevik policy toward religion more clearly manifested than in the Moslem regions of Soviet Russia. One aspect of this flexibility appeared in a prudent adaptation of the pressure of antireligious propaganda to the degree of religious feeling found in the several Moslem communities of the republic. Another appeared in the cautious, often piecemeal, implementation of acts and decrees which purposed to separate the church from the state and the church from the school and to eliminate other customary prerogatives and prescripts of the Moslem faith. Instances of local excesses in the enforcement of antireligious measures were not uncommon in Moslem regions, particularly during the period of revolution and civil war, but where the withdrawal of Moslem privileges and property excited mass resistance or otherwise discomforted the Soviet government these privileges were ultimately restored to the congregation of the faithful.

The universality of belief among the native population of these regions necessitated a temporary relaxation of the conditions of membership in the Communist Party. Despite the obvious contradiction between Party membership and religious belief, many Moslems found their way into Party ranks during the early years of Soviet rule. To some extent, the influx of Moslems stemmed from the difficulty of local Party bodies in distinguishing between religious convictions and nationality in recruiting members; to a greater extent it was a consequence of tacit encouragement from the central Party organs which were responsible not only for promises of protection for Moslem institutions[5] but for the formation under the Party Central Committee of a central Moslem Bureau and the establishment of Moslem sections of the Communist Party on the local level. In point of fact, a short-lived school of thought flourished within Party circles which sought unsuccessfully to foster the notion that Communism and Islam were complementary rather than antithetical philosophies of life.[6]

Although the policy of allowing adherents of the Moslem faith to enter the Party was basically an expedient aimed at winning popular native support for the Party and the Soviet order during the civil war period, it was nevertheless the cause of considerable uneasiness among orthodox Communists. No sooner had the Soviet regime consolidated itself in power than an opposition emerged which contended that the large incidence of believers among the native Bolsheviks in the Moslem regions constituted an incipient threat to Bolshevik principles and eventually to the Soviet authority itself. These charges were partially substantiated by complaints from the localities that native Party functionaries were making a public display of religious sentiment and were resisting Party efforts to undermine traditional Islamic institutions.[7]

Despite these and other local infractions of Party discipline in

[5] See especially the "Appeal to the Working Moslems of Russia and the East," *Izvestiia,* December 5, 1917. Text reproduced in William Henry Chamberlin, *The Russian Revolution, 1917–1921* (New York, 1935), I, 484–86.

[6] See especially the declaration of Sultan-Galiev at the Seventh All-Russian Congress of Soviets. *Sed'moi Vserossiiskii S'ezd Sovetov Rabochikh, Krest'ianskikh, Krasnoarmeiskikh i Kazach'ikh Deputatov (5–9 dekabria, 1919 goda v Moskve). stenograficheskii otchet* (Moscow, 1920), pp. 15–16. A similar line of reasoning also emerged among the Bolsheviks in Central Asia. See P. Antropov, "Pervyi S'ezd Kommunisticheskoi Partii Turkestana," in Istpart Sredazbiuro Ts.K., V.K.P.(b), *Revoliutsiia v Srednei Azii* (Tashkent, 1929), I, 18.

[7] Safarov complained bitterly of the "pollution" of Central Asian Communist organizations by religious elements at the Tenth Party Congress. *Protokoly s'ezdov i konferentsii Vsesoiuznoi Kommunisticheskoi Partii (b): Desiatyi S'ezd R.K.P.(b), mart, 1921 g.* (Moscow, 1933), p. 195. Agabekov, who was in Central Asia in 1925, also remarked that the native Communists divided their time "between trade, praying in the mosques and attending to public business." Georges Agabekov, *OGPU, the Russian Secret Terror* (New York, 1931), p. 136.

areas where the conflicting demands of Islam and Communism upon individual loyalty crossed, the Party did not alter its moderate policy greatly. The theses of the Fifth Congress of the Communist Party of Turkestan, which were characteristic of Bolshevik thinking of the period, limited the requirement of "freedom from religious prejudices" to Europeans and "fully conscious and responsible Moslem workers" who were candidates for responsible positions. An educational program whose purpose was the development of class consciousness was the sole weapon authorized for use in the struggle against the religious predilections of rank-and-file Moslem Bolsheviks.[8] The Party hewed closely to the attitude expressed in these theses throughout the early and middle twenties. In contrast to its increasingly stern policy of weeding out Europeans who entertained religious biases, the Party scrupulously avoided eliminating Moslems on the score of religious persuasion.[9]

The same circumspection which distinguished the Bolshevik attitude toward admission of Moslems into the Communist Party characterized the efforts of the Soviet government to destroy the temporal privileges of Islam. Nonetheless, the attitude of the Party toward its members and that of the state toward the citizenry differed in one important respect. The Party, for reasons which are apparent, could not adopt a neutral posture toward religion within its ranks. On the other hand, the Soviet state, guided by the old socialist precept that the state must regard religion as a private affair, did not bring the right of religious belief into question. In his article on "Socialism and Religion," Lenin had supported this viewpoint as early as 1905 and, on the basis of it, had laid the foundation of future Soviet policy toward religion:

The state should not concern itself with religion nor should religious societies be linked with state authority. Every person should

[8] From the theses of the Fifth Congress of the Communist Party of Turkestan. Text in Georgii Safarov, *Kolonial'naia revoliutsiia: opyt Turkestana* (Moscow, 1921), p. 139.

[9] The cautious policy toward Moslem Communists is well illustrated in the Party purge in Turkestan in 1922. Whereas more than 1,500 Europeans were expelled from the Party on charges of religious conviction, not a single native was ousted for this cause. See "Partiinaia chistka v Turkestane," *Zhizn' Natsional'nostei*, No. 8 (14) (April 26, 1922), pp. 9–10.

be completely free to profess whatever religion he pleases or to profess no religion at all, that is, to be an atheist, which every socialist usually is. No distinction whatsoever is to be made between citizens in respect to their rights which are dependent upon their religious faiths. . . . Complete separation of church from state—this is what the socialist proletariat demands of the modern state and church.[10]

These propositions became the fundamental principles of Soviet state policy in regard to religion. Toward religion itself the state maintained an attitude of calculated neutrality; toward the privileges of religious societies, it adopted a course of prompt extinction. On January 23, 1918, the Council of People's Commissars of the RSFSR promulgated a decree "On Freedom of Conscience and Religious Societies," [11] which, until supplemented by a directive of the Central Executive Committee and the Council of People's Commissars of the RSFSR of April 8, 1929, "On Religious Organizations," [12] was the principal act of government defining the legal status of religion and religious sects in the Soviet republic. This decree recognized the equality before the law of all religious sects, allowing preference to none, and permitted the celebration of every form of religious custom and ceremony providing it did not disturb the public peace or infringe upon the rights of other citizens of the Soviet republic. It specifically forbade local agencies of government the right to enact any law or order which limited the freedom of conscience of any citizen or established any kind of privilege based on denominational adherence. "Every citizen may adhere to any religion or adhere to none," Article 3 stated. "Any limitations before the law relating to adherence to any kind of faith or nonadherence to any faith are abolished."

Further articles provided for a complete secularization of the state. The observance of religious customs and ceremonies of

---

[10] From an excerpt from "Sotsializm i religiia," reproduced in Gurev, *Antireligioznaia khrestomatiia*, pp. 702–3.

[11] *Sobranie Uzakonenii i Rasporiazhenii Rabochego i Krest'ianskogo Pravitel'stva RSFSR*, 1918, No. 18, Art. 263. Text reproduced in Julius F. Hecker, *Religion and Communism: A Study of Religion and Atheism in Soviet Russia* (London, 1933), pp. 289–90.

[12] *Sobranie Uzakonenii i Rasporiazhenii, RSFSR*, 1929, No. 35, p. 353. Text partially reproduced in Hecker, *Religion and Communism*, pp. 290–93.

any kind was prohibited at any state or other public and social function; the religious oath was abolished; and the keeping of registers of births, marriages, and deaths was transferred to civil authorities. A special article forbade the evasion of civil duties on religious grounds. Intended especially to apply to religious sects which prohibited their members from participating in military service, it provided that exemption from the obligation to perform a specific duty might be granted solely on condition of the performance of some equivalent duty and then only with the permission of a people's court in each individual instance.

The major impact of the decree lay, however, in the blows it struck at the economic foundations of the church. In accordance with the principle of the separation of church from state, it prohibited the extension of any privilege or subsidy to churches and religious societies by the state or by local autonomous and self-governing bodies, and, in addition, banned compulsory collections or assessments for the benefit of these organizations. The last two articles dealt the deathblow to the economic power of the church. On the one hand, the law nationalized all existing church property; on the other, it denied the church the right to own property and by depriving it of the right of a juridic person made it impossible for the church as a corporation to accumulate property in the future. In this connection it should be noted that the Soviet government treated the church no differently from other institutions and private enterprises whose properties it also nationalized. Moreover, the law specifically provided that "buildings and objects specially designated for divine services [be] given for free use to corresponding religious societies." In short, the law was meant to strip the church of its temporal property while purporting to leave its spiritual domain intact.

The uncompromising opposition of the Soviet state toward the temporal power of the church found further reflection in the 1918 constitution of the RSFSR, Article 13 of which affirmed the principles set forth in the decree of January, 1918. "To the end of securing actual freedom of conscience in behalf of the toilers," the article read, "the church is separated from the state and the school from the church; but freedom of religious and antireligious propaganda is conceded in behalf of all citizens." [13] Upon this legal foundation the Soviet government gradually eliminated the privileges and expropriated the properties of religious institutions. Nevertheless, the government allowed expediency to dictate the pace at which the law was put into operation and it also took pains to avoid interfering with the practices of worship of the various sects. In its effect upon the power of the Russian Orthodox Church, this policy proved very effective. It not only prevented an outbreak of fanatical religious resistance but undermined the command of the church over the congregation and in 1922 finally split the clergy itself.[14] In its effect upon the strength of Islam, the policy was less successful in loosening the bonds with which Islam embraced the political, economic, and social life of the community.

In Central Asia especially, Bolshevik determination to destroy the secular prerogatives of religion collided with Moslem fanaticism almost from the outset of the revolution. Initially, Moslem religious leaders, unlike the Turkic nationalists, did not contest the right of the Soviet regime to exercise temporal power in the region. As a matter of fact, the ulema in Turkestan so misunderstood the nature of the Soviet authority that they sought to persuade the Tashkent Soviet to administer the region in accordance with the precepts of Moslem law.[15] The rejection of this overture, followed by the inauguration of a drastic Soviet policy toward religion, quickly disabused the Moslem community of the notion that a *modus vivendi* between Bolshevism and Islam was possible of achievement.

Within three months of the fall of the Provisional Govern-

---

[13] Andrei Y. Vyshinsky, *The Law of the Soviet State* (New York, 1949), p. 608. The article concerning freedom of conscience was repeated in the 1925 constitution of the RSFSR and similar formulas were included in the constitutions of all union and autonomous republics of the USSR. In 1929, largely in consequence of pressures applied by the militant atheists, the right of religious propaganda was abrogated.

[14] For an examination of the dispute between church and state during this period, see Hecker, *Religion and Communism*, pp. 189–214; Paul B. Anderson, *People, Church and State in Modern Russia* (New York, 1944), pp. 63–98; John S. Curtiss, *The Russian Church and the Soviet State* (Boston, 1953), pp. 71–153.

[15] P. Alekseenkov, "Kokandskaia Avtonomiia," in Istpart Sredazbiuro Ts.K., V.K.P.(b), *Revoliutsiia v Srednei Azii*, I, 31–32.

ment in Turkestan, the regional Soviet authority had promulgated a series of decrees and regulations which ordered the separation of the church from the school, annulled the prerevolutionary legal system, and nationalized the property of religious as well as civil institutions. This notice that the new regime was resolved to overthrow the established social order in the Moslem as well as the European community of Central Asia drove Moslem religious leaders directly into the path of counterrevolution and into association with the native nationalist movement. By mid-January, 1918, respected members of the Turkestanian ulema had risen to positions of prominence in the Kokand Autonomous Government and actually dominated it during the last stages of its existence.

From the fall of Kokand to the end of the civil war, the struggle between Islam and Bolshevism grew steadily in range and violence. The Tashkent government, redoubling its efforts to destroy the secular privileges of Islam, abolished the shariat court and other Moslem communal institutions, seized Moslem property indiscriminately, and even permitted Red Guard detachments to desecrate mosques and other holy places. Moslem leaders, on the other hand, allied themselves with the Basmachi. By furnishing the Basmachi movement with a popular religious symbolism and by inviting the faithful to take up arms against the "infidel Bolsheviks" in defense of Islam and the Shariat, they were instrumental in broadening and extending native guerrilla warfare against the Soviet regime.

The rapid expansion and intensification of open warfare between the Moslem population and the Soviet regime in Turkestan not only compounded the difficulties of the Tashkent government; it also caused embarrassment to the Moscow government which was seeking to placate Moslem minorities in Russia and to extend Bolshevik influence among Moslem nations beyond Russia's borders. In June, 1919, Moscow intervened directly, ordering the government of Turkestan to avoid policies which antagonized Moslems and particularly "to cease requisitioning Moslem property without the agreement of the regional Moslem organization." [16] These measures in themselves did not

[16] V. I. Lenin, *Sochineniia* (2d ed., Moscow, 1926—), XXIV, 811.

alter the situation basically. By the time they were put into effect the deterioration of relations between Moslems and the local Soviet regime was complete. But they did indicate that under sufficient pressure the Bolsheviks would compromise their policy, if not their attitude, toward religion in Central Asia.

The extent of the willingness of the Soviet regime to retreat became apparent toward the end of 1921. Earlier the government had offered a few sops to Moslem sentiment. The central authorities had ordered the return of the Sacred Koran of Osman, which the Tsarist government had removed from Turkestan.[17] The Central Executive Committee of the Turkestan republic decreed Friday, the weekly Moslem day of religious celebration, to be the legal day of rest in Turkestan.[18] At the same time, the Soviet government steadfastly refused to withdraw from positions already assumed in the struggle against religious privileges or to nullify the past acts of local authorities even though they outraged Moslem religious sensibilities.

However, in 1921, influenced by the general retreat into the New Economic Policy and by Enver Pasha's rapid progress in unifying and strengthening the Basmachi movement, the Bolsheviks reversed their position. The Soviet government ceased to tolerate interference with the right of worship, ordered the return to the congregations of mosques which had been seized by the state, and reduced civil intrusion into the affairs of the remaining religious establishments. Shariat justice, abolished in 1918, was reintroduced for believers. The state undertook to restore endowment property (wakf) which had been confiscated during the revolution, to reopen schools operated by Moslem teachers, and even to temper Bolshevik criticism of Moslem spiritual leaders.

These measures accomplished their immediate purpose. The

[17] Vyshinsky, *The Law of the Soviet State,* p. 607.

[18] Decree of the Central Executive Committee of the Turkestan ASSR of January 10, 1921. Reproduced in Pavel V. Gidulianov, *Otdelenie tserkvi ot gosudarstva v SSSR; polnyi sbornik dekretov, vedomstvennykh rasporiazhenii i opredelenii verkhsuda RSFSR i drugikh sovetskikh sotsialisticheskikh respublik: Uk. SSR, BSSR, ZSFSR, Uzbekskoi i Turkmenskoi* (3d ed., Moscow, 1926), pp. 61–62.

religious element, which had become the main bulwark of Basmachism, now split, and some mullahs endorsed the Soviet
regime. Of greater significance, the government made these concessions without compromising the legal foundations of the
principle of separation of church and state. In its constitution
and in a decree concerning the separation of church and state,
the Turkestan republic had reproduced verbatim the article of
the constitution of the RSFSR dealing with freedom of conscience and the decree of January 23, 1918.[19] After 1921 the government of the republic merely restricted enforcement of these
laws to the European population.

In contrast to Turkestan, the problem of adopting a double
standard in the application of legal norms relative to religion
did not arise in the republics of Bokhara and Khorezm until
after the national delimitation and the inclusion of their territories in the Uzbek and Turcoman SSR's. Throughout the
period of their existence, neither republic sought to separate
church from state. Both republics guaranteed their nationals
complete freedom of conscience subject only to the obligation
of noninterference with the utilization of the same right by
others.[20] Both undertook, moreover, to protect the civil as well
as the religious prerogatives of Islam. In Bokhara this was accomplished by a constitutional provision which invalidated any
law which might "contradict the foundations of Islam." [21] The
Second Kuraltai of the Khorezmian People's Republic committed itself to a similar policy, pledging noninterference by
the state in the affairs of the Shariat and of religious institutions,
and guaranteeing the inviolability of endowment property.[22]
These assurances of state protection for social-religious institutions disappeared after the national delimitation. The Uzbek
and Turcoman republics, into whose jurisdiction the territories
of Bokhara and Khorezm passed, immediately adopted legal

[19] *Ibid.*, p. 6.
[20] *Ibid.*, pp. 6, 36.
[21] From Article 26 of the constitution of the Bokharan People's Soviet Republic. See N. B. Arkhipov, "Bukharskaia Narodnaia Sovetskaia Respublika,"
Sovetskoe Pravo, No. 1 (4) (1923), pp. 136–37.
[22] A. Vinogradova, "Khorezmskaia Sovetskaia Narodnaia Respublika," *Zhizn'
Natsional'nostei*, No. 1 (January, 1923), pp. 189–90.

norms similar to those governing religion in the RSFSR and the former Turkestan republic.[23]

The promulgation of this legislation by no means indicated that the Soviet aim of confining Islam's impact upon the native community to the realm of spiritual affairs had been accomplished. In 1921, it is true, the Soviet regime had withdrawn most of the disabilities placed upon Moslem institutions during the revolution and civil war. These were temporary concessions intended primarily to undermine the Basmachi movement, but they were also an admission that they had failed in their attempt to compel by fiat changes in the customary social structure. After 1921 the Bolsheviks replaced the incautious policy of rigid enforcement of the principle of separation of church and state by a series of piecemeal restrictions which gradually undermined traditional Islamic social-religious institutions and paved the way for their ultimate destruction. Although the Soviet government employed this strategy to debilitate and finally abolish religious influences in every sphere of civil life, its immediate objective was the eradication of three traditional institutions— wakf or property in mortmain, the shariat or Koranic law, and the system of Islamic education—which lay at the root of Islamic secular power.

EXPROPRIATION BY DEGREE: THE ELIMINATION OF THE RELIGIOUS FOUNDATIONS

The first of these institutions, wakf, had long played an important part in the economy of Moslem states. The wakf had originated during the period of the Umayyad Caliphate (661–750) and had spread rapidly throughout the Moslem world. Islam encouraged the assignment in perpetuity of properties and their incomes for the maintenance of pious foundations. Historically, the caliphate had provided no public moneys for the establishment or preservation of mosques, *madrasa,* or seminaries, hospitals, aqueducts, and water conservation projects. These works were perforce established by individual rulers and persons of wealth who created out of their properties endowments whose revenue would be utilized to support pious foundations. These

[23] Gidulianov, *Otdelenie tserkvi ot gosudarstva v RSFSR,* p. 6.

estates were composed either of urban properties, whose rents provided a regular source of income, or of rural holdings whence revenues could be obtained from land rents or a charge on the tax revenue.

Equally important to the growth of the institution of wakf were the individual economic needs of Moslem property owners. This led to the establishment of private endowment properties or entails. Moslem rules of inheritance provided for a complete and complicated division of an estate among the heirs and denied to an owner the right to prevent an endless subdivision of his properties after death. By converting the estate into an endowment fund whose revenues would accrue to his descendants in accordance with the rule of succession, the owner was enabled to protect the integrity of his property and the possibility of its profitable exploitation.

While mismanagement by trustees tended inevitably to limit the effectiveness of the device as a means of protecting the integrity of private estates and of providing for permanent maintenance of public works, the institution of wakf satisfied a real social need within the Moslem community. The fact that between one eighth and one half of the land under cultivation in various Moslem countries had been sequestered in this manner attests to the popularity of the institution. According to postrevolutionary Bolshevik estimates, endowment properties in Central Asia comprised about 8 to 10 percent of the cultivated acreage, and the Bokharan government at one time calculated that they constituted one fifth of Bokhara's cultivated land resources.[24] This very popularity was the source of the greatest evil of the device. For one thing, it stimulated the withdrawal of large amounts of wealth from circulation and thus contributed to the impoverishment of the Moslem community as a whole. For another, it created large funds of tax-exempt property and consequently increased the tax burden borne by the citizenry at large.

Although resolved to eliminate the institution of wakf, the

[24] A. Vorobeichikov and Gafiz, "Kak prokhodila zemreforma v Uzbekistane," in I. S. Kraskin (ed.), *Zemel'no-vodnaia reforma v Srednei Azii: sbornik materialov* (Moscow, 1927), p. 51. Also M. N., "Pod znakom Islama," *Novyi Vostok,* No. 4 (1923), pp. 81–82.

Bolsheviks had been constrained at the beginning of the New Economic Policy to restore title to endowment properties which the Tashkent government had seized during the civil war. However, the Soviet regime did not commit itself to a complete reestablishment either of the property or of the rights and privileges of these institutions. In August, 1921, the Sixth Congress of the Communist Party of Turkestan consented to refrain from interference with the affairs of endowment properties which supported religious or cultural and educational institutions, but it limited this commitment to the pious foundations, and even in relation to these it made no promises for the future. The Bolsheviks also offered no guarantees of protection for private endowment property, and they specifically provided for subjection of pious endowments to the laws governing socialist land tenure in cases in which the toiling population demanded it.[25] Moreover, with the exception of an exemption granted for the year 1922 to populated endowment properties, which were not religious in character, as part of the effort to revive the economy of Turkestan, the Soviet government refused to permit tax privileges to endowments of any kind.[26]

For more than a year after the Sixth Party Congress in Turkestan, endowment properties pertaining to pious foundations were allowed to exist without precise legal status. In the course of that year Soviet troops defeated the Basmachi armies decisively at Kafrun, Enver Pasha perished in a Red ambush, and a period of relatively peaceful reconstruction opened in Central Asia. The strengthened position of the Soviet regime was reflected in a decree of the Central Executive Committee of the Turkestan republic of December 28, 1922, which guaranteed the endowment properties of pious foundations and established a system of public supervision and control over the administration of these properties.[27]

[25] Ilias Alkin, *Sredniaia Aziia: Ekonomiko-geograficheskii ocherk Kara-Kalpakstana, Kirgizstana, Tadzhikistana, Turkmenistana i Uzbekistana* (Moscow, 1931), I, 357–58.

[26] N. Fioletov, "Vakufnoe pravo v Sredne-Aziatskikh Sovetskikh Respublik," *Sovetskoe Pravo*, No. 2 (20) (1926), pp. 100–101. In 1923, the Khorezmian People's Republic also subjected endowment properties to taxation. *Izvestiia,* October 23, 1923.

[27] The text of the decree appeared originally in *Pravda Turkestana,* January

The first article of the decree formally acknowledged the right of religious, philanthropic, and cultural and educational institutions to own endowment properties and to utilize the revenues deriving from them. But later articles compromised this right seriously. The decree abolished outright populated endowment properties of an agricultural nature existing in rural areas, turned the land over to the tenants who were in occupation at the moment on the basis of the laws relating to socialist land tenure,[28] and prohibited future establishment of endowment properties consisting of arable land. It further stipulated that rents derived from structures erected on endowment properties by private individuals and institutions were not to be included in the revenues of the properties but were to accrue to local wakf and public education departments. The benefits of the decree, moreover, were restricted to pious foundations which could prove their existence prior to the October Revolution either by documentary evidence or by certification of the local Soviet executive committee.[29]

To supervise and regulate the activities of pious foundations, recognized in the decree, the Turkestan government created a Main Wakf Administration within the Commissariat of Education and a number of local wakf departments. The Main Administration, though it exercised the right to censor textbooks and to regulate the pattern of instruction in Moslem seminaries, functioned primarily as a coordinating agency in charge of supervision and guidance of the activities of local wakf departments and confirmation of their personnel and their budgets. Direct supervision over the management of endowment properties was delegated to the local departments which were commissioned to superintend the activities of administrators of endowment properties and to audit the expenditure of endowment revenues. The important power to appoint and dismiss

10, 1923. It is reproduced in Gidulianov, *Otdelenie tserkvi ot gosudarstva v SSSR*, pp. 279–80.

[28] An annotation to the article softened the impact somewhat by providing that local taxes, levied on these properties, be utilized to establish a cultural-educational fund for the requirements of education in the kishlaks.

[29] The decree nevertheless permitted the establishment of new endowment properties for philanthropic, cultural-educational, and socioeconomic needs.

wakf administrators, a function which had previously resided in the kadi, was also vested in the local departments.

The restrictions contained in the decree of December 28, 1922, not only imposed rigid limitations upon the extent and classes of endowment property which the Soviet regime would tolerate but placed the institution itself at the mercy of the state. In the exercise of its power of supervision and control over the expenditure of endowment revenues, the wakf administration also established control over the ministers of religion, whose livelihood depended upon incomes deriving from these properties. Through use of its power of appointment, it was likewise able to remove wakf administrators who were unsympathetic to the Soviet order and to replace them with willing collaborators.

The Soviet government employed these weapons so effectively, both to stifle religious criticism of Bolshevism and to further undermine the system of endowment property, that the suggestion, made on the eve of the land reform, that cultural and educational endowment property be included in the fund of land to be distributed among the peasants, evoked very little opposition. The government of the Turcoman republic seized upon the occasion to abolish endowment property completely.[30] The Uzbek government, aware of the danger of provoking a wave of fanatical religious opposition, acted more cautiously. In December, 1925, it decreed the transfer of title over all remaining rural endowment properties to the republic Commissariat of Agriculture, but specifically excluded orchards and vineyards pertaining to cultural and educational institutions, religious societies, and mosques.[31] Later regulations put an end even to these properties and a series of concurrent restrictions gradually eliminated endowment properties in the urban areas. By 1930 the Soviet government had regulated the institution of wakf out of legal existence in Central Asia. Undoubtedly, cases continued to crop up in which mullahs managed to derive income from

[30] Joseph Castagné, "La Réforme agraire au Turkestan," *Revue des Études Islamiques,* No. 11 (1928), pp. 396–97; also E. L. Shteinberg, *Ocherki istorii Turkmenii* (Moscow, 1934), pp. 116–17.

[31] Text of decree in *Sobranie uzakonenii i rasporiazhenii Uzbekskoi SSR,* No. 60 (December 31, 1925), p. 529.

endowments—sometimes by the expedient of converting them nominally into collective farms—but the wakf as an economic foundation of Moslem religious power had disappeared.

By abolishing endowment property the Soviet regime put an end to a traditional social institution which had survived the centuries without loss of popularity and without substantial change. Nevertheless, the government had avoided acting in direct opposition to Moslem opinion within Russia and to precedents being established elsewhere in the Moslem world. The conjunction of three circumstances, all of which were anterior to socialization, had created a favorable atmosphere for elimination of the institution. One was the existence of peasant land hunger which skillful Bolshevik exploitation forged into a weapon to destroy rural endowments. A second circumstance was the diminished importance of endowment property in pre-revolutionary Russia in consequence of confiscations by the Tsarist government—a factor which reduced the number of foundations affected by Bolshevik expropriations and served, moreover, as a precedent for them. The third was a general reform movement in Moslem states aimed at correcting abuses and remedying ill effects of the system. The governments of most of these states adopted measures to put endowment property back into circulation and created machinery to control and centralize administration of the property without destroying the institution. Republican Turkey went further and in effect abolished the institution in 1926 by authorizing the sale of endowment properties to communes and public institutions.[32]

THE SOVIETIZATION OF THE CUSTOMARY COURT

In concurrent efforts to undermine the customary legal foundations of the Moslem community, principally by abolishing shariat justice and the judicature which administered it, the Bolsheviks found still greater comfort in a long-term trend toward secularization of justice in Moslem countries. Traditionally, the determination of legal disputes involving violation or interpretation of the Shariat, the legal embodiment of all the religious, political, and social norms which regulated the life of

[32] Maurice Gaudefroy-Demombynes, *Muslim Institutions* (London, 1950), p. 146.

the believers, was within the jurisdiction of the kadi, a judicial official selected from among the ulema. The kadi was competent to hear cases involving matters concerning which the Koran had enacted special prescriptions; that is, marriage, divorce, care of orphans, successions, and contracts of various kinds. In criminal cases and other questions referred to him by the civil authorities, he applied the *hudud Allah* or laws and justice of Allah derived from the Koran.

Within his jurisdiction, the kadi theoretically enjoyed judicial powers of the broadest kind, but in practice Moslem governments have always sought to restrict his activities. As early as the eighth century there appeared in Moslem countries a special civil magistrate, the *muhtasib,* whose function was similar to that of the Byzantine agoranome. This marked the beginning of a kind of legal dualism in Moslem states which eventually led to encroachments by civil authority upon the sphere of the kadi's jurisdiction. In criminal matters especially, Moslem governments quickly established their right not only to execute, but to confirm, the sentences of canonical courts. The Ottoman Empire in the nineteenth century established a ministry of justice which operated side by side with the Sheikh-al-Islam,[33] to whom the kadis were nominally responsible, and republican Turkey in 1924 suppressed the kadi altogether and completely laicized the old Moslem jurisprudence. Other Moslem governments likewise took steps to modify the jurisdiction of canonical courts but only Iran followed Turkey's example and abolished the institution.[34]

The canonical courts within the Russian Empire had undergone similar modifications. In Turkestan the Tsarist government had replaced shariat law with Russian administrative law in many spheres and had reduced sharply the jurisdiction of native courts.[35] On the eve of the Russian Revolution canonical courts were strong only in Khiva and Bokhara, which were under the protection but not the administration of the Imperial

[33] The Sheikh-al-Islam was the supreme head of the ulemas and muftis in the Ottoman Empire. He performed the function of a minister of cults.

[34] Gaudefroy-Demombynes, *Muslim Institutions,* pp. 148–58.

[35] M. A. Nemchenko, "Agrarnaia reforma v Turkmenii," *Novyi Vostok,* No. 19 (1927), pp. 131–32.

government;[36] elsewhere, the competence of these courts was being gradually curtailed and jurisdiction usurped by the civil authority. Thus the stage was set for state control of the religious-judicial system even before the Bolsheviks had seized power.

But while the Tsarist regime had suppressed only those portions of shariat justice which interfered with Russian administration, the Soviet government condemned the entire Moslem legal system to extinction. Seen through the Marxist prism, the canonical court was a weapon utilized by the Moslem ruling classes to oppress and exploit the native poor and to preserve the remnants of the crumbling feudal-patriarchal mode of life. As a social institution, it was regarded by the Bolsheviks as a barrier separating the Soviet authority from the Moslem masses and hindering the execution of Bolshevik social objectives. As a legal institution, shariat law and the courts which applied it drew Bolshevik fire on the ground that they were unsuited to the requirements of Soviet policy relating to the administration of justice and constituted moreover an obstacle to the establishment of the unified people's court as the judicial organ of the proletarian dictatorship.[37]

Fundamentally, the Soviet campaign to eliminate the canonical court comprised but one phase of a broader struggle to destroy entirely the prerevolutionary system of justice in the Russian Empire and to replace it with a system based on socialist principles of justice. Fulfillment of the revolutionary objectives of the Bolshevik Party required the establishment of a new Soviet judicature which, as a frank agent of class warfare, would undertake the task of combating the foes of the revolution and of educating unstable members of the laboring classes in the responsibilities of citizenship in the Soviet state. Lenin later stressed precisely this point in his article "The Immediate Tasks of the Soviet Authority":

[36] Sev, "Zametki o Turkmenskom dukhovenstve," *Turkmenovedenie,* Nos. 3–4 (7–8) (March–April, 1928), p. 12.

[37] N. Fioletov, "Sudoproizvodstvo v Musul'manskikh sudakh (sudy kaziev) Srednei Azii," *Novyi Vostok,* Nos. 23–24 (1928), p. 213; also V. Shokhor, "Religiozno-bytovye sudy v RSFSR," *Sovetskoe Stroitel'stvo,* Nos. 8–9 (13–14) (August–September, 1927), p. 94.

Above all a new court was indispensable to the struggle against the exploiters striving to reestablish their dominance or to defend their privileges (or furtively to insinuate or fraudulently to get advanced payment on some portion thereof). But there is another and still more important task resting upon the courts if they are in reality organized on the principle of Soviet institutions—to assure the strictest development of the toilers' discipline and self-discipline.[38]

After the seizure of power, soviet governments, both at the center and in the borderlands, acted swiftly to put into effect plans for the establishment of the new Soviet system of justice. On December 7, 1917, the central government enacted a decree Concerning the Court (No. 1) which ordered the abolition of the prerevolutionary court system and the establishment of a unified system of people's courts based on "direct democratic election." An exception was allowed in the case of the justice-of-the-peace courts. Since these courts, founded during the reign of Alexander II, had been granted to the people as a concession and were competent to deal only with minor civil and criminal cases, they were permitted to continue.[39] The Soviet government, moreover, did not accompany the abolition of the old court with a corresponding abrogation of the prerevolutionary structure of law. The decree did annul all previous laws which contradicted the decrees of the All-Russian Central Executive Committee and the minimum programs of the Bolshevik and Social Revolutionary Parties. Otherwise it authorized the soviet court to act on the basis of the laws of the overthrown government in so far as they had not been abolished by the revolution and did not contradict "revolutionary conscience and revolutionary legality." [40]

This decree set the pattern for early acts establishing norms of revolutionary legality and a system of soviet courts in the border regions. Within a week of its promulgation (December 12, 1917) the Soviet government of Turkestan decreed the abolition of existing legal institutions in the region and the organization

[38] Lenin, Sochineniia (2d ed.), XXII, 424.
[39] Sobranie Uzakonenii i Rasporiazhenii Rabochego i Krest'ianskogo Pravitel'stva RSFSR, 1917, No. 4, Art. 50.
[40] I. P. Trainin, Deklaratsiia Prav Trudiashchegosia i Eksploatiruemogo Naroda (Moscow, 1938), p. 21.

of a new court by January 1, 1918. The inability of the local soviets to organize a system of people's courts within the allotted time, however, compelled the regional government to postpone enforcement of the decree indefinitely. By a decree of December 31, 1917, the Turkestan Council of People's Commissars directed suspension of the original decree until soviet courts had been established and instructed existing courts and judges to continue to discharge their functions in the interim. At the same time, it transferred jurisdiction in "political" cases from the courts to the local soviets.[41]

The Tashkent government issued no directives indicating the laws which should guide local courts in reaching verdicts and sentences and adopted no criteria for determining which cases were political. Hence the stipulation of the decree relating to political cases constituted an open invitation to the soviets to interfere at their own discretion in judicial proceedings. As a consequence, local soviets intervened freely in court business, removing cases from the jurisdiction of the courts, and on occasion, directing the courts to reach specific verdicts and to prescribe specific punishments.[42] The removal of cases from the courts to the jurisdiction of the soviets was common both in the various localities and in Tashkent. In fact, the Commission of Inquiry, created in November, 1917, by the Tashkent Council of Deputies to deal with speculation and counterrevolution, became so swamped with cases of a general nature that it returned many of them to the jurisdiction of the regular courts.[43]

In February, 1918, the Turkestan Council of People's Commissars attempted to halt the drift toward complete usurpation of the judicial function by the soviets. By a special order of February 22, 1918, it appealed to the people of Turkestan to cooperate with and support the regular courts and warned that "persons guilty of insubordination to the courts will be pun-

[41] Kh. Suleimanova, "Istoricheskii ocherk o sozdanii Sovetskikh sudov v Uzbekistane," *Sovetskoe Gosudarstvo i Pravo*, No. 3 (March, 1949), p. 62.

[42] Kh. Suleimanova, "Zarozhdenie Sovetskogo ugolovnogo prava v Uzbekistane," *Sovetskoe Gosudarstvo i Pravo*, No. 10 (October, 1948), p. 66.

[43] From a report in *Izvestiia Turkestanskogo Tsentral'nogo Ispolnitel'nogo Komiteta*, November 13, 1918. Quoted in Suleimanova, "Istoricheskii ocherk o sozdanii Sovetskikh sudov v Uzbekistane," *Sovetskoe Gosudarstvo i Pravo*, No. 3 (March, 1949), pp. 62-63.

ished in accordance with the laws of the revolutionary period." [44] Despite this and similar instructions, local soviets continued to dispense justice on their own terms and to interfere in the activities of local courts. The Tashkent government was at least partially to blame. Repeatedly it exhorted local organs of power to utilize the law to destroy the opposition of the overthrown classes and to inculcate revolutionary discipline in the masses, but it failed to establish previously the boundaries of counterrevolutionary crime.

Each local soviet had perforce to draw boundaries to its own jurisdiction and to create its own standards. The resulting confusion led many soviets to find justification for interfering in every legal dispute and to a gradual breakdown of the structure of law. During the year 1918, the Tashkent Soviet did make several crude attempts to introduce some kind of order into the growing legal chaos. A series of government decrees and instructions defined as crimes against the revolution and removed from the jurisdiction of the regular courts cases involving speculation, violations of labor discipline, participation in a counterrevolutionary movement, anti-Soviet propaganda and agitation, harboring enemies of the revolution, storage of arms, espionage, sabotage, and broadcasting false rumors.[45]

While these acts established a sort of rudimentary boundary between the jurisdictions of special and regular tribunals, they were not sufficient in themselves to eliminate the confusion which had developed in the judicial system. Having ordered the court reorganized by the decrees of December 12 and 31, 1917, the Tashkent government assumed that its work was completed, and it made no effort to publish instructions for the guidance of local organs in executing the reform or to create appellate courts above the local level. Left to their own devices, local soviets made their own reforms (or no reform at all) without reference to each other or to the regional government, thereby creating a heterogeneous system of judicial organs which lacked both uniformity and any common standard for applying the

---

[44] Suleimanova, "Zarozhdenie Sovetskogo ugolovnogo prava v Uzbekistane," *Sovetskoe Gosudarstvo i Pravo*, No. 10 (October, 1948), p. 67.

[45] *Ibid.*, pp. 68–69.

law. According to a description supplied by the regional Commissar of Justice in one of his reports,

every court acted in conformity to the desires of the [local] soviet or more truly of the given executive committee. . . . The department of justice . . . did not even know how many courts were under its jurisdiction. In accord with the whim of the executive committee, their number and composition changed with kaleidoscopic speed. With complete unexpectedness, some courts emerged and others disappeared in the various localities of the region.[46]

Not until the end of 1918, and then only upon receipt from Moscow of an instruction concerning the organization and activity of local people's courts, did the government of Turkestan attempt to restore order in the judicial system. On the basis of a federal decree of November 21, 1918, concerning the courts, as modified by a decree of January 15, 1919, the regional government undertook to establish a unified system of people's courts in Turkestan. At the local level the government ordered the creation of a system of people's courts to be composed of a president and two assessors. The principle of "direct democratic election" was suspended in favor of indirect nomination of the members of the court by local soviets, thus assuring continued dependence of the local courts upon the local governing authority. A degree of centralization was achieved, however, through the creation of a cassational instance, the Council of People's Courts, whose membership (to be composed "principally of Communists" according to the central government decree) [47] was elected from the people's courts. Moreover, the Turkestan government established a Department of Judicial Inspection within the Commissariat of Justice and commissioned it to examine cases which had been tried in people's courts.[48]

Further reforms in the judicial system occurred in 1921 and 1922. By a decree published in March, 1921, a Department of Judicial Control under the Commissariat of Justice replaced the

[46] *Ibid.*, p. 66.
[47] *Russia: The Official Report of the British Trades Union Delegation to Russia and Caucasia, November and December, 1924* (London, 1925), pp. 89–90.
[48] Suleimanova, "Istoricheskii ocherk o sozdanii Sovetskikh sudov v Uzbekistane," *Sovetskoe Gosudarstvo i Pravo*, No. 3 (March, 1949), pp. 64–65. See also Kaplan, "Sovetskaia iustitsiia v Turkestane," *Izvestiia*, November 13, 1923.

republic Department of Judicial Inspection. A substantial increase in the power of the department accompanied the change in name. Whereas the Department of Judicial Inspection had been competent only to examine court cases and decisions, its successor was authorized to give courts and tribunals guiding directives and to annul the verdicts and sentences of all courts in the republic.[49] It acted in this capacity until August, 1922, at which time Moscow ordered the establishment in the republic Central Executive Committee of a branch of the Supreme Court of the RSFSR with both cassational and original jurisdiction. With the completion of this last reform, the judicature of Turkestan began to function as a unit for the first time since the October Revolution.

Throughout this period cases involving crimes against the revolution had remained outside the jurisdiction of the regular courts. The reform of 1919 had established a system of revolutionary tribunals, composed, after the pattern of similar courts in the RSFSR, of a president and six assessors, to deal with conspiracy and counterrevolution. These acted without reference to the regular courts and without judicial regulation and supervision until the promulgation of the reform of 1921. They then fell under the supervision of the Department of Judicial Control within the republic Commissariat of Justice. After the creation of the republic branch of the Supreme Court, the revolutionary tribunals and special courts were reorganized and their activities restricted.

The reorganization of the judicature in Turkestan was accompanied by a campaign to eliminate the canonical court and weaken the structure of customary Moslem law. In its original decree of December 12, 1917, on reorganization of the judiciary, the Tashkent government had declared its intention to abolish the customary court, but it deferred action until 1919. In the Moslem people's courts which meanwhile emerged in some communities, the extreme decentralization of justice hindered the establishment of common standards of procedure and prevented the courts from developing into real agents of soviet justice.

[49] Suleimanova, "Istoricheskii ocherk o sozdanii Sovetskikh sudov v Uzbekistane," *Sovetskoe Gosudarstvo i Pravo*, No. 3 (March, 1949), p. 65.

They appear actually to have differed very little in their behavior from the canonical courts which they were intended to replace.

Toward the end of 1918, judicial reorganization again became the order of the day, but the Turkestan government still had no ready solution to the problem of replacing the customary courts with Moslem people's courts capable of promoting soviet principles of justice and acceptable to the Moslem population. At public meetings, called in order to prepare the population for introduction of the new system of justice, it was suggested that people's courts which entertained lawsuits involving Moslems should be permitted to refer in their decisions to the norms of the Shariat. Resolutions in support of this recommendation emerged also from the sessions of the Regional Conference of Trade Unions, a Conference of Moslem People's Courts, and a Congress of Soviet Jurists, which the Commissariat of Justice convoked for the special purpose of considering the question. In light of the universality of Moslem approval of shariat law, all agreed that the statute relating to judicial reorganization should contain a clause giving to Moslem people's courts "the right to refer in their verdicts and sentences to the Shariat and Adat if the norms of the latter do not contradict fundamentally the interests of the toiling people." [50] This recommendation was incorporated into the regional government's statute on the people's court.

Its inclusion produced a profound effect upon the administration of justice in Turkestan. By admitting a dual legal standard in the soviet court, the Soviet regime was compelled also to create two parallel court systems in place of the unified judicature that had been originally intended. One system dealt with the European population and decided lawsuits on the basis of Soviet legislation and, in its absence, socialist legality. The other administered justice to Moslems in accordance with those norms of the Shariat and Adat which did not contravene the laws of the Soviet government. Lacking the unifying influence of a common high court, each system—organized as a self-contained

[50] From the resolution of the Regional Congress of Soviet Jurists; quoted in *ibid.*, pp. 63–64.

unit consisting of people's courts on the local level and councils of people's courts as the cassational instance—functioned independently.

The very method by which the Soviet government handled the reorganization of the courts makes it obvious that the effect of the reform on the customary system of justice in Turkestan was more apparent than real. The name of the court was changed and a Moslem court of review superimposed upon the existing judicial structure. Otherwise, the canonical court remained pretty much what it had been before the reform. The absence of native proletarians who were acquainted with the principles of shariat law compelled the Soviet regime to retain the kadis in office—under the title of people's judges, to be sure, but invested with the same authority and substantially the same function as prior to the reform.[51] Even the inclusion of two people's assessors in the Moslem people's courts represented no significant departure from the traditional system, since the two witnesses to the law, required in the administration of shariat justice, had in practice filled the role of assessors to the kadi long before the rise of the Bolshevik power.

The organization and personnel of the Moslem people's courts of this period were decisive factors in the determination of the court's character. In theory it was the agent of soviet justice within the Moslem community; in practice it refused to take judicial notice of Soviet legislation which conflicted with the prescripts of customary law. And in cases involving marriage and family law, the Moslem people's courts openly flouted the acts and decrees of the Soviet government. In his annual report for 1919, the republic Commissar of Justice referred pointedly to violations of Soviet law committed in the native court. "The [Moslem] people's courts," he wrote, "refused to award divorces on the petition of a wife, punished by imprisonment [persons convicted of] conversing on the streets with women, equated the testimony of two women to that of one man, and sentenced to cohabitation with the husband wives who

---

[51] Suleimanova, "Zarozhdenie Sovetskogo ugolovnogo prava v Uzbekistane," *Sovetskoe Gosudarstvo i Pravo*, No. 10 (October, 1948), p. 68.

had petitioned for divorce." [52] The records of numerous trials conducted in the Moslem people's courts bore him out.[53]

In 1920 the government of Turkestan made one special effort to bring the norms of shariat law into conformity with Soviet legislation. On the initiative of the Commissar of Justice, a commission composed of Moslem jurists was created to investigate the conflicts between Moslem and Soviet law and to draft a code of laws reconciling the two systems of jurisprudence. Subsequent discovery that Soviet and customary law diverged at too many critical points to permit even the establishment of a common standard for agreement, however, led to abandonment of the project.[54] The commission nevertheless served an important purpose. Its work clearly demonstrated the futility of further pursuit of a middle course in the administration of justice in the native community and left to the government the alternative of annulling the right of reference to customary law in Moslem people's courts or of divorcing the Moslem courts from the Soviet system.

In the last analysis political expediency outweighed theoretical considerations in determining the government's decision. Motivated primarily by the desire to undermine the Basmachi movement through a policy of yielding to those of its demands which were most popular among Moslems and influenced further by the general Soviet retreat into the New Economic Policy, the Bolsheviks chose to restore in a modified form the prerevolutionary system of Moslem justice. Significantly, the revival of the canonical courts began in Fergana, the center of native guerrilla resistance to the Soviet regime, on October 6, 1921, and did not spread to other localities until some months later. The earliest legislation limited the jurisdiction of canonical courts to marriage and divorce, successions, and civil cases involving no more than 500,000 rubles (1921 value), with the added proviso that the competence of these courts was restricted to disputes which all parties agreed in advance to submit to the

---

[52] Quoted in Suleimanova, "Istoricheskii ocherk o sozdanii Sovetskikh sudov v Uzbekistane," *Sovetskoe Gosudarstvo i Pravo,* No. 3 (March, 1949), p. 65.

[53] *Ibid.,* pp. 65–67.

[54] *Ibid.,* p. 67.

kadi.[55] In August, 1922, the jurisdiction of the Moslem courts was broadened to include penal offenses involving imprisonment for not more than one year and a fine of not more than 500 gold rubles.[56]

Decrees published in May and August, 1922, temporarily systematized the organization of the resurrected native judicature and moreover furnished a transitional phase in the reversion of existing Moslem people's courts to the status of customary courts. The earlier decree charged local soviets directly with appointment of the kadis. Its successor attenuated this control somewhat by ordering election of members of Moslem courts by the entire population of affected localities under the guidance and supervision of the volost' and city executive committees. The structure of the native judicial system was thus modeled, organizationally, on that of the Soviet judicature. The May decree denominated the canonical court as a court of original jurisdiction and created a congress of kadis to serve as the cassational instance. The August decree superimposed a "Moslem division within the Council of People's Courts of the Turkestan republic" upon the existing structure and delegated to it supreme supervisory and cassational power.[57]

These shifts were evidence that the Soviet regime was seeking a formula to permit the existence of canonical courts under close Soviet supervision and to minimize their influence in the Moslem community. A new decree, of December 23, 1922,[58] established a legal personality for the customary courts, which persisted with certain alterations until the territorial rearrangement in Central Asia. The new decree tightened considerably Soviet control over the canonical courts and invoked stringent limitations upon their competence. The principle of popular

---

[55] Shokhor, "Religiozno-bytovye sudy v RSFSR," *Sovetskoe Stroitel'stvo*, Nos. 8–9 (13–14) (August–September, 1927), p. 108.

[56] *Izvestiia*, September 1, 1922.

[57] *Ibid.*; also Shokhor, "Religiozno-bytovye sudy v RSFSR," *Sovetskoe Stroitel'stvo*, Nos. 8–9 (13–14) (August–September, 1927), p. 108.

[58] Text partially reproduced in Gidulianov, *Otdelenie tserkvi ot gosudarstva v SSSR*, pp. 516–17. For a summary of other provisions see Shokhor, "Religiozno-bytovye sudy v RSFSR," *Sovetskoe Stroitel'stvo*, Nos. 8–9 (13–14) (August–September, 1927), p. 108, and Fioletov, "Sudoproizvodstvo v Musul'manskikh sudakh (sudy kaziev) Srednei Azii," *Novyi Vostok*, Nos. 23–24 (1928), p. 215.

election of the kadi was carried forward in a modified form and supplemented by provisions for his removal. The decree specified annual elections of the kadi but restricted the electorate to natives enfranchised under Soviet legislation. The voters selected two candidates for each post; the executive committee then appointed one and retained the other as a candidate. The power of removal resided in the regional executive committee, which might dismiss a kadi either upon his conviction for a criminal or political offense or upon presentation of a charge of "manifest unfitness" for office.

Increased Soviet control over appointment and dismissal of the kadi was accompanied by closer supervision of his activities and by additional restrictions upon the jurisdiction of the canonical court itself. Whereas earlier legislation had bound a defendant who had previously agreed to submit his case to the kadi to accept the jurisdiction of the canonical court, the December decree permitted him to demand removal of the case to the people's court at any time prior to announcement of the verdict. Moreover, the district people's court replaced the congress of kadis as the judicial instance of appeal; thus direct recourse to Soviet justice became available to individuals who had failed to sustain a defense within the terms of customary law. These reforms were important in that they tended to neutralize the effect of customary law while permitting its continued application. But even the application of customary law was restricted. The decree specifically forbade the canonical court to levy fines in criminal cases or to hear any civil case which involved the inheritance of landed property or was based on acts completed or authenticated by organs of the Soviet government.

The promulgation of the December decree brought the period of transition to an end. Soviet opposition to customary law and the customary court was nevertheless undiminished, and the government now addressed itself to a policy of gradually undermining and circumscribing the sphere of activity of the canonical courts. As a first step, the Central Executive Committee of the Turkestan republic published a decree ordering the retrial in people's courts of lawsuits which had been tried in canonical courts if one of the parties to a dispute petitioned for transfer of the case within one month of its decision.[59] In short, the government ruled that the mere complaint of a defeated litigant was sufficient to invalidate any verdict or sentence handed down by the kadi. The consequence was an immediate decrease in the number of cases brought before the canonical courts and a corresponding increase in the number of petitions for the transfer of cases to the people's courts.[60] "It is curious," the republic Commissar of Justice noted later, "that this petition [for transfer of a case to the people's court] always came from the weaker side and in divorce cases from the side of the wife." [61]

This act, whose effect was devastating to the prestige of the canonical courts, was soon supplemented with other restrictions which, for all practical purposes, eliminated the kadi as an effective agent for the administration of justice. In 1923 the government transferred the financial burden of maintaining the customary courts from the state budget directly to the shoulders of those citizens who favored continuation of these courts and followed this act with an order for the appointment of two people's assessors selected from the ranks of the toilers to each canonical court. New limitations on the jurisdiction of the native courts were invoked in February, 1924. Soviet legislation deprived them of jurisdiction in criminal cases and declared them incompetent to hear civil cases involving a sum greater than 25 rubles.[62]

Later in the same year the Soviet government took direct action to invalidate portions of the Shariat which conflicted with Soviet standards of justice. A supplement to the criminal code of the RSFSR, promulgated on October 16, 1924, and adopted without change by the Turkestan ASSR, outlawed the

[59] Suleimanova, "Istoricheskii ocherk o sozdanii Sovetskikh sudov v Uzbekistane," *Sovetskoe Gosudarstvo i Pravo,* No. 3 (March, 1949), p. 68.

[60] A member of the native lower class obtained an immediate advantage if he took a complaint against an upper-class Moslem to the soviet court since the soviet court openly favored the poor. Soviet courts, one Soviet official told the Central Executive Committee of the USSR, had enough revolutionary experience so that "every case will be decided in the interests of the workers and peasants." From a speech by Vinokurov in USSR, Tsentral'nyi Ispolnitel'nyi Komitet Vtorogo Sozyva, *Vtoraia Sessiia Ts.I.K.* (Moscow, 1924), p. 212.

[61] Suleimanova, "Istoricheskii ocherk o sozdanii Sovetskikh sudov v Uzbekistane," *Sovetskoe Gosudarstvo i Pravo,* No. 3 (March, 1949), pp. 68–69.

[62] *Ibid.,* p. 69.

payment of *diya* (a pecuniary indemnity paid to the victim of a criminal act or to his relatives) and forbade, on pain of imprisonment, the payment of *kalym* or bride price, enforced marriage of women, and bigamy.[63] These restrictions, in combination with the other burdens which the Soviet regime loaded upon the Moslem system of justice, accomplished their purpose. Gradually, the canonical courts declined in importance and in number, and Moslems with increasing frequency took their disputes directly to the soviet court or found means to settle them privately. In 1922 some 342 native courts had been operating in the provinces of Fergana, Zeravshan, Samarkand, and Syr-Daria; by the end of 1924 their number had decreased to 99.[64]

The efforts of the government of Turkestan to compel the gradual extinction of the customary court had no true counterpart in the republics of Bokhara and Khorezm. Each republic established a soviet judicature which included people's courts, a council of people's courts, and a supreme tribunal. But, throughout its existence, neither republic supported open competition between the soviet and the canonical courts and neither created a machinery capable of supervising closely the activity of the latter. In 1924 the Bokharan republic attempted belatedly to sovietize the canonical court. The government adopted legislation which provided for popular election of kadis under the supervision of soviet executive committees and for installation of people's assessors in canonical courts. It also introduced modified versions of the soviet criminal and criminal-trial codes and ordered the kadis to be guided by these codes in criminal cases.[65] But these acts had no practical consequence; before the government was able to implement them the republic of Bokhara had vanished in the national delimitation.

After their formation, the Uzbek and Turcoman SSR's thus

---

[63] Text in I. Lozovskii and I. Bibin, *Sovetskaia Politika za 10 let po natsional'-nomu voprosu v RSFSR: sistematicheskii sbornik deistvuiushchikh aktov pravitel'stv Soiuza SSR i RSFSR po delam natsional'nostei RSFSR (oktiabr' 1917–noiabr' 1927 g.)* (Moscow, 1928), pp. 316–18.

[64] Suleimanova, "Istoricheskii ocherk o sozdanii Sovetskikh sudov v Uzbekistane," *Sovetskoe Gosudarstvo i Pravo*, No. 3 (March, 1949), p. 69.

[65] N. N. Fioletov, "Sudy kaziev v Sredne-Aziatskikh respublikakh," *Sovetskoe Pravo*, No. 1 (25) (1927), pp. 144–45.

faced two immediate problems in regard to the judicature in those territories which had formerly belonged to the Bokharan and Khorezmian republics. One problem was to reduce the prestige and jurisdiction of the shariat courts to the low status they held in the former Turkestan republic. The other was to win the confidence of the Moslem masses in the soviet people's courts. The experience gained by the Bolsheviks in Turkestan proved useful. Both republics initiated broad propaganda campaigns to persuade the Moslem poorer classes that Soviet legislation and the Soviet judicial system gave special protection to their interests. And, as in Turkestan, they took measures to establish model people's courts, to hasten "nationalization" of the legal apparatus, to improve supervision of soviet judicial organs, and to regularize judicial procedures.

The Uzbek and Turcoman governments also moved to change the social complexion of the canonical court and to impair its effectiveness. To "sovietize" the customary court from within, the Bolsheviks managed the nomination of candidates to the post of kadi so that only "progressive" mullahs and members of the ulema (i.e., those sympathetic to the Soviet regime) would be elected to office. A series of decrees and regulations altered the legal procedures of the canonical courts "in the sense [of bringing them] into greater agreement with the tasks of Soviet construction" and established tight supervision and control over their activities.[66] That these measures succeeded was attested to by the Soviet "Commission for the Investigation of the Kishlaks and Auls."

The shariat court of the kadi [the Commission reported in 1926] has departed in many respects from the Shariat. Judging by judicial decisions, this court may qualify as a mixed soviet-shariat court. Because of the demands of life and changed relationships, the kadi without special compulsion has had to resort to the articles of our [law] code. . . . The clear imprint of the new soviet legislation lies on the present-day court of the kadi.[67]

By this time the campaign to undermine and destroy the

[66] Fioletov, "Sudoproizvodstvo v Musul'manskikh sudakh (sudy kaziev) Srednei Azii," *Novyi Vostok*, Nos. 23–24 (1928), p. 214.

[67] Quoted in Fioletov, "Sudy kaziev v Sredne-Aziatskikh respublikakh," *Sovetskoe Pravo*, No. 1 (25) (1927), p. 145.

canonical court had reached an advanced stage. In 1926 all the soviet governments of Central Asia adopted legislation which reduced these courts to the status of voluntary judicial organs. In that same year the last canonical court on the territory of the former Turkestan republic disappeared.[68] In 1927 the customary court disappeared also from Kirghizia; seventeen of them were still operating in Uzbekistan and eleven in Turkmenia early in the year, but they were in a state of near-collapse.[69] Finally, by a decree of September 21, 1927, "On Shariat and Adat Courts," the Central Executive Committee of the USSR delivered the *coup de grâce*. It forbade the creation of new customary courts anywhere on the territory of the Soviet Union, and it divorced all existing ones completely from the soviet state. The decree specifically banned the disbursement of public funds to customary courts from any budget, prohibited the execution of the decisions of these courts by public enforcement agencies, abolished the legal force of their decisions, and ordered public organs to refuse to recognize these decisions as legal documents.[70] This act, for practical purposes, put an end to the customary court. A few canonical courts did continue to exist fitfully and sometimes illegally in the more remote regions, but in later years even these were suppressed.

THE STRUGGLE AGAINST MOSLEM EDUCATION

By its successful campaign to debilitate and destroy the customary judicial system, the Soviet regime accomplished its second major objective in the struggle to exterminate the temporal privileges of the Islamic religion. The achievement of its third objective, the secularization of education, presented a more difficult problem. We have seen that the two institutions already examined, wakf and shariat justice, had been declining in importance throughout the Moslem world even before the Russian Revolution; customary methods of education, on the contrary, had hardly felt the shock of time. True, secular institutions of

---

[68] Suleimanova, "Istoricheskii ocherk o sozdanii Sovetskikh sudov v Uzbekistane," *Sovetskoe Gosudarstvo i Pravo*, No. 3 (March, 1949), p. 69.

[69] Shokhor, "Religiozno-bytovye sudy v RSFSR," *Sovetskoe Stroitel'stvo*, Nos. 8–9 (13–14) (August–September, 1927), p. 109.

[70] *Ibid.*, p. 111.

learning had emerged in some Moslem countries, but the core
of the educational system remained the *maktabs* or mosque
schools and the *madrasa* or seminaries which, operated by the
Moslem clergy, were devoted almost exclusively to the study of
Islamic dogma. Prior to the revolution, only 97 lay schools with
an attendance of less than 3,000 children were available to the
native population of Turkestan. And these offered instruction
only on the most elementary level.[71] In contrast, 7,290 *maktabs*,
whose course of instruction consisted in most cases of transcrib-
ing and memorizing passages from the Koran, provided elementary education for 69,864 children, and 375 *madrasa* with an
enrollment of 9,627 students offered instruction in the "Arab
sciences." [72]

The traditional system of native education exerted a powerful conservative influence upon the whole Moslem community.
Rooted in the traditional Moslem social order, the old-method
school naturally opposed the brotherhood of the faithful of all
ranks in God to concepts of class culture and class struggle. In
their prerevolutionary writings, the Bolsheviks made no distinction between the Moslem schools and the institutions for
religious education of other faiths. All were visualized as instruments for the defense of outworn political institutions and the
preservation of what Lenin characterized as the "Black-Hun-
dreds and clerical . . . culture of the landlords, priests, and
bourgeoisie." [73] It is obvious then that separation of the church
from the school should figure prominently in the Bolshevik demands for separation of church and state. In his essay on *Socialism and Religion,* Lenin had insisted as early as 1905 upon complete elimination of religious influences from the educational

[71] From a report by Khidyr-Aliev to the All-Russian Central Executive Committee. See *Tret'iaia Sessiia Vserossiiskogo Tsentral'nogo Ispolnitel'nogo Komiteta X Sozyva* (Moscow, 1924), pp. 105–6.

[72] N. Tiuriakulov, "Turkestanskaia Avtonomnaia Respublika," *Zhizn' Natsional'nostei,* No. 1 (January, 1923), p. 92. A course in the "Arab sciences" included
study of the commentaries of the Koran, the Tradition (*hadith*), law, the principles, grammar, lexicography, rhetoric, and literature. As in the lower schools,
the stress was on development of the memory rather than the intellectual
powers of the students.

[73] V. I. Lenin, *Natsional'nyi vopros* (Moscow, 1936), pp. 75–76.

system, and the Party thereafter incorporated this demand in its program.[74]

After the revolution, the Soviet government gave legal effect to the claim for the separation of the church from the school by the decree of January 23, 1918, "On Freedom of Conscience and Religious Societies." "The teaching of religious doctrines," Article 9 reads, "is not permitted in any state, public, or private educational institution where general educational subjects are taught." [75] The article did authorize the giving or receipt of religious instruction privately but later interpretation by the courts restricted groups receiving such instruction to three or fewer persons.[76] As a whole, the article was directed principally at the Orthodox Church since Orthodox religious instruction in the schools had been obligatory for all Orthodox pupils under the old regime. But in the long run it actually dealt a heavier blow to non-Orthodox religious groups—to schismatics, Roman Catholics, Jews, and Moslems—because these sects had customarily devoted special attention to religious education.

Although the Tashkent government followed Moscow's lead in decreeing the separation of church from school, the immediate effect of the action upon the Moslem school in Central Asia was negligible. Absorbed with the problem of its own survival, the local Soviet regime could not afford to dissipate energy in a consistent program of implementation of the law. Nevertheless, enactment of the decree and the few halfhearted attempts at enforcement added fuel to Moslem resentment against the Soviet regime. The spread of revolution and civil war also brought with it inevitably a decline in the cultural institutions of Central Asia and a general deterioration of the educational system. The Moslem school suffered staggering blows. The constant strife and the ruination of the economy, which impoverished the native community and led to large-scale dislocations of population, as well as Soviet confiscations of endowment proper-

[74] From an excerpt from "Sotsializm i religiia" in Gurev, *Antireligioznaia khrestomatiia,* p. 703.
[75] From text of decree in Yaroslavsky, *Religion in the USSR,* pp. 19–21.
[76] Anderson, *People, Church and State in Modern Russia,* p. 10.

ties, from which native educational institutions drew their support, undermined the Moslem school everywhere and virtually eliminated it from some communities.

The native educational system undoubtedly suffered great damage during this period, and the decline of the Moslem schools, though an accident of war, thus served one Bolshevik purpose. The Soviet government now faced the basic problem of winning acceptance in the native community of the principle of separation of church and school. It still had to establish its own network of soviet schools to compete with the existing religious schools and to persuade Moslems to utilize the new schools.

During the civil war the Turkestan government had made sporadic efforts to establish soviet schools in the most important centers, usually by reorganizing existing schools, but prior to 1920 these schools, chiefly in urban areas, catered primarily to the educational needs of the European population. The development of a system of soviet schools for the Moslem population dates from the Eighth All-Russian Party Congress in 1919 which instructed Bolsheviks in all parts of the Soviet state to redouble their efforts to remove religious influences from existing schools and to hasten the creation of soviet schools offering instruction in the local languages.[77] The Turkestan government now launched an ambitious program of soviet education in the Moslem community. Buttressed by financial support from Moscow after the reunification of Turkestan with Central Russia, the new program led to the establishment of secular schools not only in the urban areas but even in remote kishlaks and auls.

At the outset the native population greeted these measures with considerable resistance. In many cases Moslems refused to allow their children to attend soviet schools even when they offered the sole opportunity of formal education.[78] In the rural areas, according to Bolshevik charges, the mullahs campaigned actively against the new soviet schools and succeeded in frighten-

[77] *Vse-Soiuznaia Kommunisticheskaia Partiia v rezoliutsiiakh i resheniiakh s'ezdov, soveshchaniei i plenumov Tsentral'nogo Komiteta (1898–1932)* (4th ed., Moscow, 1932), I, 334.

[78] See report by Khidyr-Aliev in *Tret'iaia Sessiia Vserossiiskogo Tsentral'nogo Ispolnitel'nogo Komiteta X Sozyva*, p. 106.

ing the peasants away with predictions of crop failures as "God's retribution" for the reform.[79] The resistance was, nevertheless, bound to collapse. The failure of the Moslem school to recover from the effects of the civil war, largely in consequence of Soviet confiscation of its primary source of revenue, the wakfs, deprived Moslems in most localities of any alternative to the soviet school. Inevitably a conflict arose between the demands of communal solidarity, which was essential to success in the boycott of the soviet school, and the personal desire for education.

Of equal importance, the Bolsheviks represented the soviet school as an agency for providing free educational opportunities for the poorest strata of the native population, precisely those groups which had previously been deprived of educational opportunities. Thus the Soviet regime injected the element of class conflict into the individual conflicts. The Moslem community had no weapon to enforce the boycott other than the threat of heavenly wrath, and the Bolsheviks defeated that by appointing an occasional "progressive" mullah to a conspicuous post in the school system of recalcitrant districts. A brief period of resistance during 1919–20 was followed by a rapid upsurge in native enrollment in the soviet schools. By November, 1921, some 1,117 soviet schools, boasting an enrollment of 84,970 pupils, were operating in the Moslem communities of Turkestan.[80] This, to be sure, was a modest accomplishment in comparison with the potential size of native enrollment,[81] but it was a phenomenal triumph for secular education when compared with the prerevolutionary enrollment of less than 3,000 Moslem pupils in ninety-seven schools of the European type.

These early successes did not consolidate the position of the soviet school in the native community. The Soviet regime had neutralized but not destroyed the opposition to secular education; after 1920 the enemies of the soviet school bided their time, awaiting only an opportune moment in which to enter a

[79] Shteinberg, *Ocherki istorii Turkmenii*, p. 118.

[80] "Prosveshchenie Turkestana," *Izvestiia*, November 13, 1923.

[81] According to Khidyr-Aliev, the potential native enrollment in 1923 was 773,000 pupils. *Tret'iaia Sessiia Vserossiiskogo Tsentral'nogo Ispolnitel'nogo Komiteta X Sozyva*, p. 106.

new bid for public support. At the same time, the republic school system, founded on subventions from Moscow, operated on an extremely precarious financial footing. In 1922 the All-Russian Commissariat of Education, overwhelmed by the wave of economy which attended the introduction of the New Economic Policy, cut off its subsidy and made the Turkestan government wholly responsible for maintaining the local school system. Even the allocation of 40 percent of the budget of the Turkestan republic to education did not suffice to prevent disaster.[82] Many public schools had to close down and in rural areas the soviet school all but disappeared. After repeated pleas for assistance, the republic government induced the All-Russian Commissariat of Education to resume a 15,000-ruble monthly subsidy, but the delegate from Turkestan to the All-Russian Central Executive Committee called this "a drop in the bucket." He also reported that schoolteachers in Turkestan were abandoning their profession because of the government's inability to pay their salaries.[83] The school census bore him out. By September, 1923, the number of public schools available to the Moslem population in Turkestan had decreased to 678, and enrollment to 31,054.[84]

The inability of the Turkestan republic to finance a broad program of mass education without large-scale subsidization from Moscow and the pressure from the native community for a revival of traditional Moslem institutions brought to the fore in 1922 the question of removing disabilities placed upon the Moslem school. The Bolsheviks admitted readily that continued repression of native educational institutions had become unrealistic. "When you can't provide bread," the All-Union Commissar of Education, Lunacharskii, lamented, "you don't dare to take away a substitute." [85] The government leaders also believed they could prevent enemies of the Soviet regime from

[82] E. M., "Khoziaistvennyi obzor po Turkestanu," *Vlast' Sovetov*, No. 6 (September, 1924), pp. 218–19.

[83] From report of Khidyr-Aliev in *Tret'iaia Sessiia Vserossiiskogo Tsentral'-nogo Ispolnitel'nogo Komiteta X Sozyva*, p. 106.

[84] "Prosveshchenie Turkestana," *Izvestiia*, November 13, 1923.

[85] A. Lunacharskii, "Problemy obrazovaniia v avtonomnykh respublikakh i oblastiakh," *Zhizn' Natsional'nostei*, No. 1 (6) (1924), p. 32.

using the Moslem schools for the dissemination of anti-Soviet sentiments. Some believed even that a strict system of supervision, through government control of the endowment properties, might convert the Moslem school into an instrument for the propagation of Soviet ideology among the Moslem youth.[86]

This was the background of decrees enacted by the government of Turkestan in June and December, 1922, which restored Moslem rights in most endowment properties. The earlier of these decrees returned to Moslem administration the endowment properties which, prior to Soviet confiscation, had supported cultural and educational institutions, with the stipulation that their income be devoted exclusively to education. Freedom for these institutions to conduct their own affairs, however, was conspicuously absent from the decree. In place of a system of self-regulation and self-administration, the law vested in a six-member college, composed of representatives of the *madrasa,* the people's court, and the soviet school, responsibility for regulating the administration of *madrasa* and the management of endowment properties and for preventing "harmful misunderstandings and disorders" in each district.[87] The failure of the decree to establish a hierarchy of supervisory agencies nevertheless opened the way for greater decentralization and local flexibility in the administration of endowment properties than the Bolsheviks were willing to allow. Hence, in December the Turkestan government superimposed upon the existing organs of supervision and control regional wakf departments and a Main Wakf Administration under the republic Commissariat of Education, giving to the latter the sole right to select and approve textbooks for use in Moslem educational institutions.[88]

In the Turkestan republic this apparatus of control remained in effect without substantial change until the dissolution of the republic in 1924. Following the national delimitation, the same

[86] Fioletov, "Vakufnoe pravo v Sredne-Aziatskikh respublik," *Sovetskoe Pravo,* No. 2 (20) (1926), p. 96.

[87] From Decree No. 75 of the Turkestan republic of June 20, 1922. Text in *Izvestiia Turkestanskogo Tsentral'nogo Ispolnitel'nogo Komiteta,* July 4, 1922. Reproduced in Gidulianov, *Otdelenie tserkvi ot gosudarstva v SSSR,* p. 278.

[88] Decree No. 178 of the Turkestan republic of December 28, 1922. Text in *Pravda Turkestana,* January 10, 1923. Reproduced in Gidulianov, *Otdelenie tserkvi ot gosudarstva v SSSR,* pp. 279–80.

system was adopted by the Uzbek and Turcoman SSR's, thus extending it to the territories of the former republics of Bokhara and Khorezm, which had not attempted previously to curb or control the Moslem educational system. The Bolsheviks, however, never accepted the continued existence of the Moslem schools as desirable, nor were they ever entirely satisfied with the agencies set up to control them. It soon became apparent that Soviet manipulations would not convert the Moslem schools into an instrument for the dissemination of Soviet ideas and that no system of control could fully prevent their utilization of purposes hostile to the Soviet regime. Repeated demands from Moscow that religious schools be eliminated as quickly as possible intensified local Bolshevik hostility to the Moslem schools.

The Soviet regime was nevertheless in no hurry to invoke new restrictions against the Moslem schools. Their prestige within the Moslem community made them a difficult target. Local Soviet authorities, hamstrung by inadequate finances and the lack of qualified teachers, hesitated to close private institutions when they were unable to replace them with public schools. The plight of Soviet education in Central Asia was desperate during this period. According to a report in 1925 to the First Uzbek Congress of Soviets, less than 1 percent of the youth in the republic was receiving formal education and 96 percent of the population was illiterate.[89] The succeeding two years witnessed some expansion of the soviet school system,[90] but it was hardly great enough to support a frontal attack upon the Moslem schools. However, by expropriating certain categories of endow-

[89] From the report of the Uzbek Commissar of Education, Inogamov. See *Pervyi Vseuzbekskii S'ezd Sovetov Rabochikh, Dekhkanskikh i Krasnoarmeiskikh Deputatov Uzbekskoi Sovetskoi Sotsialisticheskoi Respubliki (fevral' 1925 goda)* (Tashkent, 1925), p. 70.

[90] Figures for the 1926–27 school year disclosed that 1,636 public schools with 115,973 pupils were operating and that 83,000 pupils were attending elementary schools. See *Vtoroi Vseuzbekskii S'ezd Sovetov Rabochikh, Dekhkanskikh i Krasnoarmeiskikh Deputatov Uzbekskoi Sovetskoi Sotsialisticheskoi Respubliki* (Samarkand, 1927), pp. 297–98, 301. These figures tend to be misleading, however, since they represent the total enrollment of all schools rather than those which native children attended. Figures for previous years which were broken down into European and native components show that consistently a much larger number of Europeans than of natives were enrolled in the schools.

ment property during the land reform of 1925–27, the Soviet government indirectly undermined the economic support of many Moslem schools and forced some of them to close their doors. In spite of this, over 250 of them were still operating legally in Central Asia in 1927.[91]

Consistent efforts to eliminate Moslem educational institutions were postponed to the period of the Five-Year Plans, when the Soviet government confiscated and dissolved the remaining endowment properties, thereby destroying the economic foundation of Moslem education. It reinforced these measures by rigid enforcement of separation of church from school. These attacks put an end to Moslem institutions of higher learning and forced natives of all classes to turn to the soviet school for the satisfaction of their educational needs. They did not, of course, eliminate the mosque school for, as historian John Maynard has pointed out, it would be a very active and ubiquitous administration indeed which could prevent the teaching of the Koran in the yard outside the mosque.[92]

THE ANTI-GOD MOVEMENT IN CENTRAL ASIA

Soviet policy toward Islam and Islamic institutions in Central Asia illustrates the general Bolshevik reluctance to apply persecution as a means of extirpating religion. However stern the disabilities placed upon institutions dominated by religious influences, the right to religious belief was not called into question. The Soviet government was unfriendly, even hostile, toward religion. But it declined consistently to disqualify any citizen or otherwise to punish individuals on charges of believing in religion or of holding or attending religious services. Bolshevism in power after 1917 was no less aware of the futility of legislation against "religious prejudices" than Lenin had been in 1905 when he insisted that the state, unlike the Party, should treat religious beliefs as a "private affair." [93]

Nevertheless, antireligion was and remains a basic tenet of

[91] *Ibid.*, pp. 297–98; Sev, "Zametki o Turkmenskom dukhovenstve," *Turkmenovedenie,* Nos. 3–4 (7–8) (March–April, 1928), p. 17.
[92] Sir John Maynard, *Russia in Flux* (New York, 1948), p. 435.
[93] From an excerpt from "Sotsializm i religiia" in Gurev, *Antireligioznaia khrestomatiia,* p. 702.

Bolshevism and constitutes a fundamental element in the philosophy of the Soviet state. According to its program, the Party is committed to wage a systematic and relentless struggle with religion, not by organizing the persecution of believers, but by undertaking a planned reorganization of the social and economic activities of the masses, by socialist reeducation of the toilers, by cultivating scientific knowledge, by expanding education, and by conducting antireligious propaganda. It is obvious that the Party could not have put these ambitious plans into effect without the continuous and active cooperation of the organs of Soviet government at all levels. The Party program, nevertheless, made no specific mention of the part which the state is expected to play in the struggle. But the program of the Communist International, which was equally binding upon Bolsheviks, contained a clarification:

Allowing freedom of confession and destroying the privileged position of the former state religion, the proletarian power [i.e., the state] at the same time conducts anti-religious propaganda by all possible means and reconstructs all educational work on the basis of a scientific materialistic world view.[94]

The Soviet state proclaimed and enforced the legal separation of church and state. It replaced religious education with "scientific-socialist" education in the schools. It suppressed the "counterrevolutionary" activities of religionists and established a regime of law conducive to the development of militant atheism. The actual dissemination of antireligious propaganda, except in its propagation through the schools, was left to the Communist Party and to the Societies of the Godless. Primarily centered on the European population, the antireligious movement found little support among the non-European nationalities during the first decade of Soviet rule. In point of fact, representatives of only six non-Russian nationalities were present at the First All-Union Conference of the Atheist Movement in 1926.

In Central Asia of the 1920's the Bolsheviks found no base for the development of the antireligious movement. The burden of circulating antireligious propaganda fell principally on outsiders, and the ideological struggle had to be conducted with

[94] Anderson, *People, Church and State in Modern Russia*, p. 62.

extreme circumspection. During the revolution and civil war the fear of arousing Moslem fanaticism within Turkestan and of antagonizing the Moslems of neighboring countries had prevented the Bolsheviks from publicly attacking Islam. The Communists did not even enforce the unwritten requirement of atheism as a condition of Party membership for natives in Central Asia. During the New Economic Policy, coincident with the growth of the anti-God movement in European Russia, the Bolsheviks in Central Asia entered upon a cautious and well-conceived program of ideological struggle against Islam.

Spearheaded by educated Tatar Communists imported from European Russia, the antireligious movement relied initially upon personal and group oral agitation conducted in the schools, trade unions, Komsomol, Koshchi, and other public and mass organizations. Propaganda by example and deed, not by pamphlet and lecture, was the method employed; its primary object was the conversion of at least one native in every Moslem village to atheism—a person whose very existence, Bolsheviks believed, would present a more effective challenge to religion than "dozens of lectures or talks by the most authoritative and persuasive orator." [95] We have noted that circumspection was the common denominator of all antireligious propaganda among Moslems. Propagandists and agitators avoided direct challenges to the Islamic religion as such, preferring to undermine specific religious beliefs with materialistic explanations of natural phenomena and of familiar problems of social life. The pressure put behind even this propaganda varied in direct relation to the intensity of religious belief in individual Moslem communities and among the different nationalities of Central Asia. Thus, the Turcomans, who were less devout, were subjected to a more impassioned propaganda than the fanatically religious Uzbeks. [96]

While the tactic of indirect attack upon Islam had the advantage of not outraging the religious sensibilities of Moslem believers, it also had the greater disadvantage of failing to weaken the bonds of religion in the Moslem community. Soviet records

[95] M. Sultan-Galiev, *Metody antireligioznoi propagandy sredi Musul'man* (Moscow, 1922), p. 5.

[96] Joseph Castagné, "Russie Slave et Russie Turque: les chances d'une politique islamique allemande," *Revue du Monde Musulman,* LVI (December, 1923), 237.

in the twenties provide no instances of large-scale abandonment of religion by Moslems; even individual cases of apostasy were relatively rare. It should be noted, however, that in 1927 organized and militant atheism, sponsored by the Communist Party, was still in its infancy. Renunciation of Islam became more common during the period of the First and Second Five-Year Plans. In 1932 alone some 10,000 Uzbek women cast aside the veil, an act which in Moslem Central Asia was tantamount to abandoning their religion. Nevertheless, Julius Hecker, taking note of these acts as well as of the growth of atheism among men, has attributed the trend more to social and economic causes than to the efforts of the Societies of the Godless.[97] To the women, it meant liberation from centuries-old degradation; to the men, it meant a break with the oppression which they had learned to associate with the old semifeudal and semitribal social order.

Despite Soviet rejection of administrative oppression as a means of destroying religion, the Soviet government had a well-stocked arsenal for use against the ministers of religion. Evasion of laws prohibiting religious propaganda or the giving of religious instruction to minors in groups of more than three exposed the violator to criminal prosecution. Soviet courts, in addition, have not infrequently convicted members of the Moslem clergy on charges of counterrevolution, espionage, and diversionary activities. Criminal codes adopted by the Central Asiatic republics include statutes prohibiting the usurpation of legal functions by religious organizations, the commission of "deceitful actions with the intent of arousing superstition in the masses," and compulsory observance of religious rites. Article 158 of the Uzbek Criminal Code provides, as well, the death penalty for "the use of religious prejudices for counterrevolutionary purposes." Devout Moslems have thus faced continually the threat of criminal prosecution for the violation of vaguely worded statutes. They have been deprived of customary sources of income by Soviet liquidation of endowment properties and by the legal prohibition of church tithes. Nevertheless, in Central Asia Islam has proved a thorny and deep-rooted plant.

[97] Hecker, *Religion and Communism,* p. 226.

VI

THE DRIVE FOR
ECONOMIC
EQUALIZATION

◆

IN RETROSPECT, three circumstances appear to have had special weight in influencing the Leninist wing of the Social Democratic movement to adopt an authoritarian solution to the tasks of social revolution in Russia. The inflexibility of the Tsarist autocracy had prevented the development of conditions and social forces favorable to a peaceful transformation of Russian society. The absence of legal channels for the expression of dissident political opinion prior to 1905 had favored the dominance of the "professionals" in the Russian revolutionary movement and had fostered Lenin's program for transforming the Bolshevik faction of the Social Democratic Party into a semimilitary officer corps of revolution. Equally significant was the Marxist rejection of the peasantry as the lever by which to overthrow the Imperial regime and Marxist emphasis upon the working class as the core of the revolutionary movement.

In their early struggle against the idea of peasant socialism, the Social Democrats had written off the peasantry as a revolutionary force and looked upon it as a potential enemy, a petit-bourgeois class interested principally in getting all the land and making over the state in the image of the village commune. But the strength which the Social Democrats gained by concentrating their activities upon the more accessible and theoretically more "revolutionary" working class was at the same time a source of great weakness; as late as 1913 the industrial proletariat comprised only 1.41 percent of the Russian population.[1] The numerical impotence of the working class compelled the Marxists to search for other associates in the enterprise of revolution. And the search led them back to the peasantry which, from the point of view of its numbers and its latent hostility to the Tsarist regime, constituted the section of Russian society most important to the revolutionary movement.

The simultaneous attraction and repulsion which the peasantry exercised upon Social Democrats found reflection in Lenin's preoccupation with the role of the peasant in revolution. Lenin defined the relationship between the peasantry and the proletariat as a tactical alliance formed in the interest of joint struggle for the destruction of the Tsarist regime and of all remnants of feudalism in Russian society. As he conceived it, the alliance was a temporary and conditional one, an expedient which the proletariat would adopt in order to strengthen its own position, but would reject when the "bourgeois" phase of revolution had passed. "The time will come," he once wrote, "when the period of democratic revolution will also be over, and then it will be ridiculous to speak about 'unity of will' of the proletariat and the peasantry, about a democratic dictatorship, etc. When that time comes, we shall take up the question of the socialist dictatorship of the proletariat." [2] In the interim, he warned Social Democrats to watch their ally "as though he were an enemy" [3] and, for that matter, to enter no alliance which did not guarantee the ascendancy of the proletariat.

In the heat of revolution Lenin reversed himself in 1917 on the need for a democratic phase of revolution. But the Bolsheviks carried over into the period of "social" revolution many of his principles concerning the peasantry. Foremost among them was the theory of the worker-peasant alliance under the leadership of the proletariat. Translated into terms of Soviet policy,

[1] Frank Lorimer, *The Population of the Soviet Union: History and Prospects* (Geneva, 1946), p. 22.
[2] From the essay "Two Tactics of Social Democracy" written in 1905. See V. I. Lenin, *Selected Works* (New York, n.d.), III, 101.
[3] *Ibid.,* p. 100.

it meant the institution of a regime of political tutelage by which the Party hoped to "educate" the peasant and to convert him ultimately into a socialist producer. In practice, it degenerated into the use of force against the peasant and the organization of a system of police supervision to coerce him to give up the product of his labor to the regime and later to enter into collective farms. Politically, it became an excuse to deny him an equal status in the society which emerged from the revolution and civil war.

The Bolsheviks' attitude toward the peasant question had a direct bearing on their postrevolutionary nationality policy. Stripped of those aspects which related directly to the Leninist theory of self-determination, the nationality question in Soviet Russia became little more than a special form of the peasant problem. In the course of the revolution, those non-Russian peoples who had achieved the highest degree of industrial development—the Poles, the Finns, and the Baltic peoples—managed to win their independence. What remained of the non-Russian territory was overwhelmingly rural and in most cases lacked even the rudiments of industry and of a native proletariat.

This fact alone affected profoundly not only the day-to-day policies which the Soviet government pursued toward the peoples of the borderlands but also the reaction of the borderland peoples toward the Soviet regime. True to its early promises, the Bolshevik government put a quick end to inequalities which, under the Tsarist regime, had been based upon differences in nationality. But it replaced them with new inequalities founded upon class membership. The colonial administration, composed principally of Russian civil servants and military personnel, disappeared in the cauldron of revolution. Its place was taken by a new administration dominated by proletarians who were also predominantly Russian in origin and culture. Small wonder that native populations, ignorant of the fine distinction involved, should see in the new system only a continuation of the colonial regime under a new ideological platform!

The postrevolutionary continuation of Great Russian domination of policy and administration in the non-Russian republics confronted the Soviet regime with a policy dilemma. The Bolsheviks could extend and consolidate the system of Great Russian political administration in the border regions under the guise of proletarian political tutelage and so establish an enlightened colonial system of the kind which Western European socialists had suggested—and Russian Social Democrats had rejected [4]—at the Stuttgart Congress in 1907. Or they could undertake a program of accelerated industrialization which would transform the overwhelmingly rural national republics and regions into centers of native proletarian strength. The whole logic of Marxist-Leninist theory of revolution and social reconstruction committed the Bolsheviks to the second line of action. Repeated Bolshevik repudiations of gradualism in the solution of the national question, as well as the promises of political, economic, and social equality, rendered colonial tutelage in any form repugnant to Soviet leaders. Internal Marxist compulsions, moreover, favored a grandiose effort to transform the whole Soviet state into an industrial society.

Economic reality in postrevolutionary Russia, nevertheless, set up a formidable barrier between the requirements of theory and the means of fulfilling them. By the time the Soviet government turned its attention to problems of socialist construction, the Russian economy, reduced to a state of collapse by seven years of war and revolution, was not equipped to sustain a program of rapid industrialization on a nation-wide scale. The primary task was the restoration of production in existing plants and equipment. Great Russia had no resources to spare, either in skilled manpower or material, to promote the establishment of industrial centers in the border regions. The peoples of the border regions, especially in the Eastern republics, were incapable of undertaking the construction and operation of an industrial plant of their own. They lacked physical resources essential to the task and there was no native labor force sufficiently skilled to build and operate a modern industrial establishment.

[4] For Lenin's report and analysis of the debate on the question, see V. I. Lenin, *Sochineniia* (2d ed., Moscow, 1926—), XII, 354–56.

THE ECONOMIC PROBLEM OF CENTRAL ASIA

In this respect the plight of Central Asia was typical of a general problem which confronted the Soviet regime in all the Eastern republics and regions. Its labor force was minuscule and for the most part unskilled; its industry was rudimentary; and both had all but disappeared during the revolution and civil war. Capitalist forms of industrial organization, which had first appeared toward the end of the nineteenth century, were still a novelty. Large industry was typically colonial in character; its central features were foreign ownership, principally Russian, and concentration on the primary processing of raw materials and agricultural products which were important to the industries of Central Russia.

Cotton processing dominated the industrial picture. Two hundred and one ginning mills and 19 cottonseed oil mills accounted for more than 81 percent of the total industrial value of the region in 1914.[5] Small-scale milling, tanning, and cocoon drying establishments accounted for most of the remaining industrial output. While 14 companies were engaged in the extraction of coal in the Khodjent district, production was low—63,-248 short tons in 1911—and the quality poor. German and French firms were financing oil extraction in Fergana and on Cheleken Island, but the output had reached only 306,960 short tons by 1911 and the owners showed no disposition to expand the enterprise.[6]

While the Tsarist government was interested in increasing the production of raw cotton and in exploiting other raw materials resources, it had consistently discouraged the establishment of local industrial enterprises which might compete with the factories of Central Russia. Local administrative officials frustrated

---

[5] P. I. Liashchenko, *Istoriia narodnogo khoziaistva SSSR* (Moscow, 1948), II, 550. By 1918, when the cotton industry was nationalized, Turkestan contained 251 operating ginning mills, 15 cottonseed oil mills, and 14 combination ginning and pressing mills. A. Novikov, "Khlopkovodstvo i khlopkovaia promyshlennost'," in *Vsia Sredniaia Aziia: spravochnaia kniga na 1926 khoziaistvennyi god* (Tashkent, 1926), p. 159.

[6] Liashchenko, *Istoriia narodnogo khoziaistva SSSR*, II, 552.

attempts to establish textile mills. Governor General Samsonov rejected one such petition solely on the ground that a local textile factory would create "unhealthy competition with the Russian factory owners of Ivanovo-Voznesensk, Moscow, and so on." [7] Only those branches of industry engaged in the initial processing of raw materials required by the factories and mills of the Central Industrial Region had developed beyond a rudimentary stage.

The local industrial labor force was small in numbers. Data for 1914 showed fewer than 21,000 workers employed in factory-mill industry. While more than 75 percent were natives of the region, the small minority of immigrant Russian workers monopolized the few positions which required industrial skill, received higher wages for their labor, and worked under better conditions.[8] These differences in status, which contributed to group solidarity among the European population and encouraged the dichotomy between native and Russian proletarians, favored the growth of a "colonial psychology" among Russian workers and the isolation of the Russian workingman in Central Asia from the native community.

A second factor contributing to the isolation of Central Asian industry from the local population was its failure to contribute to the well-being of the native community in any significant way. Ownership was concentrated in the hands of Great Russian and foreign interests, and output served the needs of Central Russia. Central Asia still depended largely upon local cottage industry for the supply of many manufactured items. But its native cottage industry was declining rapidly under the impact of Russian factory competition. Because of its inability to compete with textiles imported from Great Russia, kustar' textile production, except in silk weaving, had all but ceased by the eve of the revolution. The local silk weaving industry, likewise, faced eventual extinction in competition with a developing Great Russian silk industry, although as late as 1910 it was still able to produce for export as well as for local needs. In that year there were in

[7] Quoted in A. Khavin, *Sotsialisticheskaia industrializatsiia natsional'nykh respublik i oblastei* (Moscow, 1933), pp. 20–21.
[8] Liashchenko, *Istoriia narodnogo khoziaistva SSSR*, II, 552–53.

operation some 1,750 silk weaving establishments, averaging two to three workers and each producing an annual output valued at 1,300 to 1,500 rubles.[9]

The weaving of high-quality carpets, for which Central Asia was famous, was perhaps the strongest of the local cottage industries. In 1908 the Transcaspian region alone produced carpeting valued at 200,000 rubles. After the turn of the century this industry, too, had fallen into a decline caused by poorly organized distribution and by the poor quality of imported dyes, which decreased the value of the finished product.[10] These two factors reduced the income of weavers so much that many were abandoning their trade.

The plight of the carpet weavers was symptomatic of the general decline of cottage industry which continued into the period of the revolution. By the time of the downfall of the Tsarist regime, manufactured goods imported from Great Russia had almost completely displaced local products, chiefly textiles, and were threatening to drive locally made shoes, metal goods, and other products from the market. The decline of local consumer goods production was an index of the rapid pace at which Turkestan was being integrated into the Russian national economy. The effect was infinitely greater in agriculture. The demands of Russian industry had led to a precipitous shift from the production of foodstuffs to the production of cotton—a shift which not only subjected the local economy to the fluctuations of the Russian market but made Central Asia dependent upon imports of grain from Russia.

The revolution abruptly halted the process of integration. During the civil war Central Asia's economy tended to revert to the pattern which had obtained before the Russian conquest. Industrial production declined rapidly; plants fell idle for lack of fuel and raw materials or were damaged and destroyed in the course of the fighting; food crops displaced cotton and wool in agriculture. The Dutov blockade cut off Central Asia from Central Russia and prevented the exchange of cotton for grain. Cotton, needed desperately by the mills in Central Russia, piled up

[9] *Ibid.*, II, 548.
[10] *Ibid.*

in the warehouses of Central Asia. The peasants turned to producing food crops, and the ginning mills, caught in the squeeze, were compelled to curtail operations.

The decline of Central Asian industry was hastened by the rapid nationalization of existing industrial enterprises and by the institution of worker control over production. Cotton was the first commodity to feel the full weight of governmental intervention. On February 26, 1918, the Turkestan Council of People's Commissars sequestered all stocks of cotton in the region and four days later organized a Cotton Division to administer the property. Nationalization of the cotton industry followed on March 7; the government seized 296 ginning mills, 38 oil pressing and soap mills, and five wadding factories, and turned management of them over to the cotton and oil workers' trade union.[11] The expropriation of the cotton industry set the pattern for nationalizing other branches of industry and transport. In quick succession the Turkestan government seized railroads, steamship companies, the oil industry, and coal mining firms and vested their administration in appropriate labor unions.

In its feverish rush to transfer Turkestan's industrial plant and equipment into the hands of the workers, the local government had its eyes focused on Moscow. Lacking an appreciation either of the economic gulf between Great Russia and Central Asia or of the special peculiarities of local industry, it did little more than imitate the acts of the central government.[12] One immediate consequence was a withdrawal of experienced management personnel and the emergence of hastily formed factory committees, incapable of operating the expropriated industries efficiently. Another was a decline in labor discipline and productivity. Equipment fell rapidly into disrepair; absenteeism and malingering increased; an atmosphere of discouragement and defeatism spread swiftly throughout industry.

Constant shortages of raw materials forced many enterprises into periods of prolonged idleness; increasing food scarcities

[11] F. A. Diuzhev, "Zavody khlopkovoi promyshlennosti Turkestana," *Khlopkovoe Delo*, Nos. 3–4 (March–April, 1922), p. 42.

[12] Ilias Alkin, *Sredniaia Aziia: ekonomiko-geograficheskii ocherk Kara-Kalpakstana, Kirgizstana, Tadzhikistana, Turkmenistana i Uzbekistana* (Moscow, 1931), I, 349.

kept workers on short rations, impairing their efficiency; and the uncertainties arising out of War Communism undercut all initiative. Absence of administrative leadership, and the government's inability to allocate materials in short supply, aggravated the crisis. To be sure, the Tashkent government adopted Moscow's solution to the problem by creating a Regional Council of National Economy in May, 1918, and vesting in it authority to reorganize the economy of Turkestan. But the agency was unequal to the task. Rudzutak, a member of the Turkestan Commission, later sent by Moscow to investigate the agency, charged that it had actually "upset the national economy" and accused it of speculating and sheltering a huge bureaucracy which hid its incompetence and malfeasance behind a curtain of red tape.[13]

Incompetence within the highest economic agencies was but one manifestation of the breakdown of control over the economy of the region. Not only did this give rise to widespread graft and peculation—between 1918 and 1920 representatives of the Council of National Economy managed to steal 11,000,000 rubles of the agency's funds—but it encouraged empire building among lesser economic agencies of the Turkestan government. The Commissariat of Communications, for example, created what amounted to its own national economy complete with factories and mills. The metallurgical workers branched out into soap, textile, and leather manufacturing as well as mining and metals production.[14] One consequence was the hoarding of scarce materials, inflationary competition among government agencies for goods, and a wasteful disbursement of funds. These practices only intensified the economic crisis still further.

Mismanagement, thievery, precipitate nationalization, the destruction of plant and equipment attendant upon military operations and the atmosphere of crisis which beclouded every activity drove industry into rapid decline. The cotton industry was hardest hit. Farm land under cotton cultivation decreased; under the pressures of war and revolution thousands of acres of

---

[13] From a statement of Rudzutak made before the Fifth Regional Conference of the Communist Party of Turkestan. Quoted in Georgii Safarov, *Kolonial'-naia revoliutsiia: opyt Turkestana* (Moscow, 1921), p. 106.

[14] *Ibid.*

arable land were abandoned outright and irrigation systems fell into disrepair. Fear of confiscations of the harvest as well as the tremendous demand for food crops encouraged the peasants to plant their cotton fields to grain or rice.[15] Even on those farms which continued cotton production, the crop yield declined steadily as native seed replaced the more productive American varieties.[16] The reduction of the cotton harvest caused major cutbacks in the operations of ginning and oil pressing plants and ultimately forced many to close down completely. At the same time, the efficiency of operating plants decreased, falling by 1922 to one half of the 1918 level. Fuel consumption on the other hand increased, although fuel supplies were dwindling.[17] The total effect upon the ginning and oil pressing industry was staggering. At the end of the nationalization, the regional government had seized 251 operating ginning mills with 78,370 ginning saws, 15 oil pressing mills with 88 presses, and 14 combination ginning and pressing mills with 57 presses and 6,000 ginning saws. By 1921 the operating plant had decreased to 47 ginning mills with 18,500 ginning saws, two pressing mills with 24 presses, and five combination mills with 32 presses.[18] One year later a Soviet investigator reported that Turkestan possessed no more than 40 ginning and three or four oil pressing mills capable of operation.[19] Only 16 ginning and two oil pressing mills actually were in production during that year.[20]

The extracting industries of the region suffered a similar decrease in production. Coal production fell from a high of 220,-750 short tons in 1916 to a low of 124,590 tons in 1921, while

[15] By 1922, according to one Soviet investigator, the area under cotton cultivation in Central Asia had declined to the level of the 1880's. See V. V. Zaorskaia-Aleksandrova, "Tezisy doklada po promyshlennosti Turkestana," *Khlopkovoe Delo*, Nos. 1–2 (January–February, 1922), pp. 44–45.

[16] *Ibid.*

[17] Diuzhev, "Zavody khlopkovoi promyshlennosti Turkestana," *Khlopkovoe Delo*, Nos. 3–4 (March–April, 1922), pp. 44–45.

[18] Novikov, "Khlopkovodstvo i khlopkovaia promyshlennost'," in *Vsia Sredniaia Aziia*, p. 159.

[19] Diuzhev, "Zavody khlopkovoi promyshlennosti Turkestana," *Khlopkovoe Delo*, Nos. 3–4 (March–April, 1922), pp. 44–45.

[20] *Ibid.*, p. 44. Novikov, writing in 1926, gives 22 ginning mills and two pressing mills for the same period. See Novikov, "Khlopkovodstvo i khlopkovaia promyshlennost'," in *Vsia Sredniaia Aziia*, p. 159.

the extraction of other minerals declined almost to nothing.[21] The operation of processing industries, except for cotton processing, came to a complete standstill. The failure of factory-mill industry to weather the storm threw the burden of production on cottage industry; and the latter, already in a state of decline, tended to restrict its operations to the production of simple consumer articles for a limited local market.

The reopening of communications between Central Asia and Great Russia in 1919, and the assertion of Moscow's control in 1920, did not alter the trend. Cognizant of the necessity for a quick recovery, Lenin had radioed the Tashkent Executive Committee on August 30, 1919, that "the victories of the revolution and the Red Army must be used for the improvement of the economic life of Turkestan and Russia." [22] The crisis worsened steadily, reaching its peak in the period from 1920 to 1922. Neither the local authorities nor the emissaries sent by Moscow to supervise the economic agencies in Turkestan were able to check the destructive forces which the revolution had set in motion. Moreover, the central government, lacking a clear conception of Central Asia's economic problems, failed to formulate a positive program of recovery and reconstruction, one which was also attuned to local needs.

THE QUEST FOR A POLICY

The roots of Moscow's difficulty lay in the Bolsheviks' ignorance of the details of the Russian economic structure and in their preoccupation with the elemental problem of survival during the civil war. Before the revolution Lenin and other Bolshevik leaders were concerned less with the realities of administering hungry and recalcitrant people than with the problem of constructing a theory and a plan of revolution and of winning allies for their revolutionary goals. The contradiction between the

---

[21] "Turkestanskie problemy: o stroitel'nykh zadachakh," Zhizn' Natsional'-nostei, No. 27 (125) (November 26, 1921); also Tsentral'noe Statisticheskoe Upravlenie SSSR, Narodnoe khoziaistvo Soiuza SSR v tsifrakh: kratkii spravochnik (Moscow, 1924), pp. 152–53.

[22] "M. V. Frunze na Turkestanskom fronte," Krasnyi Arkhiv, No. 3 (100) (1940), pp. 42–43.

economic needs of Soviet Russia and Bolshevik promises of liberation for the non-Russian nationalities hit hard after the October Revolution. As the territories of the Empire fell away or came under hostile occupation, economic chaos spread throughout Great Russia. Shortages of material threatened to paralyze industry, and shortages of food threatened to turn the mob against the regime. At one period the Soviet government controlled less than 10 percent of the former Empire's coal supply, 25 percent of its iron foundries, 50 percent of its grain area, and 10 percent of its sugar beet area.[23]

The loss of the Ukraine, the Donbas, and the Caucasus deprived the republic of most of its sources of fuel, and the railways were compelled to convert to the use of wood fuel. The loss of the Donets Basin, the Urals, and Poland nearly eliminated the iron and steel industry. The loss of Turkestan and Transcaucasia starved out the cotton mills of Vladimir and Ivanovo-Voznesensk. Even in those segments of industry which managed to remain in operation, starvation and near-starvation reduced the intensity and efficiency of work, increased absenteeism, and encouraged thievery and peculation. Flight from the foodless towns to the villages became common and the population of the cities declined.

The loss of Great Russia's major sources of food, fuel, and industrial raw materials taught the Bolsheviks a lesson in economic geography. It convinced them that the Ukraine, the Caucasus, and Turkestan were indispensable to the existence of the Russian state. The complementary argument that Great Russia was equally indispensable to the border regions to protect them from imperialist exploitation was a natural corollary, though the Bolsheviks appear not to have formulated it fully until 1921. In the earlier period they emphasized Great Russia's need of raw materials and asserted that Great Russia, deprived of the coal, oil, and cotton of the border regions, would, at worst, collapse or, at best, fall under the economic domination of the imperialist powers.

It was probably natural for the Bolsheviks to think of eco-

[23] Maurice Dobb, *Soviet Economic Development since 1917* (New York, 1948), pp. 97–106.

nomic unity first in terms of defending the revolutionary center, a defense which, it was easy to argue, must be carried on at any cost. This logic prompted Zinoviev to propose an exchange of Russian "civilization" for the cotton, oil, and other resources of the border regions. It appears again in Frunze's triumphant announcement to the Seventh Congress of Soviets in 1919 that his armies had opened the road to the cotton of Turkestan. It finds its ultimate expression in Zatonskii's rejoinder to Stalin at the Tenth Party Congress in 1921: if the strengthening of the center required it, a policy of plunder in the borderlands would be proper and correct.[24]

The shift of emphasis from revolutionary and political problems to economic demands which often sounded like thinly disguised rationalizations for Soviet imperialism did not fail to alarm those Bolsheviks who were most closely associated with the nationality policy. As early as April, 1920, a writer in *Zhizn' Natsional'nostei* complained that, "when the question is raised of the East, of the Eastern republics, or of the republics in general, it is examined primarily through 'economic eyes.' Turkestan means cotton, lemons, etc.; Kirghizia, wool, cattle; Bashkiria, timbers, hides, cattle." [25] Six months later, Stalin was still writing in terms of an exchange of food, raw materials, and other products of the borderlands for the political, military, and organizational support of Great Russia. But his promise that the Soviet regime would reverse the previous status of the border regions and would bestow on them economic benefits which the Tsarist government had reserved to Great Russia contained the germ of a new economic policy toward the nationalities.[26]

By the Tenth Party Congress in 1921 the essential elements of a bold new program of economic assistance to the border nationalities had emerged. Reporting to the congress, Stalin pointed out that the Soviet regime had solved the problem of national inequality by securing equal rights for all the peoples

[24] *Protokoly s'ezdov i konferentsii Vsesoiuznoi Kommunisticheskoi Partii (b): Desiatyi S'ezd R.K.P.(b), mart 1921 g.* (Moscow, 1933), p. 207.

[25] *Zhizn' Natsional'nostei*, No. 11 (68) (April 18, 1920).

[26] See Stalin's article, "Politika Sovetskoi Vlasti po natsional'nomu voprosu v Rossii" (October 10, 1920), in J. V. Stalin, *Sochineniia* (Moscow, 1946—), IV, 351–63.

of the RSFSR. There remained, nevertheless, "a heritage from the past by virtue of which one nationality, the Great Russian nationality, is more developed politically and industrially than the other nationalities." [27] The true solution to the problem, he said, depended upon the rendering of all-round support and assistance to the non-Russian populations in order that they might overtake Central Russia politically, culturally, and economically.[28] Achievement of this goal, according to the resolution of the congress, required the elimination of feudal-patriarchal attitudes and the unification of the nationalities for the building up of the socialist system. In the political sphere, this meant intensification of current Soviet efforts to destroy existing "class privileges" in the native community, to remove the influence of "native exploiting elements" upon the masses, and to organize the masses around the Soviet authority. Economically, it set before the Party the complex problem of creating a native proletariat, of organizing and rationalizing small goods production through the formation of cooperatives, and of encouraging planned industrial development in the borderlands.[29]

After the Tenth Party Congress, economic equalization of the Soviet peoples through the establishment of "focuses of industry" in the border republics became a fundamental objective of Bolshevik nationality policy.[30] Nevertheless, the actual content of Soviet economic policy in the non-Russian regions was affected only incidentally and indirectly by Soviet plans for solving the nationality problem. In April, 1918, in his *Outline of a Plan of Scientific and Technical Tasks*, Lenin had indicated that Soviet economic development would rest upon an "efficient areal distribution of industry in Russia from the point of view of bringing it closer to raw materials and upon the least possible

[27] *Ibid.*, V, 35–36.

[28] *Ibid.*, V, 39.

[29] *Vse-Soiuznaia Kommunisticheskaia Partiia v rezoliutsiiakh i resheniiakh s'ezdov, soveshchaniei i plenumov Tsentral'nogo Komiteta (1898–1932)* (4th ed., Moscow, 1932), I, 457–58.

[30] The importance to the Bolshevik Party of economic development in the non-Russian republics, even within limitations imposed by the New Economic Policy, appears in the renewed emphasis on the problem at the Twelfth Party Congress and the Fourth Conference with Responsible Workers. See *ibid.*, I, 637; also *Dvenadtsatyi S'ezd Rossiiskoi Kommunisticheskoi Partii (b)* (Moscow, 1923), pp. 443–46.

waste of labor in the movement from the original processing of the raw material, through all successive stages of the manufacture of the semifinished product, up to the receipt of the finished product." [31]

The key to Soviet economic development, Lenin argued, lay in centralized planning of economic expansion. The objective of this policy was not the achievement of equality of industrial development for the individual nationalities of Russia, but rather the most efficient utilization of the economic forces of the whole Soviet state. Lenin's goal was not the creation of independent economic regions with their boundaries defined by nationality, but the establishment of a unified national economy capable of supplying the Soviet republic "independently in all the main categories of raw material and industry." [32] In this analysis, Lenin treated the Soviet state as an economic unity whose parts history had forged into a single whole. Even as he wrote, the centrifugal pull of nationalistic ambitions was tearing the Russian state asunder.

Several years later Stalin seized upon precisely the same point to justify reunification of the independent Soviet republics and the formation of the USSR. At the Tenth Congress of Soviets (December, 1922), in describing the conditions which had led to the reunification of the territories of the former Russian Empire, Stalin gave an important place to what he called the "natural, historically established" division of labor among the various republics and regions of the Soviet federation:

This division of labor . . . cannot be expunged with one stroke of the pen. It was created historically by the whole course of economic development of the federation. This very division of labor which renders the full development of individual districts impossible while the republics remain separated obliges the republics to unite into a single economic whole. [33]

Bolshevik policy was keyed to strengthening the economic interdependence of the territories of the Soviet federation. It

[31] Lenin, *Sochineniia* (2d ed.), XXII, 434.
[32] *Ibid.*
[33] *Desiatyi Vserossiiskii S'ezd Sovetov Rabochikh, Krest'ianskikh, Krasnoarmeiskikh i Kazach'ikh Deputatov (23–27 dekabria 1922 goda)* (Moscow, 1923), p. 185.

sought to accentuate the existing division of labor by encouraging regional specialization. This consideration was never overlooked in planning measures to promote the economic equalization of the non-Russian peoples. Despite this guiding concept, which opposed the development of self-sufficient local economies in the borderlands, Bolshevik policy offered a prospect of ultimate economic gain for the non-Russian nationalities through reversing the Tsarist policy of protecting the industries of Great Russia and discouraging industrial development elsewhere. "It is inconceivable," the plan of the State Commission for Electrification pointed out, "that the rationalization of our industry will not be accompanied by a significant transfer of industry to the East in order to permit bringing manufacturing industry as close as possible to basic sources of raw material or fuel for general economic reasons." [34]

It was within the limits set by these considerations of general policy that the Soviet government approached the problems of economic reconstruction and socialist industrialization in Central Asia. Broadly speaking, it set out to restore prerevolutionary levels of production in industry and agriculture and to create stable economic foundations for the creation of a socialist economy. Making good the losses sustained in the revolution and civil war called for rebuilding destroyed and damaged railways and irrigation systems, encouraging the peasants to return to the production of technical crops, and recovering prerevolutionary levels of production in processing and extracting industries. The primary purpose was to restore Central Asia to its prewar status as a supplier of technical crops and raw materials for the industries of Great Russia.

The Soviet leaders also directed economic recovery toward laying a foundation for establishing a socialist economic order. They applied political and economic pressure to promote rapid development of the socialist and cooperative sectors of the economy while consistently restricting and discouraging private enterprise. And they undertook to create new cadres of skilled and unskilled native workers by introducing programs of technical

[34] Quoted in S. S. Bal'zak, V. F. Vasiutin, and Ya. G. Feigin, *Economic Geography of the USSR* (New York, 1949), p. 141.

training and encouraging the transfer of surplus labor from agriculture to the revived industries. Through a program which emphasized the collectivization and mechanization of the production process and the construction of new factories and mills for the processing of local materials, the Bolsheviks began to prepare for socialist industrialization in Central Asia and the development of regional industrial specialization.

In terms of the resources and technical skills available in Central Asia, the program was extremely ambitious. Its success depended upon centralized coordination and planning in the economy, the channeling of industrial efforts toward specific goals, and constant checking on fulfillment by public agencies. It also required a limited utilization of private capital and initiative. While the retreat to the New Economic Policy permitted the revival of a private sector in the economy and the reappearance of the private producer and trader, the state reserved control of the "commanding heights" of the economy, maintaining its monopoly in basic industry,[35] transport, communications, and foreign trade. Private entrepreneurs were restricted to less important sectors of trade and industry. Within these limitations, rigidly enforced through taxation and government supervision, private capitalism performed two functions which were important to the regime and which hastened economic recovery. It released the state from the necessity of pouring its limited funds into the manufacture of many types of consumer goods; and increased revenues obtained through high taxation of private businesses gave additional resources for use in the reconstruction of socialist industry, communications, and transport. Further, the rate of recovery of private industry served as a ready criterion of progress in restoring the basic operations of the socialist sector. In fact, the pressure of competition between public and private enterprises compelled state industry to adopt cost accounting and other standard business practices in order to keep pace.

In Central Asia, as elsewhere in Soviet Russia, the introduction of the New Economic Policy, adopted at the Tenth Congress of

[35] According to Lenin's definition, basic industry included large-scale industry and industries which processed goods for other industries.

the Communist Party (March, 1921), marked the beginning of
an economic revival. The Turkestan government now denation-
alized one half of the enterprises which it had seized during the
civil war,[36] and the governments of Bokhara and Khorezm followed suit in 1922. None of these republics restored the so-called
basic industries—cotton processing and minerals extraction—to
private ownership. However, denationalization freed native capital of most of the restrictions imposed by the revolutionary government, and it removed most of the obstacles to a revival of local
cottage industry.

Local authorities even tended to permit free enterprise to
extend its sphere of activity beyond limits considered appropriate by Party leaders. The Second Congress of the Communist
Party of Bokhara in 1922 adopted a program which called for
the denationalization and leasing to private businessmen of industrial enterprises in order to encourage private enterprise in
both industry and trade.[37] A similar inclination of the Turkestan government to encourage the development of private capital beyond "reasonable" bounds occasioned a sharp reminder
from Moscow that the New Economic Policy in no wise signified
"the opening of a free field of activity to native trade and money
capital." [38]

While local deviations of this kind from the economic course
charted in Moscow were fairly common during the early period
of the New Economic Policy, the danger of an invasion of private capital into the socialist sector of the economy was actually
negligible. For one thing, political agencies responsible only to
Moscow constantly supervised or guided the activities of the local
officials, and economic commissariats and agencies of the central
government exercised a large measure of control over critical
sectors in the local economy. A review of the constitutional and
treaty relationships between the RSFSR and the governments of
the Central Asian republics shows the pervasiveness of Moscow's

[36] *Zhizn' Natsional'nostei,* No. 5 (11) (April 1, 1922).
[37] K., "Vtoroi S'ezd (Kuraltai) Bukharskoi Kommunisticheskoi Partii," *Zhizn'
Natsional'nostei,* No. 6 (135) (February 16, 1922).
[38] From a circular letter of the Central Committee, All-Russian Communist
Party (b) to the Communist Party of Turkestan (January, 1922). Quoted in
E. B. Genkina, *Obrazovanie SSSR* (Moscow, 1947), p. 98.

economic dominance. The grant of autonomy which defined Turkestan's status in the Soviet republic reserved to the government of the RSFSR exclusive jurisdiction over foreign trade and made the republic commissariats of finance, communications, posts and telegraph, and supply, and the republic Council of National Economy each responsible both to the federal commissariats of the same name and to the local government.[39]

A similar degree of central control was established over the economies of Bokhara and Khorezm. Economic agreements, concluded between them and the RSFSR between 1920 and 1923, drew them completely into the Russian economic orbit. These relationships were strengthened by the formation of the Central Asiatic Economic Council in March, 1923. This agency, from its headquarters in Tashkent, not only acted as a superior planning agency for Central Asia's agriculture, irrigation, state trading, and cooperatives, but assumed direct responsibility for unifying the regions' monetary systems, foreign trade, transport, and communications.[40]

After the national delimitation and the incorporation of the Uzbek and Turcoman republics into the USSR, the All-Union Central Executive Committee issued a new regulation which vested the Central Asiatic Economic Council with supreme economic authority in Central Asia and brought it directly under control of the government of the USSR. It charged the Economic Council with responsibility for the creation of a unified economic plan for the Central Asian republics and the supervision of the execution of those phases of all-union plans which concerned Central Asia. It also authorized the agency to issue directives to agencies which supervised the economies of the individual republics and autonomous regions, to adopt measures to hasten the economic development of Central Asia, to supervise directly the activities of institutions and enterprises having regional significance for Central Asia, and to arbitrate economic disputes between individual republics. Although six representatives from each of the republics of the region sat on the Eco-

[39] See above, pp. 76–77.
[40] For a description of the development of economic relations between the RSFSR and the republics of Bokhara and Khorezm prior to the national delimitation, see above, pp. 70–75.

nomic Council, the agency was responsible directly and solely to the All-Union Council of People's Commissars, which appointed the chairman and confirmed the appointments of three sub-chairmen of the council. The regulation also provided for appointment to the Economic Council of representatives of the all-union commissariats of worker-peasant inspection, labor, foreign and domestic trade, transport, and posts and telegraph, the commander of the Central Asiatic military district, and the Central Asiatic Bureau of the All-Union Council of Trade Unions.[41]

The existence of the Central Asiatic Economic Council and other central agencies in the region indicates clearly that the operation of the Soviet economy depended fully as much upon central control of local economic activity as it did upon state ownership and supervision of the "commanding heights." Through these agencies, Moscow was able to keep in close contact with developments in the farthest reaches of the Soviet state. Of greater significance, the agencies were transmission belts which geared local economic development to the requirements of central planning and consistently integrated local economic operations into the pattern of all-union activity.

The Moscow government, of course, made no attempt to introduce the notorious "single factory" principle[42] into the socialist sector of the economy of Central Asia. During the first years

[41] Text in I. Lozovskii and I. Bibin (eds.), *Sovetskaia Politika za 10 let po natsional'nomu voprosu v RSFSR: sistematicheskii sbornik deistvuiushchikh aktov pravitel'stv Soiuza SSR i RSFSR po delam natsional'nostei RSFSR (oktiabr' 1917 g.–noiabr' 1927 g.)* (Moscow, 1928), pp. 436–37. Also S. Ya. Gessen, "K voprosu o khoziaistvennom stroitel'stve Srednei Azii," *Sovetskoe Stroitel'stvo*, No. 1 (6) (January, 1927), p. 60.

[42] The "single factory" system, as it appeared in Soviet Russia, was an adaptation of a system of economic regulation which had arisen in Germany during the war. In its Russian manifestations, it amounted to a more or less complete "bureaucratization" of the nationalized sector of the economy. Every nationalized industry was placed under the supervision of a director who was usually selected solely on the basis of his political reliability. The director, in every instance, operated in accordance with the orders and instructions of superior coordinating agencies which, in turn, were subordinated to "central boards." This hierarchical structure culminated in the Supreme Council of National Economy. For a brief discussion and criticism of the system, see Nicholas S. Timasheff, *The Great Retreat: The Growth and Decline of Communism in Russia* (New York, 1946), pp. 109–11. For an analysis by a Soviet writer, see A. Arakelian, *Industrial Management in the USSR* (Washington, 1950), pp. 55–62.

of the New Economic Policy, actual business operations were conducted by "municipal corporations" and trusts, the former operating as local public utilities and the latter performing in ways that resembled the activities of joint stock companies in capitalist society.[43] Toward the end of the period, the state, as owner of the trusts, began to interfere directly in the productive process by creating syndicates and, in some cases, central boards above the trust, and by authorizing these agencies to fix prices, establish norms of production, and divide markets. A real central control of the economy, nevertheless, had been operative throughout the New Economic Policy and decisions on the policy level were in most cases arrived at in Moscow.

THE REVIVAL OF THE SOCIALIST SECTOR

Stated broadly, central policy during the 1920's had aimed to reverse the trend toward political and economic disintegration which had been manifested alarmingly during the last stages of War Communism. In dealing with the socialist sector of the economy in Central Asia, its purpose was to rehabilitate and develop three segments of the local economy. Of these, the reconstruction of state-owned industry was of principal importance. The restoration of the production of existing plants and equipment to prerevolutionary levels was essential both to revive the flow of raw materials to the factories and mills of the Central Industrial Region and to create stable foundations for the development of local manufacturing industries.

Progress in industrial reconstruction, moreover, determined the pace at which Bolsheviks could develop and organize a native industrial labor force. To a large extent, recruits for this labor force were expected to emerge from the ranks of the small producers who had fallen by the wayside in the economic struggle for survival. The Bolsheviks, of course, did not anticipate the early disappearance of this class, which made up the bulk

[43] Like the joint stock companies, the trusts had an administrative board, a managing director, managers of individual enterprises, and an auditing committee. They conducted operations on the basis of statutes which were similar to the articles of incorporation of the company. However, the state agency to which the trust was attached took the place of the general assembly of stockholders. This agency outlined the plan of work, supervised its execution, hired and dismissed management personnel, and exercised other policy functions.

of the native population engaged in trade and industry. Instead, they sought to extend the economic influence of the state directly over the small producer. By encouraging the development of a strong Communist-dominated and centralized cooperative movement, the Bolsheviks hoped to restrict the independence of the small producer and to harness his energies to the achievement of Party-determined goals.

Thus, during the period of the New Economic Policy, the Soviet state concentrated its energies upon the revival and expansion of state-owned industry, the creation and organization of a native industrial proletariat, and the development of a cooperative movement among small producers. In accordance with its over-all economic goals, the Soviet regime channeled its efforts toward an expansion of the socialist sector of the economy, with the ultimate objective of eliminating the vestiges of private enterprise and creating a stable groundwork for socialist industrialization. This policy offered, in Bolshevik eyes, the only basis upon which a socialist society, oriented in its totality —politically, juridically, morally, and socially—toward Marxian ideals, could emerge and endure.[44]

The state necessarily devoted a major portion of its funds and energy to the restoration of pre-1917 levels of production in "basic industry." In Central Asia this meant, first of all, a drive to revive the cotton processing industry for the needs of Central Russian textile factories, with the further goal of making Russia independent of foreign cotton. Processing of raw cotton had fallen precipitously during the civil war, and the Soviet government now concentrated its efforts on the revival of cotton cultivation and local fuel production as much as on the reorganization and expansion of cotton processing. It set favorable prices for raw cotton, sponsored loans to peasants, distributed seed, and offered other privileges in order to increase cotton planting.[45] It also established a priority in the allocation of existing fuel supplies to the cotton industry and undertook a campaign to restore fuel production to prewar levels.

[44] See P. Bulata (ed.), *Osnovy teorii Sovetskogo khoziaistva: uchebnoe posobie dlia sovpartshkol* (Leningrad, 1931), pp. 137–38.

[45] See below, pp. 312–16.

Within the cotton processing industry, reconstruction took three main paths. Initially, the Bolsheviks concerned themselves with restoring a pattern of efficient operation in active enterprises. In conformity with their general economic policy, they reintroduced the single-manager system, demanded strict observance of the norms of labor discipline by the workers, inaugurated systematic cost accounting practices, and allocated funds for the repair and replacement of worn-out and primitive machinery in operating plants. A second phase of reconstruction aimed at concentrating production and enlarging enterprises. This represented a reversal of the prerevolutionary trend toward the establishment of new enterprises rather than the expansion of existing plants and equipment. While as many as 251 ginning mills had operated in Central Asia during 1916–17, no more than 60 were active in any one year during the New Economic Policy.[46] Productive capacity of the mills, which averaged five to eight gins, nevertheless, by 1927 was approaching prewar levels. At the same time, the government set aside funds for the construction of new mills. Uzbekistan, the center of the industry, allocated 35 million rubles to the cotton ginning industry in 1925–26 alone. And most of it was expended for the construction of new mills in Andijan, New Bokhara, Charjui, Karakul, Khorasan, and other towns.[47]

The reforms, introduced during the New Economic Policy period, produced a steady revival in the ginning industry, but the goal of complete recovery of the prewar level of production was still unfulfilled when the First Five-Year Plan came into effect. Gross production rose from a mere 4 percent of the 1913 level in 1920 to 70.6 percent (116,999,600 rubles, 1913 value) in 1926–27. Increased production in the ginning industry was paralleled by a revival in the oil pressing industry and set the pace of reconstruction for all other branches of state-owned industry.

[46] A. E. Aksel'rod, "Khlopkovoe delo za 10 let (1917–1927)," *Khlopkovoe Delo,* Nos. 11–12 (November–December, 1927), p. 833.

[47] Khavin, *Sotsialisticheskaia industrializatsiia natsional'nykh respublik i oblastei,* p. 84. Plans for 1926 called for the creation of 11 additional ginning mills but lack of finances limited actual construction to five. G. Dunaev, "Planovoe khoziaistvo v Srednei Azii," *Planovoe Khoziaistvo,* No. 3 (March, 1926), p. 223.

Six pressing mills were in operation in the region in 1926–27 and their production valued at 9,670,400 rubles (1913 value) had reached 69.8 percent of the production level of 1913. The dominating role of these two branches of the cotton processing industry in Central Asia is apparent from the fact that together they accounted for 86 percent of the total gross income of state-owned industry as late as 1926–27; their recovery provided an almost exact index of the average rate of recovery in industry taken as a whole.[48]

The Soviet government's plans to establish textile centers in Central Asia likewise were characteristic of Bolshevik efforts to develop local manufacturing and to prepare the economic foundations for the achievement of socialism. As early as 1918 Lenin had urged the creation of industrial centers close to sources of raw material, and Stalin's report at the Tenth Party Congress in 1921 appears, in retrospect, as the opening shot of a campaign to hasten the industrialization of the Soviet border regions. This report[49] and the Party resolution based on it led to much discussion among Soviet economists and publicists, but in the following two years the government took no action to implement the resolution. True, after the Twelfth Party Congress in 1923 the presidium of the All-Union Council of National Economy ordered the removal of the Shuiskii cotton mill to Turkestan,[50] but the plant was still operating in Shuiskii in 1930. In 1926 the Soviet government decided to construct two 10,000-spindle experimental textile mills on sites in Ashkhabad and Fergana.[51] Upon beginning production in 1928 they be-

[48] Total recovery reached 69.6 percent of the 1913 level in 1926–27. Gessen, "K voprosu o khoziaistvennom stroitel'stve Srednei Azii," *Sovetskoe Stroitel'stvo*, No. 1 (6) (January, 1927), p. 68.

[49] See above, pp. 261–62.

[50] *Zhizn' Natsional'nostei*, Nos. 3–4 (1923), p. 204.

[51] Dunaev, "Planovoe khoziaistvo v Srednei Azii," *Planovoe Khoziaistvo*, No. 3 (March, 1926), p. 224. These two mills were designed in part to serve as a test of the feasibility of developing textile centers in Central Asia. Almost from the moment that movement of the cotton textile industry to the region was suggested, many Soviet economists had raised objections to the idea. Since it was estimated that construction of 25 factories (the number required) would cost about 300,000,000 rubles, cost alone became the basis of one complaint. Other objections were raised on the ground that Central Asia lacked a labor force sufficiently skilled to operate the mills, that the production process itself required large amounts of water, and that the temperatures of the region would

came the first modern textile mills to operate in Central Asia.[52]

During the New Economic Policy, reconstruction and development in other branches of industry, except extractive industry, followed the same pattern. Because of the difficulties encountered in reviving the salt mining and petroleum industries, extractive industry by 1926–27 was producing only 35.8 percent of the 1913 income, while industry as a whole produced 69.6 percent. The salt mining industry had almost collapsed during the revolutionary period, and the Bolsheviks, considering it to be of secondary importance, had made no concentrated effort to revive its production during the New Economic Policy.

Central Asia's petroleum industry, on the other hand, failed even to meet the test of economic utility. High production costs and poor quality of Central Asian crude oil restricted sales to the local market. Even those all-union enterprises which conducted their operations in Central Asia preferred to purchase their supplies from outside sources. As late as 1926–27 the value of Central Asian production was only 22.4 percent of the 1913 figure. In sharp contrast, production in the coal industry surged ahead of the prewar level. By 1924–25 the value of production had already surpassed the 1913 level by 42 percent and two years later it had reached 259 percent of 1913.[53]

The greatest expansion within the socialist sector of the economy took place in the development of power resources. Restoration of the production of mechanical power actually proceeded at a faster pace than electric power (see Table 6); in 1926–27 it contributed more than twice the output. The Soviet government, however, had concentrated its program of new construction on the expansion of electric power resources, chiefly in the Tashkent industrial district. Within Tashkent a diesel plant was constructed with a capacity of 2,800 kilowatts, and nearby the Bos-su and Kadyr'insk hydroelectric plants were built with a combined capacity of 16,000 kilowatts. By the end of the New

necessitate the installation of air conditioning equipment in the factories. For example, see I. Khodorov, "K probleme raionirovaniia promyshlennosti Srednei Azii," *Planovoe Khoziaistvo*, No. 1 (January, 1927), p. 194.

[52] N. B. Arkhipov, *SSSR po raionam: Sredne-Aziatskie respubliki* (2d ed., Moscow, 1928), p. 116.

[53] Gessen, "K voprosu o khoziaistvennom stroitel'stve Srednei Azii," *Sovetskoe Stroitel'stvo*, No. 1 (6) (January, 1927), p. 68.

Economic Policy a thermoelectric plant with a capacity of 8,300 kilowatts had also been completed in Fergana and construction had begun on a 12,000-kilowatt power station in Bokhara.[54]

TABLE 6

ENERGY RESOURCES OF CENTRAL ASIAN REPUBLICS

(*In Million Kilowatts*)

	UZBEKISTAN			TURKMENISTAN			TOTAL		
	Total	Me- chanical Power	Elec- tric Power	Total	Me- chanical Power	Elec- tric Power	Total	Me- chanical Power	Elec- tric Power
1925–26	36.4	25.1	11.3	5.4	1.5	3.9	41.8	26.6	15.2
1926–27	52.0	38.0	14.0	7.6	2.5	5.1	59.6	40.5	19.1

Source: Compiled from data in Gosplan SSSR, *Piatiletnii plan narodno-khoziaistvennogo stroitel'stva SSSR* (Moscow, 1930), III, 324.

Developments in cotton processing, minerals extraction, power, and transportation tell only part of the story of industrial reconstruction in Central Asia. While state-owned industry had reached 70 percent of the prewar levels, the Soviet regime had engaged most sparingly in what might be called industrial pioneering. It had made no effort to exploit Central Asia's iron deposits, nonferrous metals, rare earths, and other mineral resources, although sizable deposits were known to exist.[55] Ambitious projects for developing centers of manufacturing received very feeble implementation, while some branches, such as tanning and the preparation of leather goods, remained largely in the hands of kustar's. Of course, the Soviet government suffered from an acute shortage of funds during the period, and industrial development in Central Asia was hampered also by the lack of an industrial labor force. These difficulties compelled the Bolsheviks to choose there as elsewhere between reviving existing industries and embarking on programs of new development. They elected the former course and invested what funds were available in the expansion of industries promising the largest immediate returns.

[54] Khavin, *Sotsialisticheskaia industrializatsiia natsional'nykh respublik i oblastei*, p. 81.

[55] For a list of known mineral resources at the time, see Gosplan SSSR, *Piatiletnii plan narodno-khoziaistvennogo stroitel'stva SSSR* (Moscow, 1930), III, 321–23.

THE CAMPAIGN TO "NATIONALIZE" INDUSTRIAL LABOR

The same lack of funds and technical skills which hindered industrial growth in Central Asia during the twenties also affected Soviet plans to develop an efficient industrial labor force. During the period of War Communism, the Bolsheviks in Central Asia had ignored the problem of the efficient relationship between the size and productivity of industry and the size of the labor force. Even though industrial production was declining, they permitted, and in some cases encouraged, industrial enterprises to expand their labor force. Data collected in the course of the 1920 census of Turkestan showed a total labor force of 65,500 persons employed in some 13,731 separate industrial enterprises. The great majority were primitive kustar' establishments employing two or three persons. But there were also 34,700 persons employed in 955 state-operated factories and mills.[56] The disparity between the real labor requirements of industry and the actual size of the labor force is apparent in the decline of productivity of the individual worker, which by 1920 amounted to one fourth or one fifth of the 1913 level.[57]

The introduction of the New Economic Policy with its insistence upon industrial efficiency and its revival of business methods commonly associated with capitalist management presaged a reversal of the labor practices of the previous period. With adoption of the single-manager system and reinstatement of the criterion of profit, individual enterprises began to dismiss surplus personnel and demanded increased productivity of the remaining workers. By 1924 the productivity of labor had increased to more than 60 percent of the 1913 level, but 12,500 workers, the majority of whom had been employed in factories, were idle.[58] The labor force remaining in industry was less than half the force employed in 1920.

[56] Tsentral'noe Statisticheskoe Upravlenie SSSR, Narodnoe khoziaistvo Soiuza SSR v tsifrakh, pp. 126–27.
[57] For a comparison of worker productivity by industry, see Sredne-Aziatskoe Biuro V.Ts.S.P.S., Professional'nye soiuzy v Srednei Azii 24–25 god: otchet Sr-Aziatskogo Biuro V.Ts.S.P.S. k Pervoi Sredne-Aziatskoi Konferentsii Profsoiuzov (Tashkent, 1925), p. 62.
[58] Ibid.; also N. Presnitskii, "Rynok truda," in Vsia Sredniaia Aziia, p. 311.

The year 1924 marked the low point of industrial employment. Thereafter, industrial revival proceeded at a quickened pace; state-owned enterprises began to expand their operations and their labor force. By 1925–26 they were employing 17,400 workers and in succeeding years continued to augment their staffs.[59] Moreover, opportunities began to open up in other non-agricultural branches of endeavor. Due chiefly to the revival of industry and the extension of service to new areas, the railway employed 20,524 workers in 1926 while the construction industry had 6,382 workers on its payroll. (See Table 7.) The problem of unemployment, nevertheless, plagued Soviet author-

TABLE 7

LABOR FORCE IN CENTRAL ASIA IN 1926
(*Exclusive of Agriculture and Cottage Industry*)

INDUSTRIES	TOTAL	NATIVES		RUSSIANS	OTHERS[a]
		Total	*Uzbeks*		
Workers					
Total	98,237	49,478	32,779	32,719	16,040
Factory-Mill	18,587	7,175	4,433	7,719	3,693
Construction	6,382	2,367	1,678	2,767	1,248
Railway	20,524	2,139	1,108	14,060	4,325
Other Transport	3,375	1,223	880	1,236	916
Institutions	3,033	441	380	1,843	749
Other	46,336	36,133	24,300	5,094	5,109
Employees					
Total	98,848	23,293	17,115	54,107	21,448
Factory-Mill	4,970	730	557	2,968	1,272
Construction	1,004	35	27	779	190
Railway	8,256	164	100	6,713	1,379
Other Transport	1,484	128	97	1,023	333
Institutions	57,872	15,676	11,157	29,876	12,320
Other	25,262	6,560	5,177	12,748	5,954

Source: Compiled from data in Tsentral'noe Statisticheskoe Upravlenie SSSR, Otdel Perepisi, *Vsesoiuznaia perepis' naseleniia 1926 goda* (Moscow, 1928–29), XXXII, 2–3, 32–42; XXXIII, 2–3, 10–19; XXXVI, 206–7.

[a] Some natives included, but group is composed principally of Europeans.

ities in Central Asia throughout the 1920's[60] and was not solved

[59] Gessen, "K voprosu o khoziaistvennom stroitel'stve Srednei Azii," *Sovetskoe Stroitel'stvo*, No. 1 (6) (January, 1927), p. 67.

[60] According to data gathered by the State Planning Commission, 29.5 percent of the available labor supply was unemployed in Central Asia in 1927. By republic, the unused portions were: Uzbekistan (including Tajikistan), 30.1 percent; Turkmenistan, 33.9 percent; Kirghizia, 21.5 percent. See Gosplan, *Piatiletnii plan narodno-khoziaistvennogo stroitel'stva SSSR*, p. 323.

until the forced industrialization of the Five-Year Plan swallowed up the entire available labor supply.

While unemployment confronted the governments of Central Asia with a difficult human problem, its real gravity stemmed from its effect upon the larger issues of Soviet policy. On the one hand, it contributed to a growth of disillusionment with the Soviet regime within the ranks of labor and a rising spirit of doubt even among Communist Party workers. On the other hand, it inhibited implementation of the Bolshevik program to "naturalize" industry by creating cadres of native industrial workers. After the introduction of the New Economic Policy and the restoration of profit and efficiency as criteria of industrial performance, it was almost inevitable that the native labor force should bear the brunt of the wave of dismissals which swept through industry. The Moslem community furnished the bulk of unskilled industrial labor and this portion of the labor force could most easily be displaced when employment contracted. Doubtless, the concentration of management in European hands also influenced dismissal policy.

Hindrances to expanding the native labor force continued long after the initial period of retrenchment. Even though non-European workers suffered most in the cutbacks, the center of unemployment pressure was in the European community. Jobless natives usually were able to return to the village, find work in the old cities, or drift into other avenues of employment. No similar escape was available to Europeans. Unemployment statistics for Uzbekistan, characteristic of conditions throughout Central Asia, show that in 1924–25 over 80 percent of the unemployed were Europeans.[61] The local governments undertook to relieve the lot of the jobless by organizing collectives of the unemployed and adopting programs of ameliorative work.[62] But these were temporary expedients at best. In the long run, local officials tended, in rehiring, to give preference to members of this group.

Moscow, nevertheless, exercised a strong restraining influence upon this tendency through its continuous pressure upon the

[61] Presnitskii, "Rynok truda," in *Vsia Sredniaia Aziia*, p. 312.
[62] *Ibid.*, p. 316.

local governments to draw members of the native population into industry. The major factors in the conflict are apparent. Disregarding racial prejudice, which continued to influence the decisions of European officials in Central Asia in spite of official declarations to the contrary, local functionaries, concerned with their own immediate security, were interested in placating the European community. In contrast, the central Party leadership, motivated by long-range political considerations and committed to the policy of "naturalizing" industry, insisted that Soviet agencies draw natives into local industry. The dogmatic Bolshevik assumption that proletarians alone could furnish this base impelled the Soviet government to direct its economic policy in predominantly peasant republics, such as Turkestan, toward the creation and expansion of a native industrial labor force.

In practical application, labor policy in Central Asia tended to follow a middle course. Local officials attempted to satisfy both Moscow's demands for increasing native participation in industry and their own inclination to give preference to European job-seekers. As a consequence, native workers remained a minority in important branches of the economy (except agriculture) throughout the period. But their numbers grew and avenues of employment previously reserved to Europeans began to be opened to them. Reports from the 1926 census indicate that native workers formed a slight over-all numerical majority, but in key branches such as factory-mill industry, construction, and railway transportation, the European labor force outnumbered the native contingent (see Table 7). In Turkmenia, for example, only 306 of the 2,861 workers employed in factory-mill industry and 836 of the 8,489 railway workers were Turcomans.[63] In Kirghizia, 139 of the 1,405 factory-mill workers and three of the 450 railway workers were Kirghiz.[64] Uzbekistan, whose territory included the center of Central Asian industries, offered better opportunities to native workers; of its 14,321 factory-mill workers and 11,582 railway workers, 4,246 and 994 respectively were Uzbek in origin.[65]

[63] Tsentral'noe Statisticheskoe Upravlenie, SSSR, Otdel Perepisi, *Vsesoiuznaia perepis' naseleniia 1926 goda* (Moscow, 1928–29), XXXIII, 10–19.
[64] *Ibid.*, XXXVI, 206–7.
[65] *Ibid.*, XXXII, 2–3.

Native workers likewise were concentrated at the very bottom of the industrial ladder. The majority were illiterate and unaccustomed to factory conditions, and few of the remainder possessed sufficient industrial skill to permit an improvement of their status. In a limited effort to overcome these impediments to native advancement, the Soviet regime established technical colleges and vocational schools in the larger cities and encouraged individual enterprises to organize factory-workshop schools and model workshops. By 1926 more than 13,500 students, about half of whom were members of the indigenous nationalities, were attending these schools.[66]

Lack of education and technical skill, however, were not the only barriers to native advancement. In spite of repeated warnings—some of them from high Party agencies—the practice of discrimination persisted. As late as 1927 the report of a special investigating committee of the Central Asiatic Bureau of the Communist Party indicated that skilled native workers in Uzbekistan were being denied deserved promotions and were debarred from workers' committees, while the native labor force as a whole was isolated socially from its European counterpart.[67]

Local government agencies, stimulated by the revelations of periodic Party investigations, tried fitfully to eliminate discrimination and to suppress abuses against the native labor force. Nevertheless, the inevitable recurrence of incidents reminded non-Europeans constantly that the revolutionary changes in government had not dispelled the atmosphere of colonialism and exploitation. This, in itself, was sufficient to nullify the efforts of the Communist Party to win the respect and confidence of the native laborers. Needless to say, the mistreatment of native workers also made industrial work unattractive to Moslems. In company with the limited opportunities in industry, due to the small size of industry and the pressure of European workers for available industrial employment, native aversion to industrial labor limited the effectiveness of the Bolshe-

[66] Central Statistical Board, USSR, *Ten Years of Soviet Power in Figures, 1917–1927* (Moscow, 1927), pp. 84–85.
[67] Text partially reproduced in Mustapha Chokaiev, *Turkestan pod vlast'iu Sovetov* (Paris, 1935), pp. 31–32.

viks' program for creating a native proletarian foundation under the superstructure of Soviet power.

Logically, Communist efforts to organize native workers into trade unions would appear to depend on the ability of the regime to find a place for natives in industry. But, paradoxically, in Central Asia the movement to organize native proletarians progressed at a much quicker pace than the actual growth of a native working class.

As late as 1920 the labor unions of the region were still concentrated in the "new" or European cities and concerned themselves almost exclusively with improving the working conditions and food supply of the Russian population. In that year the Central Council of Trade Unions, in the first of a series of steps calculated to increase native representation in the unions, sent agitators into the field to organize kustar' workers.[68] Upon completion of the initial phase of the organizational campaign, the local governments enacted regulations requiring all private and cooperative enterprises to conclude collective labor contracts. These ordinances bound the enterprises concerned not only to complete contracts which fixed wages at union-determined levels but also to vest in the labor unions and their agencies complete jurisdiction over the regulation of labor conditions.[69]

The enactment of these and other legal guarantees of union rights in combination with continuing efforts to recruit artisans and handicraftsmen brought a swift increase in union membership among the native population. By the spring of 1922, almost 35,000 natives belonged to trade unions in Turkestan. Unions in Bokhara boasted a native membership exceeding 11,000, all but 700 to 800 of whom were kustar's. Even in Khorezm, the most backward of the Central Asian republics, about 20 trade unions were active. In May, 1922, the Central Council of Trade Unions put an end to the honeymoon by ordering the removal of kustar's from the union movement, and over 23,000 native

---

[68] Safarov, *Kolonial'naia revoliutsiia: opyt Turkestana*, pp. 114–15.

[69] For example, see the decree of the Turkestan ASSR of December 31, 1921, "On the Regulation of Labor in Private Enterprises." *Sobranie uzakonenii i rasporiazhenii Turkestanskoi Respubliki*, January 31, 1922, No. 293.

members were stricken from the rolls in Turkestan alone.[70] Within two years, however, the labor movement in Central Asia had recovered from the blow and the strength of the native contingent had risen to 31,516 or about 28 percent of organized labor in the region.[71] During the following years the strength of the labor unions in Central Asia increased rapidly, and by 1927 total union membership had reached 238,039, of which about one third (78,906) consisted of natives. Native strength was nevertheless concentrated in the Union of Agricultural and Forestry Workers (33,478 natives) and remained weak in the skilled trades.[72]

Despite its obvious momentum, the campaign to expand the non-European division of the trade union movement was not without its shortcomings. For one thing, the unions overemphasized the importance of mere numbers. During one of the periodic drives for membership, the trade unionists of Fergana resigned en masse and were then reentered on the rolls as new members.[73] Moreover, it was common practice also to organize the owner of an enterprise as well as his labor force.[74] In addition, the unions often adopted policies which disregarded local economic realities, such as the attempt of the Union of Agricultural and Forestry Workers to apply the eight-hour day and similar industrial practices.

[70] Sredne-Aziatskoe Biuro V.Ts.S.P.S., *Professional'nye soiuzy v Srednei Azii 24–25 god; otchet Sr-Aziatskogo Biuro V.Ts.S.P.S. k Pervoi Sredne-Aziatskoi Konferentsii Profsoiuzov*, p. 45; Turkestanskoe Biuro, V.Ts.S.P.S., *Rabota profsoiuzov Turkestana v novykh usloviiakh: otchet Turkbiuro V.Ts.S.P.S. IV Kraevoi Turkestanskoi Konferentsii Professional'nykh Soiuzov za vremia: aprel' 1922 g.–dekabr' 1923 g.* (Tashkent, 1923), pp. 4, 13; also A. Vinogradova, "Khorezmskaia Sovetskaia Narodnaia Respublika," *Zhizn' Natsional'nostei*, No. 1 (January, 1923), p. 190.

[71] Sredne-Aziatskoe Biuro V.Ts.S.P.S., *Professional'nye soiuzy v Srednei Azii 24–25 god*, p. 16.

[72] European workers outnumbered natives 3,637 to 819 in metallurgical work; 8,428 to 5,767 in textile work; 11,388 to 939 in medical-health work; 10,687 to 5,619 in educational work; 30,783 to 2,403 in railroad work; and 26,810 to 9,868 in white-collar work. Chokaiev, *Turkestan pod vlast'iu Sovetov*, pp. 28–29.

[73] Turkestanskoe Biuro, V.Ts.S.P.S., *Rabota profsoiuzov Turkestana v novykh usloviiakh*, pp. 3–4.

[74] Sredne-Aziatskoe Biuro V.Ts.S.P.S., *Professional'nye soiuzy v Srednei Azii 24–25 god*, p. 4.

While the union blunders were sometimes absurd and often irritating to non-Europeans, the real failure of trade unionism in Central Asia stemmed from the disregard of its educational function. Once recruited, native trade unionists were commonly left to shift for themselves. At best, the unions tried halfheartedly to awaken class consciousness among native workers and to indoctrinate them with the spirit of trade unionism and Communism. More often they relegated native trade unionists to the fringe of union work, permitting them no more than formal representation on factory committees and higher union agencies and isolating them politically and socially from European workers.[75]

Pressure from high Party agencies, however, compelled the local trade unions to appoint native workers in increasing numbers to district and regional councils,[76] but this was often done merely for show. In the long run, neither administrative directives nor the exposure and punishment of European trade unionists on the ground of "colonialism" and "racial prejudice" were adequate weapons in the struggle to win equality for native workers. Until the great productive efforts of the Five-Year Plans brought natives in large numbers into industry and paved the way for "nationalizing" the unions from within, native workers continued to play a secondary role in the labor movement. While actual accomplishments fell far short of the Party's announced objectives, they served as the groundwork for the expansion of the regime's industrial and political base in later years.

ORGANIZING THE ARTISANS: THE EFFORT TO PROMOTE PRODUCER COOPERATION

Difficulties like those encountered in the campaign to revive and expand state-owned industry attended Soviet efforts to organize small goods production and to "guide" native artisans and handicraftsmen onto the "path to socialism." A deep-rooted Bolshevik suspicion that the kustar' worker was a potential menace to the Soviet regime inevitably colored the government

---

[75] Chokaiev, *Turkestan pod vlast'iu Sovetov*, pp. 31–32.
[76] See above, pp. 142–45.

and Party approach to the problem. The kustar', like the peasant—and indeed the kustar' was more often than not a peasant producer—did not fit precisely into the Marxian scheme of class organization and conflict. Small goods production, in terms of Marxist-Leninist theory, did not fall within the capitalistic pattern. Since the producer owned his own means of production, there was no basis for the development of class antagonism. At the same time, small goods production was based upon private ownership of the tools of production. Although it was not itself a form of capitalism, it was the direct antecedent of capitalism —a force which, in Lenin's words, "generates capitalism and the bourgeoisie continually, hourly, daily, elementally, and on a mass scale." [77]

To attempt to eliminate the small producer from the economy, even on the ground that he was potentially dangerous to the Soviet regime, was out of the question. In the more backward parts of the country, the kustar' had traditionally supplied many of the consumer articles necessary to the well being of the local population. After the collapse of Russia's consumer goods industry and the breakdown of communications, he had become the sole source of light manufactures and processed foods in many areas. Nationalization was equally impractical if only because the small size of the individual enterprises and their wide dispersal created insurmountable administrative problems. The only course which would permit the existence of kustar' industry while also subjecting it to continuous Bolshevik influence lay through Party and government sponsorship of producer cooperatives.

Even this solution was arrived at only after considerable hesitation within Party ranks. The Soviet government, of course, had recognized the existence of producer cooperatives from the time of the October Revolution; in 1919–20 it had enacted decrees to make them dependent upon the state. But until the summer of 1921, when the government exempted industrial cooperatives with all their supplies and equipment from municipalization, the Bolshevik position had not become clear.[78] In

[77] Quoted in Bulata, *Osnovy teorii Sovetskogo khoziaistva*, p. 53.
[78] For an examination of the early development of producer cooperation and

Central Asia, the question of producer cooperatives did not arise until the meeting of the Fifth Congress of the Communist Party of Turkestan in September, 1920. Significantly, it originated during a debate on methods of reviving economic activity within the non-European community and of introducing the native masses to new forms of social production. It is significant, too, that the congress advocated a program of support to kustar' producers through opening workshops, organizing artels, and encouraging other forms of cooperation.[79]

The Tenth All-Russian Party Congress, meeting in April of the following year, also considered the question of the cooperative movement in the borderlands. Safarov, introducing the question, singled out the cooperatives as agencies which would play a "decisive role . . . in the liberation of the kustar' semi-proletarian from the exploitation of usurious trade capital" and which were particularly suited to all-round defense of the "class interests" of the native masses. The cooperative movement, he pointed out, provided the Soviet system with an instrumentality that was much closer and more sympathetic to the needs and desires of non-European peoples than existing socialist institutions—institutions which, incidentally, he likened to bureaucratic chanceries. Through the cooperative movement the Soviet regime could gradually and painlessly introduce socialist forms of production into the native community. The process was simple; kustar's would be organized initially into artisan guilds working for the free market; then into artels working for the state; and finally into proletarian industrial workers.[80]

Although Safarov's statement summarizes in substance the Bolshevik interpretation of the role of the producer cooperative in the solution of the national question, early efforts to organize kustar's in Central Asia followed a different pattern. The trade unions, taking advantage of their right to organize kustar's employed by the state, took the initiative in recruiting native artisans and craftsmen and in many cases created special

its relationship to the Soviet government, see Elsie Terry Blanc, *Cooperative Movement in Russia* (New York, 1924), pp. 228–40.

[79] Safarov, *Kolonial'naia revoliutsiia: opyt Turkestana*, pp. 114–15, 137.

[80] *Desiatyi S'ezd R.K.P.(b)*, pp. 200–202.

kustar' divisions within the general union organization. While this policy brought natives into the labor movement in large numbers, it interfered seriously with the organization and development of the cooperatives. One major difficulty arose out of the tendency to merge the cooperatives into the trade unions and hence to destroy their identity and restrict the compass of their activities. Another grew out of the unions' discovery of "class differentiation" within kustar' ranks and their consequent attempt to separate kustar' "owners" from kustar' "workers." This policy helped to maintain "proletarian purity" within the trade unions but it also isolated an important section of the kustar' group from the cooperative movement.[81]

With the introduction of the New Economic Policy, the Soviet regime counted upon an expansion of the cooperative network in the borderlands as a counterbalance to private enterprise. The continuance of these barriers to the development of industrial cooperatives, therefore, became a source of frustration to the Bolsheviks. But the All-Union Council of Trade Unions solved the problem in May, 1922, by ordering the exclusion of kustar's from the labor movement. The order brought an end to the period of labor-union domination of producer cooperation in the national republics and regions.

Producer cooperatives, nevertheless, failed to gain ground in Central Asia prior to the national delimitation. Kustar' producers, who in most cases were hostile to the system of labor discipline which prevailed in the cooperatives, resisted organization,[82] and the government, despite its declared interest in the movement, failed to give support.[83] It is of interest in this connection that 877 cooperatives with 288,331 members (including 199 producer cooperatives with 3,357 members) were in existence in Turkestan in the fall of 1923.[84] But a representative to the Central Executive Committee from Turkestan, pleading for government subsidization, commented that the organiza-

[81] "Professional'noe dvizhenie v Vostoke," *Zhizn' Natsional'nostei*, No. 1 (6) (1923), p. 17.

[82] *Zhizn' Natsional'nostei*, No. 5 (11) (April 1, 1922), p. 7.

[83] See especially report of Paskutskii to All-Russian Central Executive Committee. *Tret'iaia Sessiia Vserossiiskogo Tsentral'nogo Ispolnitel'nogo Komiteta X Sozyva* (Moscow, 1924), pp. 110–11.

[84] *Izvestiia*, November 13, 1923.

tions had no funds and existed on paper only.[85] After the national delimitation, the position of producer cooperation improved somewhat. In 1925 and 1926, republic unions of producer cooperatives were formed in Uzbekistan and Turkmenia, and in 1927 the All-Union Permanent Conference of Producer Cooperatives was organized as an administrative organ for producer cooperatives throughout the USSR.[86] The Central Asiatic republics also undertook limited commitments to aid the movement financially and otherwise. The Turcoman government created a Temporary Bureau of Aid to Kustar' Industrial Cooperatives in 1926 to assist producer cooperatives both in organizing and in procuring raw materials and tools of production.[87] Local aid was nevertheless too small to stimulate an appreciable improvement in the financial position or the productive potential of the organizations. The Central Asian republics, lacking investment capital, were helpless, and the Moscow government, insisting that every region find its own financial salvation, refused to allot credits.

The inability of local officials to procure substantial subsidies from the central government placed kustar' cooperatives in Central Asia in a paradoxical situation at the end of the New Economic Policy. Organizationally, the movement was well established in the republics of the region, but, economically, producer cooperation was an inconsequential factor even on a purely local level. In 1927 kustar' cooperatives in Uzbekistan, where the movement had gathered most momentum, accounted for only 1.3 percent of the republic's gross industrial production. By comparison, private industry, which, harassed by government restrictions and confiscatory taxation, was making its last stand, contributed 1.9 percent.[88]

[85] See remarks of Khidyr-Aliev in *Tret'iaia Sessiia Vserossiiskogo Ispolnitel'nogo Komiteta X Sozyva*, pp. 102–3.

[86] The organization was renamed the All-Union Council of Republican Centers of Producer Cooperatives in 1928. Arakelian, *Industrial Management in the USSR*, pp. 112–13.

[87] Decree of Council of People's Commissars of Turcoman SSR of March 31, 1928, "On Temporary Bureau for Aid to Kustar'-Industrial Cooperatives." *Sobranie Postanovlenii i Rasporiazhenii Raboche-Dekhkanskogo Pravitel'stva Turkmenskoi SSR*, 1926, No. 9–10, pp. 26–27.

[88] Gleb N. Cherdantsev, *Sredne-Aziatskie respubliki* (Moscow, 1928), p. 130.

In a broad sense, the experience of cooperative building in Central Asia was indicative of the whole tenor of Soviet economic development during the twenties. It was a period of slow revival and organization rather than a period in which the major objectives of Bolshevik policy could be achieved. During the first decade the Soviet government accumulated experience in industrial management and in planning, and this knowledge found application in the preparation and implementation of the Five-Year Plans. Moreover, the government introduced non-Europeans in increasing numbers to the regimen of industrial life and welded them through the trade unions and cooperatives into a social and economic support of the Soviet system.

Nonetheless, state management and control had failed to achieve the goal of economic recovery and of industrialization in the Eastern borderlands. As late as 1927 industry in Central Asia was still struggling to recapture the 1913 levels of production. Living standards were still depressed and the leap to intensive investment which the Soviet government took in 1928 compressed them still further. New industries had not appeared in Central Asia despite the insistence of Stalin and other Party leaders on the creation of "focuses of industry" in the border regions. Existing industry was small and, except for cotton processing, of purely local significance. When the USSR entered the Five-Year Plan period, the Central Asian republics were still overwhelmingly rural and agricultural.

VII

THE REVIVAL OF
AGRICULTURE

◆

WHILE Russian Social Democrats had much to say about the agrarian problem in Russia, remarkably little of it related specifically to the border regions of the Empire. Lenin believed that simple extension to the various nationalities of the right of separation would automatically open the way to the development of class antagonisms in the non-Russian countryside and thus to direct introduction of the Social Democratic agrarian program. Other Bolshevik writers, assuming that agrarian conditions in the borderlands were essentially similar to those of Great Russia and the Ukraine, likewise neglected to consider peasant problems within the context of the nationality question, and overlooked the effects both of local customs and of the colonial policies practiced by the Empire.

In Central Asia the complex of Moslem precepts and customs, upon which the Tsarist colonial administration had superimposed its own agrarian order, confronted the Soviet regime with a nearly insoluble problem. One corner of the triangular legal base was Moslem canon law, which sanctioned formal absence of private property in land and recognized the principle of sovereign ownership by the ruler or state. However, the principle that cultivated or irrigated land belonged to whoever made the improvements was firmly established in shariat law. Customary law (Adat), the second legal foundation of agrarian relationships, and actual practice had introduced other important modifications into the principle of state ownership of land. In addition to land owned directly by the government, customary practice sanctioned two other forms of land tenure. One was *miulk,* a form of private property which grew out of land grants made by the state to individuals as rewards for service and merit. The other was endowment property (wakf) which individuals and sovereigns had entrusted to pious foundations. These practices had led to the formation of large estates, which often included large tracts of uncultivated land, and to the development of landlord-peasant relationships which approximated those of manorial dependency.[1]

After the conquest of Central Asia the Tsarist administration had availed itself of these usages to seize uncultivated lands in the nomadic regions, to destroy or reduce native property rights in settled areas, and to superimpose its own agrarian order on the remains of the Moslem system of land tenure. In order to establish a large land reserve available for Russian colonization, the government sequestered large tracts of cultivated and uncultivated land in what is now Kazakhstan. New norms of land tenure reduced native holdings and opened the region to Cossack and peasant settlement. The new norms permitted the native sedentary population land allotments of up to 27 acres per person, but they made no provision for the nomadic population beyond the right to retain land occupied by buildings and plowed fields. Russian peasant settlers, on the other hand, were guaranteed 27 acres per person and Cossacks were permitted allotments of between 110 and 135 acres.

Implementation of the new land settlement led to seizure of the best land by European immigrants in a series of land grabs which continued well into the revolutionary period. With the connivance of local officials, the immigrants gradually forced native peasants onto marginal farm lands and in some districts drove them off their former landholdings altogether. In addition, the Tsarist government opened new lands to colonization by altering the landholding system of private individuals and

---

[1] P. I. Liashchenko, *Istoriia narodnogo khoziaistva SSSR* (Moscow, 1948), II, 540; Eugene Schuyler, *Turkistan* (New York, 1877), I, 298–99.

pious foundations and by extending its agrarian order to new regions in Turkestan.[2]

The effects of these changes in customary norms of land tenure were at least as important for Central Asia as the dispossession of native landholders and the emergence of large Russian settlements in the wheat-growing regions of Turkestan. One consequence was a decline in size and number of large private estates and rural endowment properties, and, with it, a virtual disappearance of "feudal" privileges in the rural areas. Another was the firm establishment of the principle of private property in land—a principle resting upon Russian recognition of land occupied by buildings and plowland as "hereditary" and at the complete disposal of its owners. It has been estimated that by 1913 about 90 percent of all irrigated land in Turkestan had become the property of private owners. A Soviet economist declares that the Russians succeeded in transplanting "new bourgeois agrarian conditions" to the region.[3]

While this view is perhaps exaggerated, it is safe to say that on the basis of the new Russian agrarian system a new land owning class had developed within the native community. Establishment of the principle of private property in land not only produced a rapid increase of the salable land fund but occasioned a rise in land prices. Inevitably, land became concentrated in the hands of wealthy landlords, some of whom were village usurers and traders, while others were successful farmers or the remnants of the old landed gentry. Thus, the imposition of Russian law contributed substantially to a real agrarian revolution in Turkestan, to the emergence of the bey, Central Asia's counterpart of the Russian kulak.

Agrarian conditions might not have changed so speedily had not the Russian market demanded ever increasing quantities of Central Asian cotton. Cotton had been cultivated there from ancient times, having been introduced from India, and a brisk trade in cotton had developed between Russia and Central Asia during the first half of the nineteenth century. In the five-

---

[2] G. I. Broido, "Materialy k istorii vosstaniia Kirgiz v 1916 g.," *Novyi Vostok*, No. 6 (1924), pp. 411–12; also O. A. Vagonov, "Zemel'naia politika tsarskogo pravitel'stva v Kazakhstane," *Istoricheskie Zapiski*, No. 31 (1950), pp. 75–78.

[3] Liashchenko, *Istoriia narodnogo khoziaistva SSSR*, II, 541.

year period between 1850 and 1855 alone Russia imported 4,875 short tons from the area. The lack of transportation as well as the poor quality of Central Asian cotton restricted Russian interest until the curtailment of American imports during the American Civil War created a crisis in the Russian textile industry.[4] In the period from 1861 to 1864, the price of cotton quadrupled. Russian demands at this time encouraged a sharp increase in cotton cultivation in Turkestan and established it permanently as a major supplier of raw cotton for the Moscow textile industry.

After the Russian conquest of Central Asia, the government took steps to expand cotton cultivation by making credit available to producers, improving methods of agriculture, and introducing the superior American cotton plant. These efforts, in company with a consistently favorable price for cotton—three to four times more profitable than cereals—led to a rapid expansion of the area under cotton. By 1890, the 233,010 acres planted to cotton met all local demands and supplied 48,211 short tons of raw cotton for Russian mills. By 1915 the area under cotton had increased to 1,762,210 acres, of which 1,463,-130 acres were planted with American seed, and the crop totaled 612,940 tons.[5]

The expansion of cotton cultivation produced far-reaching changes in the economic and social structure of Central Asia. It destroyed older forms of natural economy in the cotton-growing regions and replaced them with a money economy. The reduction of the area sown to food crops made Central Asia dependent upon imports of grain from Russia, thus hastening the integration of the region into the Russian national economy. Within the society of Central Asia these economic changes also gave impetus to an agrarian revolution for which the legal foundations had been prepared by the establishment of the principle of individual private property in land. The impact of this social revolution, it should be noted, was felt only within

[4] P. G. Galuzo, *Turkestan-koloniia (ocherk Turkestana ot zavoevaniia russkimi do revoliutsii 1917 goda* (Moscow, 1929), p. 17.

[5] Liashchenko, *Istoriia narodnogo khoziaistva SSSR*, II, 546; N. I. Balashev, *Uzbekistan i sopredel'nye respubliki i oblasti: geograficheskii i ekonomicheskii ocherk* (Tashkent, 1925), pp. 28–29.

the native community since immigrant peasants seldom took up
cotton growing. Unfamiliar with the techniques and lacking the
manpower required in cotton cultivation, they preferred to continue wheat growing. At the beginning of the cotton boom,
numerous Russian adventurers, spurred on by the prospect of
quick profits, had attempted to organize large cotton plantations, but most of these projects failed. Cotton cultivation, on
the other hand, became the common occupation of the small
native peasant, and land speculation, agricultural credit, and
share cropping provided a basis for the rise of a new landowning
class.

The causes of the new concentration of land are easy to trace.
The small grower, who cultivated by primitive methods a plot
of between five and ten acres, usually operated on a marginal
basis. After a bad harvest, easy credit at usurious rates of interest often forced him to the wall. The small peasant fell prey to
traders who were willing to purchase his land directly or to
usurers who were eager to foreclose once he had fallen behind
on his interest payments. The consequence was a rapid shift of
land into the hands of new owners, who then leased the land
back to the peasant on a share cropping basis for one half or two
thirds of the harvest.[6] Share cropping was also prevalent on the
remnants of the old "feudal" estates. While indebtedness and
primitive methods kept the Central Asian peasant on the brink
of ruin, the high price of cotton opened the way for a steady
expansion of the landholdings of the strongest group. In Fergana, where the change was most extreme, by the time of the
revolution 51 percent of the households owned three acres or
less and held only 9.8 percent of the arable land. If households
owning between three and ten acres are added to this group,

---

[6] The term which natives employed to describe a share cropper was *chairikar*.
Literally translated, it means "one fourther"; that is, a peasant who receives one
fourth of the crop harvested on the land which he leased. The widespread local
use of the term has led to the erroneous assumption by several writers of popular accounts of rural conditions in Central Asia that the one-fourth share was
usual. In actual practice, share cropping took numerous forms. At one extreme,
the cropper supplied nothing more than his labor while the lessor supplied all
the necessary seed and equipment, often including a milch cow. At the other, the
lessor contracted merely to make the land available. The size of the cropper's
share varied according to the amount of his contribution to the harvest.

81.1 percent of the rural population possessed about one third of the land. By comparison, households owning 27 or more acres of land controlled 31.3 percent of the arable land fund.[7]

On the eve of the revolution rural life was still in a state of transition. In the regions of immigrant settlement and in those of intensive cotton cultivation, capitalistic modes of landholding and production were well developed. Within the pale of Russian settlement, farms of between 400 and 540 acres were fairly common, although in the cotton regions, with predominantly native ownership, they rarely exceeded 110 to 135 acres. Side by side with these "estates" were numerous tiny farms operated on a marginal scale by debt-ridden peasants. The ranks of the landless peasantry were increasing steadily as less successful farmers fell by the wayside in the economic struggle. Nevertheless, by the time of the revolution this group was neither large enough nor desperate enough to be a political factor. Because of large manpower demands occasioned by primitive methods of cultivation, the majority could find employment as farm hands or preserved some degree of independence by leasing land as share croppers.

The seeds of social conflict which existed in many parts of the Russian countryside were weak or absent in Central Asia. Unlike the Russian landlords who lived apart from the peasantry, the native landowner was a "small man," more often than not a former cotton grower or a commission agent. He was a peasant himself and his way of life, cultural level, and religious background were hardly distinguishable from those of his hired hands. Usually he lived on the land and maintained close contact with his tenants and farm hands. The tenants, with their share in the crop, and the farm hands, who were paid in kind, were also interested in the system.[8] Islam created spiritual and social bonds between owner and worker closer than those existing among the rural population of the Eastern Orthodox community. The native village contained no open sores which the Soviet regime could readily infect with the virus of class conflict.

---

[7] A. Gurevich, "Zemel'no-vodnaia reforma v Uzbekskoi SSR (1925–1929)," *Voprosy Istorii,* No. 11 (November, 1948), pp. 50–51.

[8] L. I. Dembo, *Zemel'nyi stroi Vostoka* (Leningrad, 1927), p. 102.

In those regions where a *point d'appui* for the development of a rural class struggle did exist, the lines of cleavage invariably ran between the newly settled Russian population and the native peasantry whom the Tsarist regime had driven off the land. Agrarian conflicts in these areas inevitably took on a national coloration.

AGRARIAN POLICY IN EVOLUTION:
BOLSHEVIK PLANS AND RUSSIAN REALITIES

During the early years of the Soviet regime Bolshevik reformers were totally unprepared to deal with rural conditions in Central Asia. Lenin had based his strategy of agrarian revolution and reorganization upon conditions prevalent in rural Great Russia, and none of his immediate collaborators had attempted to translate his basic plan into terms applicable to the villages of Central Asia. In its broadest terms, the pre-1917 Bolshevik analysis of the peasant question had rested upon Lenin's application to the Russian countryside of assumptions made earlier by Marx and Engels and later by Karl Kautsky, and particularly upon the belief in the inevitability of capitalist development in agriculture. From Lenin's standpoint, the idea of by-passing capitalism in the rural areas was an "idle and reactionary dream" of petit-bourgeois democratic parties; the question was not whether capitalism would develop in the village, but what kind of capitalism.

Lenin himself saw two possible lines of development for Russian agriculture. If it followed the "Prussian" model, Russian agriculture would witness a gradual evolution of feudal landlordism into large-scale capitalist farming, with the emergence of a small class of well-to-do peasants and the expropriation and degradation of the peasant masses. The second possibility, which Lenin described as the "American" path of development, likewise required the extirpation of feudal remnants but its chief characteristic was the transformation of the patriarchal peasantry into a class of small independent farmers.[9]

The second path was, in Lenin's view, much the more desirable. It would benefit the peasants more and would hasten

[9] V. I. Lenin, *Selected Works* (New York, n.d.), III, 180–81.

the development of productive forces, ultimately opening a broader path to socialism.[10] Under Russian conditions, he argued, only a revolutionary elimination of the landlords by the peasants and a subsequent nationalization of the land could permit this line of development. Bolshevik writers have since described "nationalization" as the starting point for the transition to socialist agriculture,[11] but Lenin insisted that it was a purely "bourgeois" measure for the elimination of precapitalist rural institutions. Lenin regarded the abolition of private property in land as the most radical solution to the agrarian problem possible in bourgeois society. It would, he believed, clear away all obstacles to the investment of capital in land and hasten the development of capitalism in agriculture.[12] At the same time, it would eliminate one important category of private property in the means of production and facilitate the rise of the class struggle.

Beyond this point the position of the Bolshevik Party was highly equivocal. It wavered between a desire to establish large-scale socialist farms on the confiscated estates and to permit division of the estates among the peasantry as a price for peasant support. When the Bolsheviks approached the peasant question from the standpoint of the long-range achievement of socialism, the inclination to convert large estates into cooperative or model farms predominated. At the least, they assumed this solution would hasten the mechanization of agriculture and lead to steady increases in crop yields at a constantly diminishing cost in labor. Also, it would provide a major step toward "industrializing" agriculture and eventually toward eliminating what Marx had called the "idiocy of rural life."

While lesser Bolsheviks might dwell upon the happy prom-

---

[10] *Ibid.*, III, 184–85.

[11] See especially P. Kolomoitsev, *Krest'ianstvo i revoliutsiia* (Moscow, 1926), p. 52.

[12] Marx's theory of land rent formed the basis for the assumption that the abolition of private property would increase the amount of capital available for investment in land. Marx took the view that the purchase of land was not an investment of capital in land but the opposite: a decrease in the amount of capital available for such investment. For a sympathetic explanation of the theory, see Anna Rochester, *Lenin on the Agrarian Question* (New York, 1942), pp. 69–71.

ises of the future, Lenin never permitted himself a similar luxury for long. Being well aware of the peasants' desire to divide up the large holdings of the Imperial family, the church, and the landlords, he was cautious in expressing open support of large-scale socialist farms. In public, he criticized the expansion of small-scale peasant farming as less efficient and a hindrance to the mechanization of agriculture. Privately, he probably feared that the rise of a class of small owners would block the path to socialism. Nevertheless, Lenin was willing to consent to a "black redistribution" of the land if that was the price of getting peasant support for his revolution. This second position was made especially clear in the 1903 Party program, which advocated the transfer of confiscated lands to "democratic local government bodies" but approved division of the land among the peasants if circumstances made this second course imperative.[13] Calls for peasant initiative in seizing and dividing the land, which the Bolsheviks issued throughout 1917, showed that the Party was still willing to go along with the second solution. Even these appeals placed emphasis on the necessity for organized confiscation and preservation of the estates as a basis for large-scale agriculture.[14]

The peasant in revolution gave scant heed to Bolshevik plans for conservation of the estates and still less to the theoretical rationalizations behind the advocacy of model farms. In the squire whose large estate contrasted so vividly with his own small and scattered holding or from whom he was compelled to rent land, the peasant saw the cause of his own impoverishment. In seizure and division of the estates, he saw his salvation. He acted accordingly. Beginning with scattered and minor encroachments upon landlord rights in the spring of 1917, peasant fury mounted throughout the summer and autumn into a mighty orgy of land seizure, arson, and murder.[15] While the right-wing parties rep-

[13] Lenin, *Selected Works*, VI, 123.

[14] See especially, the resolution of the April (1917) Conference of the All-Russian Communist Party (b) on the agrarian question in *Agrarnaia politika v resheniiakh s'ezdov i konferentsii R.K.P.(b) s 1917 po 1925 god* (Moscow, 1926), pp. 12–13.

[15] For a description and analysis, see William Henry Chamberlin, *The Russian Revolution, 1917–1927* (New York, 1935), I, 242–58.

resented in the Provisional Government condemned and threatened and even the Social Revolutionaries counseled patience until the meeting of the Constituent Assembly, the Bolsheviks put aside Lenin's formulae for solving the land question and came out squarely in support of peasant seizures.

The first agrarian enactment of the Soviet government, the Decree on Land of November 8, 1917,[16] was little more than a legalization of actual changes which had occurred or were occurring in the rural areas. It was based, not on the agrarian program of the Bolshevik Party, but on a model resolution—a declaration based on 242 resolutions of peasant gatherings—of the First Congress of Soviets of Peasant Deputies. By the terms of the decree, private property in land was abolished forever and the estates together with their appurtenances were transferred to the use of those who worked them. All that remained of Lenin's plan for the creation of model farms was a provision transforming gardens, plantations, model fields, orange groves, stud farms, and similar properties into "model holdings."

As the Soviet government's chances of survival improved during the following months and years, Lenin's pre-1917 ideas began to find their way into agrarian legislation. A "Fundamental Law on the Socialization of the Land," promulgated on February 19, 1918, ordered Soviet agrarian agencies to encourage the organization of collective farms.[17] In November, 1918, the Council of People's Commissars allocated special funds to finance this program. A further decree of February 14, 1919, which anticipated the establishment of state farms and collectives on formerly intensively farmed estates and on state land, indicated that individual farming was a transitional form of production which would disappear when collective productive units were established.[18] Portents of the agrarian system which the Bolsheviks would one day impose on the entire peasant population of the USSR were thus accumulating even as civil war raged through the land.

[16] *Izvestiia*, November 8, 1917. For an English translation of the text of the Decree on Land, see Chamberlin, *The Russian Revolution, 1917–1927*, I, 474–77.
[17] N. D. Kazantsev (ed.), *Zemel'noe pravo* (Moscow, 1949), pp. 56–57.
[18] *Ibid.*, pp. 64–66.

The violent changes which took place in the rural regions of Great Russia during the revolution had no genuine counterpart in Central Asia. Following Moscow's lead, the Tashkent Soviet confiscated a number of orchards and gardens during the early months of 1918, and the Sixth Regional Congress of Soviets nationalized all land in Turkestan.[19] But no elemental movement developed to equalize land holdings by seizure and redistribution. In predominantly Moslem districts the revolution gave rise to no important changes in agrarian relationships and in regions of immigrant settlement it merely accentuated the pre-revolutionary trend toward encroachment upon native rights. The Tashkent government not only levied unbearable taxes upon the native peasantry and dispatched armed detachments from the towns to confiscate the harvest, but it opened the way to further arbitrary depredations by permitting Red Army contingents to live off the land. To add to the suffering of the Moslem villages, the government acquiesced in the seizure of native farms by mobs of European immigrant settlers.[20] Charging that the entire policy of the Turkestan government had been designed to hinder agricultural development, the Bolshevik Rudzutak reported in 1920 that European colonists had destroyed whole kishlaks and had usurped their lands.[21]

There is little doubt that the policies of the Turkestan government hastened the collapse of agriculture in Central Asia. In addition to the destruction of crops by actual fighting, the native peasantry had to endure repeated requisitions and other seizures of goods by Red Army detachments, and even the visitations of passing gangs of marauders. Many abandoned their fields altogether and fled to safer regions; others reduced their planted area to a minimum essential to their own subsistence. During the two years between 1917 and 1919, the cultivated area in Turkestan declined from 8,878,494 to 3,186,186 acres.[22]

The revolution and civil war inflicted still more lasting

[19] Ilias Alkin, *Sredniaia Aziia: ekonomiko-geograficheskii ocherk Kara-Kalpakstana, Kirgizstana, Tadzhikistana, Turkmenistana i Uzbekistana* (Moscow, 1931), I, 349.

[20] See above, pp. 38–39.

[21] Georgii Safarov, *Kolonial'naia revoliutsiia: opyt Turkestana* (Moscow, 1921), p. 106.

[22] I. G. Aleksandrov, "Narodnoe khoziaistvo Turkestana i ego vosstanovlenie," *Khlopkovoe Delo*, Nos. 1–2 (January–February, 1922), p. 24.

wounds. The great irrigation systems, which furnished the life-blood of agriculture in most of Turkestan, fell into disrepair or were destroyed. In the seven years between 1915 and 1922, irrigated land in Central Asia declined from 9,248,900 acres to 5,386,800 acres, and in Turkestan proper from 6,523,400 to 3,-212,300 acres.[23] Livestock also declined precipitously, dropping from 18,819,402 head in 1917 to 6,555,940 head in 1923.[24] In terms of numbers, most of the decrease was attributable to the destruction of nomadic herds or their removal into the desert or to Afghanistan and Sinkiang, but widespread destruction of draft animals—their numbers declined to 30 percent of prewar levels in some areas[25]—had more lasting effects upon agriculture and prevented a speedy revival after the fighting had ceased.

The civil strife and the shortsighted policies of the Tashkent government also led to a return to a natural economy. Prior to 1914 the trend had been toward regional specialization, and Central Asia had come to depend upon European Russia for its supply of grain. Even before the October Revolution, the gradual breakdown of transportation had impeded the exchange of grains for cotton, and this traffic was halted abruptly by the spread of civil war to Central Asia. This factor alone would have compelled a return to the cultivation of food crops, but the Tashkent Soviet compounded the mischief by confiscating all stocks of cotton it could lay hands on. As a consequence, the cultivation of cotton declined precipitously, while the acreage under food crops also decreased, though at a much slower pace. Between 1917 and 1919 the total planted area decreased by 64.1 percent while the sowing of food crops declined by 51.5 percent.[26]

[23] This represented a continuation and intensification of a decline in irrigation which dated from the beginning of the Great War. Statistics, compiled in 1910, showed 12,846,600 acres of irrigated land in Central Asia. Of this total, 7,581,600 acres were located in Turkestan and 4,326,000 in Bokhara. S. P. Trombachev, "Sredne-Aziatskoe vodnoe khoziaistvo," *Vestnik Irrigatsii*, V, No. 10 (October, 1927), 3–4; also Liashchenko, *Istoriia narodnogo khoziaistva SSSR*, II, 543.

[24] I. P. Trainin, *SSSR i natsional'naia problema: po natsional'nym respublikam i oblastiam Sovetskogo Soiuza* (Moscow, 1924), p. 90.

[25] K. Zubrek, "Zemledelie i irrigatsiia Khorezma v sviazi s voprosom ekonomicheskogo ob'edineniia Sredne-Aziatskikh respublik," *Novyi Vostok*, No. 3 (1923), p. 209.

[26] Aleksandrov, "Narodnoe khoziaistvo Turkestana i ego vosstanovlenie," *Khlopkovoe Delo*, Nos. 1–2 (January–February, 1922), p. 24.

By 1923 cotton planting had fallen to the level of the 1880's. While 1,463,130 acres—1,068,930 of them in Russian Turkestan —were under cotton in Central Asia in 1915, in 1922 only 138,- 855 acres of cotton were planted in Turkestan and 32,400 acres in Bokhara and Khorezm. A general reversion to the use of native seed caused a still further decline in the yield. Cotton farmers had harvested some 612,940 short tons of raw cotton in 1915, but in 1922 the crop amounted to scarcely more than 18,- 000 tons.[27]

In compounding human suffering and losses in agrarian man-power, the breakdown of the main branches of agriculture in Central Asia was even more catastrophic than any statistics can suggest. Even before the Bolshevik Revolution, the deterioration of the supply system, together with the requirements of Russia's armies, had reduced the food supplies of the region to a dangerously low level. Famine followed hard on the heels of the Soviet seizure of power. By the winter of 1919, according to Ryskulov, a Kirghiz Bolshevik, one half of the population of Turkestan was starving,[28] and entire villages had disappeared, their populations dead or scattered in flight.[29]

While the Dutov blockade, which cut off Turkestan from Central Russia, and the shortsighted policies of the Tashkent Soviet had been decisive causes of the famine, the reopening in 1919 of communications with European Russia and the re-assertion of Moscow's control over the local government brought no relief. Within Turkestan the Bolsheviks faced not only the immense problem of repairing the damage left by two years of revolution and civil war, but also the immediate task of restoring order and consolidating Soviet rule. Russia had nothing to spare for relief in this remote region; famine stalked the streets of Moscow, and Russia's total agricultural production had declined to 40 percent of the prewar level.

[27] From data appearing in Liashchenko, *Istoriia narodnogo khoziaistva SSSR*, II, 546; S. L. Zashchuk, "Khlebnaia problema v khlopkovodcheskikh raionakh Srednei Azii," *Khlopkovoe Delo*, Nos. 3–5 (March–May, 1926), p. 387; V. V. Zaorskaia-Aleksandrova, "Tezisy doklada po promyshlennosti Turkestana," *Khlopkovoe Delo*, Nos. 1–2 (January–February, 1922), pp. 44–45.

[28] From an article in *Nasha Gazeta*, No. 22 (1919), quoted in Turar R. Ryskulov, *Revoliutsiia i korennoe naselenie Turkestana* (Tashkent, 1925), p. 212.

[29] *Ibid.*, p. 78.

Famine swept through Central Asia again in 1920, in 1921, and in 1922. It struck again in 1923. Epidemics of typhus and malaria raged through Fergana, wiping out entire villages and driving the survivors to flight. Soviet investigators reported in the winter of 1923 that 400,000 people, nearly half the population of the region, were starving and that the number of famine victims was increasing.[30] Pleas for relief brought little response. In the winter of 1923 the Regional Commission to Combat Famine distributed 13,633 short tons of wheat, 3,250 tons of rice, and 2,000,000 rubles (1923 value). Prior to this, Turkstan had received no help. Even the spontaneous shift from cotton to food crops did nothing to relieve the crisis. Regardless of its own urgent needs, Central Asia was compelled to supply the central provinces of the RSFSR with grain during the famine years.[31] And the government of the Turkestan republic undertook to receive and feed 100,000 European refugees from the famine-stricken Volga regions.[32]

Under these conditions, the adoption of measures to socialize agriculture would have been futile, if not disastrous. The immediate problem was how to satisfy the most elementary needs of the impoverished and famine-pinched peasantry and to promote a revival of agricultural production. Throughout Russia, this meant restoring peaceful conditions in the countryside, and a retreat by the Bolsheviks from War Communism. In Central Asia it also meant that the Soviet regime would have to adapt its agrarian policies to the special production and social conditions which prevailed there.

In the Moslem republics the end of open warfare and the abandonment of War Communism laid the foundation for agricultural reconstruction. However, the retreat from the policy of fomenting active class conflict in the rural areas had little effect in Central Asia for the simple reason that Bolshevism had made

---

[30] A. Uralets, "Golod v Fergane," *Izvestiia*, March 20, 1923. This investigator also reported that the rural population of one district declined from 75,000 to 3,000 in the course of the famine.

[31] Alkin, *Sredniaia Aziia*, I, 352.

[32] From a report of Khidyr-Aliev at the Third Session of the Tenth Convocation of the All-Russian Central Executive Committee. See *Tret'iaia Sessiia Vserossiiskogo Tsentral'nogo Ispolnitel'nogo Komiteta X Sozyva* (Moscow, 1924), p. 101.

no inroads into the solidarity of the native community. Abandonment of forced requisitions of agricultural surpluses and adoption of the fixed tax in kind—the central feature of the New Economic Policy—paved the way for a revival of individual peasant initiative in Central Asia as elsewhere.

The further problem of shaping the new agrarian policy to conform to the peculiarities of agriculture in Central Asia was a more difficult one for the Bolsheviks. Prior to its Tenth Congress, the Communist Party appears to have made no effort to fit its agrarian program to the needs of the non-Russian peoples. Neither the Party nor the Soviet government made any attempt to interpret the Leninist program of land nationalization, division of the estates, and support of agricultural cooperation in terms of local conditions or to adapt the program of class struggle to the realities of rural life in these regions. Nor had the Bolsheviks foreseen that European colonists would use the revolution and the Soviet banner to usurp the land of native peasants and to exploit them more ruthlessly than before.

After the authority of the central government had been established in Central Asia, the new regional government adopted several measures, among them the Semirechie land reform,[33] to put an end to the worst forms of exploitation. But, aside from this act of redress, it moved but slowly to adapt Bolshevik agrarian policy to the special conditions and needs of rural Central Asia. The resolutions of the Tenth Party Congress which dealt with the future of agriculture in the non-Russian regions were couched in broad and general terms. The congress merely indicated its support of programs for organizing native toilers into cooperatives and hastening the transition of native agriculture to a "higher stage of development." The path to the second objective, it declared, lay through settling the nomadic population on the land and replacing small individual farming with planned collective plowing and harvesting.[34] These resolutions pointed to an eventual emergence of socialized forms of agriculture, but they offered no solution for immediate problems.

[33] See below, pp. 322–26.
[34] Text of the resolution in *Vse-Soiuznaia Kommunisticheskaia Partiia v rezoliutsiiakh i resheniiakh s'ezdov, soveshchaniei i plenumov Tsentral'nogo Komiteta (1898–1932)* (4th ed., Moscow, 1932), I, 457–58.

The Soviet government's effort to centralize control over agricultural policy in Moscow dates from the decree of August 4, 1921, which created a Federal Committee for Agrarian Affairs within the People's Commissariat of Agriculture of the RSFSR and authorized it to regulate agrarian matters which affected the general interests of the Russian republic. In 1922 the Soviet government broadened the competence of the Committee and placed it directly under the supervision of the All-Russian Central Executive Committee. Regulations, adopted on May 11, 1922, vested in the Federal Committee responsibility for adapting national agricultural plans to local agrarian conditions and supervising local execution of these plans, for elaborating and examining draft laws concerning agriculture, and for providing the various regions with material and technical assistance. They also provided for extending its activities to independent and friendly soviet republics.[35]

Although the Federal Committee for Agrarian Affairs was replaced by the Commissariat of Agriculture after the formation of the USSR in 1923, the impress of its activities remained on the agriculture of the border republics throughout the New Economic Policy. Its major accomplishment was to adapt the agrarian code of the RSFSR to the peculiarities of agriculture in the national republics and regions[36] and to encourage the revival of regional specialization in agriculture. It was also the agent of the Bolshevik Party in developing proto-socialist types of agricultural production among "backward" peoples.[37]

In Central Asia the Federal Committee for Agrarian Affairs was the first agency of the central government which participated regularly with local soviet bodies in seeking to restore irrigation systems, to render material, financial, and technical assistance to the native peasantry, and to revive cotton production. It established firmly the principles of federal support, supervision, and control of agriculture in the national republics and regions.

[35] E. B. Genkina, *Obrazovanie SSSR* (Moscow, 1947), pp. 83–84.

[36] The agrarian code went into effect in Turkestan on December 1, 1922, after it had been amended to fit local agrarian practices and expanded to cover the nomadic population. See Dembo, *Zemel'nyi stroi Vostoka*, p. 62.

[37] Anadoly-ogly, "Natsional'naia politika v zemel'nom voprose i sel'skom khoziaistve (Fedkomzem i ego zadachi)," *Zhizn' Natsional'nostei*, No. 2 (1923), pp. 7–12.

THE PATH OF AGRARIAN RECONSTRUCTION

A real effort to halt the downward course of agricultural production and to create favorable conditions for agricultural revival began in Central Asia only in 1921, and was centered around the restoration of destroyed and damaged irrigation works and the construction of new ones. Local concern over the rapid disintegration of irrigation had been apparent as early as 1920. A year later general interest was aroused by the publication of an ambitious five-year project designed by Georgii Rizenkampf, an engineer, calling for the irrigation of 2,411,370 acres of new land in Turkestan.[38] However, as famine raged throughout Central Asia, the irrigated area continued to contract until by 1922 it had decreased to one half the 1918 acreage. The desperate plight of agriculture and the steady encroachment of the desert upon arable land compelled the Soviet government to lay aside schemes for new projects and to concentrate on rebuilding and repairing existing irrigation systems.

These tasks were entrusted originally to the Water Department of Turkestan, and planning was confined to that republic. After the creation of the Central Asiatic Economic Council in 1923, responsibility for the development of irrigation works and the regulation of water use was transferred to the Central Asiatic Water Department, and the authority of the agency was extended to Bokhara and Khorezm. Initially, the Water Department concentrated on restoring systems serving the native community and upon introducing improved methods.[39] This was one purpose of a five-year plan of development adopted by the Central Asiatic Water Department in 1923. After the initial phase of reconstruction had been completed, the plan of irrigation envisaged three further tasks: irrigation of new lands for cotton growing, maintenance of existing works, and the irrigation of districts in Central Asia and surrounding areas for cereal

[38] Rizenkampf's plan also included estimates of cost, materials, and labor for the irrigation of 4,321,000 additional acres of land through projects of "secondary importance." See Georgii K. Rizenkampf, *Problemy orosheniia Turkestana* (Moscow, 1921), pp. 134–35.

[39] N. B. Arkhipov, *SSSR po raionam: Sredne-Aziatskie respubliki* (2d ed., Moscow, 1928), p. 47.

crops. Until the job of bringing water to existing and potential cotton-growing regions was well advanced, other irrigation projects would have to remain in abeyance.[40]

The five-year plan of 1923, in addition to giving a priority to cotton growing, gave special protection to the water rights of individual peasants and of agricultural communities. In their early forms, these statutes sought merely to regularize existing procedures for water allocation and to do away with common abuses. Tradition and the Soviet concept of water rights coincided in forbidding the purchase or sale of water and in requiring an equitable distribution of the existing supply. But bribery and favoritism were not unknown to the Moslem village; corrupt elders traded in water and otherwise used their control over its allocation as a means of self-aggrandizement. The first Soviet legislation, the water statutes enacted by the Turkestan government in February, 1921, and in August, 1922, sought to create a legal basis for curbing such practices by transforming water into state property. The statutes also defined individual rights to irrigational water as limited to the right of use and forbade the separation of water use from the use of the land which it irrigated.[41]

The foundations of the water codes which regulated the use of water in Central Asia during the latter phase of the New Economic Policy were laid in May, 1924, when the Turkestan Central Executive Committee adopted "Temporary Regulations for the Waters of the Turkestan Republic." In part the "Temporary Regulations" confirmed and defined previous water ordinances. They reaffirmed the principles of public ownership and control of water supplies, of preferential treatment for current users, and of the attachment of water to the land it irrigated.[42] The most important feature of this legislation was its establishment of the class principle as a factor in determining the rights of individuals to water use. While continuing to permit users, singly or in groups, to determine water use according

[40] I. Khodorov, "Piatiletnii khoziaistvennyi plan Srednei Azii," *Planovoe Khoziaistvo*, No. 10 (October, 1926), p. 182.

[41] Dembo, *Zemel'nyi stroi Vostoka*, p. 93.

[42] In special circumstances, however, the law permitted maintenance of the right to water separate from the land for a one-year period.

to customs which were not in contradiction with the law, it also restricted water to the "laboring use" of the population.[43] Lack of energetic enforcement stayed the impact of this provision of the law upon the Moslem community during the remainder of the lifetime of the Turkestan republic. But after the national delimitation, the governments of Uzbekistan and Turkmenia utilized the principle of "labor use" to annul or restrict drastically water rights appertaining to *miulk*, wakf, and other "non-toiling" forms of land tenure.[44]

In its initial phases the program of reconstruction centered about efforts to halt deterioration and to restore damaged irrigation facilities to operation. Stop-gap measures undertaken in Turkestan in 1922–23 restored irrigation systems servicing 963,-690 acres of land and during the following year brought water to an additional 271,810 acres. The work of these two years was completed at a cost of 11,000,000 rubles or somewhat less than ten rubles for each acre of reclaimed land. The success of these early efforts, in combination with the lingering influence of Rizenkampf's project for new irrigation, gave impetus to long-range planning. In 1923 the Central Asiatic Water Department adopted a 92,000,000-ruble[45] five-year irrigation program designed to increase the irrigated area of Turkestan to 9,150,000 acres (120 percent of the prewar area) and to restore the prewar acreage in Bokhara and Khorezm. In terms of data on irrigation compiled in 1910—and the Water Department apparently used these as the basis of its own planning—the irrigated area of Central Asia was expected to reach 14,445,000 acres by 1927–28.[46]

The goals of the five-year project were fairly modest; some

[43] Arkhipov, *SSSR po raionam: Sredne-Aziatskie respubliki*, p. 41.

[44] Joseph Castagné, "La Réforme agraire au Turkestan," *Revue des Études Islamiques*, No. 11 (1928), pp. 396–97; also I. S. Kraskin (ed.), *Zemel'no-vodnaia reforma v Srednei Azii: sbornik materialov* (Moscow, 1927), pp. 136–37.

[45] The figure of 92,000,000 rubles did not represent actual expenditures. In this total, the Water Department included the sum of 45,000,000 rubles for labor in the form of "natural service": that is, labor which peasants were required to donate in return for the privilege of using water. See report of Paskutskii to the All-Russian Central Executive Committee in *Tret'iaia Sessiia Vserossiiskogo Tsentral'nogo Ispolnitel'nogo Komiteta X Sozyva*, pp. 108–9.

[46] Prof. B. Shlegel', "Irrigatsiia," in *Vsia Sredniaia Aziia: spravochnaia kniga na 1926 khoziaistvennyi god* (Tashkent, 1926), pp. 112–13. For 1910 levels of irrigation, see Liashchenko, *Istoriia narodnogo khoziaistva SSSR*, II, 542–43.

investigators thought that more could be done, and in 1925 one expert reported that 21,294,900 acres could be brought under irrigation in Central Asia.[47] In practice, costs exceeded the planned figures and fulfillment lagged behind, forcing drastic downward revisions of the goals. By 1927 the Water Department had reduced its goal to 7,878,867 acres of land to be irrigated by the end of the period, 1928. By shifting the comparative base date to 1915—a year in which the irrigated area in Central Asia had slumped to 9,249,694 acres—it was able to report the new goal as representing a level of 85 percent reconstruction of irrigation.[48] Actual fulfillment reached 7,739,772 acres, more than 135,000 acres short of the reduced goal.[49]

The program included both the restoration of old irrigation systems and the construction of new ones. To increase arable acreage in the cotton-growing districts, the Water Department concentrated its energies there, while postponing reconstruction in other regions. Uzbekistan, the center of the Central Asiatic cotton belt, was the main beneficiary of the policy.[50] Between 1925 and 1927, over 135,000 newly irrigated acres, principally in Fergana, were opened to settlement and more than 9,000 peasant households installed on them.[51] Despite these gains, the program failed to meet planned goals in cotton production. Lack of funds, according to an Uzbek reporter at the Fourth All-Union Congress of Soviets, had prevented local governments

---

[47] Shlegel', "Irrigatsiia," in *Vsia Sredniaia Aziia,* pp. 112–13.

[48] Upravlenie Vodnogo Khoziaistva Srednei Azii, *Sostoianie i perspektivy irrigatsii v Srednei Azii* (Tashkent, 1928), p. 9.

[49] Gleb N. Cherdantsev, *Sredne-Aziatskie Respubliki* (Moscow, 1928), p. 76.

[50] The distribution of irrigated land as indicated in *ibid.,* p. 76, was as follows:

Republic	Irrigated Land (in acres)	Percentage of Total Irrigation	Percentage of Total Irrigation without Kazakhstan and Kara-Kalpakstan
Uzbek SSR	4,025,447	51.9	63.8
Tajik SSR	494,632	6.4	8.0
Turcoman SSR	802,615	10.4	12.8
Kirghiz ASSR	964,357	12.5	15.4
Kazakhstan and Kara-Kalpakstan	1,452,721	18.8	
Total	7,739,772	100.0	100.0

[51] Kraskin, *Zemel'no-vodnaia reforma v Srednei Azii,* p. 62; also *Vtoroi Vseuzbekskii S'ezd Sovetov,* pp. 270–71.

from making a real effort to enlarge irrigation.[52] The Central Asiatic republics were unable to bear the burden alone and, except for the allocation of 6,000,000 rubles in 1923, the central government had given little more than a token assistance.

The state of near bankruptcy in which the Soviet government operated during the twenties restricted its ability to undertake large-scale irrigation projects. It likewise inhibited the parallel effort to give direct assistance to peasant producers. Plans for agricultural reconstruction advanced by the Bolsheviks during the latter phase of War Communism and the early days of the New Economic Policy had emphasized the necessity for governmental distribution of seed and agricultural equipment to the most needy peasants. Very little of this direct aid reached the peasantry in Central Asia. Between 1920 and 1922, the Soviet government used famine relief funds to distribute some seed and equipment in Fergana and in other hotbeds of Basmachism.[53] After guerrilla resistance had died down the practice was discontinued.

Although the Party program for agricultural reconstruction continued to mention the distribution of seed to the poorest peasants as one aim, this was hardly more than a temporary expedient. In accordance with the underlying philosophy of the New Economic Policy, the program, in practice, emphasized the principle of government aid to those peasants who were willing to help themselves. The Soviet government was also determined to use state aid as a weapon to break the economic hold of the well-to-do peasants, usurers, and urban traders upon the poor and middle peasants, not through outright gifts, but through tax privileges, cheap agricultural credit, priority in the purchase of farming implements, and encouragement of peasant cooperatives.[54]

Through these and similar measures the Bolsheviks expected to restrict the growth of kulak farming and to assist the poorer

[52] *Chetvertyi S'ezd Sovetov* (Moscow, 1927), pp. 202–4.

[53] P. Baranov, "Polozhenie Turkestanskoi respubliki i reorganizatsiia krasnoi armii," *Voennaia Mysl'*, No. 2 (May–July, 1921), pp. 88–89.

[54] From resolutions on the peasant question adopted at the Thirteenth Conference of the All-Russian Communist Party (b). Texts in *Agrarnaia politika v resheniiakh s'ezdov i konferentsii R.K.P.(b) s 1917 po 1925 god*, pp. 49, 61.

peasants. However, the compulsion to promote a rapid recovery of agriculture even at the cost of delaying achievement of their class goals in the village curbed the Bolshevik desire to weaken and eventually to eliminate the strongest peasants. The agricultural tax, for example, was not made progressive in its impact until 1926–27. Prior to the land reform in Central Asia, agricultural credit, based on short-term transactions, was in fact more readily available to the strong than to the weak peasant.[55] In a report to the First Uzbek Congress of Soviets one critic even charged the Agricultural Bank with profiteering at the expense of the poor peasants.[56]

Progress in developing agricultural cooperatives among small and middle peasants was hardly more satisfactory. Widespread illiteracy, the absence of cadres of native cooperative workers and of native experience with cooperatives prior to the revolution, and the opposition of influential members of the Moslem community were important obstacles to their growth. Yet Soviet statistics consistently showed an expansion of agricultural cooperatives. One publicist claimed in 1923 that more than 500 primary agricultural cooperatives and 12 district associations had been organized in Turkestan.[57] Later investigation showed that the movement was strongly developed only in the European settlements and that many cooperatives existed only on paper.[58] Even at the end of the New Economic Policy, complaints were common not only that agricultural cooperatives were almost nonexistent on the local level but also that landlords, supposedly "liquidated" in the land reform, controlled many of the existing ones.[59]

During the 1920's similar consequences attended Soviet efforts

[55] E. M., "Khoziaistvennyi obzor po Turkestanu," *Vlast' Sovetov*, No. 6 (September, 1924), p. 215.
[56] *Pervyi Vseuzbekskii S'ezd Sovetov Rabochikh, Dekhkanskikh i Krasnoarmeiskikh Deputatov Uzbekskoi Sovetskoi Sotsialisticheskoi Respubliki, fevral' 1925 goda* (Tashkent, 1925), p. 52.
[57] E. M., "Khoziaistvennyi obzor po Turkestanu," *Vlast' Sovetov*, No. 6 (September, 1924), pp. 216–17.
[58] V. Lavrent'ev, "Aziia 'Inorodtsev' i Aziia sovetskikh sotsialisticheskikh respublik," *Planovoe Khoziaistvo*, No. 11 (November, 1927), pp. 208–9.
[59] For example, see A. Ikramov, "Itogi i ocherednye zadachi (doklad po 2-m Plenume Ts.K., K.P.(b) Uzbekistana v fevrale 1926 g.)," in Kraskin, *Zemel'no-vodnaia reforma v Srednei Azii*, p. 42.

to encourage the settlement of the nomadic peoples of Central Asia. Among the Turcomans, settlement had been developing successfully even before the Russian Revolution. Among the Kirghiz, however, native hostility to settlement remained strong.[60] Kirghiz peasants who turned from stock raising to sedentary forms of agriculture usually did so only through economic necessity; upon improving their status, they tended to return to their traditional pursuits. Investigations, conducted by Rumiantsev between 1909 and 1913, had shown that well-to-do Kirghiz preferred to rent out their land rather than engage in farming; Kirghiz of the "middle" rank tended to combine herding with agriculture; and only the poorest—those with no other means of subsistence—were engaged exclusively in cultivating the land.[61]

Soviet reformers, unaware of Rumiantsev's study, started out on the assumption that lack of farm land was the only real obstacle to the settlement of the nomad population. In the Kirghiz regions especially, their early activities were inspired at least partially by the expectation that a program calculated to redress the wrongs committed against the native peoples by Cossack and peasant colonizers would create a stable basis for settlement, and this consideration figured importantly in the land reform of 1921. In the course of this experiment the Soviet government drove out of Semirechie 8,084 immigrant households which had been in possession of 628,805 acres of cultivated land, with 161 villages, 95 settlements, and 175 farmsteads. It then transferred to Kirghiz nomads all the villages, land, and farmsteads along with their sown acreage, orchards, kitchen gardens, and agricultural equipment. The new "settlers" wintered there, but when spring came they gathered their flocks and trekked off to summer pastures, leaving the embarrassed Soviet officials to ponder the errors in their calculations.[62]

The Bolsheviks attributed the failure of this experiment to

[60] As late as 1925 about 64 percent of the Kirghiz people were nomadic or seminomadic, while only 24 percent of the Turcomans had not been settled. See Iu. I. Poslavskii, "Sel'skoe khoziaistvo," in *Vsia Sredniaia Aziia*, p. 126.

[61] Data reproduced in M. B. Sakharov, *Osedanie kochevykh i polukochevykh khoziaistv Kirgizii* (Moscow, 1934), p. 15.

[62] *Ibid.*, p. 21.

many causes, from "nomadic instincts" to the sinister influence of tribal leaders. But they also adopted a new approach to the problem, one which remained in effect until the Kirghiz were finally herded into collective farms in the 1930's. They continued to make land and agricultural equipment available to nomads who wished to settle permanently but gave up attempts to eliminate nomadism directly. Instead, they undertook to formalize and regularize the practice by assigning winter and summer pastures and establishing regular routes between them. These measures put an end to the rootless wandering common to many tribes and increased the importance of the winter corral period; they marked a long step toward an eventual turn to sedentary life.[63] Individual settlement was becoming more common toward the end of the twenties, particularly in districts where stock raising was possible on a year-round basis. However, the majority of nomads continued to roam until collectivization closed off the last avenue of escape from permanent settlement.

THE STRUGGLE FOR COTTON

In Central Asia the new Soviet rulers made a special effort to restore cotton cultivation to at least its prerevolutionary level. More cotton was essential both to industrial recovery of the USSR and to any industrial development in the border regions.[64] During the civil war, dwindling stocks of cotton had brought Russia's textile industry to a standstill, forcing thousands of workers out of their jobs, and a continuing low production of cotton prolonged the crisis into the 1920's. The urgent need for cotton for the textile mills of Central Russia dominated Bolshevik plans for economic recovery in Central Asia. Even before the cessation of hostilities, restoration of cotton production held first place among the goals of Soviet policy in the region.[65]

Although the Bolsheviks planned eventually to free the Rus-

[63] *Ibid.*, p. 46.

[64] See above, pp. 260–61, 270–73.

[65] See especially the report of Rykov at the Eighth All-Russian Congress of Soviets in *Vos'moi Vserossiiskii S'ezd Sovetov Rabochikh, Krest'ianskikh, Krasnoarmeiskikh i Kazach'ikh Deputatov (22–29 dekabria, 1920 goda)* (Moscow, 1921), pp. 92–93, 102–3, 112.

sian textile industry completely from its prewar partial dependence on imported cotton, early planning concentrated on
restoring the cotton yields of Central Asia to the pre-1914 levels.
As early as 1921, Rizenkampf had outlined the major avenues
of approach to reconstruction, and subsequent Soviet programs,
while divergent in detail, hewed closely to them. The immediate
requirement was to encourage peasant producers to expand their
cotton acreage to prerevolutionary levels. Second only to this
was the necessity for a campaign to intensify cotton growing
through the supply of high-yield seed and the introduction of
modern farming techniques. A third avenue of expansion was
the extension of the Central Asian irrigation system and the
creation of new cotton districts.[66]

Implementation of these policies, especially those which depended upon the cooperation of the peasantry, followed the
usual Soviet procedure of utilizing persuasive measures to win
over the majority and keeping force in reserve to convince the
wayward. The government stimulated increased production by
offering benefits and preferences to the peasant who would plant
all or most of his acreage in cotton and by artificially creating a
market structure favorable to the cotton producer. At the same
time, it openly displayed instruments of political and economic
coercion as a warning to peasants who resisted the proffered
blandishments.

From the beginning of reconstruction the Bolsheviks stressed
programs of preferential government support to cotton growers
and cotton-growing districts. As early as 1920 the central government adopted a four-year program of reconstruction work and
enacted decrees which guaranteed price supports, offered bo-
nuses to cotton producers, and provided for the organization of
cotton growing.[67] Orders were placed in the United States for
substantial quantities of American seed, which was distributed
at little or no charge in districts where producers had reverted
to the less productive native varieties of cotton. The local administration gave special privileges to cotton growers for the
purchase of seed, supplies, agricultural implements, and draft

[66] Rizenkampf, *Problemy orosheniia Turkestana*, p. 43.
[67] *Vos'moi Vserossiiskii S'ezd Sovetov*, pp. 102–3.

cattle and concentrated public reconstruction work in the cotton districts. Tax policy was enlisted to encourage increases in cotton planting. In Bokhara the government exempted from the agricultural tax all acreage planted to American seed;[68] throughout Central Asia an increase in the proportion of cotton lands meant a reduction in taxes for the farmer.[69]

The Soviet government also promoted the development of producer cooperatives among cotton growers and the provision of easier credit. Because of the long period between one year's harvest and the following year's planting, the small cotton grower, operating on the narrowest of margins, could hardly survive without access to credit. Even prosperous farmers required it. The need had existed, of course, from the beginning of Central Asia's rise as a cotton center. During the 1890's Russian commercial firms had initiated the practice of advancing sums of money, usually at the rate of one to one and a half rubles per pood of cotton (36 pounds) to small producers. Just prior to 1914, their monopoly of credit was being limited by the development of credit cooperatives, the first of which had been organized in 1909. By the eve of the war 210 credit societies and 146 cooperative savings associations with 80,500 members and net assets of 1,264,000 rubles were operating in Central Asia.[70] The cooperatives were doing much to promote the development of cotton growing but membership in them was confined largely to the more substantial elements in the Moslem community. The poor peasant, forced to seek private credit at usurious rates, tended to become entangled in debt.

After the revolution, the Turkestan government attempted to eliminate the system by doing away with private credit and with private trade in cotton. In their place it established state wholesalers and authorized them to purchase cotton directly from the producers and to finance new planting. This project was quickly defeated by the very magnitude of the task of dealing individually with tens of thousands of peasants. In 1919 the Soviet government revived the prerevolutionary cotton-growing co-

---

[68] E. M., "Khoziaistvennyi obzor po Turkestanu," *Vlast' Sovetov,* No. 6 (September, 1924), pp. 214–15.

[69] Anna Louise Strong, *Red Star in Samarkand* (New York, 1929), pp. 52–53.

[70] Liashchenko, *Istoriia narodnogo khoziaistva SSSR,* II, 548–49.

operatives, commissioning them to act as middlemen in purchasing cotton and in providing producers with credit for seed
and agricultural implements.[71] During 1919 alone 42 cooperatives with a membership of 70,000 cotton producers sprang into
being, and, of 278,564 acres under cotton, 198,450 were in the
possession of their members.[72] Despite a serious setback during
the famine year of 1922, in which membership in cooperatives
fell to 45,543 and their planted area to 116,080 acres, the movement spread rapidly. In 1923 membership climbed again to 100,-
000 and the planted area reached 340,145 acres. By 1927 the
number of cooperatives had reached 593 with 631,510 members,
with 1,665,975 acres under cotton.[73]

Although the rise of the cooperatives undoubtedly attests to
their popularity, government subsidization of cotton growing,
carried on through the cooperatives, was the central factor in
their growth. Under the New Economic Policy, with its relatively restricted range of direct government intervention, government subsidies determined the success or failure of the
campaign to expand cotton acreage. At first, the subsidy took the
form of a government commitment to support the price of cotton
at a fixed ratio to the price of grain sold on the open market.
Prerevolutionary experience had shown that cotton cultivation
increased when a price differential of 2.5 or three to one obtained between cotton and bread grains and conversely that cotton planting decreased when this proportion was unbalanced in
favor of grain.[74] With these data as a guide, the Main Cotton
Committee of Turkestan in 1922 fixed cotton prices at 2.5 times
the price of grain: that is, the Soviet government and its agencies
guaranteed to purchase all cotton offered at two and one-half
times the prices being paid for similar weights of grain on the
open market.

[71] N. P. Rogozhin, "Kooperatsiia v khlopkovom dele Turkestana," *Khlopkovoe
Delo*, Nos. 7–8 (July–August, 1924), pp. 20–21.
[72] *Ibid.*, pp. 26–28.
[73] A. E. Aksel'rod, "Khlopkovoe delo za 10 let (1917–1927)," *Khlopkovoe Delo*,
Nos. 11–12 (November–December, 1927), p. 841.
[74] A. A. Predtechenskii, "Khleb za khlopok (k vvozu khleba v Turkestan),"
Khlopkovoe Delo, Nos. 1–2 (January–February, 1923), pp. 33–35.

The fallacy in the approach is immediately apparent. Its success depended upon a relatively stable grain market, and the latter, barring complete control of the economy and arbitrary price fixing by the government, rested on adequate grain supplies. Prior to the war, grain imports from European Russia and the North Caucasus, averaging 270,848 short tons annually,[75] had maintained the cotton-grain ratio and had supported the rapid expansion of cotton growing. When the imports stopped after the revolution, grain prices skyrocketed; because of the increasingly acute grain shortage, they had actually overtaken cotton prices by the season of 1921. The Main Cotton Committee was not unaware of these conditions. In fact, it based its policy on the expectation that European Russia would export 36,113 tons of bread grains to Turkestan during the year and persisted in this policy even after it was apparent that no imports were forthcoming. The results were disastrous. Despite government promises of high prices for cotton, the cotton acreage in Central Asia slumped to the level of the 1880's. Simultaneously, the policy gave fresh impetus to the inflationary tendencies in the wheat market and drove grain prices to new highs.[76]

The experience of 1922 demonstrated forcibly that no amount of persuasion could get cotton out of Turkestan unless basic supplies of bread grain were made available. Sporadic local efforts to encourage grain plantings on unirrigated land, aimed eventually at decreasing Central Asia's dependence on imports, also date from this period. The central government now stepped up the shipment of wheat into the region, and this, together with an increase of the grain-cotton ratio to three-to-one, had the desired effect. Central Asian farmers planted 476,550 acres to cotton in 1923 and 1,290,600 acres by 1925.[77] The critical period over, the government took steps to eliminate the influence of the open market on cotton prices. Beginning with the fall of 1926, it replaced the guaranteed wheat-cotton ratio price with

[75] *Ibid.*
[76] *Ibid.*, pp. 38–39.
[77] Zashchuk, "Khlebnaia problema v khlopkovodcheskikh raionakh Srednei Azii," *Khlopkovoe Delo,* Nos. 3–5 (March–May, 1926), p. 387.

subsidized sales of bread grains to cotton growers at less than wholesale prices.[78]

This step represented more than a mere substitution of one form of subsidization for another. It was evidence of increasing confidence on the part of the state in its ability to compel the individual peasant to do its bidding. Significantly, it was connected closely with the land reform and the division of the large economically independent landholdings into tiny plots of land, incapable of supporting the smallholder recipients. The smallholders consequently became dependent for support upon the government, which rendered aid, usually in the form of advances, on condition that the peasants undertake to plant cotton on their allotments.[79] The Bolsheviks thus turned agricultural credit into a weapon which was as effective as direct subsidization had been in promoting the Soviet cotton policy. In Uzbekistan, on land allotted to the peasants, the share of land planted to cotton increased by 27 percent during the first year of the reform alone.[80]

The Soviet government pursued no aspect of its economic policy in Central Asia so relentlessly as it did the quest for cotton. Every instrument available to the state was utilized to persuade the peasant to increase his cotton acreage. Peasants whom the Bolsheviks could not persuade by subsidy and preferential treatment they coerced with economic and other pressures. Peasants who still had the temerity to resist placing their irrigated acreage under cotton or who dared to advocate openly the cultivation of other crops risked denunciation as "wreckers" or "counterrevolutionaries," with the attendant prospect of undergoing administrative reprisals or criminal prosecution.[81]

[78] Lavrent'ev, "Aziia 'inorodtsev' i Aziia sovetskikh sotsialisticheskikh respublik," *Planovoe Khoziaistvo,* No. 11 (November, 1927), p. 207.

[79] Mustapha Chokaiev, "Turkestan and the Soviet Regime," *Journal of the Royal Central Asian Society,* XVIII (1931), 415–16.

[80] Gurevich, "Zemel'no-vodnaia reforma v Uzbekskoi SSR (1925–1929)," *Voprosy Istorii,* No. 11 (November, 1948), p. 63. Data, gathered in 1927, showed that almost 84 percent of the cotton acreage in Uzbekistan and 88 percent in Turkmenia was planted by peasants whose farms were smaller than five and one-half acres. The addition of farms ranging between 5.5 and 8 acres increased these percentages to 93.8 and 97 respectively. Mikh. Katsenelenbogen, "Ob 'uklonakh' v natsional'noi politika V.K.P.(b)," *Bol'shevik,* No. 22 (November 30, 1927), p. 23.

[81] In the three years between 1924 and 1927, the Uzbek government alone

The policy brought results. Between 1922 and 1927 the area under cotton rose from 171,255 to 1,674,557 acres, more than in 1913 and within 87,650 acres of the 1915 figure. However, as one consequence of the Soviet policy of favoring the small and often inefficient producer, yields of cotton lint were well below prerevolutionary levels. Whereas the 1915 crop had produced 264,455 short tons of cotton lint, only 209,816 tons were collected in 1927, a yield of 251 pounds per acre instead of 297 pounds per acre in 1915 (see Table 8). The 1927 crop met somewhat more than half the annual requirements of Soviet textile industry.

Despite the new regime's concentration on the revival of cotton growing, the general structure of agriculture in Central Asia remained pretty much what it had been prior to the revolution. Cotton acreage expanded relatively more rapidly than did the area under other crops. By the end of the New Economic Policy cotton output had achieved prewar levels, although the total planted area was only 80 percent of prewar.[82] Rice cultivation, on the other hand, declined steadily from the prerevolutionary levels. Because it required large amounts of water —seven to nine times as much as cotton—the Soviet government actively discouraged rice planting.[83] The major branches of agriculture, however, maintained the correlation which existed prior to the war. While in 1914 farming had accounted for 77 percent and stock raising for 23 percent of the gross value of agricultural production in Central Asia, in 1925–26 farming accounted for 78 percent and stock raising for 22 percent.

Within the individual republics changes were more marked than in the region as a whole. In Uzbekistan the share of livestock production decreased from 16.5 percent in 1914 to 15 percent in 1925–26, while that of cotton cultivation increased from 38.5 to 42 percent. Stock raising also declined in Turkmenia,

appropriated 1,670,000 rubles specifically for struggle against "wreckers" who opposed the Soviet cotton policy. See *Vtoroi Vseuzbekskii S'ezd Sovetov Rabochikh, Dekhkanskikh i Krasnoarmeiskikh Deputatov Uzbekskoi Sovetskoi Sotsialisticheskoi Respubliki* (Samarkand, 1927), p. 273.

[82] S. Ia. Gessen, "K voprosu o khoziaistvennom stroitel'stve Srednei Azii," *Sovetskoe Stroitel'stvo*, No. 1 (6) (January, 1927), p. 62.

[83] Cherdantsev, *Sredne-Aziatskie respubliki*, p. 92; Strong, *Red Star in Samarkand*, pp. 52–53.

dropping from 41 percent in 1914 to 36 percent in 1925–26, but it increased in Kirghizia from 31 to 34 percent, and in Tajikistan from 44 to 56 percent.[84] These figures by no means in-

TABLE 8

EXPANSION AND EFFICIENCY OF COTTON CULTIVATION IN
CENTRAL ASIA

Years	Cotton Area in Acres	Raw Cotton in Short Tons	Cotton Lint in Short Tons	Lint per Acre in Pounds	Cotton Lint Consumed by Soviet Textile Industry in Short Tons
1915	1,762,210		264,455	297	
1924	984,460	303,403	86,418	176	220,563
1925	1,289,710	516,017	154,022	239	292,232
1926	1,412,915	506,342	154,690	219	344,825
1927	1,674,557	671,359	209,817	251	393,632

Source: Compiled from data appearing in A. E. Aksel'rod, "Khlopkovoe delo za 10 let (1917–1927)," *Khlopkovoe Delo*, Nos. 11–12 (November–December, 1927), p. 846; S. K. Kondrashov, "Ispolnenie planov po irrigatsii i khlopkovodstvu v Sredne-Aziatskoi respublike v 1924/25 g.," *Planovoe Khoziaistvo*, No. 5 (May, 1925), p. 249; Upravlenie Vodnogo Khoziaistva Srednei Azii, *Sostoianie i perspektivy irrigatsii v Srednei Azii* (Tashkent, 1928), pp. 9–10.

dicate that stock raising revived from the losses sustained during the war and revolution as quickly as did more sedentary forms of agriculture. As late as 1926–27 the livestock herds of Central Asia had reached only 71.6 percent of their prewar size, and there were only two thirds as many draft animals in the region (see Table 9).

The total picture of agricultural reconstruction in Central Asia reveals clearly a revival, and to some degree an accentuation, of basic trends which had begun under Imperial rule. Soviet policy, even more than Imperial policy, aimed to intensify regional specialization in agriculture, and it did so with even less regard for its effect on local economic life and on the welfare of the rural population. One root of the policy was a thinly disguised determination to complete without delay the economic integration of Central Asia into the Russian national economy by destroying all hope of local self-sufficiency. Another, and an equally compelling one, was the preferential fos-

[84] Alkin, *Sredniaia Aziia*, I, 359–61.

TABLE 9

REVIVAL OF LIVESTOCK BREEDING IN CENTRAL ASIA

| | IN THOUSAND HEAD | | | | IN PERCENT OF 1914 | | |
	1914	1924–25	1925–26	1926–27	1924–25	1925–26	1926–27
Uzbek SSR	7,376.5	4,401.8	4,767.4	5,176.9	59.7	64.6	70.2
Tajik SSR	2,715.5	1,763.9	1,872.1	2,050.8	64.9	68.9	75.5
Turcoman SSR	4,700.0	3,363.9	3,358.6	3,640.6	71.6	71.5	77.5
Kirghiz ASSR	4,755.7	2,794.0	2,906.1	3,132.8	58.8	61.1	65.9
Total for Central Asia	19,547.7	12,323.6	12,904.2	14,001.1	63.0	66.0	71.6
Draft Animals	2,142.7	1,284.9	1,355.2	1,448.6	59.9	63.2	67.6

Source: Compiled from data in S. Ia. Gessen, "K voprosu o khoziaistvennom stroitel'stve Srednei Azii," *Sovetskoe Stroitel'stvo*, No. 1 (6) (January, 1927), p. 64.

tering of technical crops essential to the revival of industry, even if it meant maintaining food margins at a low level.

The merits or demerits of these goals are not discussed here, but clearly the Bolsheviks pursued in Central Asia those very agrarian policies for which they had repeatedly condemned the Tsarist regime, and they pursued them with far greater vigor. It is the art of the propagandist in power to disguise embarrassing similarities between his own policies and those of the "old regime." While Soviet publicists continued to damn the Imperial government for having converted Central Asia into a "cotton colony," they were now obliged to justify a continuation and reenforcement of that policy on the basis of economic efficiency. And, indeed, when the Five-Year Plans went into operation, projects for developing food crops in the region capable of satisfying local requirements receded into the background. In terms of state planning, Central Asian agriculture had a more important economic purpose to serve: that of an "agricultural-livestock combination" producing cotton, wool, and hides for the needs of Soviet Russia's growing industry.

VIII

LAND REFORM
IN CENTRAL ASIA

◆

PRE-SOVIET Marxist doctrine concerning the peasant assumed that capitalism was an inevitable stage of development in agriculture as well as in industry, an inescapable preparation for the advent of socialism. The immediate necessity was to eliminate all vestiges of "feudalism," personified in Russia by the landlord and the large estate, which hindered the full development of capitalism in rural life. Although peasant hopes and Bolshevik plans conflicted in their ultimate goals, both Bolsheviks and peasantry desired the destruction of the landlord. This provided the basis for Lenin's concept of a proletarian-peasant alliance which, transformed into "the union of a working-class revolution with a peasant war," became the cornerstone of his grand strategy of revolution.

While this tactic brought the Bolsheviks into power in Central Russia, it did not find spontaneous support in Central Asia; there the revolution did not give rise to peasant violence against the landlords. Although the Tashkent government had nationalized the land early in 1918 and ordered the seizure and redistribution of large landholdings, it made no real effort to implement the decree.[1] The very idea of seizing the property of the landlord was incomprehensible to native peasants. Religious and communal ties, even the economic interests of the

[1] Ilias Alkin, *Sredniaia Aziia: ekonomiko-geograficheskii ocherk Kara-Kalpakstana, Kirgizstana, Tadzhikistana, Turkmenistana i Uzbekistana* (Moscow, 1931), I, 356–57.

peasants, bound the rural native community tightly together and prevented the emergence of those class antagonisms which had led in Central Russia to peasant war against the landowners. Indeed, nationalization of the land in Turkestan actually encouraged new seizures by European immigrants of the lands of the native peasantry, in continuation of the land seizures which had erupted with special virulence after the Kirghiz rebellion of 1916. In the Semirechie region especially, European settlers organized themselves into soviets after the revolution, confiscated lands belonging to the local population, and transferred them to "communes" and "artels" of Russian immigrants.[2]

THE FIRST STEP: EPISODE IN SEMIRECHIE

Not until 1919, when Moscow reasserted its authority in Turkestan, did local officials undertake any program to reverse the practice of immigrant seizures of land from the native peasantry. The first attempts to solve this question coincided with a revival of Soviet interest in the East. By 1920 the major danger from foreign intervention was over in the West, and the White Armies of Kolchak and Denikin had been defeated. When the expected wave of proletarian revolutions in Western Europe had failed to materialize, Soviet policy turned decisively to the East in an effort to strengthen the Soviet regime in Russia's Eastern borderlands and to support anti-imperialist movements in the colonial countries. The new policy was designed, in part, to right the wrongs committed against the natives of Central

---

[2] E. Zel'kina, *Ocherki po agrarnomu voprosu v Srednei Azii* (Moscow, 1930), pp. 70–71. This particular issue came up as early as the Sixth Congress of Soviets of Turkestan in October, 1918. The Commissar of Agriculture, reporting that the law on socialization of the land had had no effect, complained that volost' soviets had refused to implement it or were interpreting it to the detriment of the native population. I. Zelenskii, "O zemel'no-vodnoi reforme v Srednei Azii (doklad na plenume Sredazbiuro Ts.K. V.K.P.(b) ot 14 marta 1925)," in I. S. Kraskin (ed.), *Zemel'no-vodnaia reforma v Srednei Azii: sbornik materialov* (Moscow, 1927), p. 11. But nothing was done to remedy the situation. The Tashkent government, confronted by more formidable problems, lost interest in the question and Russian colonists continued to seize native lands. So flagrant were the actions of European settlers that Safarov charged later that the Russian kulak had used the revolution to grow fat on the life and blood of the Kirghiz agricultural workers. *Protokoly s'ezdov i konferentsii Vsesoiuznoi Kommunisticheskoi Partii (b): Desiatyi S'ezd R.K.P.(b), mart 1921 g.* (Moscow, 1933), p. 197.

Asia before and during the revolution. Another aim was to transform the "national revolution," which the revolution had touched off in Central Asia, into an antifeudal revolution.

In 1920 the Soviet press began stressing the need for a revolution among the non-Russian peasantry and for the seizure of "excess" lands which were in the hands of kulaks.[3] Neither the publicists nor the government, however, were prepared to demand an agrarian revolution within the native community. Stalin himself confined his attacks upon large landowners in the national republics and regions to the "predatory Great Russian kulaks" and limited Party interference to supporting the native peasants in ridding themselves of "kulak colonizers." [4] The first Bolshevik plan to introduce the idea of land reform into Central Asia was a program to return to the natives the lands which had been seized by colonists after the 1916 rebellion and to organize on these lands communes and artels of landless and small peasants.

By a decree of March 4, 1920, the government of Turkestan ordered immigrants to return to their former owners all lands confiscated after the revolution.[5] This was followed on June 29, 1920, by a resolution of the Central Committee of the Communist Party of Turkestan enjoining all Bolsheviks to put an end to hostility between the European and native populations and to eliminate patriarchal-feudal survivals which lingered on in the native community. It demanded the confiscation of all lands seized by the Immigration Administration or arbitrarily taken by the immigrants from the Kirghiz, and its redistribution among Kirghiz peasants and refugees—the so-called *dugan* who had fled into Sinkiang after the rebellion of 1916.[6] The Ninth Regional Congress of Soviets, meeting in September, 1920, re

[3] As one example, see G. Broido, "Turkestanskie problemy," *Zhizn' Natsiona¹ nostei*, No. 23 (80) (July 18, 1920).

[4] J. V. Stalin, *Sochineniia* (Moscow, 1946—), V, 25–26.

[5] Alkin, *Sredniaia Aziia*, I, 357–58.

[6] *Ibid.*, I, 356–57. The provision was repeated verbatim in the theses of the Fifth Congress of the Communist Party of Turkestan. In a companion effort to undermine the economic and social foundations of the native community, the theses further demanded that surpluses of cattle be taken from well-to-do natives and divided among the poor. From the text of the Theses of the Fifth Congress of the Communist Party of Turkestan as reproduced in Georgii Safarov, *Kolonial'naia revoliutsiia: opyt Turkestana* (Moscow, 1921), p. 137.

inforced this decision by stripping immigrant peasants of special privileges and ordered the return to the natives of all lands seized after the revolt of 1916. At the same time, the congress abolished private property in land and directed the distribution of nationalized lands according to the principle of equalized land tenure: first, among share croppers and agricultural workers; second, among landless peasants; and, last, among soviet farms, agricultural communes, artels, and cooperatives.[7]

In practice the Soviet government did not attempt at that time to introduce the principle of equalized land tenure into the native community, but it took immediate steps to eliminate the Russian kulak in the Kirghiz regions. By May, 1921, the Soviet regime had seized some 687,841 acres of land from European colonists and had redistributed it to 13,000 native households. Over 601,000 acres of the land were given to Kirghiz nomads and the rest allotted to Kazakhs and Uzbeks. These reform measures affected only a small part of the region—Semirechie, Jetysuisk, and part of Syr-Daria. There was no land reform within predominantly non-Russian regions.[8]

In its first phase the land reform in Central Asia pursued national rather than class objectives. It sought not so much to reorganize agrarian relations among the Moslems as to effect a public reversal of the colonial policies of the Tsarist regime. Atabaev, who reported to the Tenth Congress of Soviets of Turkestan on the progress of the land reform, emphasized this facet of the program:

Our land policy was directed to the liquidation of the consequences of the colonial policy of the autocracy, the "arbitrary seizures," and to the struggle against the colonizing mood of the Russian village. . . . As regards the promulgation of the land reform in regions with an overwhelmingly native population engaged in agri-

---

[7] S., "Zemel'naia reforma v Uzbekistane," *Vlast' Sovetov*, IX, No. 7 (February 14, 1926), 8; also Zel'kina, *Ocherki po agrarnomu voprosu v Srednei Azii*, pp. 71–72.

[8] S., "Zemel'naia reforma v Uzbekistane," *Vlast' Sovetov*, IX, No. 7 (February 14, 1926), 8; A. Gurevich, "Zemel'no-vodnaia reforma v Uzbekskoi SSR (1925–1929)," *Voprosy Istorii*, No. 11 (November, 1948), pp. 55–56; M. B. Sakharov, *Osedanie kochevykh i polukochevykh khoziaistv Kirgizii* (Moscow, 1934), p. 21.

culture, the leading Soviet and Party agencies did not approach the solution of this question.[9]

With minor exceptions[10] the reform bore no semblance of a class struggle. The very procedures which the Soviet government followed in redistributing the property of colonists militated against the development of class conflicts within the native community. The confiscated land was turned over to tribal or communal units for disposition by them rather than being presented outright to individual peasants. Tribal chieftains thus became the real arbiters of the reform and in some cases utilized it for their own aggrandizement. Even where personal profit was not a motivating factor, they distributed land without reference to Soviet laws on the labor basis of land tenure. These and other "distortions" of the principle of Soviet land reform inevitably drew the fire of prominent Central Asian Bolsheviks. At the Eleventh Congress of Turkestan Soviets in 1922, Rudzutak claimed that the land reform had been carried out "mechanically" and had failed to reach the non-Russian masses. Even the lands taken from the Russian immigrant population, he charged, had not been distributed completely among the natives. Ryskulov argued further that failure to follow up the legal grant of land with measures designed to consolidate the new holdings as effective economic units was defeating the purpose of the reform even when the provisions of the law were observed.[11] Another major hindrance to improvement in the lot of native settlers arose from the lack of agricultural equipment and the failure of the Soviet regime to aid the needy households.[12] Consequently, most recipients of confiscated land were

[9] Kraskin, *Zemel'no-vodnaia reforma v Srednei Azii*, p. 12.

[10] The Bolsheviks had extended the legal effect of the Soviet agrarian code to districts populated predominantly by Uzbeks, Tajiks, and Turcomans but attempts to put its provisions into effect were generally unsuccessful. Fergana proved to be something of an exception. Here grass-roots uprisings, spearheaded by poor peasants, led to the seizure of some 5,500 acres of land from Moslem landowners. But the risings were unorganized and carried on without Soviet aid or Party directives. E. Zel'kina, "Zemel'naia reforma v Srednei Azii," *Revoliutsionnyi Vostok*, No. 3 (1927), p. 152.

[11] S., "Zemel'naia reforma v Uzbekistane," *Vlast' Sovetov*, IX, No. 7 (February 14, 1926), 8.

[12] The delegate from Turkestan, Khidyr-Aliev, who reported on the reform to

ill-prepared to manage their new allotments and within two or three years had lost them to the large owners.[13]

While the land reform in 1921 did not remove the economic sources of impoverishment in the native rural community and failed to weaken communal cohesiveness, it had considerable importance politically. As Ryskulov pointed out at the Twelfth Party Congress in 1923, the Bolshevik Party and the Soviet power had in effect abolished national inequality in the countryside. By putting an end to kulak privileges and distributing to native peasants surpluses of land which had belonged to European colonists, the Soviet regime, in his opinion, had established political equilibrium.[14] Other Soviet observers agreed with his analysis. The policy was, from the Bolshevik standpoint, the best form of education toward native acceptance of the Soviet regime since it contributed materially to strengthening the trust of the native peoples toward the Russians and to awakening class consciousness among the rural poor. Hence, the argument ran, it encouraged the development of an alliance of the toilers of the local nationalities with the Great Russian people and promoted what Stalin had often called the friendship of peoples in the USSR.

The land reform in Semirechie was not the only attempt to solve agrarian problems in Central Asia during this period. In both Bokhara and Khorezm the Bolsheviks supported weak and unsuccessful steps to divide up lands which had belonged to the former ruling groups. In 1921 the Khorezmian government ordered the division of some 675,000 acres, seized from the deposed Khan of Khiva and his relatives, into plots averaging two acres for distribution among poor and landless peasants.[15] But

the All-Russian Central Executive Committee, took special pains to explode the popular notion that the government could solve the problems of the poor peasants merely by dividing the land among them. Pointing out that the average annual income of peasant households in many districts did not exceed 70 rubles, he insisted that the only solution lay in putting the peasants on the land at state expense; that is, by government supply of free seed, livestock, and agricultural implements. *Tret'iaia Sessiia Vserossiiskogo Ispolnitel'nogo Komiteta X Sozyva* (Moscow, 1924), p. 104.

[13] Zel'kina, *Ocherki po agrarnomu voprosu v Srednei Azii*, p. 73.

[14] *Dvenadtsatyi S'ezd Rossiiskoi Kommunisticheskoi Partii (bol'shevikov)* (Moscow, 1923), p. 470.

[15] A. Vinogradova, "Khorezmskaia Sovetskaia Narodnaia Respublika," *Zhizn' Natsional'nostei*, No. 1 (January, 1923), p. 188.

little of the land actually got into the hands of this group. Widespread evasion as well as political favoritism left most of the nationalized land in the possession of a few large owners. Traditional economic and social relationships, moreover, were completely untouched.[16]

In Bokhara the Revolutionary Committee, which held power prior to the organization of a "people's government," adopted a most revolutionary decree on land nationalization. It ordered all endowment and emirate lands, as well as landed property belonging to officials of the former regime and large landowners, together with their livestock and equipment, to be distributed among the peasants.[17] In practice the Bokharan government nationalized only properties which had belonged to the Emir of Bokhara and to important members of his official family, and very little of these lands was distributed among poor and landless peasants.[18] Of still greater concern to Bolshevik observers, the transfers of property which followed the revolutions both in Bokhara and in Khorezm made no change in customary rural institutions or in the prerevolutionary agrarian pattern.

Neither the revolution nor its aftermath had brought about an agrarian revolution. The principle of private property in land remained in effect, despite numerous decrees and regulations to the contrary issued by the governments of the Central Asian republics, and the economic distance between rich and poor remained as sharp as it had been prior to the revolution. Initial measures to divide the land had not touched the interests of native landowners, nor bettered the position of the poorer peasants. The latter, Bolshevik observers charged, not without some exaggeration, were even worse off than before the revolution, while the kulaks and the middle peasants with working capital had improved their position appreciably.[19]

[16] K. Zubrek, "Zemledelie i irrigatsiia Khorezma v sviazi s voprosom ekonomicheskogo ob'edineniia Sredne-Aziatskikh respublik," *Novyi Vostok*, No. 3 (1923), pp. 210–12.

[17] Text of decree in A. Mashitskii, "Materialy po istorii Bukharskoi revoliutsii," *Vestnik Narodnogo Komissariata Inostrannykh Del*, Nos. 4–5 (April–May, 1922), pp. 127–28.

[18] Gurevich, "Zemel'no-vodnaia reforma v Uzbekskoi SSR," *Voprosy Istorii*, No. 11 (November, 1948), pp. 55–56.

[19] *Ibid.*, pp. 53–54; see also report of Khidyr-Aliev in *Tret'iaia Sessiia Vserossiiskogo Tsentral'nogo Ispolnitel'nogo Komiteta X Sozyva*, p. 102.

Comparative statistics for 1917 and 1925 tended to disprove these claims. The poorest group, it is true, had not bettered its status as a result of the revolution, but the strongest groups had decreased considerably in numbers. In the Fergana valley, the center of cotton growing, 51 percent of all households in 1925 had 2.5 acres or less and owned only 9.8 percent of the cultivated land in the area. This group together with the middle households, which held an average of seven acres, was cultivating about one third of the valley. On the other hand, landowners possessing over 27 acres and constituting 3.5 percent of all households controlled over 31 percent of the farmed area.[20] In other districts where cotton growing was less developed, the differentiation was much less marked.

The majority of the large landowners in Turkestan were immigrants from among the "nouveaux riches"—kishlak usurers, city and village traders who had bought up land or seized it from the poor in payment of debts. Some of the large landed properties in Turkestan belonged to descendants of the feudal gentry who had increased their landholdings through purchase, usury, and other means. The economic and social distinctions between rich and poor were weaker in Bokhara and Khorezm, where traditional types of land tenure remained in force and a patriarchal pattern was the rule. Such distinctions were also slight in many parts of the Turcoman provinces, where communal land ownership continued to exist.[21]

Political considerations aside, feudal and semifeudal relationships constituted, in the Soviet view, a direct threat to the development of the productive forces of Central Asia and to the improvement of the peasant economy. Private property in land, the presence of what the Bolsheviks characterized as large *pomestie*-type land tenure,[22] the remnants of feudal and patriarchal

[20] Zel'kina, "Zemel'naia reforma v Srednei Azii," *Revoliutsionnyi Vostok,* No. 3 (1927), p. 152; see also Kraskin, *Zemel'no-vodnaia reforma v Srednei Azii,* pp. 12–17.

[21] Soviet investigators have said that the incidence of landlessness trebled in the Turcoman regions in the period from 1914 to 1917, and that the number of households having a better status also decreased. See M. A. Nemchenko, "Agrarnaia reforma v Turkmenii," *Novyi Vostok,* No. 19 (1927), p. 127.

[22] The designation *pomestie* was for the most part a deliberate misnomer, which the Bolsheviks cultivated in order to stir up resentment. Something approximating the system did exist in parts of Turkmenia where remnants of *miulk*—large landed estates which local rulers had awarded to individuals,

relationships between landlord and peasant, and a backward system of tilling the land were some of the obstacles to the Soviet program, as were the customary and complicated regulation of land utilization and the rules of water tenure, which in some cases dated back to the era of Khudoiar Khan.[23]

THE PREPARATION FOR THE REFORM

Although land redistribution was not expected to solve all the problems of agriculture in Central Asia, the Bolsheviks believed that it would clear away remnants of the "feudal" and patriarchal regime in the village, would open the way for the development of cooperative forms of production, and would improve the lot of the poorest peasants immediately. Land reform was to be the precursor of a future Soviet agriculture.[24] It was to complete the "bourgeois-democratic" revolution in the non-Russian village, to purge land relationships of feudal and tribal survivals, and to deliver a blow at growing "capitalist" elements which had emerged in the cotton districts.

In this sense, land reform represented the second phase of revolution among the backward peoples of Soviet Russia. Cutting away the bonds of Tsarist imperialism and transforming the former colonies into "autonomous" soviet republics had completed the first phase, thus, allegedly, resolving the political phase of the national question and launching the Eastern peoples on a path of noncapitalistic development. The second stage, according to Bolshevik concepts, entailed the deepening of the revolution and completion of its "bourgeois task"—that is, the extirpation of tribal, feudal, and patriarchal vestiges in the countryside through nationalizing and redividing the land.[25]

often in payment for special services to the state—survived the revolution. In Bolshevik propaganda, however, the term was applied to farms in excess of 150 to 200 acres, whatever their origin.

[23] One Bolshevik writer found five major "contradictions" which impeded the revival of agriculture: the lack of adequate means of production among the poor peasants, the small parcelized landholdings, the survival of precapitalistic forms of agriculture, the need for credit facilities, and the growing overpopulation of the rural areas. Alkin, *Sredniaia Aziia*, I, 364–65.

[24] Quoted in Joseph Castagné, "La Réforme agraire au Turkestan," *Revue des Études Islamiques*, No. 11 (1928), pp. 393–94.

[25] Zel'kina, *Ocherki po agrarnomu voprosu v Srednei Azii*, p. 87; also I. D. Vermenichev, "Ob agrarnoi reforme v Srednei Azii," *Agrarnye Problemy*, No. 2 (November, 1927), p. 64.

The Bolsheviks had these objectives plainly in view as the partial land reform of 1921 was being completed. The Twelfth Congress of Turkestan Soviets now took up the question of carrying the land reform into the predominantly native regions. Delegates complained that the land-and-water issue had not been settled and demanded that state lands now being rented to the peasants and properties belonging to large landowners should be divided among the landless peasantry. One deputy remarked pointedly that where there was no reform there had been no revolution.[26]

The congress declared land reform to be the primary objective of Soviet policy. Noting the growing impoverishment of the poorest peasants, it demanded eventual confiscation of landholdings belonging to beys, to the state, or to religious institutions, and their distribution among the poor.[27] The Soviet government was not yet ready to act. First it had to persuade the peasantry to support a revolutionary redivision of property. Notwithstanding a rash of proreform petitions, many of them the work of local Party committees, which flooded Tashkent after the close of the congress, the Bolsheviks were well aware that the traditional and religious authority of the feudal lords, the beys, and the mullahs was still virtually unbroken. The idea of seizing the land from the rich landowners, or, even worse, of violating endowment properties, was completely alien to the native peasantry. Ties were not only feudal but patriarchal. The bey, the mullah, and the peasant belonged to the same tribe or clan, and often had identical interests. Before reform measures could be initiated, a period of "education" and investigation was necessary. The Bolsheviks needed first to drive wedges into the native community. They also had to prepare leaders and organizers from among the native population, persons who would get a sympathetic hearing from the peasants.

Here the peasant union, the Koshchi, came to the fore.[28] Wedded, from its emergence in 1919, to the cause of land redistribution, it was an ideal instrument for encouraging peasant

[26] Zelenskii, "O zemel'no-vodnoi reforme v Srednei Azii," in Kraskin, *Zemel'no-vodnaia reforma v Srednei Azii*, p. 14.
[27] *Ibid.*
[28] See above, pp. 146–53.

opposition to large landowners. During the land reform of 1921, the Koshchi had been largely responsible for the isolated peasant seizures of property belonging to native landlords in Fergana and Syr-Daria, and it had used the actual shortage of arable land in all parts of Central Asia to encourage the growth, among poorer peasants, of hostility toward the beys. As early as 1921, extensive efforts were undertaken to sow seeds of hatred toward the landlord and to recruit poor and landless peasants, agricultural workers, and herdsmen into the Koshchi. Actual preparation for the direct seizure of the landlords' property was delayed until 1923. The first step was to tighten the ranks of the organization through a gigantic purge which swept out more than 113,000 potential dissenters.[29]

From this point forward land reform became the major issue for the Koshchi. Adopting the slogan of "full utilization of the exploiters' land" and demanding the right to use fallow agricultural lands, the organization began working toward a complete reorganization of landholding. Wherever the Koshchi was able to recruit a mass following strong enough to act on its own, it encouraged the peasants to take the law into their own hands. Seizures of land which occurred during these outbursts enjoyed the tacit approval of the Soviet government; in practice, their permanence depended upon the strength of the movement within the particular region. Since there were no written records of land ownership, the legal right to confiscated acreage rested on the testimony of the local peasantry. Where the Koshchi were strongly entrenched, the landowner had no real chance to protest. In districts frequented by Basmachi bands, and in areas where the landowner had many friends, he was usually able to recover his property by force and often able to inflict bloody retribution upon peasant squatters. Expropriations were successful in districts where class divisions were sharpest and peasant land hunger most acute. Fergana, the center of rural overpopulation in Turkestan, became the focal point of arbitrary land seizures, but the idea spread quickly. Even in Bokhara and Khorezm scattered seizures occurred, and

[29] S. Itsyna, "Bedniatskie organizatsii na Sovetskom Vostoke i ikh zadachi," *Sovetskoe Stroitel'stvo*, Nos. 2–3 (1925), pp. 226–27.

though there were no large-scale expropriations, the demand for a land reform continued to grow among the poorest groups everywhere.

Although the carefully nourished unrest was spreading quickly, the Soviet government still refrained from ordering a full-scale program of agrarian reform in Central Asia. In many districts the structure of local soviet government remained weak, and traditional political and social institutions showed surprising vitality. The peasantry persisted in returning members of "hostile classes" to elective office and often were able to insinuate enemies of the Soviet system into the Bolshevik Party. Tribal and patriarchal exclusiveness gave rise to national frictions, which in turn strengthened tribal and communal solidarity and inhibited the growth of class conflict within the community. Soviet and Party leaders adopted a cautious posture, lest transfers of land and water from one clan to another lead to outbreaks of intertribal warfare.

The completion of the national delimitation in 1924 was the signal for a renewed effort to develop class consciousness among the poor peasantry, and Stalin himself ordered immediate intensification of the campaign for a revolutionary redivision of the land. The Uzbek republic, he pointed out in a message to the First Congress of the Communist Party of Uzbekistan in February, 1925, "can become a powerful force in the Orient only if the condition of the peasants is fundamentally improved and the small tenants are liberated from the bondage of the beys. I have no doubt," he added, "that the Communists of Uzbekistan will not spare their strength for the promotion of these tasks." [30] In response, republican Party and Soviet authorities throughout Central Asia conducted a swift purge of the local soviet apparatus and the Communist Party organizations. Elections to Soviet bodies were held in the fall; where investigation proved them to be "premature"—that is, where anti-Soviet elements had been returned to office—they were run off a second time. The Party also ordered a reexamination of the credentials of Party members in the primary Party or-

[30] Gurevich, "Zemel'no-vodnaia reforma v Uzbekskoi SSR," *Voprosy Istorii*, No. 11 (November, 1948), p. 57.

ganizations and many antiproletarian elements were eliminated.[31]

Simultaneously, the Bolsheviks undertook to weaken the position of the rich and to undermine traditional institutions which
stood in the way of agrarian revolution. One approach to this
problem was through attacking endowment properties. While
the Soviet government abjured the liquidation of the wakf—a
measure which Bolshevik zealots had advocated at the beginning of the twenties[32]—it went on chipping away at the foundations of that institution. In 1922 the Turkestan government
ordered that all rural endowment properties be placed at the
disposition of the peasants and that tenure on them be regulated
by Soviet agrarian law, although endowment properties appertaining to mosques and Moslem educational institutions remained in Moslem possession.[33] The reform was not enforced
consistently. Many rural endowment properties remained in
the hands of their traditional administrators until the actual
land reform. Even then, vineyards and orchards belonging to
cultural and educational institutions or mosques were excluded
from confiscation and retained their previous status until the
period of collectivization.

Soviet treatment of rural endowment property illustrates the
triumph of the practical side of policy over the long-range requirements of Bolshevik doctrine. Tactical considerations,
which influenced Soviet policies toward land reform, required
the attack upon traditional institutions to be made on a level
which would avoid exciting widespread public resistance.

Similar considerations determined the Bolshevik approach to
the problem of encouraging class differentiation and stimulat-
ing class warfare in the villages. Simply stated, the objective
of Soviet planning for land reform in Central Asia was to promote a war over the land between the multitude of poor peasants and the relatively small number of landlords, without harm-

[31] Kraskin, *Zemel'no-vodnaia reforma v Srednei Azii*, p. vii.
[32] For example, see report by Skachko, a delegate from Turkestan, in *Pervyi
S'ezd Narodov Vostoka* (Petrograd, 1920), p. 192.
[33] Decree No. 75 of the Turkestan republic of June 20, 1922; published originally in *Izvestiia TurkTsIK*, No. 143 (July 4, 1922); reproduced in Pavel V.
Gidulianov, *Otdelenie tserkvi ot gosudarstva v SSSR* (Moscow, 1926), p. 278.

ing the interests or exciting the hostility of the small independent farmer, the so-called middle peasant. In Central Asia, the initial, and in some ways the crucial, problem was one of definition. Serfdom and its aftermath had made these distinctions crystal clear in Russia proper, but in Central Asia history had created no sharp lines of demarcation between the rich and middle peasant and between the middle and the poor. Unlike the situation in prerevolutionary Russia, there were no large landlord estates in Central Asia. There were no landowning courtiers representing a special caste, hostile ideologically to, and differentiated culturally from, the mass of the peasantry. The *barin* (nobleman) landlord had never emerged in Central Asia. Large feudal property had disappeared after the Russian conquest and only a few vestiges of it still persisted. Here the large landowner usually came from the village and, culturally and spiritually, was bound up closely with the peasantry. His estate seldom exceeded 110 to 135 acres and in many cases contained no more than 30 acres.[34] Because of this, the task both of "discovering" the bey and of setting the poor peasant against him constituted a difficult problem.[35]

Inevitably, there were differences within the Party regarding the class structure of the Central Asian village. Some extremists, rejecting the entire concept of neutralizing the middle peasantry, insisted that the government classify all peasants possessing more than three acres of land as "large landowners." Compliance with this demand, which was little more than an invitation to renewed civil war, would have made the property of well over half the peasants in Central Asia subject to expropriation. Despite immediate Soviet rejection of this approach, some Koshchi organizations, influenced by local Bolshevik zealots, undertook

[34] Bolshevik writings give evidence that the intuitive approach figured prominently in Soviet determination of who in Central Asia was and who was not a large landowner. Witness Stalin's question to Ikramov at the Fourteenth Party Conference: "And will you explain what a bey is?" The answer: "A bey is a strong kulak. The beys are the stronger owners and they are also usurers and commission agents who were middlemen between Russian capital and the local economy before the revolution." *Chetyrnadtsataia Konferentsiia Rossiiskoi Kommunisticheskoi Partii (bol'shevikov)* (Moscow, 1925), p. 49.

[35] Vermenichev, "Ob agrarnoi reforme v Srednei Azii," *Agrarnye Problemy*, No. 2 (November, 1927), pp. 74–75; also L. I. Dembo, *Zemel'nyi stroi Vostoka* (Leningrad, 1927), p. 102.

to seize the properties of small farmers.[36] Such outbursts were infrequent and in many cases merely provided a convenient disguise for the settlement of village grudges.

Extremism found its exponents in a small group of left-wing Bolsheviks. The deviation toward leniency in regard to the rich peasant was far more common in the republican Party and Soviet councils. In addition to apathy and outright opposition to the idea of land reform, neither of which was uncommon, the rank and file, and even some members of the Party hierarchy, did not understand the political and social implications of Soviet land redistribution. Many believed that land reform was the instrument of a sort of social justice in the rural community, that it would produce an economic leveling in the village conducive to the interests of all yet also destructive of every form of exploitation. Others argued that no reform at all was necessary since the root of rural impoverishment did not lie in the shortage or maldistribution of land but in a shortage of irrigation. The remedy was the expansion of irrigation even if the cost to the government for irrigating one new acre of land was twice that of seizing an acre from the bey and delivering it to his tenant.

While these and similar arguments had no effect on the ultimate Soviet decision to reorganize the agrarian system in Central Asia, their rejection gave emphasis to the real purposes of the reform. The Bolshevik objective was neither equality for all nor the promotion of social harmony. Lenin had castigated such goals long ago as "petit-bourgeois reformism" characteristic of the "viewpoint of the well-wishing official" who seeks to rise above the class struggle. Land redistribution was, on the contrary, a weapon in the hands of the Bolsheviks to be used for deepening and aggravating the class struggle.[37] In turning the peasant against the landlord, the Bolsheviks were not aiming merely to put an end to historically derived inequalities in the countryside; they sought rather to destroy the landlord as a political, economic, and social force in the village. Much as they

[36] Kraskin, *Zemel'no-vodnaia reforma v Srednei Azii*, p. xi.
[37] Ikramov, "Itogi i ocherednye zadachi (doklad po 2-m plenume Ts.K., K.P.(b) Uzbekistana v fevrale 1926 g.)," in *ibid.*, p. 31.

had earlier insisted upon "blowing up" the state so that no vestige of its influence might remain to infect the new government, they now were determined to "blow up" the community, to destroy the very warp and woof of the customary social pattern. The land reform was to be an instrument for cutting the peasant loose from every tie with the past. By destroying every competing authority it sought to make the Soviet system the only source of guidance in the village.

Violent upheaval lay at the root of this concept of land reform, but the Party planned to channel its course so that land redistribution would be carried through with a maximum of effectiveness and a minimum of opposition and of property destruction. It rejected the idea of a "black redistribution," such as had occurred in Russia proper, and proposed an "organized agrarian revolution" from above, set going and controlled at all times by the Soviet state. Not a peasant war against the landlords, but an organized elimination by the Soviet state of every vestige of the "feudal" past—this was the purpose and the method of Soviet agrarian reform in Central Asia.[38]

This, the first large-scale Soviet experiment in carrying out an agrarian revolution from above, was so important that a special commission, attached directly to the Central Committee of the All-Union Communist Party, was appointed to work out its details. Stalin, who had just reached the apex of the Party hierarchy, and Kalinin, chairman of the presidium of the All-Union Central Executive Committee, were among its members.[39] The commission's proposals, presented in October, 1924, defined the nature and extent of the proposed reform and gave detailed instructions for its execution. The Bolshevik organizations in Central Asia were ordered to take immediate steps to eliminate feudal and tribal survivals in land and water use, to seize and distribute among poor and landless peasants the property and equipment of large landed estates, to expropriate farm lands from members of the "large and middle urban bourgeoisie," to seize the acreage of village kulaks in excess of norms

[38] Vermenichev, "Ob agrarnoi reforme v Srednei Azii," *Agrarnye Problemy*, No. 2 (November, 1927), pp. 64–65.

[39] Gurevich, "Zemel'no-vodnaia reforma v Uzbekskoi SSR," *Voprosy Istorii*, No. 11 (November, 1948), pp. 57–58.

permitted by Soviet agrarian law, and to consolidate the holdings of small and landless peasants.[40]

Tactical directives designed to minimize destruction to agricultural property while maximizing the effectiveness of the reform constituted the real genius of the proposals. The very first paragraph directed the republic governments to hold nationalization decrees in abeyance until the harvests were in. Succeeding paragraphs cautioned against attempts to introduce Soviet agrarian law throughout Central Asia at one stroke, and ordered the reform promulgated on a district-by-district basis, the timing to be determined in each case by prior success in "cleansing" and strengthening the local Soviet apparatus and in creating broad peasant support for expropriations. The directives specifically warned against promulgating the reform "from above" by sending outsiders into the village to seize and redistribute land. Such an approach, they pointed out, would not only facilitate evasion of the reform but would endanger the success of the underlying purposes of the reform, the isolation of the rich peasant from the rest of the community.

While this program established the method and extent of the land reform, Party leaders did not regard it as a complete substitute for local initiative. The republic Party and Soviet agencies were also directed to bring the agrarian code of the USSR into conformity with local agricultural peculiarities. The central committee of each national Party organization was to establish a commission, including specialists on agriculture, to work out detailed measures for the execution of the reform. In addition, republic Party organizations were directed to submit monthly progress reports to the Central Committee of the Party's Central Asiatic Bureau in Moscow.

THE AGRARIAN REVOLUTION IN UZBEKISTAN

The instructions of the Central Committee of the Communist Party were published in October, 1925. Scarcely a month later, the Second Congress of the Communist Party of Uzbekistan demanded immediate nationalization of the republic's land and

[40] Text in Zelenskii's report to the plenary session of the Party's Central Asiatic Bureau. See Kraskin, *Zemel'no-vodnaia reforma v Srednei Azii*, pp. 24–27.

water resources and called for a revolutionary redistribution of rural property.[41] At an Extraordinary Session, held at the beginning of December, the Uzbek Central Executive Committee decreed the nationalization of all lands, forests, waters, and natural resources within the confines of the Uzbek SSR. To forestall anticipated evasions of the consequences of nationalization, it also forbade future purchases or sales, exchanges, mortgages, or other transfers of agricultural property.[42] A further decree set the pattern for redistribution of the land.[43]

The bulk of the land fund marked for distribution to the peasants was to come from complete expropriation of the properties of "nonlaboring" households and partial seizure of lands belonging to well-to-do peasants. Absentee landlords and village residents who possessed land without actually working it constituted the "nonlaboring" category. For households engaged directly in farming, the decision depended on the size of the individual holding. This was not uniform for all regions of the republic; depending on the value and productivity of farming land, the norm varied from province to province and from district to district. In Fergana, farms which exceeded 110 acres were considered estates subject to total confiscation, while those between 20 and 110 acres were subject to partial seizure. In Samarkand and Tashkent, however, the Soviet government set similar limits at 135 and 27 acres.

In addition to increments to be acquired from these properties, the government ordered inclusion in the land fund of state-owned lands administered by the republic Commissariat of Agriculture, farm lands belonging to Moslem cultural and educational institutions, agricultural properties in escheat, and lands on which the Soviet government had expended state funds to establish new irrigation works. The bulk of these properties was reserved for distribution among poor and landless peasants —tenant farmers, poor smallholders, and agricultural workers —but local authorities were also ordered to accord special privi-

[41] Gurevich, "Zemel'no-vodnaia reforma v Uzbekskoi SSR," *Voprosy Istorii*, No. 11 (November, 1948), pp. 57–58.

[42] Text reproduced in Kraskin, *Zemel'no-vodnaia reforma v Srednei Azii*, pp. 163–64.

[43] Text in *ibid.*, pp. 165–67.

leges to the families of Red Army men, elected officials, teachers, and government functionaries. The government allowed even small traders and low-ranking Moslem clerics to participate in the redistribution.

Only as the Soviet government enlisted peasant support for the land reform did it take steps to enforce the norms of land confiscation and redistribution. At first it undertook land reform only in the three central provinces of Fergana, Tashkent, and Samarkand, where it had had its best success in promoting class hostility and in establishing a large network of local soviets and Party organizations. In the remaining regions, formerly part of the Bokharan and Khorezmian People's Republics, the influence of traditional leaders and of the patriarchal pattern was still strong and class distinctions were hardly visible. The Soviet regime had not acquired much influence over the poor peasants, and in some areas Basmachi bands were active and military repressions in full swing. In these districts anti-Soviet feeling was so rife that the government postponed the election of local soviets until the beginning of 1926. And even then the electorate often returned anti-Soviet candidates to office. Under these circumstances, the government postponed implementation of the land redistribution until it could first consolidate Soviet authority and then proceed to arouse the poor peasants against the landlords. In the Bokharan oasis (Zeravshan province) the Bolsheviks had to put off the agrarian reform until the end of 1926. In the three outlying provinces of Uzbekistan, Surkhan Daria, Kashka Daria, and Khorezm, where anti-Soviet feeling flourished and Basmachi guerrillas operated into the late 1920's, the Soviet government put the reform into effect only at the beginning of 1929.[44]

Even in the central provinces of Fergana, Tashkent, and Samarkand, promulgation of the agrarian reform was not followed immediately by a redistribution of property. Instead, it marked the beginning of an intensive campaign of proreform propaganda, into which the Bolsheviks threw all their resources. Local soviets, Party agencies, and Koshchi organizations cho-

[44] Gurevich, "Zemel'no-vodnaia reforma v Uzbekskoi SSR," *Voprosy Istorii*, No. 11 (November, 1948), p. 59.

rused demands for an early seizure of the landlords' land and organized the peasants in preparation for it. The rural areas were deluged with posters and pamphlets. Agitators, usually in groups of fives, and often accompanied by native musicians and singers, traveled from village to village, stirring up smallholders, farm hands, and share croppers, and organizing "spontaneous" demonstrations of poor peasants against the landlords. The president of the Uzbek republic, with other commissars, stumped the countryside. Along less flamboyant lines, Bolshevik organizers convoked peasant village assemblies to explain the scope and method of the reform. They also called regional conferences of share croppers and poor peasants, at which Party and Soviet leaders delivered inflammatory speeches on the reform.[45]

Throughout the propaganda campaign, the Bolsheviks showed a particular deference to religious traditions, most strongly rooted in the villages. The agitators avoided any display of antireligious sentiment and constantly cited Islamic law and tradition in support of redistribution. Government proclamations quoted chapter and verse from the Koran and other sacred books of Islam to prove that the owner must himself till his land, and, if he was unable to do so, he must renounce his land in favor of him who was able.

Hence [reads a proclamation] the measures directed by the Soviet government toward supplying the landless peasants with surplus lands and toward freeing the serfs from age-long humiliation and bondage—such measures shall never be unlawful according to the Islamic religion.[46]

To reinforce the appeal, a corps of Moslem devouts who approved the land reform was organized and dispatched to the countryside. Other sympathetic Moslems were set to work grinding out reams of pro-Soviet literature, including one pointed

---

[45] *Ibid.*, p. 65; also Vorobeichikov and Gafiz, "Kak prokhodila zem-reforma v Uzbekistan," in Kraskin, *Zemel'no-vodnaia reforma v Srednei Azii*, pp. 52, 88–89.

[46] Quoted in Joshua Kunitz, *Dawn over Samarkand: The Rebirth of Central Asia* (New York, 1935), p. 190.

question-and-answer series purporting to prove conclusively that the land belonged to those who tilled it.[47]

The agitational campaign was effective among the poorest peasant groups, and many poor peasants and agricultural workers took an active part in the promulgation of the reform. The middle group was divided and to some extent took the side of the large landowners. Many in this group feared that a campaign to seize their own lands and equipment would follow on the heels of the expropriation of the beys. This fear was stimulated by extremist demands for the seizure of holdings above three acres, and considerable agitation was required to overcome the resistance of the middle peasantry. In reality, the determination of the extent of confiscation was based on the rent structure rather than upon an arbitrary acreage. The line between the well-to-do and middle peasants was drawn on the basis of statistics which showed the point at which farmers customarily began to rent out parcels of their land. In most cases, farms in excess of 15 to 30 acres, depending upon local conditions, fell into the well-to-do category.[48]

While all agencies and organizations which supported the Soviet system took part in the preparatory phases of the reform, its actual execution was concentrated in the hands of land-and-water commissions, headed by a central commission which had been created by the republic Central Executive Committee in December, 1925.[49] It was responsible for directing the execution of the reform, organizing regional commissions, determining the manner in which the reform was to be introduced, establishing

[47] Vorobeichikov and Gafiz, "Kak prokhodila zem-reforma v Uzbekistan," in Kraskin, *Zemel'no-vodnaia reforma v Srednei Azii,* pp. 65–72. So bitter became the hostility between Moslems who supported the reform and those who opposed it that it created a schism in the religious groups. According to the claims of Soviet observers, the dispute even planted the seeds of doubt in the minds of believers and encouraged apostasy in some localities. *Ibid.,* pp. 71–72.

[48] For an explanation of the procedures followed by the Bolsheviks in determining the line between the large and middle peasant as well as the data on which the division was based, see *Vtoroi Vseuzbekskii S'ezd Sovetov Rabochikh, Dekhkanskikh i Krasnoarmeiskikh Deputatov Uzbekskoi Sovetskoi Sotsialisticheskoi Respubliki* (Samarkand, 1927), pp. 222–25.

[49] Text of the decree in Kraskin, *Zemel'no-vodnaia reforma v Srednei Azii,* pp. 168–71.

norms for the division of the land, distributing credit, and mediating disputes between regional commissions. Below it were regional commissions for the individual provinces. These agencies were to adjudicate disputes between districts, collect and distribute agricultural equipment and farming implements, issue deeds to property, and guide, instruct, and coordinate the activities of lower agencies. Among the latter agencies, district commissions, organized by decree of the responsible regional commission, were primarily concerned with agitation, while the county commissions were the actual instruments for carrying out the reform on the local level.

The commissions consisted almost exclusively of Party members, totaling over 1,200 members or 80 percent of the total Party membership. The overwhelming majority were city dwellers, many of them European in origin, who were dispatched to the localities only for the duration of the reform.[50] The very manner in which the commissions were constituted thus revealed anew the inherent Bolshevik distrust of the peasant. Despite careful cultivation of the seeds of class conflict in the village and despite propaganda campaigns for land redistribution extending over several years, the Soviet regime still doubted the capacity or willingness of the peasants to put into effect the principles of the reform without close and unremitting proletarian "leadership."

To the peasantry the packing of the commissions with city folk made the reform appear as a proletarian raid against the countryside and underscored the fact that the reform was being imposed without regard to the self-determined desires of the rural population. The weaknesses of the reform apparatus were recognized by the Bolsheviks, who set about enlisting peasant cooperation by creating local "committees of assistance" from among the peasant population. In nearly every village government-summoned assemblies of the poor selected ten-to-fifteen-member commissions of share croppers, agricultural workers, and in some cases middle peasants. Lacking administrative au-

---

[50] Ikramov, "Itogi i ocherednye zadachi," in *ibid.*, p. 33; also Gurevich, "Zemel'no-vodnaia reforma v Uzbekskoi SSR," *Voprosy Istorii*, No. 11 (November, 1948), p. 65.

thority of their own and operating under the supervision of the county land commissions, the "committees of assistance" drew up lists of local nontoiling households, their landholdings and agricultural equipment, and sometimes took part in the expropriation proceedings.[51] The commissions were organized most quickly and easily in Fergana, while in Tashkent and Samarkand the peasants of many localities refused to participate.[52]

Peasant resistance nevertheless failed to slow down the momentum of the movement. The Bolshevik strategists had timed the formation of the land-and-water commissions and of the peasant committees to climax the final propaganda onslaught, and they now pressed forward with the expropriations. The first step was liquidation of "nontoiling" households. By December 15, 1925, the Soviet government had driven the owners of farms exceeding 110 acres in Fergana and 135 acres in Tashkent and Samarkand from their properties and had completed the sequestration of their land, livestock, and agricultural equipment. Next to fall victim to government seizure were the lands of traders and absentee landowners whose holdings exceeded 10 acres. By January 1, 1925, this phase of the confiscation program was over, and the land commissions proceeded step by step to deprive resident peasants of holdings in excess of norms permitted by Soviet agrarian law.[53]

Through careful organization and intensive preparation, the Soviet regime had succeeded so well in isolating from their com-

[51] The Committees of Assistance, which operated in Uzbek villages during the land reform, appear to have been modeled closely upon the famous "Committees of the Poor" which served the Soviet government so well at the height of the revolution and civil war. Like the Committees of the Poor, the Committees of Assistance were used to ferret out hidden agricultural supplies and equipment and to assist the government in confiscating them. They also fulfilled the function of organizing poor peasants for participation in the reform and of disseminating propaganda on the village level. For explanation of the tasks of the Committees of Assistance, see Vorobeichikov and Gafiz, "Kak prokhodila zem-reforma v Uzbekistan," in Kraskin, *Zemel'no-vodnaia reforma v Srednei Azii,* p. 55. A brief description of the Committees of the Poor is included in Andrei Y. Vyshinsky, *The Law of the Soviet State* (New York, 1948), p. 440.

[52] Kraskin, *Zemel'no-vodnaia reforma v Srednei Azii,* pp. 33–34, 90.

[53] Vorobeichikov and Gafiz, "Kak prokhodila zem-reforma v Uzbekistan," in *ibid.,* pp. 58–69; Gurevich, "Zemel'no-vodnaia reforma v Uzbekskoi SSR," *Voprosy Istorii,* No. 11 (November, 1948), pp. 60–61; report of Ikramov in *Vtoroi Vseuzbekskii S'ezd Sovetov,* p. 222.

munities groups marked for expropriation that the program of land seizure was carried out almost without incident. In most localities armed opposition was hopeless, but the landowners, forewarned by prolonged and intensive Soviet preparation for the reform, adopted subtle tactics of resistance. Attempts to evade the effects of the reform were widespread, took numerous forms, and were often successful. Some property owners sought to forestall expropriation by dividing their estates among sons, relatives, and other persons. Others divided portions of their land voluntarily among share croppers and poor peasants in order to create opposition to the reform and avoid total expropriation. Still others hid their livestock and agricultural equipment. Some landholders ceased renting land to share croppers so that they could claim to be working it themselves. Others sold agricultural equipment to poor peasants at low prices in order to salvage something. A few even attempted to distribute their properties among share croppers on condition that the latter return them after the reform had been completed.[54]

In some localities, opposition retarded the progress of the expropriations and reduced somewhat the size of the land fund which accrued to the state. Such losses notwithstanding, the government managed to create a fund of 580,864 acres for distribution among poor peasants. In the three central provinces—Samarkand, Tashkent, and Fergana—and in Zeravshan, where the reform was promulgated a year later, some 117,339 acres were seized from 594 landlord households. The government likewise expropriated 3,302 acres from large traders, 154,950 acres from households with land in excess of the legal norm, and 91,343 acres from urban dwellers. In addition, 74,139 acres accrued from state lands, endowment property, and socialized land, 11,512 from property in escheat, and 128,301 from other

[54] Kraskin, Zemel'no-vodnaia reforma v Srednei Azii, pp. 33–34, 56–57, 72–74. Opposition to the land reform was not confined solely to the property owners of Central Asia. Considerable friction also developed within official Soviet circles. In particular, Party cells and Koshchi organizations on the local level tended to hang back. Official reports from Samarkand indicated that more than 20 percent of the volost' executive committees and village soviets took no active part in the execution of the reform and in many cases these agencies sought to hinder it. See Vorobeichikov and Gafiz, "Kak prokhodila zem-reforma v Uzbekistan," in ibid., pp. 117–19.

sources. In all, some 25,216 households were affected adversely by the land reform.[55]

The beneficiaries of this fund were 66,000 small and landless households.[56] The first to secure land were the numerous tenant farmers. Members of this group received outright the plowlands which they had worked prior to the reform. The next share went to the hired hands. What remained was assigned to tenants whose original holdings were below the norms established for the given locality. Smallholders who already owned land but did not also work on shares did not participate in the redistribution[57] but, instead, received preference in the allotment of newly irrigated land. Newly settled households received the additional benefit of long-term credits for the purchase of cattle, farm implements, seed, and building equipment, which the state had obtained through confiscation and through a fund of 10,000,000 rubles set aside in the budget for this purpose.[58]

The consequences of the reform, in terms of altering the structure of land tenure, were relatively slight. Although Soviet investigators claimed that postreform households were almost universally in the middle peasant group, the agricultural census of 1927 showed that the average household possessed only eight acres of land and slightly less than one draft animal. With this figure as a basis for determining the middle household, the data in comparison with statistics gathered in 1924 showed an increase of 10 percent in the number of households in this class, an increase of 14.5 percent in their planted area, and 17.8 percent in the number of draft animals owned by them. On the other hand, the percentage of landless peasants had declined from 4.3 to 0.5 percent and the number of very small holdings

---

[55] From report of Ikramov in *Vtoroi Vseuzbekskii S'ezd Sovetov*, p. 223; see also Zel'kina, "Zemel'naia reforma v Srednei Azii," *Revoliutsionnyi Vostok*, No. 3 (1927), p. 159.

[56] The second major phase of the land reform which took place in 1929 resulted in the distribution of over 108,000 additional acres of land to 13,000 poor households in Surkhan Daria, Kashka Daria, and Khorezm provinces. The net consequence of the whole reform was the distribution of nearly 690,000 acres of land to more than 79,000 peasant households. Gurevich, "Zemel'no-vodnaia reforma v Uzbekskoi SSR," *Voprosy Istorii*, No. 11 (November, 1948), pp. 61–62.

[57] Kraskin, *Zemel'no-vodnaia reforma v Srednei Azii*, pp. 60–61.

[58] Gurevich, "Zemel'no-vodnaia reforma v Uzbekskoi SSR," *Voprosy Istorii*, No. 11 (November, 1948), p. 62.

(those possessing three acres or less) from 38.1 to 34.3 percent. The group of those owning three to eight acres, conversely, had increased by 7 percent, and those owning eight to 24 acres by 3 percent.[59] While actual landlessness had all but disappeared in the rural areas, few peasants came out of the reform strong enough to subsist without further aid from the state.

THE LAND REFORM IN TURKMENIA

The land reform in Turkmenia followed much the same lines as in Uzbekistan, apart from a number of distinctive features resulting from special forms of land tenure peculiar to the Turcoman tribes. As in Uzbekistan, the Soviet government had first introduced Soviet agrarian legislation considerably in advance of the actual land reform. The First Congress of Soviets of the Transcaspian region, which convened in 1920 soon after the civil war had ended, recommended, and the regional Executive Committee decreed, the nationalization of the land, the transfer to the regional water department of authority to distribute water among districts and villages, and the outlawing of the purchase and sale of land and water.[60]

The most revolutionary aspects of the decree were the extension of the right to land-and-water allotments to male peasants who had reached their sixteenth birthday and the abolition of feudal estates (*miulk*). The former provision was intended to do away with the traditional practice of restricting land-and-water rights to married peasants. The goal of the latter was abolition of the remnants of "feudalism" in the rural areas of Transcaspia. However, further provision that the confiscated properties be transferred to village communes for distribution among poor and landless peasants might actually have strengthened the existing system of communal land tenure, which also was an object of Soviet suspicion. In practice, however, none of the provisions had any real effect upon land relations in the region, since the government made no effort to enforce compliance with its decree. Adoption of the New Economic Policy in 1921 postponed indefinitely plans to promote an agrarian revo-

[59] From data in *Vtoroi Vseuzbekskii S'ezd Sovetov*, pp. 221–24; Zel'kina, "Zemel'naia reforma v Srednei Azii," *Revoliutsionnyi Vostok*, No. 3 (1927), p. 162.

[60] E. L. Shteinberg, *Ocherki istorii Turkmenii* (Moscow, 1934), pp. 114–15.

lution, and the government did not revive them until completion of the national delimitation of Central Asia.

In 1925, upon the issuance of the general directive of the Central Committee of the Communist Party, a congress of secretaries of the Communist Party organizations of Turkmenistan voted to proceed immediately to nationalize rural landholdings. The congress attacked particularly the traditional forms of land-and-water tenure based on communal forms of land ownership and on customary procedures of allotment for use. Land-and-water rights, it declared, should be granted solely and inalienably to toiling peasants.[61]

Following the decisions of the congress, the Turcoman Council of People's Commissars proceeded to vest the ownership of rural property in the agricultural toilers of Turkmenia. The new regulation, issued by the Soviet government of Turkmenia on September 24, 1925,[62] ordered government confiscation of agricultural land belonging to merchants, absentee owners, Moslem clergymen, herdsmen, and others who did not cultivate their possessions by means of their own labor. The act not only reaffirmed the previous Soviet abolition of feudal property (*miulk*) but ordered the liquidation of endowment property. In a blow aimed at the very foundation of the tribal commune, it annulled the *sanachik* (communal land tenure with periodic repartition) and directed specifically that confiscated land be transferred to the peasants as individuals rather than as members of the community.

As in Uzbekistan, the extent of the reform in Turkmenia was limited. Only in the Merv and Poltoratsk districts did the Soviet government undertake a full-scale redistribution. In Bairam Ali, the reform was restricted to a distribution of state-owned lands among landless peasants, while in those regions of Turkmenia which had constituted part of the republics of Bokhara and Khorezm, political factors led the government to postpone all action.[63] Turkmenian practice also followed that of Uzbekistan in the creation of central, okrug, and district land-and-

---

[61] Zelenskii, "O zemel'no-vodnaia reforma v Srednei Azii," in Kraskin, *Zemel'no-vodnaia reforma v Srednei Azii*, p. 10.

[62] Text in *ibid.*, pp. 179–80.

[63] Castagné, "La Réforme agraire au Turkestan," *Revue des Études Islamiques*, No. 11 (1928), pp. 396–97.

water commissions to execute the provisions of the decree on land redistribution.[64] Instead of peasant "committees of assistance," the government organized village land commissions, each composed of three peasants selected at a meeting of the village assembly.[65] The overt function of these committees, which operated under the supervision of district land-and-water commissions, was to lead the village proletarians and peasants in carrying out the reform. Their real purpose was to develop a center of opposition to the tribal commune within the commune itself and, in Soviet terms, to convert the reform into a "class struggle" between the tribal leaders and the bulk of the peasantry.

Except in a few localities where the commune was already in a state of decay, this was a most difficult assignment. The Bolsheviks of Turkmenia had to cope not only with the absence of a social and cultural gulf between tribal elders and rank-and-file peasants but also with a real paucity of exploitable factors of economic inequality in the village. Land, in most cases, was the property of tribes, not of individuals, and inequality was an inequality of groups rather than of individuals. Tribal units which had settled the land first laid claim to the best land and asserted the right to special privileges in water use. Because they protected the interests of the clan as a whole, tribal leaders were more strongly entrenched than were the landowners of Uzbekistan, and they had a stronger grip on the loyalties of the people. At election time Turcoman peasants persisted in returning their traditional leaders to office, and even local Party members habitually consulted them before acting upon Party directives.

Soviet determination to utilize land reform as a bludgeon to impose a system resembling private property in land not only incurred the wrath of the customary leaders but often provoked the organized resistance of the commune. Particularly furious outbursts occurred in districts where the government ordered the transfer to one tribe of lands which had belonged to another.[66] Even in districts where no such transfers were contem-

---

[64] Text of ordinance in Kraskin, *Zemel'no-vodnaia reforma v Srednei Azii*, pp. 181–84.

[65] *Ibid.*, p. 152.

[66] *Ibid.*, p. 154.

plated, tribal elders succeeded in converting the reform into a struggle for consolidating the clan and promoted the development of intertribal frictions. Overleaping the boundaries of the commune itself, the struggle raged through the councils of the village soviets, the Koshchi, and even the Party organizations. So successful were the tribal maneuvers that they nearly compelled the Bolsheviks to reexamine the whole agrarian question in the region. Almost a year passed before Soviet agitators were able to convert the struggle between tribes into a struggle for land within the individual tribal unit.[67]

The actual division of the land took place between 1925 and 1927. For the purpose of determining the extent of postreform land tenure the Turcoman government fixed the maximum norms of land at seven acres per household in Poltoratsk and 13.5 acres in Merv.[68] As a result of the redistribution of property, 32,777 new farms were created, 10,056 of them belonging to formerly landless peasants and 22,721 to small peasants. At the same time, 2,289 households were driven from the land entirely, and the farms of 15,271 others were diminished in size.[69] Of greater importance, the reform put an end to tribal property in land and water and in so doing destroyed the tribal commune. It also ended the division of the land into *miulk* and *sanachik*, and by guaranteeing each household one share of contiguous farming property it abolished farming on scattered strips. By enforcing the principle of land utilization by the toilers, the Soviet regime removed the burden of bride price which customary marriage laws had imposed on the poorest peasants.[70]

Completion of land redivision in the two regions of Turkmenia and the four central agricultural regions of Uzbekistan brought to a close the first stage of the land reform in Central

---

[67] Shteinberg, *Ocherki istorii Turkmenii*, pp. 117–18; Castagné, "La Réforme agraire au Turkestan," *Revue des Études Islamiques*, No. 11 (1928), pp. 394–95.

[68] As in Uzbekistan, the norms of allowable land ownership were based upon the fertility of the soil and the pressure of rural overpopulation within individual districts. Kraskin, *Zemel'no-vodnaia reforma v Srednei Azii*, p. iv; Castagné, "La Réforme agraire au Turkestan," *Revue des Études Islamiques*, No. 11 (1928), pp. 369–70.

[69] From data in Nemchenko, "Agrarnaia reforma v Turkmenii," *Novyi Vostok*, No. 19 (1927), p. 139.

[70] Kraskin, *Zemel'no-vodnaia reforma v Srednei Azii*, pp. 154–56.

Asia. A second phase opened in 1927 in those provinces which the Bolsheviks had considered politically unripe during the initial period of reform. Although the reform was not completed in the most remote regions until 1929, one year after the campaign for collectivization had begun in Russia, it was a repetition, in methods and consequences, of the earlier reform. In their total impact, the changes which the agrarian reform had wrought in the rural communities of Central Asia were considerably more profound than those produced by the October Revolution itself. The revolution had destroyed one set of political institutions and created another to replace them. But its shocks, concentrated at the higher levels of government, were only dimly perceived in the villages. The land reform, bent upon destruction of the very social and economic institutions which undergirded traditional Moslem society, shook the rural community to its roots.

In this sense, the reform served effectively its principal purpose as a weapon of class struggle in the countryside. The Bolsheviks used every weapon to promote and intensify this aspect of the reform in order to encourage what Rykov called the "October Revolution" in Central Asia.[71] The land reform became exactly this—an October Revolution executed according to a precise plan and completed at a precise rate of progress. By destroying customary categories of land tenure, it eliminated semifeudal conditions in the rural areas and destroyed the traditional foundations of village unity.[72] It did not, however, destroy "capitalistic" elements in the village.[73] These, personified in the independent smallholder, continued to exist until the collectivization drive put an end to the independent farmers.

Whether the reform benefited the peasant immediately or ultimately remains an open question. Certainly, as Soviet publicists have pointed out repeatedly, it put an end to the renting of land, freeing the poor peasants of payments aggregating from

[71] Quoted by Ikramov in his report on land reform before the Second Uzbek Congress of Soviets. *Vtoroi Vseuzbekskii S'ezd Sovetov,* p. 226.

[72] V. Lavrent'ev, "Aziia 'inorodtsev' i Aziia sovetskikh sotsialisticheskikh respublik," *Planovoe Khoziaistvo,* No. 11 (November, 1927), p. 205.

[73] Ikramov's report in *Vtoroi Vseuzbekskii S'ezd Sovetov,* p. 227.

25 to 28 million rubles a year.[74] In the three central regions of Uzbekistan, the number of households which rented land dropped from 42.5 percent to 5.6 percent after the reform. Another consequence was a rapid increase in the area under cultivation and a wider distribution of draft animals and agricultural equipment.[75]

Such positive factors notwithstanding, the reform failed to satisfy the land hunger of the poor peasants. In the Uzbek regions, for example, only 22 percent of the needy households received land as a result of the reform.[76] The small size of the land fund seized from the landowners, as well as the scarcity of newly irrigated lands, compelled the government to reduce drastically the size of allotments below that originally projected. While the Soviet regime had expected to distribute land parcels of seven to thirteen and one-half acres, it actually was able to pass out shares ranging only from one and one-fourth to six acres.[77] Instead of improving the lot of the peasantry, the breaking up of large farms into small plots tended to increase the number of needy smallholders. Thus the land reform increased the proportion of smallholders incapable of self-support.[78]

The Bolsheviks nevertheless advanced their goal of promoting equality in the countryside. The agrarian reform in Central Asia was a part of the larger process of social leveling up and leveling down, of destroying the advantages and privileges

[74] A. Khavin, *Sotsialisticheskaia industrializatsiia natsional'nykh respublik i oblastei* (Moscow, 1933), p. 79.

[75] Gurevich, "Zemel'no-vodnaia reforma v Uzbekskoi SSR," *Voprosy Istorii*, No. 11 (November, 1948), p. 68.

[76] *Ibid.*, p. 62.

[77] Mustapha Chokaiev, "Turkestan and the Soviet Regime," *Journal of the Royal Central Asian Society*, XVIII (1931), 415.

[78] Another disability placed upon the peasant grew out of the legal regime which came into being with the land reform. Although the Soviet government deeded land shares over to the peasants in property, it compromised seriously the uses to which this property might be put. While the peasant possessed the right to transfer title to his share to his descendants and could lease it to another for a specified period under certain circumstances, he could not legally purchase new land or sell or mortgage his allotment. Both Uzbekistan and Turkmenia had adopted agrarian codes which were modeled closely on the agrarian code of December 1, 1922, of the RSFSR, and these governed peasant use of the land. For a discussion of the latter code, see N. D. Kazantsev (ed.), *Zemel'noe Pravo* (Moscow, 1949), pp. 70–78.

which had often accrued to one segment of society at the expense of others. The fact that the application of this process to rural Central Asia could not also guarantee greater security to the peasant, either as an individual or as a member of the community, was due to conditions which it was largely beyond the ability of the Soviet regime to alter. The major problem was an extreme rural overpopulation arising principally from an acute shortage of arable land. The government could neither expand the land fund rapidly through new irrigation works nor create a local industrial base large enough to siphon off excess rural population in sufficient numbers to relieve the pressure. Leveling up and leveling down, however desirable as a Soviet social goal, thus amounted in practice to a leveling of all into poverty and dependence.

That too served a purpose. In the economic field the Soviet government used peasant dependence on public support to enforce increased sowing of cotton. Politically, the government used it in the 1920's to strengthen peasant loyalty to the soviet system and in the 1930's to compel these same peasants to enroll in collective farms.

IX

THE REVOLUTION
IN CULTURE

◆

THE LATE Sir John Maynard once observed that half the causes of the Russian Revolution resided in the policy of the Tsars toward their non-Great Russian subjects. Certainly the sentiment of Great Russian national chauvinism which flourished under Alexander III and Nicholas II aggravated the national disunity which afflicted the Empire during its latter years. The disastrous consequences of this policy stood as a warning to the Soviet government against the compulsory assimilation of non-Russian peoples to the dominant Great Russian culture. To be sure, sentiments of Great Russian cultural superiority survived the revolution but Bolshevik leaders condemned their overt expression. Their philosophy was broad enough to find room for cultural-national diversity within the greater unity to be created in the process of "building socialism."

Prior to the Bolshevik seizure of power, Russian Marxists had reserved some of their severest criticism for proponents of a federal structure based on national autonomy. Lenin had repeatedly condemned national-cultural autonomy in those days as "the most pernicious nationalism." [1] And Stalin, who had had personal experience in Transcaucasia, had warned that it would deliver the masses "to the mercy of reactionary mullahs." [2] Len-

[1] V. I. Lenin, *Natsional'nyi vopros* (Moscow, 1936), p. 64.
[2] From Stalin's essay, *Marxism and the National Question,* written in 1913. J. V. Stalin, *Sochineniia* (Moscow, 1946—), II, 351.

in's prerevolutionary rejection of national-cultural autonomy had served as a stout ideological weapon in his bitter struggles against the Bundists and the Ukrainians and in his polemics against the Austrian Marxists. For Lenin, national culture had no positive values. If anything, it constituted a betrayal of proletarian internationalism, since it tended to strengthen the ties between the bourgeois and working classes of the individual nationalities. The interests of the working classes, on the other hand, required a fusion of the workers of all nationalities into unified proletarian organizations capable of opposing the bourgeoisie of every nation.

Lenin assumed the existence of two nations within every nationality, one of them a nation of toilers, the other a nation of landlords and bourgeoisie. The two, he insisted, were separated by an unbridgeable ideological and cultural gulf.

There are two national cultures in every national culture. There is the Great Russian national culture of the Purishkeviches, the Guchkovs, and the Struves, but there is also a Great Russian culture which is characterized by the names of Chernyshevskii and Plekhanov. There are likewise the very same two cultures among the Ukrainians, in Germany, France, among the Jews, and so on.[3]

In prerevolutionary Russia, groaning under the rule of the bourgeoisie and the landlords, national culture, he argued, usually meant the culture of the landlords, the priests, and the bourgeoisie. To this culture Lenin opposed "An International Culture of Democracy and the World Workers' Movement," consisting of the democratic and socialistic elements in every national culture.[4]

Lenin's rejection of cultural autonomy as a form of national relations within a bourgeois-dominated state did not mean that he also rejected it in a socialist setting. The initial efforts of Bolshevik leaders to create within the Soviet state a structure of government expressing national diversities within the larger context of "proletarian" or Communist Party unity caused some consternation and considerable confusion within Party ranks. Certain Bolsheviks, perceiving the dawn of a socialist era, de-

[3] Lenin, *Natsional'nyi vopros,* pp. 75–76.
[4] *Ibid.,* p. 76.

manded the immediate dying out of nations and of national differences. "One Language, One Culture"—a slogan which Lenin had rejected in 1913—again became popular and again met the opposition of Party leaders. Others, aware of the Party's practical refusal of the right of separation to peoples who could not win it by force of arms, sought to revive and reinterpret the old slogan of national-cultural autonomy. At the Tenth Party Congress, Safarov presented such a formula. In affirmation of Stalin's earlier reservation of the right of self-determination to the toilers, he asked Bolshevik support for the "national-cultural self-determination" of the toiling masses among the backward nationalities.[5] Although the key to Safarov's proposal resided in the differentiation of the culture of the poor from that of the rich, Stalin himself opposed it on the ground that it was a "Bundist formulation" of the problem.[6]

The idea of national culture, it should be observed, was no longer repugnant to the Party. Stalin based his rejection of Safarov's formula primarily on its revival of the embarrassing slogan of self-determination. The concept of cultural autonomy which was central to it, however, was carried forward and later elaborated in Stalin's famous slogan, "Proletarian in Content, National in Form." Speaking before the graduating class at the Communist University of the Toilers of the East in 1925, Stalin pointed out that

proletarian culture does not abolish national culture but gives it content. And on the contrary, national culture does not abolish proletarian culture but gives it form. The slogan of national culture was a bourgeois slogan when the bourgeoisie was in power, and the consolidation of nationalities took place under the aegis of the bourgeois order. The slogan of national culture became a proletarian slogan when the working class came into power and the consolidation of nationalities began to take place under the aegis of the Soviet power.[7]

Freedom to develop nationally combined with guidance from the center constituted the essence of cultural autonomy as de-

[5] *Protokoly s'ezdov i konferentsii Vsesoiuznoi Kommunisticheskoi Partii (b): Desiatyi S'ezd R.K.P.(b), mart 1921 g.* (Moscow, 1933), pp. 203–4.
[6] *Ibid.,* p. 216.
[7] Stalin, *Sochineniia,* VII, 138.

fined by Communist leaders. The key to the slogan lay in the "proletarian content" which, reduced to practice, meant little more than the use of national languages to propagate the teachings of Marxism-Leninism among the toilers of all nationalities.[8] As one Soviet writer put it,

The struggle of the classes in culture finds expression in the struggle between national and international culture, between the national community and the class community which ends in the victory of the latter only in a socialist society, in which the elements of international culture become the ruling culture of society, in which "the community of the class idea embraces the whole of society." [9]

The goal was clearly ideological integration, not uniformity in the use of language or in the external details of life. In other words, unlike the Tsars who attempted to extinguish alien cultures by destroying languages, the Bolsheviks undertook to use these languages to imbue all peoples with the principles of the international culture of Bolshevism. Hence, they sought to develop national languages as the shortest way to infuse the masses of all nations with Bolshevik principles and to promote a "cultural revolution" throughout the USSR.

SOVIET EDUCATION: THE THIRD FRONT
OF THE PROLETARIAN DICTATORSHIP

The basis of this revolution lay in a prolonged process of education and reeducation of the masses; its goals were the destruction of the customary ideological structure of society and the remolding of the minds of men on a gigantic scale. All education in the Soviet state, as Lunacharskii, the first Commissar of Education, declared at the Tenth Party Congress, could be "only Communist and no other," and all science and all art, indeed, all modes of human expression, must be "imbued with a Communist spirit." [10] In pursuing this aim, the Bolsheviks inevitably began to equate men with other forms of raw material, as objects devoid of innate personality and individuality. Like other raw

[8] For a concise Soviet statement to this effect, see Ia. Mushpert and E. Fainberg, *Komsomol i molodezh' natsional'nykh men'shinstv* (Moscow, 1926), pp. 6–8.

[9] V. Vaganian, *O natsional'noi kul'ture* (Moscow, 1927), p. 22.

[10] *Desiatyi S'ezd R.K.P.(b)*, p. 157.

materials, they could be shaped to fit the needs of Soviet society. Ideological training and retraining through constant propaganda and agitation could forge a "new man" freed from "bourgeois" prejudices and thus capable of creating a Communist society.

No one realized better than Lenin that education is a total process. All institutions of Soviet society were expected to participate in the broad program of reshaping human values. But, from the outset of Bolshevik rule, the special agency of cultural reformation was the Soviet educational system. Conceding primacy only to the Bolshevik Party and the Soviet apparatus of government in the task of developing a new way of life in the Soviet republic, Lunacharskii boldly called it "the third front" of the proletarian dictatorship.[11]

Immediately after the Bolshevik seizure of power, the Soviet regime began its efforts to remold the educational system. Its primary goals were the elimination of illiteracy, the introduction of universal compulsory instruction, the separation of church and school, and the organization of a system of adult education. In 1918 the Fifth Congress of Soviets proclaimed the principle of free and equal access to educational facilities for the workers and poorest peasants, in Article 17 of the first constitution of the RSFSR. It also eliminated prerevolutionary restrictions based on sex, race, or nationality,[12] thereby laying the legal foundation for developing state-supported systems of education for the national minorities of the RSFSR.

Soviet efforts to extend educational opportunities to the non-Russian peoples date from May, 1918, when the Commissariat for National Affairs created a cultural and educational commission to be responsible for all curricular and extracurricular affairs among the non-Russian populations. Serving as an intermediary between the Commissariat for National Affairs and the Commissariat for Education, the commission expended more than 56,000,000 rubles for educational purposes during the second half of 1918. It undertook the publication of textbooks

[11] *Ibid.*, p. 156.
[12] Andrei Y. Vyshinsky, *The Law of the Soviet State* (New York, 1948), pp. 582–83.

in twelve different languages and established informal educational centers in thirteen national regions. The Commissariat of Education, jointly with the Commissariat for National Affairs, began forming divisions of education for the national minorities on the provincial, regional, and district levels; these divisions were to organize schools and other cultural and educational institutions for various national groups, as well as exercising direct control over their curricula.[13]

In this preparatory stage, few Soviet schools were actually opened in the non-Russian regions. The educational rights of non-Russian peoples were not clearly defined until after the creation of a Department of Education for National Minorities within the Commissariat of Education in late 1918 and until a decree of the Soviet government authorized all nationalities in the RSFSR to organize courses of study in their own languages, both in the unified labor schools and in the higher schools. The decree also ordered the opening of schools for national minorities in all districts where twenty-five or more pupils of a given age group resided. Instruction in the native language was guaranteed, although pupils were also required to study the language of the majority in the region, which in most cases was Russian.[14]

Although civil war conditions seriously hindered Soviet efforts to implement the provisions of the decree, its enactment was indicative of increasing government interest in the development of a broadly based educational system in non-Russian republics and regions. The program of the Communist Party, adopted at the Eighth Congress in March, 1919, called for transformation of the school "from an instrument of the class domination of the bourgeoisie into an instrument for the complete suppression of the division of society into classes, into an instrument for the Communist regeneration of society." As a militant molder of Soviet culture, the school was expected to participate actively

[13] I. I., "Delo prosveshcheniia natsional'nykh men'shinstv," Zhizn' Natsional'-nostei, No. 6 (December 15, 1918); also N. Mansvetov, "Velikaia Oktiabr'skaia Sotsialisticheskaia Revoliutsiia i sozdanie Narodnogo Komissariata po Delam Natsional'nostei," Voprosy Istorii, No. 8 (August, 1949), pp. 23–24.

[14] G. Mansurov, Za kul'turnoe stroitel'stvo natsional'nostei (Moscow, 1927), pp. 16–17.

both in "rearing a generation capable of achieving Communism" and in extending and deepening the "ideological, organizational, and educational influence" of the proletariat over semiproletarian and nonproletarian elements in the population.[15]

Although the Party program did not deal specifically with the development of a Soviet educational system in the non-Russian regions of the Soviet state, its adoption brought this problem to the fore. Writing in *Zhizn' Natsional'nostei,* Stalin insisted that elimination of "cultural limitedness and social backwardness" among the borderland peoples was a fundamental task of the Soviet government. The solution to the problem, he wrote, lay in Soviet organization of a "rich network" of schools and educational institutions and in development of oral and printed Soviet agitation.[16] The problem was examined in detail by the Eighth All-Russian Congress of Soviets. Acknowledging the lack of educational opportunities in many parts of Russia, the congress ordered the immediate development of a broad network of elementary, middle, and higher schools in the non-Russian districts, as well as other measures designed to hasten the "leveling up" of the cultural institutions of the non-Russian peoples with those of the "advanced" nationalities.[17] This policy was reinforced some three months later, in March, 1921, by a resolution of the Tenth Party Congress on developing cultural and educational institutions in national republics and regions.[18]

EDUCATING MOSLEMS: THE STRUGGLE FOR THE SOVIET SCHOOL

Prior to 1920, local Soviet authorities in Central Asia had given scant attention to the most elementary problems of educating non-Russian populations in a Soviet spirit. The government of

[15] From the twelfth section of the program of the All-Russian Communist Party (b), "In the Field of Public Education." Text in *Vsesoiuznaia Kommunisticheskaia Partiia (b) v rezoliutsiiakh i resheniiakh s'ezdov, konferentsii i plenumov Ts.K., 1898–1935* (5th ed., Moscow, 1936), I, 333–34.

[16] J. V. Stalin, "Nashi zadachi na Vostoke," *Zhizn' Natsional'nostei,* No. 7 (15) (March 2, 1919).

[17] Text of directive reprinted in I. Lozovskii and I. Bibin, *Sovetskaia politika za 10 let po natsional'nomu voprosu v RSFSR: sistematicheskii sbornik deistvuiushchikh aktov pravitel'stv Soiuza SSR i RSFSR po delam natsional'nostei RSFSR (oktiabr' 1917 g.–noiabr' 1927 g.)* (Moscow, 1928), pp. 297–99.

[18] Text of resolution in *Desiatyi S'ezd R.K.P.(b),* p. 279.

Turkestan had merely enacted laws requiring the secularization of education and had made sporadic efforts to establish soviet schools in the largest centers. But the government did not enforce separation of church and school in the native community, and secular schools catered primarily to the needs of the immigrant population. As late as 1920, not a single nonreligious native school existed in Semirechie, Transcaspia, and Amu-Daria. Budget allocations for cultural and educational purposes were weighted heavily in favor of the European community. As Broido complained in an article in *Zhizn' Natsional'nostei,* the Commissariat of Education had allocated no more than one sixth of its primary school budget for the education of native children.[19]

By 1920 the focus of Soviet policy was shifting from West to East and Lenin's prerevolutionary projects for encouraging colonial revolutions were beginning to figure prominently in Bolshevik planning. The sense of urgency which was becoming manifest in Soviet dealings with Eastern peoples within and outside of Russia presaged a reversal of the past practices of officials in many of the non-Russian localities. In Central Asia especially, educational opportunities now began to be opened to the Moslem peoples. The government of Turkestan, supported by generous subsidies from Moscow, embarked upon an ambitious program of school construction. By October 1, 1921, 2,333 educational institutions were in operation. These consisted of 1,965 primary schools with 165,700 pupils, 58 secondary schools with an attendance of 7,450, 203 kindergartens with 24,175 pupils, and 107 other schools with student bodies totaling 7,840.[20] A month later 72 more new schools were functioning and the total number of Soviet schools of all descriptions had reached 3,405; of these, 1,288 with 90,350 students served the European population and 1,117 with 87,970 pupils served the Moslem community. By the end of the year there were 2,680 Soviet educational institutions in the republic.[21]

In terms of the larger goals of Soviet education in the non-

[19] G. Broido, "Turkestanskie problemy," *Zhizn' Natsional'nostei,* No. 23 (80) (July 18, 1920).
[20] *Zhizn' Natsional'nostei,* No. 10 (16) (May 3, 1922).
[21] *Izvestiia,* October 26, November 13, 1923.

Russian regions these accomplishments represented no more than a small beginning. At the end of 1921 the public school system in Turkestan was still insufficient to satisfy even the most elementary educational needs of the local population. Even so, the program of school expansion was beyond the economic capacity of the government of Turkestan. When, at the beginning of 1922, Moscow's subsidy was withdrawn—a victim of the retrenchment which attended the introduction of the New Economic Policy—the foundation melted away from under the program of educational expansion. In many regions educational institutions closed their doors, and the village school, the backbone of Soviet education in the Moslem community, almost disappeared. The financial inability of local governments to support an expanding program of Soviet education impeded even a return to the 1921 levels. In 1923, when the Turkestan government assigned 40 percent of its entire budget to education, it was able to support only 1,669 educational institutions.[22] Of this number, 991 with an enrollment of 66,000 served the European community and 673 with an enrollment of 31,000 served the Moslem population.[23]

Even granting financial limitations which greatly hampered the development of Soviet education in Turkestan, a comparison of facilities and enrollments indicates a Soviet failure to achieve anything approaching equality of educational opportunity for the non-Russian population. Europeans had one third more public schools than Moslems, and European schools accommodated twice as many pupils. Although ten times more native children were attending European-type schools in 1923 than before the revolution,[24] only a token effort was being made to satisfy the educational needs of the non-Russian peoples. A literacy survey showed that only 21 Kirghiz, 18 Uzbeks, and six Turcomans per thousand could read or write, while 353 Euro-

[22] E. M., "Khoziaistvennyi obzor po Turkestanu," *Vlast' Sovetov*, No. 6 (September, 1924), pp. 218–19.

[23] *Izvestiia*, November 13, 1923.

[24] Data presented before the All-Russian Central Executive Committee by Khidyr-Aliev, a delegate from Turkestan, indicate that only 97 "new method" schools with a combined student body of 2,986 persons served the Moslem community of Turkestan in the prewar period. See *Tret'iaia Sessiia Vserossiiskogo Tsentral'nogo Ispolnitel'nogo Komiteta X Sozyva* (Moscow, 1924), pp. 105–6.

peans per thousand in the republic were literate.[25] School census figures, moreover, indicated the presence in the republic of 773,-000 native children of school age as against 118,000 European children in the same category.[26]

Despite the great disparity in educational opportunities there was much resistance to suggestions for a more equitable distribution of local educational funds. Local officials preferred to throw a large share of the burden of supporting non-Russian public schools onto the Moscow government. Repeated pleas for aid did win Turkestan a monthly subsidy of 15,000 rubles from the All-Russian Commissariat of Education but this money could not even provide teachers' salaries.[27] Sharp criticisms of the central government's failure to support local cultural and educational institutions were made at the Fourth Conference with Responsible Workers. Admitting that school facilities in Turkestan were inadequate, that local administrative institutions had not been "nationalized," and that the culture remained low, Stalin counseled patience. "If it is impossible in two or three, or even in ten years, to elevate Russian culture," he pointed out, "then how can we demand a speedy elevation of culture in non-Russian regions which are backward and almost illiterate?" [28] The answer was obvious. Lack of funds for the building of schools, for the provision of textbooks and other supplies, as well as the absence of qualified teachers, rendered impossible a rapid expansion of the educational system not only in Central Asia but in Great Russia itself.

Responsibility for the slow development, however, did not rest solely with the central government. Soviet officials reported that all native institutions of soviet education were in much worse condition than the Russian school system and local officials were paying little attention to improving them. Trained personnel was practically nonexistent and textbooks in the national languages failed to satisfy local needs.[29]

[25] *Izvestiia*, November 13, 1923.

[26] From report of Khidyr-Aliev in *Tret'iaia Sessiia Vserossiiskogo Tsentral'nogo Ispolnitel'nogo Komiteta X Sozyva*, p. 106.

[27] *Ibid.*

[28] Stalin, *Sochineniia*, V, 307–8.

[29] G. Ul'ianov, "Pervyi vserossiiskii s'ezd Sovnatsmenov," *Zhizn' Natsional'nostei*, No. 2 (1923), pp. 109–10.

Similar problems confronted Soviet educational authorities in the people's republics of Bokhara and Khorezm. In these republics, however, a slower initial pace of expansion permitted the educational system to avoid setbacks such as had occurred in Turkestan. By its treaties with both republics the Soviet government had promised to support the development of public school systems by subsidizing education, loaning teachers and instructors, and providing printing presses, textbooks, and literature.[30] These funds, materials, and personnel formed the chief source of support for the educational systems of Bokhara and Khorezm during their early years. The republics began to contribute substantially from their own revenues only in 1923, when the Bokharan republic allocated one fourth of its budget to education. In its 15 libraries, some 10,000 volumes had been collected. In Khorezm, 40 Soviet schools—one of them a normal school—with a combined student body of 2,000 were in operation. Nearly all of these schools, however, were on the primary level and students desiring higher education had to attend Russian institutions in Tashkent or Moscow.[31]

A review of the general development of the public school systems in these republics and in Turkestan indicates that a lack of funds was the principal factor inhibiting their growth. In allocating limited educational funds, local Soviet authorities were compelled to choose between creating a new public school system in the native community and protecting an existing system in the European community. That decisions tended to favor the latter course can be ascribed only in part to lingering survivals of "Great Russian chauvinism" among European administrators. A normal desire to protect established teaching staffs and facilities cannot be discounted. Over and above that, formidable obstacles confronted Soviet educational planners who sought to establish the Soviet school in the native community. In addition to the absence of adequate funds, there was the necessity for overcoming widespread Moslem resistance to Soviet education.

[30] S. Iakubovskaia, *Ob'edinitel'noe dvizhenie za obrazovanie SSSR (1917–1922)* (Moscow, 1947), p. 125.
[31] Joseph Castagné, "Russie slave et Russie turque: les chances d'une politique islamique allemande," *Revue du Monde Musulman*, LVI (December, 1923), 198; also *Zhizn' Natsional'nostei*, No. 4 (10) (March 21, 1922).

The Soviet regime also faced the problem of recruiting and training teachers capable of working in the local languages and within the native community. And it had to find a way to overcome the great obstacles to mass education presented by the character of the written languages of Central Asia.

The problem of preparing native teaching personnel was an extremely difficult one. Ninety-five out of a hundred Moslems could not meet the mere test of literacy. The native intelligentsia was small in numbers and was generally hostile to the Soviet regime. Because of their association with the anti-Soviet nationalist movement or with deposed governments, many native intellectuals had been forced to flee the country. Others, members of the ulema, sided with the religious community in its struggle against lay interference in the education of Moslem children. The few pro-Soviet native intellectuals tended to find employment in government and Party work which had little direct bearing upon the development of a public educational system in the non-Russian community.

The Soviet government, for its part, did little to overcome these obstacles. Despite repeated proclamations of dismay in regard to the shortages of native teaching personnel, it offered no inducements, either financial or social, sufficient to attract educated Moslems in large numbers into the teaching profession, and it made little effort to recruit and train future pedagogues. By 1923–24, only three schools were training teachers in the Turkestan republic;[32] none was equipped to serve adequately the needs of the many national groupings in the region. The Kirghiz, for example, were without native teachers until after the national delimitation. Public education—what little there was of it—was carried on in the Turkic, Kazakh, Uzbek, or Tatar languages. Even after the delimitation, teacher preparation consisted of a three-month short course.[33] The Tajiks had no schools at all, and the Turcomans very few.[34] At the end of 1925

[32] G. Ul'ianov, "K voprosu o podgotovke uchitel'stva natsional'nykh men'-shinstv," Narodnoe Prosveshchenie, Nos. 11–12 (1924), p. 79.

[33] From a report of the Kirghiz delegate, Tokbaev, in XIII Vserossiiskii S'ezd Sovetov: stenograficheskii otchet (Moscow, 1927), p. 434.

[34] Pervyi Vseuzbekskii S'ezd Sovetov Rabochikh, Dekhkanskikh i Krasnoarmeiskikh Deputatov Uzbekskoi Sovetskoi Sotsialisticheskoi Respubliki, fevral' 1925 goda (Tashkent, 1925), p. 51.

there were only 4,158 teachers in the republics of Uzbekistan and Turkmenia.[35] And this number increased very slowly in succeeding years.

Ten years after the revolution there was still no corps of native teachers adequate to satisfy even the most elementary educational needs of the non-Russian peoples. Teacher training had not proved amenable to Bolshevik shock tactics. In the long run, qualified native teaching staffs could emerge only out of expanding educational facilities and opportunities. Such cadres are themselves the products of broadening educational opportunity; and their growth, in Soviet Russia as elsewhere, depended directly upon the general progress of the broad program of cultural leveling up of backward nationalities to which both government and Party were committed. Throughout the twenties, the whole program was hamstrung by the absence of funds for cultural and educational purposes in the national republics and regions, by the extremely low levels of literacy inherited from the prerevolutionary period, and, not least, by opposition among native religious leaders and nationalists to the secularization and sovietization of culture and education.

In the Moslem regions, moreover, the written language constituted a formidable barrier to cultural and educational progress and, by extension, a barrier to achievement of the goals of Soviet nationality policy. Because mastery of the Arabic script alone requires years of study,[36] public education, despite government support, was financially beyond the reach of the masses. Hence it constituted a hindrance not only to popular cultural development but to the fulfillment of Soviet plans for creating an industrial society and for training the masses to participate actively in Soviet political, economic, and social life.

Suggestions for language reform as one solution to the problems of popularizing education and combating illiteracy had

[35] Central Statistical Board, USSR, *Ten Years of Soviet Power in Figures, 1917–1927* (Moscow, 1927), p. 89. No breakdown of this figure into its European and native components was available.

[36] Additional difficulties arose from the application of the Arabic alphabet to the Turkic languages. Whereas Arabic script contains only three vowels, there are eight vowel sounds in the Turkic tongues. Consequently, unrelated words were often rendered identically in the written form, and even highly educated Turks often found correspondence from friends and colleagues undecipherable.

gained prominence among Moslems even before the Russian Revolution. A movement for replacing the Arabic alphabet with a more readily comprehensible orthography was one outgrowth of the surge of nationalism which had enveloped the Moslem world after 1908. Despite the vigorous opposition of Moslem teachers and scholars, its influence had spread quickly through the ranks of nationalistically inclined Moslem intellectuals in the Russian Empire. The movement was, nevertheless, ineffective in Russia until Bolshevik revolutionists in power were able to assert their demands for secularized and compulsory education and to lay the groundwork for a system of mass "polytechnic" training. Even during the civil war, suggestions for language reform—preferably by way of Latinization of the Arabic alphabet—found favor in Bolshevik Party circles, and in 1919 the Soviet government, as a matter of convenience, replaced Arabic characters with their Latin equivalents on the telegraph circuits in Azerbaijan.[37] Soviet support of a general language reform increased significantly during the early twenties, but the central government refused to interfere directly in the matter. Its interest was confined rather to unofficial sponsorship of a Moslem reform committee whose principal tasks were to devise a Latinized alphabet and to prepare modernized grammars and dictionaries. Moscow interceded only to the extent of offering financial assistance to local governments which adopted the new orthography. The decision for reform itself was left in each instance to the individual Moslem republics and regions.

The Turkic peoples in the Caucasus region were the first to adopt the new characters. Azerbaijan accorded the Latinized alphabet official status in 1924 and by 1927 the entire popular literature of the North Caucasian peoples had been reprinted in a Latinized form.[38] Introduction of the reform proceeded at a slower pace in other Moslem regions. Resistance was greatest among the Tatars, who boasted the most highly developed culture among Russia's Turkic peoples. The republics of Central

---

[37] R., "Kul'turnaia zadacha revoliutsii na musul'manskom Vostoke," *Zhizn' Natsional'nostei*, No. 1 (99) (July 13, 1920).

[38] Avrahm Yarmolinsky, *The Jews and Other Minor Nationalities under the Soviets* (New York, 1928), p. 173.

Asia likewise hesitated until the late twenties. A number of schools in the Tashkent region adopted the Latin alphabet during 1927–28,[39] but the governments of Uzbekistan and Turkmenia expressed no official attitude on the matter until mid-1928. Then both republics ordered a complete replacement of Arabic characters with the Latinized alphabet in all public schools, soviet cultural institutions, and official documents.[40]

While this reform was perhaps the most important single act of the republic governments in opening up educational opportunities to the native population of Central Asia, it was not introduced soon enough to produce practical results in the twenties. Between 1926 and 1928, enrollment in the public schools of Uzbekistan increased only from 131,185 to 175,750, and in Turkmenia from 29,926 to 36,370. Even these figures do not represent a true picture of increases in native enrollment since Soviet statisticians had abandoned the practice of classifying European and native student bodies separately. The level of educational opportunity, in any case, continued to be low for both European and native children. At the beginning of 1927 Uzbekistan boasted only 1,850 general and professional educational institutions of all types, and Turkmenia had only 530. The total student bodies respectively were 143,741 and 34,873. In Uzbekistan 90 schools with a student population of 15,407 were of a professional type, and 1,761 with 128,334 pupils were on the preschool, primary, and secondary levels. Turkmenia had only 31 professional schools with 2,876 students, and 499 nonprofessional schools with 31,997 pupils.[41] On the higher levels particularly, the overwhelming majority of the students were of European origin. In 1927–28 only 10 percent of the student body of higher educational institutions in Uzbekistan were natives of Central Asia. Of a student body of 4,000 to 5,000

---

[39] Joseph Castagné (ed.), "Le Mouvement de latinisation dans les républiques soviétiques musulmanes et les pays voisins (documents de presse russe)," *Revue des Études Islamiques,* No. 11 (1928), p. 575.

[40] *Ibid.,* p. 574; also *Izvestiia,* June 3, 1928.

[41] From statistical data appearing in Central Statistical Board, USSR, *Ten Years of Soviet Power in Figures,* pp. 84–85, and Central Administration of Economic and Social Statistics of the State Planning Commission of the USSR, *Socialist Construction in the USSR* (Moscow, 1936), pp. 451–52. These figures exclude "political educational" centers.

students in the Central Asiatic State University in Tashkent, only 350 were natives.[42]

That formal educational opportunities in the non-Russian localities were not greater in 1927 than they were is not, in itself, a valid ground for criticizing the Soviet government. If anything, the main fault lay in an overambitious program rather than in a lack of zeal. Against that, the first ten years of Soviet rule saw the firm establishment of two crucial principles: that of equal educational opportunity without regard to race or nationality and that of education as the right of all, not the privilege of a few. In the test of performance too, the Soviet government achieved a creditable record; not only were non-Russians going to school in 1927 in far greater numbers than ever before, but opportunities were open for them at every educational level from the highest to the lowest.

THE MEANS OF ADULT EDUCATION

Through the public school the government and the Party sought to rear a new generation steeped in the ideals of Marx and Lenin and capable of achieving the stage of Communism. But education also had immediate objectives to serve: to convert into socially productive members of Soviet society illiterate and semi-illiterate adults whose ignorance prevented them from participating actively in political, economic, and social reconstruction; and to mobilize, indoctrinate, and organize the masses for fulfillment of the immediate tasks of building up the socialist state. These were tasks best fulfilled through the development of adult education and a centralized and disciplined periodical press.

"Political literacy" (*politgramota*), the term most commonly associated with adult education in the Soviet Union, was considered from the first days of Bolshevik rule to be an integral part of the general system of Soviet education. Originally the task of developing nonacademic educational institutions and procedures was assigned to the Commissariat of Education, since

[42] A. Rysakoff, *The National Policy of the Soviet Union* (New York, n.d.), p. 52; Mustapha Chokaiev, "Turkestan and the Soviet Regime," *Journal of the Royal Central Asian Society*, XVIII (1931), 418–19.

the Bolsheviks conceived of adult education primarily as an instrument of mass political growth and cultural broadening. Direct responsibility for the creation of local centers of adult education and the preparation of personnel to man them resided initially in a Nonacademic Division of the commissariat.

While it is impossible within the limits of this study to trace the ramifications of the development of adult education in Soviet Russia, it must be noted that the movement subsequently divided itself into two major branches. One of these was devoted principally to the training of leaders to serve the dictatorship of the proletariat on all levels of Soviet and Party life. The importance of this kind of educational work both to the continuance and extension of the Bolshevik Party's monopoly of political power and to fulfillment of the Party's programmatic objectives led inevitably to its concentration in Party hands.[43] The second branch was to prepare the workers and peasants on a mass scale for active participation in Soviet life; it too was under the jurisdiction of the Nonacademic Division and of its successor, the Political Education Division of the Commissariat of Education. During the civil war, this division had sponsored the establishment of libraries, worker's clubs, schools for illiterates, and even "people's universities." In the period of reconstruction it broadened its activities to include the founding and maintenance of peasant reading rooms and of schools for semiliterate and literate workers and peasants, as well as supporting the educational programs of numerous mass organizations and institutions.

The Soviet leaders considered success or failure in eliminating illiteracy as the crucial test of mass adult education.[44] Not only did inability to read and write handicap the workman in his factory tasks, but it also denied him any effective participation in political life. Even simple slogans do not have the desired effect if workers and peasants cannot read.

A Bolshevik program to provide elementary educational op-

[43] Several of the educational institutions which functioned under direct Bolshevik Party control are examined above, pp. 133–36.

[44] For Lenin's comments on the hopelessness of attempting to construct a Communist society in an illiterate country, see V. I. Lenin, *Sochineniia* (2d ed., Moscow, 1926—), XXV, 395.

portunities for all illiterate adults and youths over fifteen had been outlined at the First All-Russian Congress on Nonacademic Education in May, 1919, which proposed the establishment of some 50,000 to 60,000 elementary schools for adults[45] as well as the creation of literacy schools offering three-month courses of instruction within all existing cultural institutions of the RSFSR.[46] A decree promulgated in December, 1919, "Concerning the Elimination of Illiteracy among the Population of the RSFSR" ordered all illiterates between 18 and 50 to learn their letters; the Commissariat of Education and its local branch agencies were to mobilize all literates for this campaign.[47] In June, 1920, an All-Russian Extraordinary Commission to Abolish Illiteracy (*Likbez*) was created, with authority to guide and coordinate the training program on all its levels.[48]

In these early decrees the Soviet government assumed that general laws and regulations concerning education would apply equally to all the peoples of the RSFSR and did not treat illiteracy in the non-Russian republics and regions as a special problem. Originally the Commissariat for National Affairs had assumed responsibility for establishing literacy schools as well as workers' and peasants' clubs, people's universities, libraries, and other cultural and educational institutions in the non-Russian regions.[49] In addition, an instruction of the Council of People's Commissars, of April, 1920, ordered the formation of national commissions for the abolition of illiteracy, for the purpose of supporting the work of local departments of public education and organizing worker-peasant control over adult educational institutions.[50]

---

[45] The resolution itself did not specifically ask creation of a stated number of schools but it did seek the establishment of one school for each district with 3,000 or fewer population.

[46] A. M. Ivanova, *Chto sdelala Sovetskaia Vlast' po likvidatsii negramotnosti sredi vzroslykh* (Moscow, 1949), pp. 12–13.

[47] Specifically exempted from the provisions of the decree were persons serving in the armed forces or employed in militarized industries. Text of decree reprinted in *ibid.*, pp. 91–92.

[48] *Ibid.*, p. 14.

[49] Mansvetov, "Velikaia Oktiabr'skaia Sotsialisticheskaia Revoliutsiia i sozdanie Narodnogo Komissariata po Delam Natsional'nostei," *Voprosy Istorii*, No. 8 (August, 1949), p. 21.

[50] Text of instruction in Narodnyi Komissariat po Delam Natsional'nostei, RSFSR, *Politika Sovetskoi Vlasti po natsional'nomu voprosu za tri goda, 1917–xi–1920* (Moscow, 1920), pp. 158–59.

Within the non-Russian regions the efforts of the central government to combat illiteracy had little effect during the civil war, apart from the creation of a scattering of literacy schools toward the end of the period. Until the Fifth Congress of the Turkestan Bolshevik Party, in September, 1920, demanded "heroic measures" against Moslem illiteracy,[51] local officials had made no effort to encourage programs of adult education in the native community. Even then the organization of courses of study, the provision of equipment and facilities, and the recruiting of teachers proceeded at an extremely slow pace. By 1923 only 200 literacy schools were operating in the Turkestan republic, mainly in the urban areas.[52] The program was continually handicapped by the lack of financial support, and also by the widespread resistance in the rural areas from local Soviet officials and Party secretaries—often illiterate themselves—who were either generally suspicious of cultural and educational activities or had more immediate uses for the limited funds at their disposal.[53]

Faced by the wide gulf between policy and its execution, the government now began to provide more substantial support. The practice of allocating educational subsidies to non-Russian republics from the All-Russian budget, suspended in 1922, was partially resumed in 1923. Republic governments increased their support to the campaign against illiteracy and also required district, county, and local soviets to allocate specific proportions of their own budgets for the same purpose. For example, a decree promulgated in February, 1926, by the Turcoman Government ordered local governmental agencies to devote 25 percent of their budgets to combating illiteracy.[54]

Special attention was also given to methods for expanding literacy in the rural areas. The itinerant school began to serve

[51] Georgii Safarov, *Kolonial'naia revoliutsiia: opyt Turkestana* (Moscow, 1921), p. 138.

[52] G. Neradov, "Narodnoe prosveshcheniia na okrainakh," *Izvestiia,* January 24, 1923.

[53] See report of Syrtsov in *Chetyrnadtsataia Konferentsiia Rossiiskoi Kommunisticheskoi Partii (bol'shevikov),* p. 33; also E. M., "Khoziaistvennyi obzor po Turkestanu," *Vlast' Sovetov,* No. 6 (September, 1924), p. 219.

[54] A decree of the Turcoman Central Executive Committee of February 27, 1926, "On the Liquidation of Illiteracy." Text in *Sobranie postanovlenii i rasporiazhenii raboche-dekhkanskogo pravitel'stva Turkmenskoi SSR,* No. 8 (June 1, 1926), pp. 4–5.

as the major vehicle of literacy training for the villages. Bolshevik Party members were ordered to learn reading and writing on pain of expulsion from the Party, and local soviets and their departments of public education were made responsible for spreading literacy. The Turcoman government adopted a ten-year plan for the abolition of illiteracy among urban dwellers between the ages of 18 and 35 and among rural inhabitants between 14 and 30 by the end of 1934.[55] Party and Soviet agencies attacked the problem with great zeal. By 1925 over 1,500 literacy schools were operating in the three major republics of Central Asia,[56] and, in 1926, some 53,323 adults were attending literacy classes.[57]

In addition to the attack on illiteracy, the Central Asiatic republics organized general educational courses to raise the "cultural and political level" of adults in the urban centers. Libraries, clubs, cottage reading rooms, and "peasant houses" had been established in numerous towns and villages. By October, 1928, over 150 itinerant and permanent motion-picture theaters were operating in the republics of Turkmenia and Uzbekistan.[58]

All these programs and institutions had one clearly defined objective: to destroy survivals of the old society and supplant them with the ideals of Communism. On every level adult education stressed the study of the class struggle, the Bolshevik Party, and the unique role of the Soviet Union in world politics. Even in the literacy schools political indoctrination predominated, and elementary readers were usually compilations of

[55] "Likvidatsiia negramotnosti v Turkmenistane i Uzbekistane," *Vlast' Sovetov*, IX, No. 9 (February 28, 1926), 12.

[56] These figures, broken down on a republican basis, include 160 schools in Turkmenia, 207 in Kirghizia, and 1,155 in Uzbekistan. See *ibid.*, p. 12; M. Mukhitdinov, "Politiko-prosvetitel'naia rabota v natsional'nom razreze," *Kommunisticheskoe Prosveshchenie*, No. 2 (20) (March–April, 1925), p. 37.

[57] In that year, 34,739 adults were attending these schools in Uzbekistan, 11,084 in Turkmenia, and 7,500 in Kirghizia. Data for Kirghizia were taken from a census conducted at the beginning of 1926, whereas those for Uzbekistan and Turkmenia indicate the status of those republics in November, 1926. See Central Statistical Board, USSR, *Ten Years of Soviet Power in Figures*, pp. 84–85; Ivanova, *Chto sdelala Sovetskaia Vlast' po likvidatsii negramotnosti sredi vzroslykh*, p. 30.

[58] Central Statistical Board, USSR, *Ten Years of Soviet Power in Figures*, pp. 84–85; Central Administration of Economic and Social Statistics of the State Planning Commission of the USSR, *Socialist Construction in the USSR*, pp. 460–61.

slogans.[59] Libraries, clubs, reading rooms, and Red Corners provided the newly literate with access to the printed word and were designed to drive home socialist precepts.

In this respect the Soviet periodical press played an extremely important role. Because printed matter furnished virtually the only medium of communication between the central government and the non-Russian peoples during the early phases of the revolution, the speedy development of a vernacular press in the languages of the national minorities was especially urgent. Publishing was, in fact, one of the major functions of the Commissariat for National Affairs, which was responsible for translating government decrees and Party literature into the non-Russian languages and for promoting the growth of a diversified vernacular press. Initially, this activity was handicapped by a serious lack of qualified writers and translators as well as by the absence of adequate printing facilities. However, by the end of 1919, its national commissariats and departments were printing some sixty newspapers in various non-Russian languages and dialects and had struck off more than 700 different books and pamphlets with a total imprint of 11,000,000 copies.[60]

In the borderlands of the former Empire the Bolsheviks exhibited a lively concern for the creation of a non-Russian press, more than for the development of any other means for reaching the non-Russian masses. At their first postrevolutionary congress in June, 1918, the Bolsheviks of Turkestan, who were almost callously indifferent to the educational needs of the Moslem community, went on record in favor of the development of a native-language press.[61] At the time the rise of a vernacular press in Turkestan was not feasible, but the period of the New Eco-

[59] Early lessons in the literacy schools involved the reading of such slogans as "We will bring freedom to the world," "Defense of the revolution is the duty of all toilers," "We are neither slaves nor masters," and so on. In later lessons, simple textual discussions of political questions were introduced. See Ivanova, *Chto sdelala Sovetskaia Vlast' po likvidatsii negramotnosti sredi vzroslykh,* pp. 27–28.

[60] Mansvetov, "Velikaia Oktiabr'skaia Sotsialisticheskaia Revoliutsiia i sozdanie Narodnogo Komissariata po Delam Natsional'nostei," *Voprosy Istorii,* No. 8 (August, 1949), p. 22.

[61] P. Antropov, *Materialy i dokumenty I S'ezda Kompartii Turkestana* (Tashkent, 1934), p. 44.

nomic Policy witnessed a rapid increase both in number and in circulation of native-language newspapers and periodicals.

At the beginning of 1922, two vernacular newspapers, one of which, *Kyzyl Bairak*, was published by the Turkestan Central Executive Committee and edited by a Tatar Bolshevik, were appearing regularly.[62] In March, 1923, *Izvestiia* reported that eight newspapers and seven periodicals were being published currently in the languages of the peoples of Turkestan. The vernacular press soon developed a marked degree of specialization in accordance with the usual Soviet pattern. Two newspapers and two magazines were published specifically for the nomadic peoples; one was directed to a peasant audience; another newspaper, *Zhiskeirat*, was aimed at the native youth.[63]

Despite its rapid growth, the vernacular press in Turkestan had not yet developed into a mass press. Inadequate finances, constant shortages of newsprint, and the absence of a large literate audience narrowly restricted its impact upon the Moslem community. The combined circulation of 11 non-Russian newspapers in the republic had reached only 36,600 copies daily by the end of 1923. Newspaper circulation climbed to over 80,000 copies in 1925 and in August, 1927, to over 107,000. Increases in circulation were accompanied by an expansion of the press in size and diversity. In 1927 and 1928, 19 newspapers and 24 magazines aimed at diverse audiences were appearing regularly in Central Asia.[64]

The rapid expansion of the native-language press in Central Asia created numerous problems in the area of Bolshevik guidance and control. Initially, the Party sought to exercise close supervision by putting the more important newspapers and periodicals in charge of Bolsheviks recruited among better educated Moslem groups, in particular, the Volga Tatars. One weakness of this procedure was that the editors, often unacquainted with the nuances of local speech, were unable to pre-

[62] Joseph Castagné, "Le Bolchévisme et l'Islam: les organisations soviétiques de la Russie musulmane," *Revue du Monde Musulman*, LI (October, 1922), 71.
[63] *Izvestiia*, March 3, 1923.
[64] Central Statistical Board, USSR, *Ten Years of Soviet Power in Figures*, p. 95; Komissiia po Izucheniiu Natsional'nogo Voprosa, Kommunisticheskaia Akademiia, *Natsional'naia politika V.K.P.(b) v tsifrakh* (Moscow, 1930), p. 301.

vent publication of misleading and distorted articles. For example, the Uzbek-language newspaper of the Turkestan Central Executive Committee, *Kyzyl Bairak,* for a time bore the legend "Vagrants of the World Unite." [65] The subsequent transfer of responsibility to native editors brought with it other pitfalls. As late as 1927, the Party's Central Asiatic Bureau criticized the national press on four major grounds: its failure to give due heed to Party work; its failure to exercise due surveillance over the activities of Party, Soviet, and public agencies; its failure to reflect accurately and consistently the life of the workers; and its commission of political errors and "deviations." [66]

Deviations, failures, and errors notwithstanding, the vernacular press of Central Asia was then and later the principal instrument for educating, indoctrinating, and organizing the non-Russian peoples for participation in the task of building up and strengthening the Soviet state. Its function was to teach the workers and peasants new forms of work, to watch over the activities of public agencies and institutions, to educate young and old alike in the demands of Soviet citizenship. As Stalin remarked of the entire Soviet press, it was the unique instrument through which the Party spoke daily, hourly, with the working class in exactly the way it needed.[67] Like the Russian-language press, the native-language press was designed, with all other instruments of Soviet education and culture, to convert all the peoples of Russia into builders of socialism and eventually into willing citizens of a Communist community. In this and other respects, Soviet cultural autonomy was largely an autonomy of externals, and its prime concern was to inculcate a common standard of perception, belief, and action in all citizens through propaganda presented in their native languages. In the hands of the Party, moreover, even those institutions which reflected nationality functioned primarily as tools for the transmission of socialist culture and ideology and for winning popular support for the aims of the Party.

[65] Castagné, "Le Bolchévisme et l'Islam," *Revue du Monde Musulman,* LI (October, 1922), 71.

[66] Sredne-Aziatskoe Biuro Ts.K., V.K.P.(b), *Resoliutsii i postanovleniia XII Plenuma (24–27 ianvaria 1927 g.)* (Tashkent, n.d.), pp. 17–18.

[67] See G. Aleksandrov *et al., Politicheskii slovar'* (Moscow, 1940), p. 422.

In Central Asia only the foundations of this program had been laid during the twenties. The Soviet program of cultural reformation was still in its initial phase. A vernacular press had been created, but it had not yet achieved a status of equality with Russian-language newspapers and periodicals which were also being published in the region. Institutions for mass formal and informal education were neither sufficiently numerous nor adequately staffed to satisfy the needs of the local peoples or the aims of the regime. Remote districts, which for the most part had barely heard the whisperings of the new era, had experienced none of the educational and cultural uplift which it promised. As late as 1928, Soviet planners were still complaining of the "insufficient development of mass education" and the "extremely low level of general culture" throughout Central Asia.[68] Nevertheless, what had been accomplished became the basis of the far more ambitious and effective Five-Year Plans.

[68] From the Five-Year Plan control figures for 1928–29. Quoted in W. P. and Zelda K. Coates, *Soviets in Central Asia* (New York, 1951), p. 113.

X

THE PATTERN OF
SOVIET NATIONALITY
POLICY

◆

THE OCTOBER REVOLUTION had given rise to a fundamental shift in the Bolshevik doctrine of self-determination, which cut itself adrift from the concept of national liberation within a bourgeois setting and, instead, adopted as its goal the concept of national equality within a socialist system. Confronted at every quarter of the compass with the claims of national groups for independence or for broad grants of political autonomy, the Bolshevik Party adopted what seemed to be the only practical, yet also revolutionary, solution to the difficult problem of maintaining the territorial integrity of the former Russian state. In terms of doctrine, it now argued that the interests of the workers required the largest possible state and that, conversely, only enemies of the Soviet system would seek to destroy the existing unity. This was coupled with a deep-seated belief that the elimination of national inequality and discrimination would put an end to separatist tendencies, would undermine the idea of nationalism, and would ultimately make way for the rise of the truly internationalist outlook and the culture of socialism.

Nothing in these beliefs was inconsistent with the prerevolutionary ideals of Bolshevism. The idea of equality itself lay at the roots of Marxist philosophy, and Bolshevik leaders had always condemned discrimination on the ground of nationality, race, or color. Their postrevolutionary thinking, however, carried the idea of national equality far beyond the mere removal of legal disabilities which the imperial regime had practiced against many non-Russian peoples. The Soviet regime now undertook to bring the former subject peoples up to the political, economic, and cultural level of the Great Russian proletariat.

Soviet leaders visualized national equalization as a general process of educational and political development through which native workers and peasants would rise to the forefront of political life in their own republics and regions. They regarded the growth of national cultures under Bolshevik aegis as a means both to satisfy national aspirations and to enrich the international culture of socialism. The essence of the concept was economic, and its primary goal an equalized distribution of industry throughout the Soviet territory. This was the most revolutionary aspect of the post-October nationalities program. It foresaw a complete reversal of past policies, which had treated Russia's borderlands as mere suppliers of food and raw materials for the factories of Central Russia. The construction of industries in the non-Russian regions, it seemed to Bolshevik planners, would hasten the destruction of the historic contrast between industrial Great Russia and its agricultural colonies, would ultimately lead to the disappearance of the vestiges of Tsarist Russia's colonial legacy, and would facilitate the consolidation of Soviet power.

RUSSIANIZATION AND REVOLUTION: THE SYNTHESIZING PROCESS

By its nature, the process of eliminating the historical maldistribution of Soviet Russia's productive and cultural resources was not amenable to Bolshevik shock tactics. The program of equalization was unquestionably conceived in honesty and later accomplishments were substantial, but the path to fulfillment was beset with difficult obstacles. Many of these derived from Bolshevik philosophy; equally formidable ones sprang from Great Russia's heritage of preponderance over the non-Russian and especially over the non-Slavic populations and from the geographical dispersion of Russians and Ukrainians throughout nearly every territory and region of the USSR. And the impact of these limitations was intensified both by the numerical weakness and relative backwardness of the non-Russian nationalities and by the absence of any source of unity in the Soviet state outside the Great Russian national core.

To these limiting forces Soviet doctrine and practice added its own peculiar contradictions. After the Bolsheviks had come to power, they assiduously promoted and fostered new inequalities which contrasted sharply with the concept of national equality and in the long run operated to hinder achievement of that goal. For one thing, Soviet policy deliberately developed and strengthened inequalities between the toilers of every nationality and their former "exploiting" classes. In the former colonies of the Tsarist Empire, however, the exploiting groups were often the only ones which had awakened to political consciousness and which possessed educational qualifications permitting easy and effective entry into active political and administrative life. But the revolutionary government, bent on exercising its policy of class rule, aimed to exclude them from these spheres.

Another gulf arose from Bolshevik reliance upon the proletariat as the bulwark of Soviet power and its suspicion of the peasantry as an incipient petit-bourgeois class and a potentially counterrevolutionary force. While the policy of favoring members of the working class had no special implications for Soviet nationality policy in European Russia, it bore directly on the execution of that policy in the Asiatic borderlands. In most of these regions, the division between proletarian and peasant corresponded almost precisely to the line between European and native. By inference, Soviet support of proletarian domination constituted an endorsement of continuing Russian control of the critical positions in local political, administrative, and economic agencies. The symbols and content of the old Imperial domination had vanished in the revolution but the figure of the Russian or Russianized administrator tended to remain. Consequently, a regime of European political tutelage over the native people, very similar in content to the concept of an enlightened colonial administration, actually sprang into being.

The Bolsheviks, it is true, viewed the system as a temporary device to protect non-Russian toilers against their own exploiters
and to hasten the transition of backward peoples to socialism.
The regime was nonetheless real; and, as later developments
showed, it tended more and more to entrench and perpetuate
itself.

Although these factors in themselves created formidable obstacles to the realization of the Bolshevik ideal of an equal federation of equal peoples, they were not alone decisive. Ultimately,
the outcome of Soviet nationality policy depended upon the
resolution of the central conflict in Bolshevik doctrine and
policy between authoritarian and antiauthoritarian approaches
to the remaking of human society. On the one hand, Marxist
thought, as it had developed within and outside of Russia, had
aspired to generally democratic political and social goals; and
the goals themselves had stressed the sharing of political power
and responsibility with the masses. The dictatorship of the proletariat itself was envisaged less as an instrument of permanent
oppression than as a temporary vehicle for the rule of the overwhelming majority over a small minority of former exploiters.
In the period of transition from capitalism to socialism, moreover, the soviets were expected to serve as agencies for training
the masses to participate in the process of decision making at
every level.

The authoritarian aspect of Bolshevik doctrine, on the other
hand, grew, in part, out of Lenin's early recognition of two
facts of Russian political life: the working class in Tsarist Russia itself constituted only a tiny minority in the total population;
and the self-determined goals of the workers diverged at critical
points from the aims of the Bolshevik wing of the Social Democratic Party. These factors were at least partially responsible for
Lenin's frequent demands for greater centralism and discipline
in the Social Democratic revolutionary movement; they found
concrete embodiment in his concept of the Bolshevik Party as a
highly centralized elite formation, operating under the iron
discipline of a well-trained military formation.

After the seizure of power, this aspect of ideology received
fresh reinforcement. The assumption of political responsibility

alone doubtless fostered a greater consolidation of authority, and this tendency grew rapidly in the atmosphere of continual crisis which seemed to compel ever greater discipline and ever greater centralization of power in the hands of the few. The very fact that the October Revolution had given a minority of workingmen dictatorial power over the majority of peasants strengthened the prerevolutionary Leninist concept of dictatorship as a means to "educate" the masses to socialism under Bolshevik tutelage. Both Lenin and Stalin spoke repeatedly of the Soviet regime as a giant school of Communism in which millions of workers and peasants could study under Bolshevik guidance so that they might eventually learn to rule. It was quite in accordance with the objectives of Soviet nationality policy to extend the application of this concept to the non-Russian republics and regions.

That most of these regions had felt little of the social impact of the great revolution added a second compelling motivation for keeping the reins of guidance and control tightly held in the hands of European proletarians. In many of these territories customary sources of property and authority had survived the revolution intact. The revolution itself, concentrated in the political and administrative centers, had spent its force upon the European settlements. On the whole, its challenges to the indigenous social structure proved to be weak and ineffectual. Where native discontent had existed, it had usually focused itself upon European immigrants and colonial administrators or found expression in intercommunal and intertribal frictions. Even the most "revolutionary" members of the indigenous nationalities seldom expressed more than nascent middle-class tendencies.

After establishing their political control the Bolsheviks faced the problem of breaking down traditional loyalties in the native community and creating new loyalties to the Soviet regime and to its aims. In this sense, the "October" phase of revolution lasted through the first decade of Soviet rule in Central Asia, and it consisted, not of a violently destructive and spontaneous outburst against old inequalities, but a carefully executed and centrally directed Bolshevik campaign to undermine gradually the traditional structure of social myth and institution and to destroy the solidarity and imperviousness of the native community. The essence of the process was a highly coordinated and centralized program whose pace and direction was rigidly controlled by superior Party and governmental agencies.

Throughout this period Bolshevik leaders commonly argued that the thoroughgoing domination of the political and administrative apparatus by Europeans would disappear as soon as the enemies of the Soviet regime had been removed from places of influence or authority and the masses had been educated to loyalty to the new order. Nonetheless, the constantly growing concentration of power at the Great Russian center tended to harden the system of European control and to perpetuate old inequalities. After the first blush of freedom and decentralization in 1917, government by the masses and through the soviets had given way increasingly to government by centralized administrative agencies. Later developments witnessed a continuous strengthening and extension of bureaucratic practices and procedures as a substitute for more democratic forms of mass initiative. The effect upon nationality policy was clear almost from the beginning. Just as the Great Russian nationality dominated all others in the Soviet state and formed the core around which all the Soviet peoples were rallied, so also the core of the bureaucratic machine was Russian in origin and in spirit. Inevitably the machine became a powerful agency of Russianization.

For one thing, the non-Russian nationalities, many of whom were primitive peoples without political experience and most of whom were barely literate, could not contribute effectively to the administrative apparatus. Native intellectual classes were often minuscule in size and many of the intelligentsia were disqualified from participation in the Soviet regime because of their hostility toward the Bolsheviks. While programs of training and education were undertaken in the 1920's to prepare cadres of native workers for responsible posts in government and administration, the process of preparation was by its nature a prolonged one. During the crucial formative period of administrative organization, these groups played no significant role. By the time they entered the system, procedures had been adopted and standards set, and these were inevitably Great Russian in provenance and character. Aside from these disabilities, the mere mechanics of selection and advancement of non-Russian personnel in a predominantly Great Russian apparatus tended to favor those individuals who most readily adapted themselves to the Great Russian outlook.

These same centralizing and Russianizing tendencies were also at work in other agencies of the Soviet state. Foremost among them was the Red Army, which was principally Russian in composition even in the national republics and regions. While fitful efforts were undertaken after the Twelfth Party Congress in 1923 to organize native militias in a few of the more backward republics, these attempts were later abandoned, and existing units were absorbed into the Red Army. The trend to standardization and centralization was reinforced by the character of the trade unions, the youth movements, and all other mass organizations whose membership cut across national boundaries in the USSR. Not the least, the Bolshevik Party, which consciously subordinated the nationality principle to a monolithic doctrine and organization, was a powerful agency of centralization and Russianization. In all these agencies of power, the paramount emphasis was upon unity and centralism, and these objectives, in practice, reinforced Great Russian predominance.[1] Not only did Russian or Russianized Communists control the upper levels of their organizational structure, but in the more backward national republics and regions Russians frequently outnumbered natives even in the primary or local organizations.

The centralizing influence of the Soviet power structure was accentuated as time wore on by the inevitable blending of Russia's historical traditions with the ideological myth structure of Bolshevism. Russian nationalism, although submerged in the first outburst of revolutionary enthusiasm, did not disappear as a force in Russian life, nor, for that matter, had it lost its magic even for all the members of the Bolshevik Party. In addition, with the return of peaceful conditions and the recon-

[1] For a brief discussion, see Edward Hallett Carr, *The Bolshevik Revolution, 1917–1923* (New York, 1951–53), I, 367–70.

ciliation of many members of the former ruling classes with the Soviet regime—and with their frequent return to work within the bureaucracy—traditional Russian symbols and attitudes were absorbed into Soviet life and thought.[2]

The trend toward a reconciliation of Bolshevik nationality doctrine and practice with many of the symbols of Russia's historical past was complemented by Marxist assumptions concerning the world-wide solidarity of the working class and the eventual rise of an international culture of socialism. The Soviet rejection of national self-determination as a solution to the nationality problem in Russia had strengthened the ideal of national assimilation as the ultimate goal of Bolshevik policy, but doctrine gave no clear indication of the content of the socialist culture into which the peoples of Russia were to be drawn. In terms of Bolshevik responses, three lines of possible development were conceivable. One path was indicated by Lenin's view that a socialist culture would emerge from a natural process in which each Soviet nation would contribute the best elements of its own culture to the formation of a truly international culture of socialism. On the other hand, left-wing sentiment rejected nationalism and national self-determination as incompatible with the goal of international proletarian solidarity and unconsciously equated the symbols of Marxist internationalism with the living institutions of Great Russian culture in its postrevolutionary content.

In the first years after the Bolshevik revolution, these alternatives were the focus of numerous intra-Party disputes concerning the role of nationality in the Soviet state.[3] With the passage of time, both tended to give way to a third approach which both rejected the left-wing denial of nationality and abandoned the general thesis of a spontaneous growth of social-

[2] Lenin himself had been greatly disturbed by the fear that "specialists" who had been brought into the administrative machine as a temporary expedient would ultimately use their influence to transform the Soviet machine into an instrumentality for a return to the past. At the Eleventh Congress in 1922, he had warned the Party that responsible Communists were not managing the bureaucracy. Without knowing, they were being "managed" by bourgeois and aristocratic elements which had found their way into the administrative apparatus. See V. I. Lenin, *Sochineniia* (2d ed., Moscow, 1926—), XXVII, 244–45.

[3] See above, pp. 351–56.

ist culture. In part, this attitude was an outgrowth of the ideological compulsion to give precedence to the proletariat as
against the peasantry; this tendency, translated into the terms
of Soviet nationality policy, was tantamount to a guarantee of
preference to the Great Russian component. Stalin himself
stood squarely on this platform at the Twelfth Party Congress
in 1923. "The political foundation of the dictatorship of the
proletariat," he pointed out then, "is constituted first and chiefly
by the central regions which are industrial and not by the borderlands which represent peasant lands." [4]

In retrospect, the congress appears to have constituted a turning point in the Bolshevik approach to Russia's nationality
problem. Hitherto, the main weight of the Party's attacks
against nationalism had been directed against Great Russian
chauvinism. After 1923 the focus shifted subtly to an attack
on manifestations of local nationalism, on the efforts of non-
Russian leaders to preserve the identity of their national institutions and cultures and to protect the non-Russian populations against continuing encroachments by Moscow upon their
political, economic, and cultural traditions and interests. The
Bolshevik hierarchy continued to condemn crude displays of the
Great Russian national spirit, but, as Kalinin declared openly,
the object of Soviet policy was now "to teach the people of the
Kirghiz steppe, the small Uzbek cotton grower, and the Turkmenian gardener to accept the ideals of the Leningrad
worker." [5]

The methods by which the Soviet government implemented
its nationality policy served to strengthen the trend toward Russian predominance. The numerous small autonomous units
established by the Bolsheviks were too weak numerically and
often too primitive to develop independent cultural institutions
capable of resisting Moscow's influence. Even in the more advanced regions Soviet policy tended to isolate each national
group from contact not only with kindred nationalities beyond
the Soviet borders but also with peoples of similar cultures
within the USSR. All-out opposition to Pan-Turkic and Pan-

[4] J. V. Stalin, *Sochineniia* (Moscow, 1946—), V, 265.
[5] M. Kalinin, *Za ety gody* (Moscow, 1929), III, 385–86.

Islamic tendencies in the Eastern borderlands were directed initially against the formation of non-Russian centers of political opposition to the Soviet regime, but it also served to inhibit the growth of any larger cultural unities sufficiently strong and enduring to resist Great Russian domination.

During the 1920's Marxist doctrine as well as day-to-day problems of administration led the Bolsheviks to adopt numerous practices which tended to perpetuate and often to reinforce national inequality. In some degree, these tendencies reflected the continuing inability of the Soviet regime to eliminate "actual" national inequalities in political, economic, and cultural life. They were also a reflection of the growing centralization of power in its Great Russian center and of the steady bureaucratization and Russianization of central and local administrative agencies. The leap to intensive industrialization during the 1930's resulted in intensifying this trend but it did not also balance it with massive progress in Soviet nationality policy.[6] The 1930's brought great gains in the fight against illiteracy among the non-Russian peoples and in assimilating new cadres of native workers into the local governmental and administrative apparatus. Yet Russians continued to dominate critical agencies—the ministries of internal affairs and state security, the ministries of justice, and the state banking and economic planning agencies—in the non-Russian republics. The crucial factor, however, was the general trend toward greater reliance upon the Great Russian national core as the principal bulwark of the Soviet state. Party resolutions, to be sure, continued to inveigh against Great Russian chauvinism but these appeals were less pressing and less insistent than they had been in the

---

[6] In the economic field especially, achievements during the first two Five-Year Plans lagged well behind early Soviet expectations. Construction of the first two cotton mills in Central Asia had not begun until 1928, and nine years later, at the end of the second plan period, the old industrial centers were still producing 95 percent of all cotton cloth manufactured in the USSR. The gross output of all large-scale industry reached 1,915 million rubles in 1937; this was almost six times the production of 1913, but similar industry in the RSFSR had increased eight and one-half times to a gross output of 65,948 million rubles during the same period. In 1937, too, local industry in the republics of Central Asia and Kazakhstan accounted for only 2.2 percent of the total production in the USSR while the central regions and Leningrad Oblast were producing 53 percent. S. S. Bal'zak, V. F. Vasiutin, and Ya. G. Feigin, *Economic Geography of the USSR* (New York, 1949), pp. 154, 206, 338.

past. By the mid-1930's the portents of a new "Soviet patriotism" frankly recognizing the Great Russian nation as *primus inter pares* among the Soviet peoples were unmistakable.

Although the Bolshevik approach to nationality problems within the USSR does not constitute a certain index of future developments in these areas, it does indicate a strong Soviet tendency toward an antidemocratic resolution of them. The probability, moreover, has been strongly reinforced by philosophical considerations which go back at least to Lenin's break with the so-called bourgeois theory of national self-determination. Whatever the merits of Lenin's counter-thesis that the Russian Revolution had transformed the essence of the national question from a demand for political liberation to a demand for equality within the socialist order, it led ultimately to a Bolshevik denial of national claims and to the emergence within the USSR of a narrowly circumscribed form of national-cultural autonomy. This solution permitted a limited sphere of national initiative. But its essence was the dissociation of politics from nationality, and the substitution of promises of economic advancement for the political rights which would have made possible the defense of national customs and institutions. From a technical standpoint, this approach may have permitted the Soviet regime to make more rapid progress toward equalizing the nations of Russia than might have been possible under different circumstances. Great strides have been made in the development and utilization of native languages, in the elimination of illiteracy, in the involvement of minority peoples at least in the routine phases of political and administrative activity, and in the development of industrial centers in the non-Russian regions.

But the gains arising from these advances have not always or often been advantageous to the populations of the non-Russian republics. The development of the non-Russian languages and the expansion of literacy have enabled the central government and Party agencies to propagate more easily their own doctrines, slogans, and directives, but rigidly centralized controls have circumscribed narrowly the development of native social and cultural institutions. Increasing native participation in local administrative and political organs has been accompanied by a steady concentration of the crucial processes of decision making in centralized agencies located in Moscow. Nor has industrial development been adjusted with regard to the economic requirements or interests of local populations. In the absence either of political checks upon the power of central government or of real safeguards for national interests, Soviet policy has given rise to new forms of exploitation which in the context of Russia's nationality problem may only be described as Soviet colonialism.

In the last analysis, the failure of the Soviet regime to achieve a solution to Russia's nationality policy which would also admit a degree of tolerance of and respect for human dignity and regional aspirations has grown from causes other than the defects of Soviet nationality policy and doctrine. If the non-Russian peoples in the USSR have felt the sting of Communist police terror, oppression, and exploitation, their burdens have in many respects been no greater than those borne by the Great Russian nation. Mistrust of the popular masses and disbelief in their revolutionary capacities, arising from Lenin's early recognition of the broad divergence between the spontaneous goals of the people and the revolutionary aims of Marxism, runs threadlike through the whole history of Bolshevism in Russia. In Lenin it found expression in the theory and practice of a revolutionary elite which would not only lead the masses through a revolutionary seizure of power but would retain absolute command of the state and its agencies during the transition to socialism. Under Stalin it led to a consolidation of totalitarian forms of political, economic, and social organization and to the development of a bureaucratic system of administration which treated individuals and nations solely in terms of their usefulness to the Soviet state and the Communist movement. In the end, it gave birth to a doctrine and policy that seeks to cast all men and all nations into a single mold, into a single submissiveness to the vagaries of an arbitrary central will. And under its domination the original Marxist promise of human liberation from exploitation and degradation seems destined to remain beyond the reach of Soviet man.

BIBLIOGRAPHY

Only the principal sources used in the foregoing study appear in this bibliography. Works utilized incidentally or cited no more than twice in the text and articles which appeared in publications with a newspaper format are cited fully as they occur in the text.

1. DOCUMENTARY SOURCES

Agrarnaia politika v resheniiakh s'ezdov i konferentsii R.K.P. (b) s 1917 po 1925 god (Agrarian Policy in the Decisions of the Congresses and Conferences of the Russian Communist Party [b] from 1917 to 1925). Moscow, 1926.

Aleksandrov, G., *et al. Politicheskii slovar'* (Political Dictionary). Moscow, 1940.

Antropov, P. G. *Materialy i dokumenty I S'ezda Kompartii Turkestana* (Materials and Documents of the First Congress of the Communist Party of Turkestan). Tashkent, 1934.

Bol'shaia Sovetskaia Entsiklopediia (Great Soviet Encyclopedia). Several volumes. Moscow, 1926–33.

Dimanshtein, S. M. (ed.). *Revoliutsiia i natsional'nyi vopros: dokumenty i materialy* (The Revolution and the Nationality Problem: Documents and Materials). Vol. III. Moscow, 1930.

Gidulianov, Pavel V. *Otdelenie tserkvi ot gosudarstva v SSSR: polnyi sbornik dekretov, vedomstvennykh rasporiazhenii i opredelenii verkhsuda RSFSR i drugikh sovetskikh sotsialisticheskikh respublik: UkSSR, BSSR, ZSFSR, Uzbekskoi i Turkmenskoi* (The Separation of the Church from the State in the USSR: A Complete Collection of Decrees, Departmental Orders and Decisions of the Supreme Court of the RSFSR and Other Soviet Socialist Republics: The Ukrainian SSR, the Belorussian SSR, the TSFSR, and the Uzbek and Turcoman SSRs). 3d ed. Moscow, 1926.

Gosplan SSSR. Piatiletnii plan narodno-khoziaistvennogo stroitel'-stva SSSR (The Five-Year Plan of National Economic Construction in the USSR). Vol. III. Moscow, 1930.

Istoriia Sovetskoi Konstitutsii v dekretakh i postanovleniiakh Sovetskogo Pravitel'stva 1917–1936 (The History of the Soviet Constitution in the Decrees and Enactments of the Soviet Government 1917–1936). Moscow, 1936.

Kommunisticheskaia Akademiia, Komissiia po Izucheniiu Natsional'nogo Voprosa. Natsional'naia politika V.K.P.(b) v tsifrakh (The Nationality Policy of the All-Union Communist Party [b] in Figures). Moscow, 1930.

Konferentsii Vsesoiuznoi Kommunisticheskoi Partii (b). Stenograficheskie otchety (Conferences of the All-Union Communist Party [b]. Stenographic Reports).

—— Chetyrnadtsataia Konferentsiia Rossiiskoi Kommunisticheskoi Partii (bol'shevikov) (The Fourteenth Conference of the Russian Communist Party [Bolshevik]). Moscow, April 27–29, 1925. Moscow, 1925.

—— XV Konferentsiia Vsesoiuznoi Kommunisticheskoi Partii (b) (26 oktiabria–3 noiabria, 1926 g). (The Fifteenth Conference of the All-Union Communist Party [b], October 26–November 3, 1926). Moscow, 1927.

Kraskin, I. S. (ed.). Zemel'no-vodnaia reforma v Srednei Azii: sbornik materialov (The Land and Water Reform in Central Asia: A Collection of Materials). Moscow, 1927.

Lozovskii, I., and I. Bibin (eds.). Sovetskaia politika za 10 let po natsional'nomu voprosu v RSFSR: sistematicheskii sbornik deistvuiushchikh aktov pravitel'stv Soiuza SSR i RSFSR po delam natsional'nostei RSFSR, oktiabr' 1917 g.–noiabr' 1927 g. (Soviet Policy for Ten Years concerning the Nationality Question in the RSFSR: Systematic Collection of the Operative Acts of the Governments of the USSR and the RSFSR concerning Nationality Affairs in the RSFSR, October, 1917–November, 1927). Moscow, 1928.

Mashitskii, A. "Materialy po istorii Bukharskoi revoliutsii" (Materials on the History of the Bokharan Revolution), Vestnik Narodnogo Komissariata Inostrannykh Del, Nos. 4–5 (April–May, 1922), pp. 122–36.

"M. V. Frunze na Turkestanskom fronte (vvodnaia stat'ia komdiva F. Novitskogo)" (M. V. Frunze at the Turkestan Front [Introductory Article by Divisional Commander F. Novitskii]), *Krasnyi Arkhiv*, No. 3 (100) (1940), pp. 36–78.

Narodnyi Komissariat po Delam Natsional'nostei RSFSR. Politika Sovetskoi Vlasti po natsional'nomu voprosu za tri goda, 1917–xi–1920 (The Policy of the Soviet Government on the Nationality Question for Three Years, November, 1917–November, 1920). Moscow, 1920.

Orakhelashvili, M. D., and V. G. Sorin. Dekrety Oktiabr'skoi Revoliutsii (pravitel'stvennye akty, podpisannye ili utverzhdennye Leninym kak predsedatelem Sovnarkoma): Vol. I, Ot Oktiabr'skogo perevorota do rospuska Uchreditel'nogo Sobraniia (Decrees of the October Revolution [Governmental Acts, Signed or Confirmed by Lenin as Chairman of the Council of People's Commissars]: Vol. I, From the October Revolution to the Dissolution of the Constituent Assembly). Moscow, 1933.

Pervyi S'ezd Narodov Vostoka, Baku, 1–8 sent. 1920 g. stenograficheskie otchety (The First Congress of the Peoples of the East. Baku, September 1–8, 1920. Stenographic Reports). Petrograd, 1920.

Rasshirennyi Plenum Ispolkoma Kommunisticheskogo Internatsionala (21 marta–6 aprelia, 1925 g.): stenograficheskii otchet (Enlarged Plenum of the Executive Committee of the Communist International [March 21–April 6, 1925]: Stenographic Report). Moscow, 1925.

Sabanin, A. V. (ed.). Sbornik deistvuiushchikh dogovorov, soglashenii i konventsii, zakliuchennykh s inostrannymi gosudarstvami (Collection of Acting Treaties, Agreements, and Conventions Concluded with Foreign States). Vols. I–IV. Moscow, 1924–28.

Sbornik deistvuiushchikh dogovorov, soglashenii i konventsii, zakliuchennykh RSFSR s inostrannymi gosudarstvami (Collection of Acting Treaties, Agreements, and Conventions Concluded between the RSFSR and Foreign States). 5 vols. Moscow, 1921–23.

S'ezdy Rossiiskoi Kommunisticheskoi Partii (bol'shevikov). Stenograficheskie otchety (Congresses of the Russian Communist Party [Bolshevik]. Stenographic Reports). After the Thirteenth Congress, the Party bears the name All-Union (Vsesoiuznaia) Communist Party (b).

—— Sed'moi S'ezd Rossiiskoi Kommunisticheskoi Partii (6–8–go marta, 1918 goda) (Seventh Congress of the Russian Communist Party, March 6–8, 1918). Moscow, 1923.

S'ezdy Rossiiskoi Kommunisticheskoi Partii (*cont.*)

—— VIII S'ezd Rossiiskoi Kommunisticheskoi Partii (bol'shevikov), Moskva, 18–23 marta, 1919 (Eighth Congress of the Russian Communist Party [b]. Moscow, March 18–23, 1919). Moscow, 1919.

—— Deviatyi S'ezd Rossiiskoi Kommunisticheskoi Partii (29–go marta–4 aprelia, 1920 g.) (Ninth Congress of the Russian Communist Party [b], March 29–April 4, 1920). Moscow, 1919.

—— Protokoly s'ezdov i konferentsii Vsesoiuznoi Kommunisticheskoi Partii (b): Desiatyi S'ezd R.K.P. (b), mart 1921 g. (Protocols of the Congresses and Conferences of the All-Union Communist Party [b]: Tenth Congress of the Russian Communist Party [b], March, 1921). Moscow, 1933.

—— Protokoly s'ezdov i konferentsii Vsesoiuznoi Kommunisticheskoi Partii (b): Odinnadtsatyi S'ezd R.K.P. (b) (Protocols of the Congresses and Conferences of the All-Union Communist Party [b]: Eleventh Congress of the Russian Communist Party [b]). Moscow, March 27–April 2, 1922. Moscow, 1936.

—— Dvenadtsatyi S'ezd Rossiiskoi Kommunisticheskoi Partii (bol'-shevikov), 17–25 aprelia 1923 g. (Twelfth Congress of the Russian Communist Party [b], April 17–25, 1923). Moscow, 1923.

—— XV S'ezd Vsesoiuznoi Kommunisticheskoi Partii (b), 2–19 dekabria, 1927 g. (Fifteenth Congress of the All-Union Communist Party [b], December 2–19, 1927). Moscow, 1928.

S'ezdy Sovetov RSFSR. Stenograficheskie otchety (Congresses of Soviets of the RSFSR. Stenographic Reports).

—— Tretii Vserossiiskii S'ezd Sovetov Rabochikh, Soldatskikh i Krest'ianskikh Deputatov (Third All-Russian Congress of Soviets of Worker, Soldier, and Peasant Deputies). Petrograd, January 10–18, 1918. Peterburg, 1918.

—— Piatyi Vserossiiskii S'ezd Sovetov Rabochikh, Krest'ianskikh Soldatskikh i Kazach'ikh Deputatov: Moskva, 4–10 iiulia, 1918 g. (Fifth All-Russian Congress of Soviets of Worker, Peasant, Soldier, and Cossack Deputies. Moscow, July 4–10, 1918). Moscow, 1918.

—— 7-i Vserossiiskii S'ezd Sovetov Rabochikh, Krest'ianskikh, Krasnoarmeiskikh i Kazach'ikh Deputatov (5–9 dekabria, 1919 goda v Moskve) (Seventh All-Russian Congress of Soviets of Worker, Peasant, Red Army, and Cossack Deputies, December 5–9, 1919, at Moscow). Moscow, 1920.

—— Vos'moi Vserossiiskii S'ezd Sovetov Rabochikh, Krest'ianskikh, Krasnoarmeiskikh i Kazach'ikh Deputatov (22–29 dekabria, 1920 goda) (Eighth All-Russian Congress of Soviets of Worker, Peasant, Red Army, and Cossack Deputies, December 22–29, 1920). Moscow, 1921.

—— Desiatyi Vserossiiskii S'ezd Sovetov Rabochikh, Krest'ianskikh, Krasnoarmeiskikh i Kazach'ikh Deputatov (23–27 dekabria 1922 goda) (Tenth All-Russian Congress of Soviets of Worker, Peasant, Red Army, and Cossack Deputies, December 23–27, 1922). Moscow, 1923.

—— XII Vserossiiskii S'ezd Sovetov (Twelfth All-Russian Congress of Soviets). Moscow, 1925.

—— XIII Vserossiiskii S'ezd Sovetov (Thirteenth All-Russian Congress of Soviets). Moscow, 1927.

S'ezdy Sovetov SSSR. Stenograficheskie otchety (Congresses of Soviets of the USSR. Stenographic Reports).

—— I S'ezd Sovetov Soiuza Sovetskikh Sotsialisticheskikh Respublik (30 dekabria, 1922 g.) (First Congress of Soviets of the USSR, December 30, 1922). Moscow, 1922.

—— Vtoroi S'ezd Sovetov Soiuza Sovetskikh Sotsialisticheskikh Respublik (Second Congress of Soviets of the USSR). Moscow, January 26–February 2, 1924. Moscow, 1924.

—— Tretii S'ezd Sovetov Soiuza Sovetskikh Sotsialisticheskikh Respublik (Third Congress of Soviets of the USSR). Moscow, May 13–20, 1925. Moscow, 1925.

—— Chetvertyi S'ezd Sovetov (Fourth Congress of Soviets). Moscow, April 18–26, 1927. Moscow, 1927.

S'ezdy Sovetov Uzbekskoi SSR. Stenograficheskie otchety (Congresses of Soviets of the Uzbek SSR. Stenographic Reports).

—— Pervyi Vseuzbekskii S'ezd Sovetov Rabochikh, Dekhkanskikh i Krasnoarmeiskikh Deputatov Uzbekskoi Sovetskoi Sotsialisticheskoi Respubliki, fevral' 1925 goda (First All-Uzbek Congress of Soviets of Worker, Peasant, and Red Army Deputies of the Uzbek SSR, February, 1925). Tashkent, 1925.

—— Vtoroi Vseuzbekskii S'ezd Sovetov Rabochikh Dekhkanskikh i Krasnoarmeiskikh Deputatov Uzbekskoi Sovetskoi Sotsialisticheskoi Respubliki (Second All-Uzbek Congress of Soviets of Worker, Peasant, and Red Army Deputies of the Uzbek SSR). Samarkand, 1927.

Shapiro, Leonard (ed.). Soviet Treaty Series: A Collection of Bilateral Treaties, Agreements and Conventions, etc., Concluded between the Soviet Union and Foreign Powers. Vol. I, 1917–1928. Washington, 1950.

Sobranie postanovlenii i rasporiazhenii raboche-dekhkanskogo pravitel'stva Turkmenskoi SSR (Collection of Enactments and Decrees of the Worker-Peasant Government of the Turcoman SSR).
Ashkhabad, 1926–27.

Sobranie uzakonenii i rasporiazhenii rabochego i krest'ianskogo
pravitel'stva RSFSR (Collection of Statutes and Decrees of the
Worker and Peasant Government of the RSFSR). Moscow, 1917—.

Sobranie uzakonenii i rasporiazhenii Turkestanskoi Respubliki
(Collection of Statutes and Decrees of the Turkestan Republic).
Tashkent, January–May, 1922.

Sobranie uzakonenii i rasporiazhenii Uzbekskoi SSR (Collection of
Statutes and Decrees of the Uzbek SSR). Samarkand, 1925–27.

Spravochnik Narodnogo Komissariata po Delam Natsional'nostei
(Reference Book of the People's Commissariat for Nationality
Affairs). Moscow, 1921.

Sredne-Aziatskoe Biuro Ts.K. V.K.P.(b). Rezoliutsii i postanovleniia
XII Plenuma (24–27 ianvaria 1927 g.) (The Resolutions and
Enactments of the Twelfth Plenary Session, January 24–27, 1927).
Tashkent, n.d.

Sredne-Aziatskoe Biuro V.Ts.S.P.S. Professional'nye soiuzy v Srednei
Azii 24–25 god: otchet Sr.-Aziatskogo Biuro V.Ts.S.P.S. k 1-i
Sredne-Aziatskoi Konferentsii Profsoiuzov (Trade Unions in Cen-
tral Asia in 1924–25: The Report of the Central Asiatic Bureau
of the All-Union Central Council of Trade Unions for the First
Central Asiatic Conference of Trade Unions). Tashkent, 1925.

Statisticheskii Otdel, Tsentral'nyi Komitet V.K.P.(b). Sotsial'nyi i
natsional'nyi sostav V.K.P.(b) (The Social and National Composition of the All-Union Communist Party [b]). Moscow, 1928.

Tsentral'noe Statisticheskoe Upravlenie SSSR. Fabrichno-zavodskaia
promyshlennost' SSSR v 1925/26 gody (The Factory-Mill Industry
of the USSR in 1925–26). Moscow, 1927.

—— Narodnoe khoziaistvo Soiuza SSR v tsifrakh: kratkii spravochnik (The National Economy of the USSR in Figures: A Short
Reference Guide). Moscow, 1924.

Tsentral'noe Statisticheskoe Upravlenie SSSR, Otdel Perepisi. Vse-
soiuznaia perepis' naseleniia 1926 goda (The All-Union Census of
1926). Vols. XXXII, XXXIII, XXXVI. Moscow, 1928–29.

Tsentral'nyi Ispolnitel'nyi Komitet RSFSR. Stenograficheskie otchety (Central Executive Committee of the RSFSR. Stenographic
Reports).

—— Protokoly zasedanii Vserossiiskogo Tsentral'nogo Ispolnitel'-

nogo Komiteta Sovetov R., S., Kr. i Kaz. Deputatov II Sozyva (Protocols of the Sessions of the All-Russian Central Executive Committee of the Soviets of Worker, Soldier, Peasant, and Cossack Deputies of the Second Convocation). October 27–December 29, 1917. Moscow, 1918.

—— Vtoraia Sessiia Vserossiiskogo Tsentral'nogo Ispolnitel'nogo Komiteta X Sozyva (Second Session of the All-Russian Central Executive Committee of the Tenth Convocation). Moscow, 1923.

—— Tret'iaia Sessiia Vserossiiskogo Tsentral'nogo Ispolnitel'nogo Komiteta X Sozyva (29 oktiabria–3 noiabria, 1923 g.) (Third Session of the All-Russian Central Executive Committee of the Tenth Convocation, October 29–November 3, 1923). Moscow, 1924.

—— Vserossiiskii Tsentral'nyi Ispolnitel'nyi Komitet XI Sozyva: Vtoraia Sessiia (All-Russian Central Executive Committee of the Eleventh Convocation: Second Session). Moscow, 1924.

Tsentral'nyi Ispolnitel'nyi Komitet SSSR. Stenograficheskie otchety (Central Executive Committee of the USSR. Stenographic Reports).

—— Sozyv I. Vtoraia Sessiia Tsentral'nogo Ispolnitel'nogo Komiteta Soiuza Sovetskikh Sotsialisticheskikh Respublik, 6 iiulia, 1923 g. (First Convocation. Second Session of the Central Executive Committee of the USSR, July 6, 1923). Moscow, 1923.

—— Sozyv II. Vtoraia Sessiia Ts.I.K. (Second Convocation. Second Session of the Central Executive Committee). Moscow, 1924.

—— Sozyv II. Tret'iaia Sessiia Tsentral'nyi Ispolnitel'nyi Komitet (Second Convocation. Third Session, Central Executive Committee). Moscow, 1925.

Turkestanskoe Biuro, V.Ts.S.P.S. Rabota profsoiuzov Turkestana v novykh usloviiakh: otchet Turkbiuro V.Ts.S.P.S. IV Kraevoi Turkestanskoi Konferentsii Professional'nykh Soiuzov za vremia: aprel' 1922 g.–dekabr' 1923 g. (Work of the Trade Unions of Turkestan in New Conditions: Report of the Turkestan Bureau of the All-Russian Council of Trade Unions to the Fourth Regional Conference of Trade Unions for the Period April, 1922–December, 1923). Tashkent, 1923.

Upravlenie Vodnogo Khoziaistva Srednei Azii. Sostoianie i perspektivy irrigatsii v Srednei Azii (The Status and Perspectives of Irrigation in Central Asia). Tashkent, 1928.

Vse-Soiuznaia Kommunisticheskaia Partiia (b) v rezoliutsiiakh i resheniiakh s'ezdov, soveshchaniei i plenumov Tsentral'nogo

Komiteta (1898–1932) (The All-Union Communist Party [b] in Resolutions and Decisions of the Congresses, Conferences, and Plenums of the Central Committee, 1898–1932). 4th ed., 2 vols. Moscow, 1932.

Vse-Soiuznaia Kommunisticheskaia Partiia (b) v rezoliutsiiakh i resheniiakh s'ezdov, konferentsii i plenumov Ts.K., 1898–1935 (The All-Union Communist Party [b] in Resolutions and Decisions of the Congresses, Conferences, and Plenums of the Central Committee, 1898–1935). 5th ed., 2 vols. Moscow, 1936.

Vsia Sredniaia Aziia: spravochnaia kniga na 1926 khoz. god (All Central Asia: Reference Book for the 1926 Economic Year). Tashkent, 1926.

2. BOOKS, TREATISES, PAMPHLETS, AND ARTICLES

Aksel'rod, A. E. "Khlopkovoe delo za 10 let (1917–1927)" (The Cotton Industry for Ten Years, 1917–1927), *Khlopkovoe Delo,* Nos. 11–12 (November–December, 1927), pp. 825–47.

Aleksandrov, I. G. "Narodnoe khoziaistvo Turkestana i ego vosstanovlenie" (The National Economy of Turkestan and Its Rehabilitation), *Khlopkovoe Delo,* Nos. 1–2 (January–February, 1922), pp. 23–36.

Alkin, Ilias. Sredniaia Aziia: ekonomiko-geograficheskii ocherk Kara-Kalpakstana, Kirgizstana, Tadzhikistana, Turkmenistana i Uzbekistana (Central Asia: An Economic and Geographic Sketch of Kara-Kalpakstan, Kirghizia, Tajikistan, Turkmenia, and Uzbekistan). Vol. I. Moscow, 1931.

Alymov, A., and S. Studenikin. "Sovetskii federalizm i demokraticheskii tsentralizm" (Soviet Federalism and Democratic Centralism), *Sovetskoe Gosudarstvo,* Nos. 1–2 (1933), pp. 13–20.

Anadoly-ogly. "Natsional'naia politika v zemel'nom voprose i sel'skom khoziaistve (Fedkomzem i ego zadachi)" (Nationality Policy in the Agrarian Question and Agriculture [The Federal Commissariat for Agriculture and Its Tasks]), *Zhizn' Natsional'-nostei,* No. 2 (1923), pp. 7–12.

Ananov, I. N. "K preobrazovaniiu Sredne-Aziatskikh respublik" (Toward the Reformation of the Central Asiatic Republics), *Sovetskoe Pravo,* No. 4 (16) (1925), pp. 132–38.

—— Mestnye organy Sovetskoi vlasti (The Local Agencies of the Soviet Government). Moscow, 1925.

—— Ocherki federal'nogo upravleniia SSSR (Outlines of the Federal Administration of the USSR). Moscow, 1925.

Anderson, Paul B. People, Church and State in Modern Russia. New York, 1944.

Arkhipov, N. B. "Bukharskaia Narodnaia Sovetskaia Respublika" (The Bokharan People's Soviet Republic), *Sovetskoe Pravo*, No. 1 (4) (1923), pp. 133–39.

—— SSSR po raionam: Sredne-Aziatskie respubliki (The USSR by Districts: The Central Asiatic Republics). 2d ed. Moscow, 1928.

Arkhippov, Konst. "Tipy sovetskoi avtonomii" (Types of Soviet Autonomy), *Vlast' Sovetov*, Nos. 8–9 (August–September, 1923), pp. 28–44; No. 10 (October, 1923), pp. 35–56.

Bailey, Lt. Col. F. M. Mission to Tashkent. London, 1946.

Balashev, N. I. Uzbekistan i sopredel'nye respubliki i oblasti: geograficheskii i ekonomicheskii ocherk (Uzbekistan and Contiguous Republics and Regions: A Geographic Sketch). Tashkent, 1925.

Bal'zak, S. S., V. F. Vasiutin, and Ya. G. Feigin. Economic Geography of the USSR. New York, 1949.

Baranov, P. "Polozhenie Turkestanskoi respubliki i reorganizatsiia Krasnoi Armii" (The Status of the Turkestan Republic and the Reorganization of the Red Army), *Voennaia Mysl'*, No. 2 (May–July, 1921), pp. 82–95.

Baranskii, N. Ekonomicheskaia geografiia Sovetskogo Soiuza: obzor po oblastiam Gosplana (The Economic Geography of the Soviet Union: A Survey by Regions of the State Planning Commission). Moscow, 1926.

Baykov, Alexander. The Development of the Soviet Economic System: An Essay on the Experience of Planning in the USSR. New York, 1947.

Beichek, G. "Shkoly-peredvizhki v Srednei Azii" (Itinerant Schools in Central Asia), *Kommunisticheskaia Revoliutsiia*, No. 8 (April, 1926), pp. 66–72.

Belotskii, M. Kirgizskaia Respublika (The Kirghiz Republic). Moscow, 1936.

Bloom, Solomon Frank. The World of Nations: A Study of the National Implications of the Work of Karl Marx. New York, 1941.

Bolotov, S. "Iz istorii 'Osipovskogo' miatezha v Turkestane (s predisloviem G. Lelivicha)" (History of the "Osipov" Mutiny in

Turkestan [Foreword by G. Lelivich]), *Proletarskaia Revoliutsiia,* No. 6 (53) (June, 1926), pp. 110–37.

Bozhko, F. Grazhdanskaia Voina v Srednei Azii (The Civil War in Central Asia). Tashkent, 1930.

Broido, G. I. "Eshche o soiuze 'Koshchi' " (More on the "Koshchi"), *Zhizn' Natsional'nostei,* No. 5 (1923), pp. 15–27.

—— "Osnovnye voprosy natsional'noi politiki" (Fundamental Problems of Nationality Policy), *Zhizn' National'nostei,* Nos. 3–4 (1923), pp. 3–9.

Brun, Capt. A. H. Troublous Times: Experiences in Bolshevik Russia and Turkestan. London, 1931.

Bulata, P. (ed.). Osnovy teorii Sovetskogo khoziaistva: uchebnoe posobie dlia sovpartshkol (Basic Theories of the Soviet Economy: A Textbook for Soviet and Party Schools). Leningrad, 1931.

Carr, Edward Hallett. The Bolshevik Revolution, 1917–1923. Vol. I. New York, 1951.

Castagné, Joseph. "La Réforme agraire au Turkestan," *Revue des Études Islamiques,* No. 11 (1928), pp. 361–99.

—— "Le Bolchévisme et l'Islam; les organisations soviétiques de la Russie musulmane," *Revue du Monde Musulman,* LI (October, 1922).

—— Les Basmatchis: le mouvement national des indigènes d'Asie Centrale. Paris, 1925.

—— "Le Turkestan depuis la révolution russe," *Revue du Monde Musulman,* L (June, 1922), 28–73.

—— "Russie slave et Russie turque: les chances d'une politique islamique allemande," *Revue du Monde Musulman,* LVI (December, 1923).

Castagné, Joseph (ed.). "Le Mouvement de latinisation dans les républiques soviétiques musulmanes et les pays voisins (documents de presse russe)," *Revue des Études Islamiques,* No. 11 (1928), pp. 559–95.

Central Administration of Economic and Social Statistics of the State Planning Commission of the USSR. Socialist Construction in the USSR. Moscow, 1936.

Central Statistical Board, USSR. Ten Years of Soviet Power in Figures, 1917–1927. Moscow, 1927.

Chaikin, Vadim. K istorii Rossiiskoi Revoliutsii, vypusk I, Kazn' 26 Bakinskikh komissarov (History of the Russian Revolution: Vol. I, The Execution of the Twenty-six Baku Commissars). Moscow, 1922.

Chamberlin, William Henry. The Russian Revolution, 1917–1921. 2 vols. New York, 1935.

Chanyshev, A. "O soiuzakh 'Koshchi' " (On the "Koshchi"), *Sovetskoe Stroitel'stvo,* Nos. 4–5 (1926), pp. 124–26.

Chekalin, N. "Sobytiia v Khorezmskoi Respublike" (Occurrences in the Khorezmian Republic), *Voennaia Mysl',* No. 1 (January–April, 1921), pp. 227–29.

Cherdantsev, Gleb N. "Raionirovannaia Sredniaia Aziia" (The Districting of Central Asia), *Planovoe Khoziaistvo,* No. 7 (July, 1927), pp. 245–56.

—— Sredne-Aziatskie respubliki (The Central Asiatic Republics). Moscow, 1928.

Cherniavskii, E. Sailaular-saili: Prazdnik vyborov (Sailaular-saili: The Election Holiday). Tashkent, 1927.

Chokaiev (Chokai-ogly), Mustapha. "Turkestan and the Soviet Regime," *Journal of the Royal Central Asian Society,* XVIII (1931), 403–20.

—— Turkestan pod vlast'iu Sovetov (Turkestan under the Soviet Authority). Paris, 1935.

Dembo, L. I. Zemel'nyi stroi Vostoka (The Agrarian Order of the East). Leningrad, 1927.

Dervish. "Bukharskaia Sovetskaia Narodnaia Respublika" (The Bokharan Soviet People's Republic), *Zhizn' Natsional'nostei,* No. 1 (January, 1923), pp. 195–200.

Dimanshtein, S. "Bor'ba na ideologicheskom fronte v Srednei Azii" (The Struggle on the Ideological Front in Central Asia), *Revoliutsiia i Natsional' nosti,* No. 12 (58) (December, 1934), pp. 21–35.

Diuzhev, F. A. "Zavody khlopkovoi promyshlennosti Turkestana" (Cotton Mills in Turkestan), *Khlopkovoe Delo,* Nos. 3–4 (March–April, 1922), pp. 42–48.

Dobb, Maurice. Soviet Economic Development since 1917. New York, 1948.

Dunaev, G. "Planovoe khoziaistvo v Srednei Azii" (Planned Economy in Central Asia), *Planovoe Khoziaistvo,* No. 3 (March, 1926), pp. 217–28.

Durdenevskii, V. N. Ravnopravie iazykov v Sovetskom stroe (Equality of Languages in the Soviet System). Moscow, 1927.

Engels, Friedrich. The Origin of the Family, Private Property and the State. New York, 1942.

Etherton, Col. P. T. In the Heart of Asia. London, 1925.

Eudin, Xenia Joukoff. "Soviet National Minority Policies, 1918–1921," *Slavonic and East European Review,* XXI (1943), 31–55.

Fami-Rusal'. "Narodnoe prosveshchenie v Turkrespublike" (Public Education in the Turkestan Republic), *Zhizn' Natsional'-nostei,* Nos. 3–4 (1923), pp. 98–107.

Fioletov, N. N. "Sudoproizvodstvo v Musul'manskikh sudakh (sudy kaziev) Srednei Azii" (Legal Procedure in the Moslem Courts [Kadi Courts] of Central Asia), *Novyi Vostok,* Nos. 23–24 (1928), pp. 204–17.

—— "Sudy kaziev v Sredne-Aziatskikh respublikakh" (The Kadi Courts in the Central Asiatic Republics), *Sovetskoe Pravo,* No. 1 (25) (1927), pp. 132–46.

—— "Vakufnoe pravo v Sredne-Aziatskikh sovetskikh respublik" (The Law on Endowment Property in the Central Asiatic Soviet Republics), *Sovetskoe Pravo,* No. 2 (20) (1926), pp. 84–103.

Fischer, Louis. The Soviets in World Affairs: A History of the Relations between the Soviet Union and the Rest of the World. 2 vols. Princeton, 1951.

Gasilov, G. V. (ed.). Prosveshchenie natsional'nykh men'shinstv v RSFSR (The Education of National Minorities in the RSFSR). Moscow, 1928.

Gaudefroy-Demombynes, Maurice. Muslim Institutions. London, 1950.

Genkina, E. B. Obrazovanie SSSR (The Formation of the USSR). 2d ed. Moscow, 1947.

Gessen, S. Ya. "K voprosu o khoziaistvennom stroitel'stve Srednei Azii" (The Problem of Economic Construction in Central Asia), *Sovetskoe Stroitel'stvo,* No. 1 (6) (January, 1927), pp. 58–78.

Ginzburg, S. B. "Basmachestvo v Fergane" (Basmachism in Fergana), *Novyi Vostok,* Nos. 10–11 (1925), pp. 175–202.

Goikhbarg, A. G. "O Turkestanskoi Konstitutsii" (On the Turkestan Constitution), *Proletarskaia Revoliutsiia i Pravo,* Nos. 8–10 (November 15–December 15, 1918), pp. 19–35.

Gor'kii, M., Vs. Ivanov, I. Mints, and F. Kolesov (eds.). Voina v peskakh: Grazhdanskaia Voina v Srednei Azii (War in the Desert: The Civil War in Central Asia). [Moscow], 1935.

Gurev, G. A. Antireligioznaia khrestomatiia: posobie dlia propagandistov, prepodavatelei i uchashchikhsia (Antireligious Reader: A Textbook for Propagandists, Teachers, and Students). 4th ed. Moscow, 1930.

Gurevich, A. "Zemel'no-vodnaia reforma v Uzbekskoi SSR (1925–

1929)" (The Land and Water Reform in the Uzbek SSR, 1925–1929), *Voprosy Istorii,* No. 11 (November, 1948), pp. 50–69.

Gurvich, Prof. G. S. Osnovy Sovetskoi konstitutsii (Fundamentals of the Soviet Constitution). 2d ed. Moscow, 1922.

Iakubovskaia, S. I. Ob'edinitel'noe dvizhenie za obrazovanie SSSR (1917–1922) (The Unification Movement for the Formation of the USSR, 1917–1922). Moscow, 1947.

Iranskii, S. "Tendentsii v razvitii organizatsionnykh form torgovli SSSR so stranami Vostoka" (Trends in the Development of the Organizational Forms in the Trade of the USSR with the Countries of the Orient), *Torgovlia Rossii s Vostokom,* Nos. 1–2 (January–February, 1925), pp. 3–6.

Istpart Sredazbiuro Ts.K., V.K.P.(b). Revoliutsiia v Srednei Azii (The Revolution in Central Asia). Vol. I. Tashkent, 1928.

Itsyna, S. "Bedniatskie organizatsii na Sovetskom Vostoke i ikh zadachi" (Organizations of the Poor Peasants in the Soviet East and Their Tasks), *Sovetskoe Stroitel'stvo,* Nos. 2–3 (1925), pp. 219–36.

Ivanova, A. M. Chto sdelala Sovetskaia vlast' po likvidatsii negramotnosti sredi vzroslykh (What the Soviet Government Did to Eliminate Illiteracy among Adults). Moscow, 1949.

Karpych, V. "K istorii vozniknoveniia Turkmenskoi SSR" (The History of the Origin of the Turcoman SSR), *Turkmenovedenie,* Nos. 10–11 (14–15) (October–November, 1928), pp. 37–52.

—— "Revoliutsionnyi put' Turkmenistana (i o nepravil'nom tolkovanii 'Turkmeny i Revoliutsiia')" (The Revolutionary Path of Turkmenistan [and the Wrong Interpretation of "The Turcomans and the Revolution"]), *Turkmenovedenie,* No. 1 (5) (January, 1928), pp. 6–15.

Katsenelenbogen, Mikh. "Ob 'uklonakh' v natsional'noi politike V.K.P.(b)" (On Deviations in the Nationality Policy of the All-Union Communist Party [b]), *Bol'shevik,* No. 22 (November 30, 1927), pp. 19–31.

Kazantsev, N. D. (ed.). Zemel'noe pravo (Agrarian Law). Moscow, 1949.

Khavin, A. Sotsialisticheskaia industrializatsiia natsional'nykh respublik i oblastei (The Socialist Industrialization of the National Republics and Regions). Moscow, 1933.

Khodorov, I. "K probleme raionirovaniia promyshlennosti Srednei Azii" (The Problem of Districting the Industry of Central Asia), *Planovoe Khoziaistvo,* No. 1 (January, 1927), pp. 189–202.

Khodorov, I. (cont.)

—— "Natsional'noe razmezhevanie Srednei Azii" (The National Delimitation of Central Asia), Novyi Vostok, Nos. 8–9 (1925), pp. 65–81.

—— "Piatiletnii khoziaistvennyi plan Srednei Azii" (The Five-Year Economic Plan for Central Asia), Planovoe Khoziaistvo, No. 10 (October, 1926), pp. 181–98.

Khodzhaev, Faizulla. K istorii revoliutsii v Bukhare (History of the Revolution in Bokhara). Tashkent, 1926.

—— "O Mlado-Bukhartsakh" (The Young Bokharans), Istorik Marksist, No. 1 (1926), pp. 123–41.

Khromykh, K. "Sozdanie fronta revoliutsii v Srednei Azii. Khorezmskaia respublika" (The Creation of the Revolutionary Front in Central Asia. The Khorezmian Republic), Voennaia Mysl', No. 1 (September, 1920), pp. 283–98.

Kolomoitsev, P. Krest'ianstvo i revoliutsiia (The Peasantry and the Revolution). Moscow, 1926.

Kolychevskii, I. "Bukhara" (Bokhara), Voennaia Mysl', No. 1 (September, 1920), pp. 299–309.

Kondrashov, S. K. "Ispolnenie planov po irrigatsii i khlopkovodstvu v Sredne-Aziatskoi respublike v 1924–25 g." (Fulfillment of the Plans for Irrigation and Cotton Growing in the Central Asiatic Republic in 1924–25), Planovoe Khoziaistvo, No. 5 (May, 1925), pp. 247–53.

—— "Sredne-Aziatskoe razmezhevanie" (The Delimitation of Central Asia), Planovoe Khoziaistvo, No. 4 (April, 1925), pp. 255–63.

Korbe. "Sovety Srednei Azii" (The Soviets of Central Asia), Revoliutsiia i Natsional'nosti, No. 12 (58) (December, 1934), pp. 54–59.

Kotliarevskii, Prof. S. A. "Pravovoe polozhenie avtonomnykh respublik" (The Legal Status of Autonomous Republics), Sovetskoe Pravo, No. 6 (18) (1925), pp. 37–45.

—— SSSR i soiuznye respubliki (The USSR and Allied Republics). Moscow, 1924.

Kozlov, T. S. "Anglichane v. Zakaspii" (The English in Transcaspia), Turkmenovedenie, Nos. 7–8 (11–12) (July–August, 1928), pp. 33–56.

—— Krasnaia Gvardiia i Krasnaia Armiia v Turkmenii (istoricheskaia spravka ob organizatsii i etapakh bor'by) (The Red Guard and the Red Army in Turkmenia [Historical Information on Organization and the Stages of Struggle]). Ashkhabad, 1928.

Krylov, S. B. "Istoricheskii protsess razvitiia Sovetskogo federal-

BIBLIOGRAPHY 403

izma" (The Historical Process of the Development of Soviet Federalism), *Sovetskoe Pravo*, No. 5 (11) (1924), pp. 36–66.

Kryl'tsov, I. I. "Zakonodatel'stvo Sredne-Aziatskikh sovetskikh respublik" (The Legislation of the Central Asiatic Soviet Republics), *Sovetskoe Pravo*, No. 5 (29) (1927), pp. 130–38.

Ksenofontov, F. Uzbekistan i Turkmenistan: k voprosu ob ikh vkhozhdenii v SSSR (Uzbekistan and Turkmenia: On the Problem of Their Entrance into the USSR). Moscow, 1925.

Kunitz, Joshua. Dawn over Samarkand: The Rebirth of Central Asia. New York, 1935.

Kushner (Knyshev), P. Gornaia Kirgiziia (sotsiologicheskaia razvedka) (Mountainous Kirghizia [A Sociological Survey]). Moscow, 1929.

Lammens, H. Islam: Beliefs and Institutions. New York, n.d.

Lavrent'ev, Vl. "Aziia 'inorodtsev' i Aziia sovetskikh sotsialisticheskikh respublik" (The Asia of the "Foreigners" and the Asia of the Soviet Socialist Republics), *Planovoe Khoziaistvo*, No. 11 (November, 1927), pp. 197–214.

Lenin, Vladimir I. Collected Works. London, 1927—.

—— Imeprialism, the Highest Stage of Capitalism—a Popular Outline with New Data. Edited by E. Varga and L. Mendelsohn. New York, 1940.

—— Natsional'nyi vopros (The Nationality Question). Moscow, 1936.

—— Selected Works. 12 vols. New York, n.d.

—— Sochineniia (Collected Works). 2d ed., 30 vols. Moscow, 1926–32.

—— State and Revolution. New York, 1932.

Liashchenko, P. I. Istoriia narodnogo khoziaistva SSSR (History of the National Economy of the USSR). Vol. II. Moscow, 1948.

Lorimer, Frank. The Population of the Soviet Union: History and Prospects. Geneva, 1946.

Lunacharskii, A. "Problemy obrazovaniia v avtonomnykh respublikakh i oblastiakh" (Problems of Education in the Autonomous Republics and Regions), *Zhizn' Natsional'nostei*, No. 1 (6) (1924), pp. 31–33.

M., E. "Khoziaistvennyi obzor po Turkestanu" (An Economic Survey of Turkestan), *Vlast' Sovetov*, No. 6 (September, 1924), pp. 214–20.

Maiskii, I. Vneshniaia politika RSFSR, 1917–1922 (The Foreign Policy of the RSFSR, 1917–1922). Moscow, 1922.

Mansurov, G. Za kul'turnoe stroitel'stvo natsional'nostei (Toward the Cultural Construction of the Nationalities). [Moscow], 1927.

Mansvetov, N. "Velikaia Oktiabr'skaia Sotsialisticheskaia Revoliutsiia i sozdanie Narodnogo Komissariata po Delam Natsional'nostei" (The Great October Socialist Revolution and the Creation of the People's Commissariat for Nationality Affairs), *Voprosy Istorii*, No. 8 (August, 1949), pp. 9-29.

Marx, Karl, and Friedrich Engels. Capital, the Communist Manifesto and Other Writings. New York, 1932.

—— Manifesto of the Communist Party. New York, 1932.

—— Selected Correspondence, 1846–1895. New York, 1942.

Mashitskii, A. "K istorii revoliutsii v Bukhare" (The History of the Revolution in Bokhara), *Vestnik Narodnogo Komissariata Inostrannykh Del*, Nos. 3–4 (May, 1921), pp. 24–37; Nos. 5–6 (July, 1921), pp. 70–83.

Maynard, Sir John. Russia in Flux. New York, 1948.

Mindlin, Z. "Kirgiz i revoliutsiia" (The Kirghiz and the Revolution), *Novyi Vostok*, No. 5 (1924), pp. 217–29.

Mirkin, Z. (ed.). K desiatiletiiu interventsii: sbornik statei (The Tenth Anniversary of the Intervention: A Collection of Articles). Moscow, 1929.

Moore, Barrington, Jr. Soviet Politics—the Dilemma of Power. Cambridge, 1950.

Mukhitdinov, M. "Politiko-prosvetitel'naia rabota v natsional'nom razreze" (Political-Educational Work in the National Connection), *Kommunisticheskoe Prosveshchenie*, No. 2 (20) (March–April, 1925), pp. 20–26.

—— "Sistema narodnogo obrazovaniia v natsional'nom razreze" (The System of Public Education in the National Connection), *Narodnoe Prosveshchenie*, No. 4 (April, 1925), pp. 73–78.

Muraveiskii, S. (V. Lopukhin). Ocherki po istorii revoliutsionnogo dvizheniia v Srednei Azii (Sketches on the History of the Revolutionary Movement in Central Asia). Tashkent, 1926.

—— "V bor'be za kadry v Srednei Azii" (In the Struggle for Cadres in Central Asia), *Kommunisticheskaia Revoliutsiia*, No. 17 (September, 1926), pp. 62–73.

Mushpert, Ia., and E. Fainberg. Komsomol i molodezh' natsional'nykh men'shinstv (The Communist League of Youth and the Youth of the National Minorities). Moscow, 1926.

N., M. "Pod znakom Islama" (Under the Badge of Islam), *Novyi Vostok*, No. 4 (1923), pp. 72–97.

Narodnyi Komissariat po Delam Natsional'nostei. Natsional'nyi vopros i Sovetskaia Rossiia (Soviet Russia and the Nationality Question). Moscow, 1921.

Nazarov, P. S. Hunted through Central Asia. London, 1932.

Nemchenko, M. A. "Agrarnaia reforma v Turkmenii" (Land Reform in Turkmenia), *Novyi Vostok*, No. 19 (1927), pp. 121–39.

—— Dinamika Turkmenskogo krest'ianskogo khoziaistva (The Dynamics of the Turcoman Peasant Economy). Poltoratsk (Ashkhabad), 1926.

—— "Natsional'noe razmezhevanie Srednei Azii" (The National Delimitation of Central Asia), *Mezhdunarodnaia Zhizn'*, Nos. 4–5 (1924), pp. 67–92.

Nepesov, G. "Vozniknovenie i razvitie Turkmenskoi Sovetskoi Sotsialisticheskoi Respubliki" (The Emergence and Development of the Turcoman Soviet Socialist Republic), *Voprosy Istorii,* No. 2 (February, 1950), pp. 3–24.

Ocherki revoliutsionnogo dvizheniia v Srednei Azii: sbornik statei Feizuly Khodzhaeva, E. Fedorova, T. Ryskulova, S. Ginsburga (Sketches of the Revolutionary Movement in Central Asia: Collected Articles of Feizulla Khozhaev, E. Fedorov, T. Ryskulov, and S. Ginsburg). Moscow, 1926.

Pavlovich, M. (M. Vel'tman). Revoliutsionnyi Vostok (The Revolutionary Orient). Vol. I. Moscow, 1927.

—— "Vserossiiskaia Nauchnaia Assotsiatsiia Vostochnogo Vedeniia" (The All-Russian Scientific Association of Eastern Learning), *Zhizn' Natsional'nostei,* No. 1 (January, 1923), pp. 267–71.

Piontkovskii, S. Grazhdanskaia Voina v Rossii (1918–1921 g.g.): khrestomatiia (The Civil War in Russia [1918–1921]: Readings). Moscow, 1925.

Plekhanov, P. "O rassloenii Turkmenskogo aula" (On the Stratification of the Turcoman Village), *Planovoe Khoziaistvo,* No. 5 (May, 1928), pp. 287–98.

Podurovskii, A. "Gornaia promyshlennost' Turkestana, ee razvitie i sovremennoe sostoianie" (The Mining Industry of Turkestan, Its Development and Present Status), *Voennaia Mysl',* No. 1 (January–April, 1921), pp 134–57.

Popov, N. N. Natsional'naia politika Sovetskoi vlasti (The Nationality Policy of the Soviet Government). Moscow, 1927.

Prager, P. "K postanovke voprosa o nekapitalisticheskom puti razvitiia otstalykh stran" (Toward a Formulation of the Question of the Noncapitalistic Path of Development of Backward Countries), *Proletarskaia Revoliutsiia*, No. 5 (100) (May, 1930), pp. 55–94; No. 6 (101) (June, 1930), pp. 73–102.

Predtechenskii, A. A. "Khleb za khlopok (k vvozy khleba v Turkestan)" (Grain for Cotton [Toward the Import of Grain into Turkestan]), *Khlopkovoe Delo*, Nos. 1–2 (January–February, 1923), pp. 31–43.

Radzhapov, S. "Etapy razvitiia Sovetskogo gosudarstvennogo stroia v Srednei Azii" (The Stages of Development of the Soviet State Order in Central Asia), *Sovetskoe Gosudarstvo i Pravo*, No. 11 (November, 1948), pp. 61–67.

Reisner, M. "Soiuz Sotsialisticheskikh Sovetskikh Respublik" (The Union of Socialist Soviet Republics), *Vlast' Sovetov*, Nos. 1–2 (January–February, 1923), pp. 9–24.

Rizenkampf, Georgii K. Problemy orosheniia Turkestana (Problems of Irrigation in Turkestan). Moscow, 1921.

Rochester, Anna. Lenin on the Agrarian Question. New York, 1942.

Rogozhin, N. P. "Kooperatsiia v khlopkovom dele Turkestana" (Cooperation in the Cotton Business of Turkestan), *Khlopkovoe Delo*, Nos. 7–8 (July–August, 1924), pp. 20–31.

Ronin, S. L. "Stalinskoe uchenie o natsii i o mnogonatsional'nom sovetskom gosudarstve" (Stalinist Doctrine concerning the Nation and the Multinational Soviet State), *Sovetskoe Gosudarstvo i Pravo*, No. 2 (February, 1950), pp. 1–15.

Rozenblium, B. L. "O rasprostranenii deistviia mezhdunarodnykh dogovorov, zakliuchennykh Soiuzom SSR i otdel'nymi respublikami na vnov' vstupaiushchie v SSSR respubliki" (On the Extension of the Action of International Treaties, Concluded between the USSR and the Individual Republics Which Recently Entered the USSR), *Sovetskoe Pravo*, No. 5 (29) (1927), pp. 98–107.

Rozner, V. "Vysshaia partiinaia shkola v Turkestane" (The Higher Party School in Turkestan), *Kommunisticheskaia Revoliutsiia*, Nos. 11–12 (35–36) (October 1, 1922), pp. 182–85.

Russia: The Official Report of the British Trades Union Delegation to Russia and Caucasia, November and December, 1924. London, 1925.

Rysakoff, A. The National Policy of the Soviet Union. New York, n.d.

Ryskulov, Turar R. Kirgizstan (Kirghizia). Moscow, 1935.

—— Revoliutsiia i korennoe naselenie Turkestana (The Revolution and the Native Population of Turkestan). Tashkent, 1925.

S. "Zemel'naia reforma v Uzbekistane" (The Land Reform in Uzbekistan), *Vlast' Sovetov*, No. 7 (February 14, 1926), pp. 8–10; No. 8 (February 21, 1926), pp. 9–10.

Safarov, Georgii. Kolonial'naia revoliutsiia: opyt Turkestana (The Colonial Revolution: Turkestan's Experience). Moscow, 1921.

—— Marx and the East. New York, 1934.

—— Problemy Vostoka (Oriental Problems). Petrograd, 1922.

Said Alim Khan. La Voix de la Bourkharie opprimée. Paris, 1929.

Sakharov, M. G. Osedanie kochevykh i polukochevykh khoziaistv Kirgizii (The Settlement of Nomadic and Seminomadic Households in Kirghizia). Moscow, 1934.

Sev. "Zametki o Turkmenskom dukhovenstve" (Notes on the Turcoman Clergy), *Turkmenovedenie*, Nos. 3–4 (7–8) (March–April, 1928), pp. 15–20.

Shokhor, V. "Religiozno-bytovye sudy v RSFSR" (Religious and Customary Courts in the RSFSR), *Sovetskoe Stroitel'stvo*, Nos. 8–9 (13–14) (August–September, 1927), pp. 94–114.

Shteinberg, E. L. Ocherki istorii Turkmenii (Outlines of the History of Turkmenia). Moscow, 1934.

—— "Sredneaziatskoe razmezhevanie i protsess natsional'noi konsolidatsii" (The Central Asiatic Delimitation and the Process of National Consolidation), *Revoliutsiia i Natsional'nosti*, No. 12 (58) (December, 1934), pp. 47–54.

Shutemov, A. "Itogi i perspektivy Sovetskogo stroitel'stva v Turkmenistane" (The Results and Perspectives of Soviet Construction in Turkmenia), *Vlast' Sovetov*, No. 13 (March 28, 1926), pp. 5–7; No. 14 (April 4, 1926), pp. 2–4.

Skalov, G. "Ekonomicheskoe ob'edinenie Sredne-Aziatskikh respublik, kak faktor natsional'noi politiki" (The Economic Unification of the Central Asiatic Republics as a Factor of Nationality Policy), *Zhizn' Natsional'nostei*, No. 5 (1923), pp. 40–45.

—— "Opyt klassovogo rassloeniia v usloviiakh Turkestana (soiuz 'Koshchi')" (The Experience of Class Stratification in Turkestan Conditions [the Koshchi]), *Zhizn' Natsional'nostei*, No. 2 (1923), pp. 34–41.

—— "O soiuze 'Koshchi'" (On the "Koshchi"), *Zhizn' Natsional'nostei*, No. 5 (1923), pp. 15–27.

—— "Revoliutsiia v Khive 1920 goda" (The Khivan Revolution of 1920), *Novyi Vostok*, No. 3 (1923), pp. 241–57.

Skalov, G. (*cont.*)

—— "Sotsial'naia priroda basmachestva v Turkestane" (The Social Character of Basmachism in Turkestan), *Zhizn' Natsional'nostei,* Nos. 3–4 (1923), pp. 51–61.

Soloveichik, D. "Revoliutsionnaia Bukhara" (Revolutionary Bokhara), *Novyi Vostok,* No. 2 (1922), pp. 272–88.

Stalin, J. V. Leninism. 2 vols. New York, 1932–33.

—— Marxism and the National and Colonial Question. New York, n.d.

—— Sochineniia (Collected Works). Vols. I–XIII. Moscow, 1946–51.

Stasevich. "Natsional'nyi sostav naseleniia RSFSR" (The National Composition of the Population of the RSFSR), *Zhizn' Natsional'-nostei,* No. 1 (6) (1924), pp. 129–62.

Strong, Anna Louise. Red Star in Samarkand. New York, 1929.

"Struggle for Soviet Ashkhabad, The. The Beginning of the Civil War in Transcaspia" (Translated from *Turkmenovedenie,* October, 1930), *Journal of the Royal Central Asian Society,* XVIII (1931), 620–23.

Suleimanova, Kh. "Istoricheskii ocherk o sozdanii Sovetskikh sudov v Uzbekistane" (An Historical Sketch on the Creation of Soviet Courts in Uzbekistan), *Sovetskoe Gosudarstvo i Pravo,* No. 3 (March, 1949), pp. 61–69.

—— "Zarozhdenie Sovetskogo ugolovnogo prava v Uzbekistane" (The Origin of Soviet Criminal Law in Uzbekistan), *Sovetskoe Gosudarstvo i Pravo,* No. 10 (October, 1948), pp. 65–69.

Sultan-Galiev, M. Metody antireligioznoi propagandy sredi Musul'-man (Methods of Antireligious Propaganda among Moslems). Moscow, 1922.

Ter-Pogos-Avetisov. "Nashi ekonomicheskie vzaimootnosheniia s Bukharoi v proshlom i nastoiashchem" (Our Past and Present Economic Relations with Bokhara), *Voennaia Mysl',* No. 2 (May–July, 1921), pp. 227–36.

Timasheff, Nicholas S. The Great Retreat: The Growth and Decline of Communism in Russia. New York, 1946.

Tiuriakulov, N. "Turkestanskaia Avtonomnaia Respublika" (The Turkestan Autonomous Republic), *Zhizn' Natsional'nostei,* No. 1 (January, 1923), pp. 86–95.

Towster, Julian. Political Power in the USSR, 1917–1947. New York, 1948.

Trainin, I. P. Deklaratsiia Prav Trudiashchegosia i Eksploatiruemogo Naroda (The Declaration of the Rights of the Toiling and Exploited Peoples). Moscow, 1938.

—— SSSR i natsional'naia problema: po natsional'nym respublikam i oblastiam Sovetskogo Soiuza (The USSR and the Nationality Problem: Through the National Republics and Regions of the Soviet Union). Moscow, 1924.

Trombachev, S. P. "Sredne-Aziatskoe vodnoe khoziaistvo" (The Central Asiatic Water Economy), *Vestnik Irrigatsii,* V, No. 10 (October, 1927), 3–8.

Trotsky, Leon. Stalin: An Appraisal of the Man and His Influence. New York, 1941.

Turubiner, A. M. Gosudarstvennyi stroi RSFSR (konspekt lektsii) (The State Order of the RSFSR [Synopsis of a Lecture]). Moscow, 1923.

—— "Konstitutsii Turkestana, Kryma, Dagestana" (The Constitutions of Turkestan, the Crimea, and Daghestan), *Vlast' Sovetov,* No. 1 (April, 1924), pp. 133–36.

Ul'ianov, G. "K voprosu o podgotovke uchitel'stva natsional'nykh men'shinstv" (The Problem of Preparing Teachers of the National Minorities), *Narodnoe Prosveshchenie,* Nos. 11–12 (1924), pp. 79–85.

—— "Pervyi Vserossiiskii S'ezd Sovnatsmenov" (The First All-Russian Congress of Soviets of the National Minorities), *Zhizn' Natsional'nostei,* No. 2 (1923), pp. 102–13.

—— "Politprosvetrabota sredi natsmen" (Political Educational Work among the National Minorities), *Kommunisticheskoe Prosveshchenie,* No. 2 (26) (March–April, 1926), pp. 36–41.

Vaganian, V. O natsional'noi kul'ture (On National Culture). Moscow, 1927.

Vasilevskii. "Fazy Basmacheskogo dvizheniia v Srednei Azii" (The Phases of the Basmachi Movement in Central Asia), *Novyi Vostok,* No. 29 (1930), pp. 126–41.

Vermenichev, I. D. "Ob agrarnoi reforme v Srednei Azii" (On the Land Reform in Central Asia), *Agrarnye Problemy,* No. 2 (November, 1927), pp. 61–83.

Viktorov, Vl. "Kommunisticheskii Universitet Trudiashchikhsia Vostoka" (The Communist University of the Toilers of the East), *Zhizn' Natsional'nostei,* No. 1 (January, 1923), pp. 261–66.

Vinogradova, A. "Khorezmskaia Sovetskaia Narodnaia Respublika" (The Khorezmian Soviet People's Republic), *Zhizn' Natsional'-nostei,* No. 1 (January, 1923), pp. 181–94.

Vorshev, V. "Osnovnye etapy razvitiia partorganizatsii Turkmenistana" (The Basic Stages of the Development of the Party Organization in Turkmenia), *Revoliutsiia i Natsional'nosti,* No. 12 (58)
(December, 1934), pp. 68–80.

Vyshinsky, Andrei Y. The Law of the Soviet State. Translated by
Hugh W. Babb. New York, 1948.

Wolfe, Bertram D. Three Who Made a Revolution. New York,
1948.

Yaroslavsky, Emelian. Religion in the USSR. London, 1932.

Zaitsev, P. "Provedenie izbiratel'noi kampanii v Uzbekistane" (Conduct of the Election Campaign in Uzbekistan), *Vlast' Sovetov,* X,
No. 9 (February 27, 1927), 10–14.

Zaorskaia-Aleksandrova, V. V. "Tezisy doklada po promyshlennosti
Turkestana" (Theses of a Report on the Industry of Turkestan),
Khlopkovoe Delo, Nos. 1–2 (January–February, 1922), pp. 42–46.

Zashchuk, S. L. "Khlebnaia problema v khlopkovodcheskikh raio-
nakh Srednei Azii" (The Grain Problem in the Cotton-growing
Districts of Central Asia), *Khlopkovoe Delo,* Nos. 3–5 (March–
May, 1926), pp. 386–97.

Zel'kina, E. Ocherki po agrarnomu voprosu v Srednei Azii (Sketches
on the Agrarian Question in Central Asia). Moscow, 1930.

—— "Zemel'naia reforma v Srednei Azii" (The Land Reform in
Central Asia), *Revoliutsionnyi Vostok,* No. 3 (1927), pp. 133–67.

Zinger, L. Natsional'nyi sostav proletariata v SSSR (The National
Composition of the Proletariat of the USSR). Moscow, 1934.

Zorin, A. N. Revoliutsionnoe dvizhenie Kirgizii (severnaia chast')
(The Revolutionary Movement in Kirghizia: The Northern
Part). Frunze, 1931.

Zubrek, K. "Zemledelie i irrigatsiia Khorezma v sviazi s voprosom
ekonomicheskogo ob'edineniia Sredne-Aziatskikh respublik" (The
Agriculture and Irrigation of Khorezm in Connection with the
Question of the Economic Unification of the Central Asiatic
Republics), *Novyi Vostok,* No. 3 (1923), pp. 208–19.

3. NEWSPAPERS AND PERIODICALS

Agrarnye Problemy (Agrarian Problems).

Bol'shevik (Bolshevik). Theoretical journal of the Central Committee of the All-Union Communist Party (b).

Istorik Marksist (The Marxist Historian). Journal of the Institute
of History of the Academy of Sciences of the USSR.

Izvestiia Sovetov Deputatov Trudiashchikhsia SSSR (News of the Soviets of Toilers' Deputies of the USSR).

Journal of the Royal Central Asian Society.

Khlopkovoe Delo (The Cotton Industry). Journal of the Main Committee for the Cotton Industry of the Supreme Council for the National Economy of the USSR.

Kommunisticheskaia Revoliutsiia (The Communist Revolution). Organ of the Agitation-Propaganda Section of the Central Committee of the All-Union Communist Party (b).

Kommunisticheskoe Prosveshchenie (Communist Education). Journal of the Principal Committee on Political Education of the People's Commissariat for Education of the RSFSR.

Krasnyi Arkhiv (The Red Archives). Publication of the Central Archive of the RSFSR.

Mezhdunarodnaia Zhizn' (International Life). Journal of the People's Commissariat for Foreign Affairs.

Narodnoe Prosveshchenie (Public Education). Journal of the People's Commissariat for Education of the RSFSR.

Novyi Vostok (The New Orient). Journal of the All-Russian Scientific Association of Eastern Learning.

Planovoe Khoziaistvo (Planned Economy). Political-economic journal of the State Planning Commission.

Pravda (Truth). Organ of the Central Committee and the Moscow Committee of the All-Union Communist Party (b).

Pravda Vostoka (Truth of the Orient).

Pravo i Zhizn' (Law and Life).

Proletarskaia Revoliutsiia (Proletarian Revolution). Publication of the Russian Communist Party (b).

Proletarskaia Revoliutsiia i Pravo (The Proletarian Revolution and the Law). Journal of the People's Commissariat of Justice of the RSFSR.

Revoliutsiia i Natsional'nosti (The Revolution and the Nationalities).

Revoliutsionnyi Vostok (The Revolutionary Orient).

Revue des Études Islamiques.

Revue du Monde Musulman.

Sovetskoe Gosudarstvo (The Soviet State). Organ of the Institute of Law of the Academy of Sciences of the USSR and the All-Union Institute of Juridical Sciences of the Ministry of Justice of the USSR. After 1939, the journal appeared under the title *Sovetskoe Gosudarstvo i Pravo* (The Soviet State and Law).

Sovetskoe Pravo (Soviet Law). Journal of the Institute of Soviet Law.

Sovetskoe Stroitel'stvo (Soviet Construction). A publication of the Central Executive Committee of the USSR.

Svobodnyi Turkestan (Free Turkestan). A Tashkent newspaper devoted to independent socialist thought. Suspended and later revived under the title *Novyi Turkestan* (The New Turkestan).

Torgovlia Rossii s Vostokom (Russia's Trade with the Orient). Journal of the All-Union Eastern Chamber of Commerce.

Turkestanskaia Pravda (Turkestan Truth).

Turkmenovedenie (Turcoman Learning). Journal of the Institute of Turcoman Culture.

Vestnik Irrigatsii (The Herald of Irrigation).

Vestnik Narodnogo Komissariata Inostrannykh Del (Herald of the People's Commissariat for Foreign Affairs).

Vlast' Sovetov (Authority of the Soviets). Organ of the People's Commissariat for Internal Affairs of the RSFSR.

Voennaia Mysl' (Military Thought). Organ of the Central Asiatic Military District.

Voprosy Istorii (Questions of History). Journal of the Institute of History of the Academy of Sciences of the USSR.

Zhizn' Natsional'nostei (Life of the Nationalities). Journal of the People's Commissariat for Nationality Affairs.

INDEX

◆

Adat, use of, to support Soviet policy, 171; use of, in Moslem people's courts, 229; agrarian principles in, 288–89

Adult Education, organization of, 368–69; program of, in RSFSR, 369–70

Afghanistan, support of Basmachi by, 41–42

Agitation, see Propaganda

Agrarian Affairs, Federal Committee for, 303

Agricultural and Forestry Workers, Union of, membership of, 144–45, 150, 281; competition of, with Koshchi, 150–51

Agricultural Bank, 309

Agricultural cooperatives, in Central Asia, 309

Agriculture, collapse of, in Turkestan during civil war, 37–39, 298–300; distribution of, in Central Asia, 100–105; emphasis on cotton growing in, 290–91; Lenin's theory of capitalist development in, 294–95; revival of, in Central Asia, 301–2; centralization of control over, 303

Agriculture, People's Commissariat of, 303

Agriculture, Turkestan Commissariat of, role of Koshchi in, 147, 148

Aksakal (elder), 84

Aktiubinsk, emergence of Communist Party in, 124

Alexander II, 224

All-Russian Extraordinary Commission to Abolish Illiteracy, 370

All-Russian Moslem Council, 119

All-Union Commissariats, representation of, in Central Asia, 123

Alphabet reform, prerevolutionary Turkic support for, 365–66; completion of, in Soviet Union, 366–67

Amu-Daria region, 69, 96, 360

Andijan, 41, 271

Anti-Duhring, 206

Apostasy, 248

Armenia, treaty relations of, with RSFSR, 61–62

Artisans, see Kustar's

Ashkhabad, 272; revolt in, in June, 1918, 27; activities of Commissar Frolov in, 27–28; Soviet capture of, 30; emergence of Communist Party in, 124

Ashkhabad Soviet, 27

Astrakhan, 119

Atabaev, Kajgisiz, on Semirechie land reform, 324–25

Atheist Movement, First All-Union Conference of, 246

Azerbaijan, treaty relations of, with RSFSR, 61–62; alphabet reform in, 366

Bailey, Lt. Col. F. M., 33

Bashkir Autonomous Soviet Socialist Republic, 179

Basmachi movement, 157, 167; causes of, 34; emergence of, 40–41; nationalistic elements in, 40–41; relations of, with anti-Soviet Europeans, 41; peasant support of, 41; growth of, 49–50; religious elements in, 50, 213; Enver Pasha assumes leadership in,